HOME FOOD

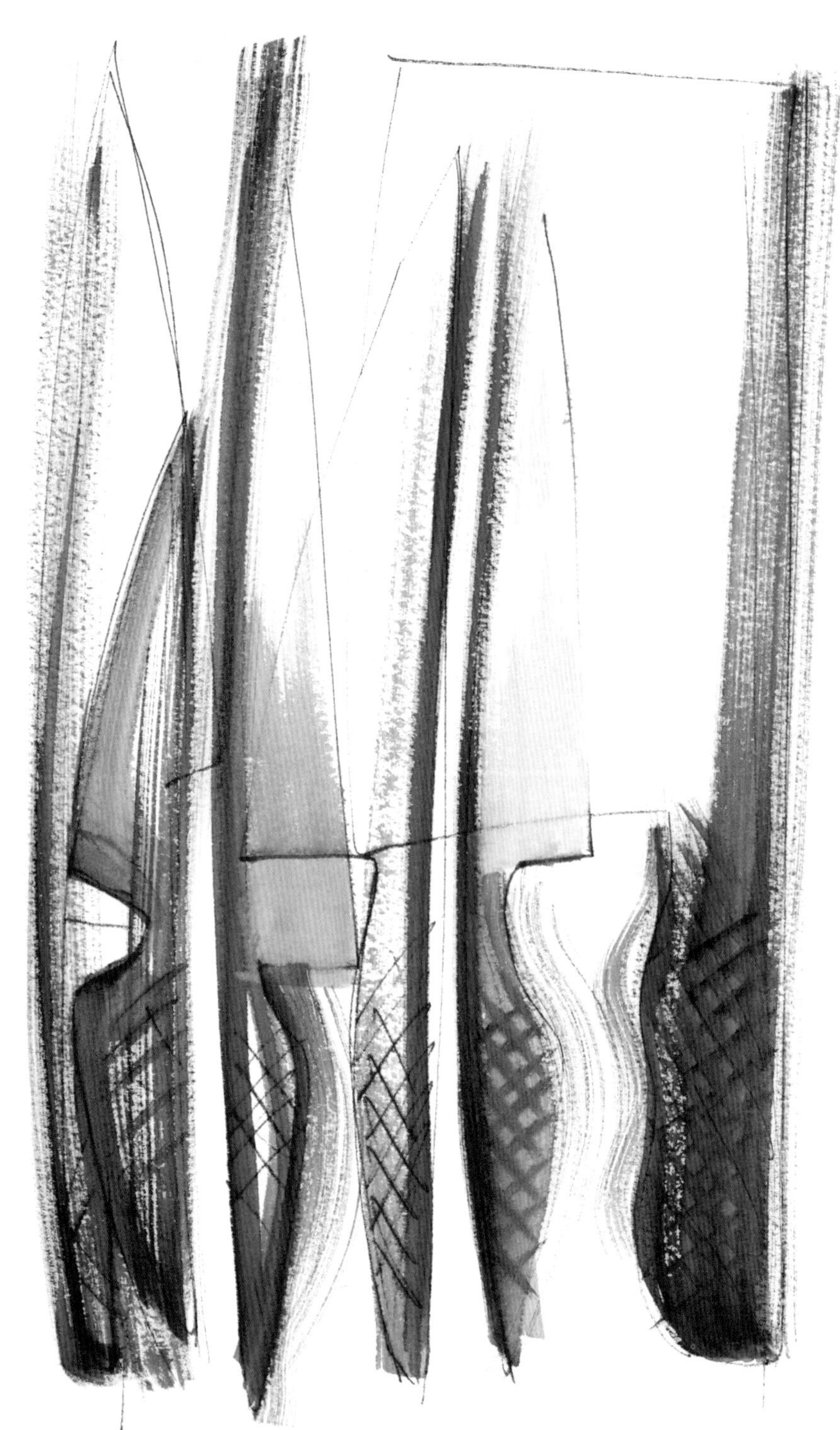

HOME FOOD

Exploring the World's Best Cooking

Richard Whittington

Drawings by Brian Ma Siy

CASSELL

In memory of my wife, Pippa
1948–1992
With love and gratitude

This edition first published in the UK in 1999 by
Cassell,
Wellington House,
125 Strand,
London WC2R 0BB
www.cassell.co.uk

Both metric and imperial quantities are given. Use either all metric or all imperial, as the two are not necessarily interchangeable.

Project Editor: Deborah Taylor
Edited by Lewis Esson
Proofread by Annie Lee
Indexed by Hilary Bird
Designed by Hugh Adams and Frank Barron, AB3 Design
Drawings by Brian Ma Siy
Photography by James Murphy
Food for photography by Janet Smith assisted by Jo Barry

British Library Cataloguing-in-Publication Data
A catalogue record for this book is available from the British Library.

ISBN 0-304-35077-X

Colour Separation by Tenon & Polert Colour Scanning Ltd.
Printed and bound in Italy by New Interlitho

Contents

Taste First

Home Food is a voyage around the world in one cookbook, a journey which puts together dishes reflecting the best of each of the places it visits. 'Overseas', 'foreign' or 'abroad' mean the same thing whichever country you are a national of and provide the contexts which make 'foreign' food authentic. They describe anywhere you did not grow up, a place which is excitingly different. *Home Food* is a celebration of that difference, of those differences, a recognition that food is identified by the place it comes from and this helps make it special.

What is 'home food'? Well, for a start, it is not restaurant food, though restaurant food is a vital catalyst in the essential change and development of today's domestic cooking. Without the impact of what innovative chefs do, home food becomes codified and ridiculously partisan, locked in a box of endless repetition. Food is a living thing and needs to change if it is not to be compartmentalized. However, the nature of the symbiotic relationship between home food and restaurant food must be viewed with some reservations, because it is not all good news that trickles down from the professional kitchen. The recent fascination with chefs and restaurant cooking has been sending some confusing messages, particularly in their performance on television. I believe television has an ultimately corrosive effect on good food and good food writing because it is in the nature of the medium to concentrate on celebrity and visual effect.

This, in turn, impacts on publishing – which increasingly packages cookbooks around television 'celebrity chefs'. Since television cannot, of itself, communicate what something tastes or smells like, or spend time on the detail of its preparation, directors inevitably focus on bravura displays, manual dexterity and things like knife skills, which have nothing whatsoever to do with the taste, balance or integrity of a dish. If the chef does not have a vocabulary to articulate nuances and subtleties, the quality of the information contributed is poor or, in some cases, irrelevant and misleading.

A universal TV food cliché takes the chef/presenter to a distant and exotic place and has him or her perform against a spectacular or entertaining backdrop, though it has to be said that a sausage charcoal-grilled on top of Ayers Rock will be no different from one barbecued in a backyard in Slough. Too often our chef is encouraged to think his every exaggerated word and gesture is hysterically funny when, in reality, the performance has me and everybody I know reaching for the remote control.

We live in the world of food as game show, as exhibitionism and as voyeurism. I recognize that comedic food presentation is not really designed to be cooked from and is a pure construct of ratings-driven programming, but this formula's success does make it harder and harder for people to finance television that takes food seriously, and because television and cookbook publishing are increasingly indivisible, the publishing footprint contracts. When substance is absent and celebrity rules, we may see an entire hugely expensive series with multiple international locations tied down to one piece of cooking kit with the inevitable consequence of boiling water on a barbecue and frying fish cakes in a wok.

There are honourable exceptions to such nonsense. Jacques Pépin is a genius, while Peter Gordon is a natural and exceptional communicator. Both make you want to turn on the stove and pick up a knife, and both can write about their subject with honesty and love. I can think of no higher praise.

The useful lessons of the professional kitchen for the majority of private cooks are not to do with the charisma or otherwise of an individual chef, but with planning and delivery – the essential *mise-en-place* which makes service in a restaurant environment possible. These are the tricks of the trade, by which everything that can possibly be done in advance is done, so that the last-minute preparation is restricted to one or two items, the exercise being one of compilation and presentation on the plate just before a dish exits the kitchen, the part referred to as 'on the pass'. Which reminds me of a little ditty once recited to me by Mary Hayley Bell: 'First lady forward, second lady pass, third lady's finger up the fourth lady's...'. But I digress.

These organizational skills are important concerns for anybody who wishes to entertain, since the approach – with its attendant disciplines and emphasis on planning – helps get food to the table on time and with a minimum of panic, the very things that so often are the death of a dinner or lunch party. They are not, in themselves, a formula for excellent food, however, as anybody who has eaten badly in a restaurant will attest. The disgusting meal you choked over paying for was undoubtedly prepared with dazzling knife-work and much shouting of 'yes chef', but then, technique and slavish discipline can never substitute for good taste.

Of course, there are areas of overlap between the professional and domestic kitchen, but this should not obscure the fact that there are many dishes which are best cooked at home, often slow food as opposed to fast. If we have the time to indulge in lengthy preparation and take pleasure in doing so, then where is the harm? And if the precision of the *chiffonnade* or *brunoise* is absent, this will surely not affect the taste without which good food cannot be good food. Taste first, taste second and taste last. Everything else is window dressing.

Home Food is personal because it is a book about the food I have enjoyed eating as well as cooking. Both experiences have to be a pleasure, because I am never again going to cook something I don't want to cook or eat myself. I suspect that this is not as obvious as it sounds. I look at a lot of books and wonder how the author could like everything suggested. Some of the contrasts are too odd. I look at a recipe and know that, while I'll try most things, I won't like it. I knew I was not going to like the sheep's eyeball in Saudi Arabia, and I was right. That is an extreme example, as was the slippery sea slug I ate with shuddering distaste in Japan. I sensed the texture was not for me, but I tried it, confirming my worst suspicions.

My attitude to food today is not the response of a child arbitrarily refusing to taste something, but a judgement based on many years eating and learning. Most of us start out with a good palate which, if we are unlucky, becomes damaged by early abuse. Enduring good taste comes from learning to discriminate. If I see on a menu a custard flavoured with liquorice – or, worse, lavender – I know it is a mistake. I was once offered a rosemary crème brûlée. I did not need to put it in my mouth to know that this was a bad idea, an attempt to inject novelty where none was needed, a failure on the part of the chef – out of immaturity or simply not having sat down and eaten a full portion.

N'est pas gourmand qui veut, Brillat-Savarin acidly noted. In other words, it is not enough to aspire. You have to educate your palate and that does not conveniently come with the territorial donning of a uniform or the acquisition of a title. And sadly there will always be an element of vocation. Some people will never cook well no matter how many lifetimes of effort they put in. On the most practical level, many grotesqueries would be avoided in the professional kitchen if more than a teaspoon was consumed when judging a dish, a point incidentally as true of over-salting. If you are hot and sweating and taste only a teaspoon of something, your palate's judgement is inaccurate because you are dehydrated and crave salt along with liquid.

Other dangers are to be found with much of what is dubbed fusion food, and I say this as one who wrote a book with Martin Webb about modern Australian cooking called *Fusions*, though when I look back at it, few of the dishes really were. A menu can sustain several different national influences, but cross-cultural combining in one dish is a dangerous game and can all too easily become confusion on the plate. Lemon grass and kaffir lime leaves, when transplanted into a Western tradition, can taste all too easily like a bar of soap or cheap perfume, while the incontinent use of Sichuan pepper has all the charm of a dish sauced with Vick's Vapour Rub. An excessive use of star anise or five-spice powder will queasily bring incense out of the cathedral and into your mouth.

Without good taste you evince distaste and without balance you have discomfort and distortion. Balance is the antithesis of self-conscious presentation. I am not impressed if the sauce is pearled in equidistant and precisely uniform blobs around the circumference of a plate or the food built into towers that crash messily when prodded with a fork. Home food must always strive to retain natural balance and, when it does, it looks appealing on the plate without the necessity of being teased into an unnatural elevation or arranged into patterns with the cook's fingers. This is the good food of common sense and all our senses are involved in its enjoyment.

A response to something may be conditioned by emotion or irrationality or aesthetic sensibility or, of course, hunger. I will never eat anything called a 'bake', a 'purse' or a 'parcel'. If I see something so described then I pass. In the post today came a flyer from a new and expensive restaurant touting for trade. Among other delights, the sample menu offered me 'lamb parcel with Covent Garden parcels'. My response to that as I threw it in the bin was to utter, very loudly, the last word of Mary's little rhyme.

My kind of home food reflects national themes with recipes that are designed for entertaining and sharing, food that people who care about eating well in different countries cook for their families and friends. It is about always cooking with a generous spirit, not the same thing as spending heavily on ingredients. Skill is inevitably involved, though often it is time that is the most precious commodity the cook has to spend.

In almost every dish I have imposed my will, because food does not stand still. There was never a precise moment when it was universally agreed that one formula was the only way of doing something, though from this generalization I exclude the scientific and essential precision of the pastry cook. All the dishes can be prepared in a simple kitchen or on the most basic barbecue. Gadgets are kept to a minimum, though I have assumed the ownership of a food processor and an electric mixer, a ridged grill pan, bamboo steamers and an overhead grill.

I have considered changing perceptions about healthy eating, something sneered at by a hard core of food writing reactionaries, all of whom have been blessed with efficient metabolisms, something God did not give me. It seems mad for those of us who do gain weight when we eat too much fat not to recognize that Mexican food, for example, in its most traditional expressions uses lots of lard, as does Vietnamese cooking, though I believe Southeast Asian cooks today are increasingly turning to groundnut oil.

Excessive consumption of saturated fat is now widely believed to be one of death's more effective preparatory tools and while it is probably too late to make any difference to me, I see good reason to take it into account when working on dishes that others will eat. The portion sizes of Brazilian and Argentinian meat dishes are heart-stopping in scale. Arab and Indian puddings and sweets can be unbearably sweet to a palate that consciously reduces sugar intake, while Japanese food is very high in salt. Much Indian food uses alarming amounts of clarified butter, now implicated in the high incidence of cardiovascular disease in the British Asian community.

Led by chefs like the brilliant Alain Ducasse, French cuisine has become less fat-saturated in recent times, but the amounts of butter called for can still shock the uninitiated. My interpretations are generally lighter without, I hope, losing the national character of the food. This is not, however, low-fat cooking in a medical sense, but lower-fat cooking. The distinction is important, for this is not a diet book but a book about good food that coincidentally restricts the amount of saturated fat used.

I hate it when people become obsessed with fat, demanding in restaurants their dressings and sauces 'on the side', or – please not – an egg white omelette and hold the sodium. I'd rather eat a dog biscuit. We can use less fat without ruining the food. The flavours can remain big and bold and authentically of the country from which they originate or that has inspired their creation.

Few would dispute that the most exciting thing to have happened to home cooking in the last ten years is the ready availability of ingredients and fresh produce from around the world. Our increasingly international larder has paved the way for a global kitchen in which cooks trained in one cultural idiom seek inspiration from the world at large. This multiculturalism is often dubbed eclectic, for the dishes that result are fusions that mix the flavours and spicing of one place with ingredients from another. It is a place where one country can meet another on the same plate to good effect – I think of Tetsuya's Japanese/French cooking in Sydney – but it is also a minefield for the unwary. Here the cook must seek balance and should always be judged harshly when the essential knowledge and sensitivity required are absent. The exercise is not one of 'mix-and-match' but the application of good taste and knowledge in depth, bloody difficult for anybody to get right.

There is an inevitable reaction against fusion cooking, with some food writers and restaurant critics dismissing it out of hand, having failed to understand that cooking fusions have been around for hundreds of years. One thinks of the Spanish and Portuguese in South and Central America and the Arabs in Spain, Portugal and Sicily. We talk about Mediterranean food as if it was one thing, when the reality is vastly more complex in its cultural cross-fertilization. When we refer to a Mediterranean diet, what we really infer is more fish and less meat, the generous use of olive oil rather than butter, the inclusion of pungent herbs with some eaten raw as salads, and an appreciation of fruit and vegetables as primary rather than secondary ingredients. This is influencing the way more and more people eat. It is not a fad or a fashion, but a continuing force for change in the way we eat and, it seems, the basis of a healthy diet, though what that may be is medically redefined at regular intervals.

People talk about Indian food, a description of massive generalization, for the cooking of the sub-continent is regionally diverse. A vegetarian meal in Kerala bears little resemblance to the tandoor roast meats of the far north, as different in style and execution as a Parisian brasserie lunch is from the food eaten in a Sicilian trattoria. Yet the spices of the East, many of which started their life in Central America, have been a part of British and Mediterranean cooking for hundreds of years.

The distinctive flavours of peppercorns, of coriander, cumin and fennel seeds are today no longer 'foreign', but an integral part of our food cultures and, in Britain for example, there are more Indian restaurants than any other kind, more even than fish and chip shops. The Chinese takeaway may not often be the best exponent of that country's cooking, but it is nationally ubiquitous here, and has had a huge impact, helping change people's tastes, often serving fish and chips as well as Chinese dishes, an example of crossover at a grass-roots level.

We may have overdosed wildly on Southeast Asian flavours but, put in perspective, they have brought a lasting and valuable legacy, for when used with restraint and only when appropriate, they permit subtle variations on much loved themes. The Eastern Mediterranean and North Africa have brought their own distinct flavours and cooking techniques, too. We have welcomed them all and they have changed us for the better.

Home Food sets out to be a book with international relevance, not one written solely for a British market. That being said, and while I have lived in the USA and France, I am British and I believe it is time we stopped playing down the strengths of our present culinary revolution. Britain, particularly London, is a great place to be interested in food and cooking. The roots of our food are global and while, at the time of writing, the flavours of Southeast Asia and, increasingly, North Africa, hold sway in fashionable restaurants, they are clearly neither the beginning nor the end, but only part of an ongoing process in which successive waves of immigrants have helped change the way we do things as their cultures have met and become part of our own.

Happily, this has not meant the loss of national cooking, whether it be Italian, Greek, French, Moroccan, Thai, Malaysian, Japanese, Indian or, of course, British. The cooking styles of different nationalities have been allowed to retain their unique identities as we have learned to appreciate their differences rather than seeking to subsume them, thereby providing us with constant points of comparison against which the significance of new directions can be judged. It is within their own national or geographic frameworks that they give a continuing springboard for new ideas – not to them but to us.

Let us not forget that there is a pendulum effect in cooking trends. As soon as Southeast Asian food becomes ubiquitous it becomes unfashionable, prompting a strong swing of interest back to the national dishes it temporarily displaced. Galangal in the ascendant only stimulates a rediscovery of suet a stop or two down the line. And if you want to know where I think people are going to seek inspiration next, then it must be South America.

I have written *Home Food* based on a learning path that has meandered for thirty years, experience which I believe is a microcosm of what has happened to the food we eat in recent times. This is a book which spans the globe but, inevitably, with many omissions since it is based on my own preferences. The number of recipes is not the same for each country or continent, because I have found more things that are interesting to work with in one place than in another. In some cases I have been drawn to specific regions as, for example, in the USA, where I have mostly chosen the distinctive flavours of the Louisiana kitchen... I am not trying to cover every base, just food that turns me on.

The book also reflects the way we eat when we go out to restaurants or order takeaway meals. Thus, a Cantonese lunch menu may be followed in the evening with a light Provençal supper. The next day a Moroccan menu or a Tamil vegetarian feast. After that, we may move to Cyprus or Brazil, eat Thai noodles on Saturday, a Venezuelan *cruzado* of poached meats on Sunday. Because I fell in love with Australia and was knocked out by the quality of the food I ate there, I have included recipes which I think are representative of its contemporary cooking. Whatever its national influence, the focus throughout is on ease of preparation, the essential simplicity, the lack of contrivance. Above all else, I hope this is a book about real food which keeps the idea of the food tasting of itself at the forefront, wherever it comes from.

Eating well is an integral part of living in the present. The opportunity to enjoy good food is always with us and it is no more difficult or expensive to have a good meal than a bad one. Good food does not have to be fancy. It can be as basic as a piece of bread and a slice of cheese or sausage, an omelette and a glass of wine. If we failed yesterday to eat well and with pleasure, then that particular opportunity will never come again. But then, in all things, the attitude with which we enter each day will to a large extent determine how much joy we find there. Wherever we come from and wherever we live – the two no longer automatically being the same thing they once invariably were – we can embrace a multitude of foreign influences when deciding what will be our daily bread, for which I give heartfelt thanks.

I hope that you will enjoy the flavours and ideas which have entertained my family, my friends and me, and will find sufficient substance in *Home Food* to put some new good things on the table.

Richard Whittington

Introduction to the Recipes

When writing recipes an irritatingly obvious statement to one person is an obscure reference to another. This pushes the writer to include everything in the method, while fighting constantly not to offend by over-simplification or to sound condescending. I have tried to limit the most basic information and hope that by doing so have struck an acceptable balance rather than an awkward compromise.

I have assumed that the reader knows what boiling water is – *pace* Delia – and with the exception of Japanese *dashi* broth, how to make stocks which I have decided not to describe in detail. For anybody who has never killed and cooked a live crab or lobster, I suggest you read Rick Stein on the subject. I have written about it in other books but his knowledge and its clear explanation cannot be improved upon. All of the recipes can be cooked with simple equipment, though I have assumed access to both a food processor and a food mixer. A rice steamer is a very useful piece of kit, though obviously not vital, though to my way of thinking, bamboo steaming baskets are. They are cheap, aesthetically pleasing and have many uses. An ice-cream maker is also desirable but, now we can buy excellent ice-cream, certainly not essential.

The issue of what food looks like on the plate is something which should emerge naturally from the way a recipe communicates the process. I dislike food that has been much handled to make a self-conscious presentation and particularly loathe the current restaurant obsession with tall food built into precarious towers with the help of tubes, or with decorating the edges of the plate with dribbles of oil, finely chopped herbs or – in the case of puddings – icing sugar or cocoa powder dusted over a template of a fork or the chef's initial, any or all of them making me reach for a gun. Such practices are offensive enough in restaurants and certainly have no place in home cooking. When the food in a recipe brings the elements together on the plate in harmony, that dish looks good. I do use flat-leaf parsley, coriander and celery leaves and chives to finish dishes, but they are all there to be eaten. The word 'garnish' is an ugly one, but only incorrect when interpreted as a purely visual effect. A garnish in the French sense can be something very substantial. When used to describe the last-minute addition of herbs, this must never be added automatically, for while they give visual impact they more importantly deliver flavour and contrasting texture.

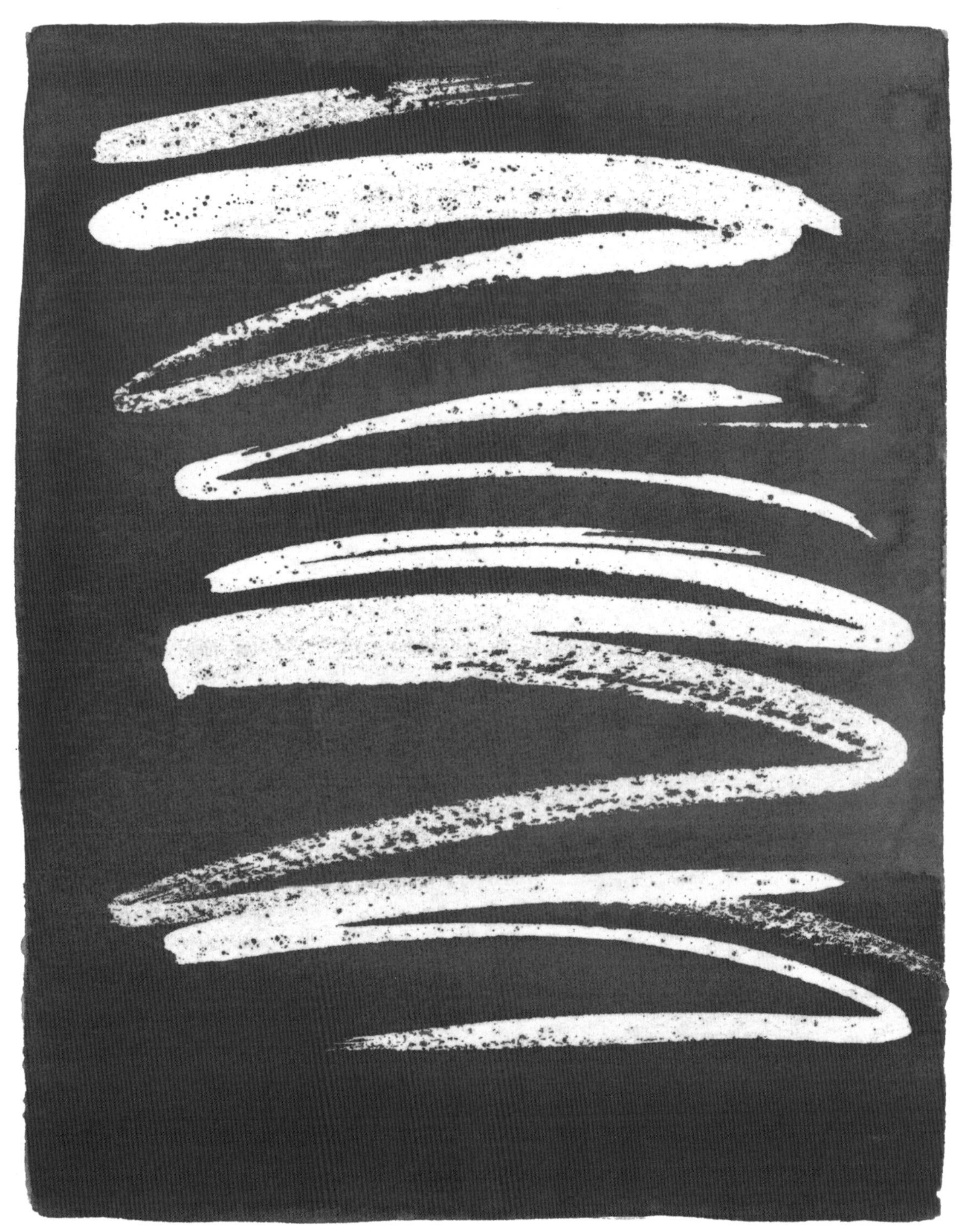

Chapter 1
Soups

Essentially broth

Soups, whatever their national origin, can precede a main course from somewhere else, in the same way that desserts from anywhere can follow on from a savoury dish originally from the other side of the world without any awkward lurch or cultural dissonance. I imagine that this is because of the role played by broth in the former and sugar in the latter.

Perhaps more than any other of the categories of cooked food that we eat, soup has the capacity to expand naturally into a one-dish meal. This is particularly true of the soups of China and Southeast Asia, where they do not, in any case, normally precede a meal – indeed, they often are the meal. One thinks of classics like duck soup noodles and *tom yam gung*. In a European context, the addition of bread and butter on the side and the possibility of concluding with cheese or a salad make soup more than a stepping stone to bigger and better things. I especially enjoy clear broths into which one can add things as availability and fancy dictate.

A perfectly balanced consommé is a creation of great beauty and complexity. My fridge is never without jellied chicken stock, its ongoing production an automatic part of my kitchen routine. A weak chicken consommé can be used even with fish, though it should not always be included in vegetable soups. These benefit from vegetable stock or even water.

WATERCRESS SOUP

Watercress is in the process of being rediscovered. Not that it ever went away, but there was certainly less of it about in restaurants after 1970, when its presence as a garnish for grilled steaks ceased to be automatic as chefs became conscious of the winds of presentational change blowing from across the Channel. Whether this preceded or succeeded a drop in consumption of watercress as a salad leaf eaten at home is debatable.

Whatever the reason, people rather forgot about it – which is a pity, because it shares a number of characteristics with the more fashionable and expensive rocket, having a strong clean flavour and a distinctively peppery finish. This makes it a particularly appropriate complement for any plain grilled fish or meat, or to cut the richness and fattiness of fried foods. A bunch of watercress goes well with fish and chips, for example, as good a reason for eating it as its indisputably healthy characteristics.

The great joy of watercress is to be found in its raw state, the texture and colour being integral to its enjoyment, and both are adversely affected by cooking. An acceptable half-way house is to be found in this soup, where the watercress is not cooked but rather puréed and warmed through. Bunches of watercress vary in size but, typically, a bunch will weigh 115 g (4 oz).

serves 4-6
225 g (8 oz) onions, sliced
45 g (1½ oz) unsalted butter
800 g (1¾ lb) potatoes, peeled and thinly sliced
600 ml (1 pint) milk
bunch of watercress, including stems
salt and pepper
4–6 tbsp double cream

Sweat the onions in the butter over a low heat until soft and translucent. Add the potatoes and turn to coat.

Pour in the milk followed by 600 ml (1 pint) of water and bring to the boil. Season with a little salt and cook until the potatoes are just done.

Transfer the contents of the pan to a food processor, together with the watercress (reserving 4 perfect leaves for garnish) and blitz to a purée.

Taste and add a little more salt and some pepper if you think it needs it, though the watercress is already quite peppery. If the purée is too thick, thin with a little hot water.

Serve at once in warmed bowls, zig-zagging the cream across the surface and placing one of the reserved whole watercress leaves in the centre of each. If you cannot serve immediately, keep warm over the lowest heat, but only briefly, or the impact of the watercress flavour will be diminished and the green will turn khaki.

CARROT AND CORIANDER SOUP

This has become a commercial cliché, insipid and gutless in its absence of coriander flavour. Now that it is easier to buy coriander with the roots on, you can make a much better soup. It is the roots that give a terrific depth of flavour, with the addition of chilli and lemon giving it an edge. It is very good chilled.

serves 6
175 g (6 oz) diced onion
4 tbsp olive oil
3 garlic cloves, finely chopped
1 scotch bonnet or habanero chilli, shredded
60 g (2 oz) washed coriander roots, chopped, plus whole leaves for garnish
600 g (1¼ lb) carrots, diced

1.5 litres (2¾ pints) light chicken or vegetable stock
salt and pepper
juice of ½ lemon
150 ml (¼ pint) crème fraîche

Sweat the diced onion in the olive oil until soft, then add the chopped garlic, shredded chilli and coriander roots. Continue to cook, stirring, for 2–3 minutes. Turn the carrots in the pan with the other ingredients. Pour in the stock, season with salt and pepper, and simmer for 30 minutes.

Transfer to a processor and blitz to a purée, adding the lemon juice and crème fraîche through the feeder tube as you do so. Chill for at least 4 hours, tasting and adjusting the seasoning after adding the cream.

Serve in large chilled soup bowls, scattered with a few whole coriander leaves.

CHILLED PEA SOUP WITH CRÈME FRAÎCHE

This is a cold soup for the summer, though it also works when served hot. If you have fresh peas from the garden use them, but frozen petits pois are sweetest. Canned peas just won't hack it. You can also use frozen leaf spinach but, if so, do not blanch it.

Crème fraîche crops up from time to time in this book. It can be used to thicken savoury sauces and soups, and has a unique flavour that is both astringent and smooth at the same time. It is made from double cream mixed with buttermilk, which is then heated gently for several hours until it thickens and stabilizes, acquiring its distinctive tangy taste.

serves 4
salt and pepper
175 g (6 oz) shallots, peeled
60 g (2 oz) unsalted butter
300 g (10½ oz) spinach leaves, destalked
500 g (1 lb 2 oz) frozen peas
850 ml (1½ pints) chicken stock
1 tsp caster sugar
150 ml (¼ pint) crème fraîche
8 basil leaves, torn, to garnish

Bring a large pan of salted water to the boil. Cut the shallots across into thin slices and then cut these into small dice.

Put the butter in a frying pan over a low heat and sweat the shallot dice until soft. Cut the stems from the spinach, then plunge the leaves in the rapidly boiling water for 20 seconds. Refresh in cold water, drain and reserve.

Stir the peas into the shallots and continue to cook for 2–3 minutes, stirring, then add the stock. Bring to the boil, lower the heat and simmer for 10 minutes if the peas are fresh. (If frozen they will need no simmering.)

Transfer to a food processor with the spinach and blitz to a purée. Pass through a sieve into a bowl, pushing through as much of the purée as you can. Add the sugar and season generously with salt and pepper. Leave to cool, then chill for at least 4 hours or overnight.

Just before serving, stir in the crème fraîche, adding a little milk as well if the soup is too thick. Adjust the seasoning, if necessary. Ladle into chilled bowls and serve with torn basil leaves scattered on top.

SAVOY CABBAGE AND POTATO SOUP

If you have some mashed potatoes left over, this soup is made very quickly, but only add them when the cabbage is done. For such an uncomplicated dish it has delicate and complex flavours.

serves 4
6 spring onions, thinly sliced
3 tbsp olive oil
2 garlic cloves, finely chopped
900 g (2 lb) potatoes, diced
600 ml (1 pint) chicken stock
½ Savoy cabbage, outer leaves and base stalk removed
freshly grated nutmeg
salt and pepper
handful of flat-leaf parsley leaves
extra-virgin olive oil, to dress
4 tbsp crème fraîche, to finish

Sweat the onions in the olive oil until soft. Add the garlic and cook, stirring, for 1 minute. Then add the diced raw potatoes, the stock and 600 ml (1 pint) water. Bring to the boil and cook for 10 minutes, mash, then add the shredded cabbage and season to taste with nutmeg, salt and pepper. Continue to cook until the potatoes disintegrate and you have a purée flecked with cabbage.

Chop the parsley finely and stir it in. Cook for a further minute, then ladle into large warmed soup bowls. Dress with zig-zags of extra-virgin olive oil and float a spoonful of crème fraîche in the middle.

RASAM

Rasam is the chilli-hot soup of Southern India and Sri Lanka which is characterized by sour tamarind, the partially dried seeds and pods of the tamarind tree. You buy it in packets, peeled and deseeded, which you should press to make sure it is pliant. If it has gone hard, then it has dried out and you will not be able to extract much pulp. The pulp is soaked and the extract strained through a sieve; it is this tamarind water that is used in cooking, the leftover solids being discarded. Though when dried they are apparently very good for polishing brass, something I have never felt the urge to check out.

The other defining ingredient of *rasam* is curry leaves, which can be bought fresh or dried from some Asian grocers. They actually smell like a compound curry powder and impart a really fabulous flavour that is unique. I always keep a bag in the freezer, because they are quite difficult to find fresh and fresh are superior to dried. They are especially good in sambars and vegetable curries like avial.

Rasam is supposed to be very hot, but there is little to be gained from using authentic levels of chilli if your guests go puce in the face and do lots of hand-flapping and panting. I once cooked a Thai green curry for Sky News and you would have thought from the fuss the presenters made that I had tried to kill them. To spare your own feelings, if not those for whom you are cooking the *rasam*, find out how they are with well-spiced food. If they are going to be weedy then make something else.

You can make tamarind water fresh each time, by soaking the pulp and seed mixture in warm water, then rubbing it between your fingers. The approximate ratio of water to solids is 10:1. Alternatively, you can make a larger amount and freeze it. This has the dual benefits of immediacy and the extraction is done when the tamarind pulp is relatively fresh.

To do so, break 500 g (1 lb 2 oz) of it into lumps, put into a bowl and pour over 1.1 litres (2 pints) of boiling water. Leave to steep for an hour or overnight. Strain through a sieve, pressing the pulp with the back of a wooden spoon to extract as much liquid as possible. Pour this liquid into ice-cube trays and freeze, transferring the cubes to a zip-lock bag so you will always have it to hand when you need it. You can now also buy bottles of tamarind water, the most effortless solution to always having some to hand.

serves 6
115 g (4 oz) dal (split peas)
2 tsp ground turmeric
5-cm (2-inch) piece of root ginger, peeled and cut into thin strips
2 tsp coriander seeds
4 ripe plum tomatoes, blanched and peeled
500 g (1 lb 2 oz) canned plum tomatoes, puréed
2 tbsp tamarind water (see above)
6 garlic cloves
16 fresh curry leaves
6 hot red chillies, shredded
30 g (1 oz) coriander leaves, stems and roots
1½ tsp salt
3 tbsp groundnut or sunflower oil
115 g (4 oz) shallots, thinly sliced
2 tsp black mustard seeds
2 tsp cumin seeds

Put the dal in a large pan with 1.1 litres (2 pints) of water, the turmeric and the ginger. Bring to the boil, cover with a lid, lower the heat and simmer for 45 minutes. Check occasionally to make sure it does not dry out, stirring in more water if it does. Remove from the heat.

Toast the coriander seeds in a dry pan over a low heat for 3–4 minutes, grind to a powder and reserve.

Quarter the peeled fresh tomatoes, putting the pulp in a saucepan and reserving the pieces. Add the puréed canned tomatoes to the pulp in the pan with 850 ml (1½ pints) of water, the tamarind water, 4 garlic cloves, finely chopped, 8 of the curry leaves, the chillies, the ground coriander, a handful of coriander stems and roots, coarsely chopped, and the salt. Bring to the boil, cover with a lid, lower the heat and simmer for 1 hour.

Skim out 300 ml (½ pint) of the liquid from the top of the dal and add to the tomato pan with 4 tablespoons of the dal. Blitz this mixture in a food processor, then pass through a sieve into a clean pan, pushing through as much of the solids as you can with a spoon.

In a frying pan, heat the oil until hot but not smoking. Fry the shallots quickly until they start to soften. Cut the remaining 2 garlic cloves into paper-thin slices and toss them in the oil with the shallots, mustard seeds, cumin seeds and 8 remaining curry leaves. As the garlic browns and the seeds start to pop, pour and scrape into the soup. Chop a handful of coriander leaves and stir in with the reserved tomato pieces. It should be very liquid. Add water if needed.

Leave to stand off the heat, covered with a lid, for 5 minutes to allow the flavours to mix and develop. The leftover dal can be stir-fried with onions and garlic to make the soup more robust or added to another soup. In any case, serve with lots of whole coriander leaves on top.

COCONUT AND PIGEON PEA SOUP WITH HAM

Pigeon peas can be bought from West Indian markets, or you can substitute black-eyed peas.

serves 4–6
350 g (12 oz) pigeon peas or black-eyed peas, soaked overnight
1 ham hock
225 g (8 oz) onions, chopped
3 garlic cloves, cut into paper-thin slices
1 bay leaf
1 tsp dried chilli flakes
30 g (1 oz) coriander, with stems and roots, tied in a bunch
salt and pepper
600 ml (1 pint) chicken stock
300 ml (½ pint) coconut milk

In separate saucepans, cover the peas and ham hock with cold water and bring to the boil. Throw this water away and put the ham and peas in the same pot. Add the onion, garlic, bay leaf, chilli flakes, coriander stems and roots, and pepper.

Pour over the stock and then top up with cold water to cover. Bring to the boil, lower the heat and simmer for 1½ hours.

Remove the ham hock to a board. Remove and discard the bay leaf and coriander stems and roots.

As soon as it is cool enough to handle, remove all the meat from the hock and shred. Chop the coriander leaves finely. Add the coconut milk to the peas and stir in the ham and coriander, only adding salt if you think it needs it.

Simmer for 5 minutes before ladling into large, warmed soup bowls to serve.

FENNEL SOUP WITH FRESH BORLOTTI

Speckled like tiny birds' eggs and nestling in their elegant violet-streaked pods, fresh borlotti beans are irresistible. Borlotti rank amongst the most beautiful vegetables in the world and I noticed that Marcella Hazan chose to be photographed shelling them for the cover of her most recent book, *Marcella Cucina*. You will need about a kilo (2 lb) of borlotti in their pods to produce enough beans to serve 4 people.

In this soup, the fennel is puréed, with the borlotti cooked separately and presented whole in the middle of the dish. Most fennel is sold trimmed of its frond-like leaves. Ideally you will find some left untrimmed as, finely chopped, a spoonful of these makes the perfect garnish. If you are unable to obtain fennel fronds, then substitute finely chopped parsley to coat the beans.

serves 6

675 g (1½ lb) fennel (with fronds if possible)
150 g (5 oz) onions
3 tbsp olive oil
60 g (2 oz) butter
115 g (4 oz) potato, diced
1 garlic clove, chopped
1.25 litres (2¼ pints) vegetable stock
salt and pepper
3 tbsp mascarpone cheese
3 tbsp dry white wine
about 350 g (12 oz) shelled borlotti beans
600 ml (1 pint) boiling water

Dice the fennel and onions into 1-cm (½-inch) chunks and sweat these in the olive oil and half the butter in a saucepan over a low heat, stirring occasionally, until softened – but do not allow to colour.

Add the potatoes and garlic, and continue to cook for a minute. Add the stock, season with salt and pepper and bring to the boil. Turn down the heat and simmer until the vegetables are tender, 15–20 minutes.

Purée in a food processor with the mascarpone, then taste and adjust the seasoning. Return to the pan over the lowest heat to keep warm.

While the vegetables are cooking, in another pan, place the wine over a high heat. When bubbling hard, add the beans and cook, stirring until the wine evaporates. Immediately add the boiling water and cook for about 12 minutes, or until just done. Season to taste and drain, then return to the pan. If you have them, finely chop enough fennel fronds to give 1 tablespoon. Add to the beans with the remaining butter and turn with a spoon to coat.

Ladle the purée into large warmed bowls, mounding the beans in the middle.

A few snipped pieces of fennel frond may be scattered over.

GARLIC AND POTATO SOUP

This is best made with the first, intensely flavoured, wet garlic of the season, but old garlic is fine, the latter giving a more mellow flavour. Because it is completely cooked in broth the flavour of the garlic will never be overpowering.

serves 6
675 g (1½ lb) garlic
1.1 litres (2 pints) chicken or vegetable stock
225 g (8 oz) onion, diced
60 g (2 oz) butter
300 ml (½ pint) dry white wine
350 g (12 oz) mashed potato
salt and pepper
extra-virgin olive oil, to dress
finely snipped chives, to garnish

Cut the tops off the heads of garlic and discard. Simmer the garlic heads in the stock for 30 minutes.

During the last 20 minutes of this simmering, sweat the onion in the butter until soft and translucent.

Remove the garlic from the stock and, when cool enough to handle, squeeze out the cloves (which will have softened almost to a paste) into the onion and discard the skins.

Stir the garlic into the pan with the onion and fry gently together for 2–3 minutes. Pour in the wine, bring to the boil, lower the heat and simmer for 5 minutes.

Add the stock, stir in the mashed potato, season with salt and pepper and simmer gently for a final 5 minutes before serving.

Serve dressed with extra-virgin olive oil in a zigzag on the surface and scattered with finely chopped chives.

ORZO SOUP WITH FENNEL AND ONION

Orzo is Italian for pearl barley, the husked, steamed and coarsely ground grain that cooks to a gelatinous and thickened finish and which used to feature widely in simple British dishes, where it provided cheap bulk more than flavour, a typical example being its inclusion in neck of lamb stew.

It is suddenly a fashionable ingredient, I suspect because of its pretty Italian name. Is there a restaurant called Orzo? If not, there soon will be. Orso already exists in London, as does Riva. There will also hopefully be one called Rima for young media folk.

serves 4
400 g (14 oz) fennel bulbs
400 g (14 oz) onion
115 g (4 oz) pearl barley
1 garlic clove, chopped
salt and pepper
extra-virgin olive oil, to dress and serve
grated Parmesan cheese, to serve

Cut off the fronds from the fennel and reserve, then cut the bulb into small dice. Thinly slice the onions.

Put 1.5 litres (2¾ pints) of water into a large pan and bring to the boil. Stir in the fennel, onion, garlic, barley and 1 teaspoon of salt. Lower the heat, cover with a lid and simmer for 50 minutes.

Measure out 600 ml (1 pint) of the soup into a food processor or liquidizer and blitz to a purée. Return this to the pan. Stir in and continue cooking over a moderate heat, uncovered, for 8–10 minutes, stirring from time to time. It will be very thick. If too solid, add boiling water. Taste, adding salt and pepper as you like.

Serve in large warmed bowls, with a zig-zag of oil on top, scattering the finely chopped fennel fronds over. Offer more extra-virgin olive oil and grated Parmesan at the table for people to help themselves.

THREE BEAN CHUPE

Puréed white beans flavoured with bacon and aromatics are served with whole black and red beans, the chupe being finished with caramelized garlic, olive oil and a scattering of finely chopped fennel to give an attractive presentation. When fresh beans, like borlotti, are available you can replace either the black or red beans to good effect. If you can't get fennel with its fronds attached, scatter over chopped chives or parsley.

serves 4–6
150 g (5 oz) white haricot beans, soaked overnight
85 g (3 oz) black beans, soaked overnight
85 g (3 oz) red kidney beans, soaked overnight
225 g (8 oz) piece of smoked streaky bacon in a piece
2 bay leaves
1 tsp dried chilli flakes
5 tbsp olive oil
150 g (5 oz) onion, diced
1 head of fennel, diced, plus the fronds for garnish
2 celery stalks, diced
salt and pepper
1.25 litres (2¼ pints) chicken stock
3 garlic cloves, cut into paper-thin slices
1 tsp caster sugar

In separate saucepans, bring each of the types of bean to the boil. Throw away and replace the water for the haricot and black beans. Add the bacon, bay leaves and chilli flakes to the haricots. Boil the red beans vigorously for 10 minutes before replacing the water. Simmer all the beans for about an hour or until just done. Discard the bay leaves and reserve the bacon.

Put 3 tablespoons of the oil in a frying pan over a low heat and sweat the onions, fennel and celery in this until soft, stirring at regular intervals.

When done, transfer to a food processor. Drain the haricots and add. Season with salt and pepper. Purée, adding the chicken stock through the feeder tube. Add some bean liquor as well, if the purée is too thick. Pour into a saucepan, add the whole red and black beans and bring to a simmer. Shred the cooked bacon and stir in. Simmer for 5 minutes, stirring from time to time.

Fry the garlic gently in the remaining olive oil, stirring until it starts to brown. Sprinkle over the sugar and cook for a few more seconds.

Ladle the soup into large warmed soup bowls. Zig-zag a little extra-virgin olive oil on top and scatter over the fried garlic and some finely chopped fennel fronds.

LEEK AND PUMPKIN SOUP WITH WHITE WINE AND SALT PORK

It was in Macon that I ate this soup and was told that pumpkin is often used in southern Burgundy for its ability to thicken liquid dishes rather than for its flavour. This makes sense, for the taste is scarcely assertive. The inclusion of salt pork rather than bacon is deliberate. This is the *petit salé* used in larger quantities in the recipe on page 126. The soup can, of course, be made without it, though this rather misses its point.

Choose a bone-dry white Burgundy for the wine, which can also be drunk with the soup. Soup generally is a killer of decent wine, but I am not suggesting you use a fine Chablis. Supermarkets sell OK generic white Burgundy, fine for the soup and to drink with it. If you don't like the idea, then a glass of dry sherry is delicious with any soup.

serves 6
225 g (8 oz) Petit Salé (salt pork, page 125)
75 g (2¾ oz) unsalted butter
115 g (4 oz) onions, diced
275 g (10 oz) leeks, sliced
275 g (10 oz) potatoes
275 g (10 oz) pumpkin, rind removed and deseeded
300 ml (½ pint) dry white wine
salt and pepper
chives, to garnish

If the pork is very salty, cover it with cold water and bring to the boil. Throw this water away and rinse the pork under cold running water before proceeding.

Cut the pork into 5-mm (¼-inch) dice and sweat in a saucepan with 60 g (2 oz) of the butter until the pork fat runs and the pork starts to colour. Add the onion and leeks, and continue to cook until they are soft and translucent.

Cut the potatoes and pumpkin into 3-cm (1¼-inch) chunks and add to the pan. Pour in the white wine and bring to the boil. Add 1.25 litres (2¼ pints) of water and season with pepper. Return to the boil, lower the heat and simmer for 25–30 minutes. Taste and add salt if necessary. Transfer to a food processor and purée. Rinse the pan and return the soup to it.

To serve, whisk in the remaining butter. Ladle into large warmed bowls and snip some chives in the middle of each.

BEAN CREMA WITH PANCETTA AND BAY LEAVES

Dried bay leaves can be powerful and intrusive, so we usually add them with restraint. In this Pugliese soup, bay leaves are used quite deliberately in larger quantities, but they must be fresh and are first blanched in boiling water and then traditionally served on top of the soup, though they are not to be eaten! Finely chopped celery leaves are stirred in to improve the flavour, but are not essential.

serves 4
325 g (11½ oz) dried borlotti or cannellini beans, soaked overnight
2 dried bay leaves
115 g (4 oz) pancetta in a piece
5 tbsp extra-virgin olive oil
175 g (6 oz) onions
115 g (4 oz) carrots
115 g (4 oz) celery stalks, trimmed, plus a handful of leaves
1 garlic clove, chopped
4 fresh bay leaves
1.1 litres (2 pints) chicken or vegetable stock
salt and pepper

Bring the beans to the boil, throw away the water and cover with fresh cold water by 2.5 cm (1 inch). Bring back to the boil, add the dried bay leaves, lower the heat and simmer gently for 1–1¼ hours, until the beans are tender.

Dice the pancetta and fry it gently in 3 tablespoons of the olive oil until it starts to brown. Dice the onion, carrot and celery and sweat with the pancetta until the onion is soft and translucent. Then add the garlic and cook for 2 minutes more. Stir into the beans after they have been simmering for 30 minutes.

Pour boiling water over the fresh bay leaves in a small bowl and leave for 5 minutes.

Drain the beans, pancetta and vegetables, reserving some of the cooking liquid and discarding the cooked dried bay leaves. Put the beans in a food processor and liquidize, pouring the stock through the feeder tube. If too thick, add spoonfuls of the cooking liquid until you have the consistency of pouring cream. Return this purée to the saucepan and taste, seasoning with salt and pepper. Bring to the boil, turn down the heat and simmer for 5 minutes.

Finely chop the celery leaves and stir in. Simmer for 5 minutes and ladle into large warmed soup bowls. Zig-zag the remaining olive oil on top and put a fresh bay leaf in the middle of each bowl before serving.

SMOKED HADDOCK CREAM

Cullen is a small fishing port on the southern shore of the Moray Firth, 'skink' the Scottish word for broth, hence 'cullen skink', the Scottish name for this dish. I do not like the kind of restaurants which insist on calling dishes by their ancient names or describing them in fake Olde Englishe calligraphy on the menu and never forget that partan bree rhymes with twee. Cullen skink, however, is a proper title for smoked haddock cream if you want to go down that road.

There are many recipes for it, though all include smoked haddock, potatoes and cream in varying amounts. There is really no need to buy the best Finnan smoked haddock for soup. You will be paying for a lot of bones and making unnecessary preparation for yourself, so just buy properly smoked haddock fillets. Using the same method, a nice smoky soup can be made with kipper fillets.

serves 4-6

225 g (8 oz) onions, diced
30 g (1 oz) unsalted butter
500 g (1 lb 2 oz) floury potatoes, peeled and diced
850 ml (1½ pints) milk
salt and pepper
1 bay leaf
500 g (1 lb 2 oz) smoked haddock fillets
300 ml (½ pint) single or double cream
3 tbsp chopped flat-leaf parsley

Sweat the onion in the butter until soft and translucent, then stir in the potato dice and turn to coat. Pour in the milk. Season with plenty of pepper and a little salt. Add the bay leaf, stir, bring to the boil and immediately lower the heat to simmer. Continue to simmer for 15–20 minutes, or until the potato dice are just cooked.

Remove any pin bones and skin from the smoked haddock fillets, then cut into bite-sized pieces. Add to the pot with the cream and a handful of chopped parsley. Return to a simmer and cook for 3 minutes.

Discard the bay leaf and serve at once, in large warmed bowls, scattered with a little more of the chopped parsley.

SHELLFISH CONSOMMÉ WITH PRAWN CAKES

The light prawn dumplings are floated in a clear broth flavoured with a hint of star anise.

serves 4

500 g (1 lb 2 oz) frozen raw tiger prawns, with heads and shells
salt and pepper
4 shallots, chopped
2 garlic cloves, finely chopped
5-cm (2-inch) piece of root ginger, peeled and chopped
1 star anise
2 tbsp rice vinegar
12 black peppercorns
2 tbsp fish sauce
1 sachet (7g) dashi-no-moto (page 30)
15 g (½ oz) coriander, leaves and stalks
white of 1 egg
½ tsp dried chilli flakes
1 tbsp soy sauce

Defrost the prawns slowly. Remove the heads and peel off the shells. Cut along the back and remove the intestinal thread. Put the prawns in ice-cold heavily salted water and rub gently between your fingers for a minute. This removes any freezer taint and improves their flavour and texture.

Put the heads and shells, the shallots, garlic, ginger, star anise and vinegar in a pan and add 1.5 litres (2¾ pints) of water. Bring to the boil, skim, lower the heat, add the peppercorns and simmer for 30 minutes.

Pass through a fine sieve into a clean pan and add the fish sauce and *dashi* granules. Keep hot over a low heat or, if more convenient, leave to cool and then chill for a few hours until needed.

Put a large pan of lightly salted water on to bring to the boil.

Put the prawns, coriander (reserving some whole leaves for garnish), egg white, chilli flakes and soy sauce in a food processor. Season with pepper and pulse-chop to a thick purée. Use a dessertspoon to remove walnut-sized balls of the mixture and poach these in the boiling salted water for 2 minutes, when they will have bobbed to the surface.

Transfer to warm bowls, ladle over the broth and scatter over some whole coriander leaves.

MUSSELS IN MILK AND WHITE WINE BROTH

Mussel soup, if thickened at all, is usually cooked with cream. Milk makes for a less rich and more delicate finish. The dish is made in two stages. If more convenient, the mussels may be cooked a day ahead and refrigerated until needed.

serves 4

300 ml (½ pint) dry white wine
1 kg (2¼ lb) cleaned mussels
10 red shallots, thinly sliced
60 g (2 oz) unsalted butter
850 ml (1½ pints) full-fat milk
20 saffron threads
2 tbsp finely chopped flat-leaf parsley
115 g (4 oz) dry mashed potato
salt and pepper

Put the white wine in a wide shallow pan and bring to the boil. Add the mussels, cover with a lid and cook, shaking from time to time, until they open, about 3 minutes. Strain through a sieve, reserving the liquor.

Reserve 12 mussels in their shells and shuck the rest.

Sweat the shallots in the butter until soft and translucent. Add the reserved wine and mussel liquor, the milk, saffron and parsley. Bring to the boil, lower the heat and beat in the mashed potato. Simmer for 5 minutes. Taste and season with salt and pepper, then add the shucked mussels and simmer for 2 minutes.

Put 3 mussels in their shells in the centre of each warmed soup bowl and ladle over the soup.

CLAM CHOWDER

The first time I ever heard of clam chowder was in *Moby Dick*, where Herman Melville describes Ishmael waxing lyrical over the bowl he ate at the Try Pots Inn on his first night in New Bedford: 'Oh! sweet friends, hearken to me. It was made of small juicy clams, scarcely bigger than hazelnuts, mixed with pounded ship biscuits, and salt pork cut up into little flakes; the whole enriched with butter.' Since those days, chowder has lightened somewhat.

Green bacon rather than salt pork is more common, diced potato and onions play an important part and the stew is more likely to be thickened with flour than ship's biscuits or, more luxuriously, with cream. In a reference back to the original ship's biscuits, little salty crackers are served with chowder for people to crumble into their bowls at the table.

This chowder is based on the recipe given by Fanny Farmer in her famous and eponymous cookbook, widely regarded as the *sine qua non* in such matters. The large quahog or steamer clams of Massachusetts, which are minced because they are tough, are hard to come by in Britain, so use the smaller local carpetshell variety which are also called 'palourdes'. Apparently the only place quahogs are found is along the Solent, where it is thought they established themselves from ones thrown overboard with kitchen rubbish from incoming American cruise liners.

One of the best clam chowders I have tasted is served by Legal Seafood, a Boston-based chain of restaurants the slogan of which is, 'If it ain't fresh, it ain't legal,' and which is currently expanding at a rate of knots, like some high-class burger chain. Beware, Legal, beware. Founder George Berkowitz says that he reckons the Legal clam chowder is the best in the business. 'We sell about seven hundred gallons of clam chowder each week at our restaurants and take-out counters. The reason for its popularity is simple. We use only the best ingredients and plenty of them. Don't try and economize by cutting back on the amount of clams or cream because the chowder will never taste as flavourful as ours.' Well maybe so, Mr Berkowitz, maybe so.

serves 4 as main course, 6 as first course

1 kg (2¼ lb) carpetshell clams
3 tbsp dry white wine
60 g (2 oz) unsalted butter
225 g (8 oz) salt pork (page 125), cut into fat matchsticks
450 g (1 lb) onions, diced
1.5 litres (2¾ pints) fish or shellfish stock or water
2 small carrots, peeled and diced
2 celery stalks
450 g (1 lb) potatoes, peeled and diced
1 bay leaf
salt and pepper
freshly grated nutmeg
150 ml (¼ pint) double cream
1 tbsp chopped flat-leaf parsley
oyster or saltine crackers, to serve

Wash the clams, then put them in a pan with the wine and half the butter. Cover with a lid and cook over a moderate heat, shaking, until they are all open. Leave until cool enough to handle.

Shuck the clams, discarding the shells, put them in a bowl with the buttery juices from the pan and reserve.

Fry the salt pork matchsticks gently in a large pan with the remaining butter until the fat runs and they start to brown. Add the diced onions and fry with the bacon until they soften. Pour over the fish or shellfish stock or water and stir in the carrots, celery and potatoes. Put in a bay leaf, season with salt, pepper and grated nutmeg and bring to the boil. Lower the heat and simmer gently, stirring from time to time, until the potatoes are almost done.

Add the clams, double cream and chopped parsley. Taste, adjust the seasoning and simmer for a few more minutes before serving with oyster or saltine crackers.

CARPETSHELL CLAM AND FRESH BORLOTTI BEAN SOUP

Most of us encounter borlotti beans in their dried form, but fresh beans in the pod are now more widely available in season. A kilo (2 lb) of fresh beans in their pods will yield about 450 g (1 lb) of shelled beans. You can use any small clams. They are cooked separately and added in their shells just before serving. Inexpensive mussels can be substituted for the more expensive clams, though it makes it a very different dish.

serves 4
1.35 kg (3 lb) fresh borlotti beans
1.75 litres (3¼ pints) shellfish stock
150 ml (¼ pint) olive oil
225 g (8 oz) red shallots, thinly sliced
2 garlic cloves, chopped
½ tsp dried chilli flakes
salt and pepper
500 g (1 lb 2 oz) small clams
30 g (1 oz) flat-leaf parsley

Put a pot of water on to heat to the boil. Shell the beans and cook until just done, about 12 minutes, drain and reserve. While they are cooking, put the shellfish stock to heat to a simmer in another pan.

Put the olive oil in a shallow pan over a low heat. Stir the shallots into the oil and cook gently for 5 minutes until softened.

Mix the garlic with the chilli flakes.

Put the beans into the fish stock to warm through. Taste and season with salt and pepper.

Rinse the clams, discarding any that are open or cracked. Turn up the heat under the oil to medium and, when the oil is very hot, stir in the garlic and chilli flakes, followed by the clams. Cover with a lid and shake. They will cook very quickly and are done as soon as they have all opened, which will only take a minute or two. Remove from the heat and stir in the finely chopped parsley.

Ladle the beans and broth into 4 large warmed soup bowls. Ladle the clams with their oil and cooking liquid in the centre of each and serve at once. A large empty bowl for the shells and finger bowls are a good idea.

JAPANESE BROTHS

Japanese soups are mostly based on konbu seaweed and bonito flakes (page 162) or on soya bean paste (miso, page 162). There are instant soup base mixes available and, of these, I find *dashi-no-moto* particularly useful – tiny granules which make a delicious, slightly smoky broth with the addition of hot water, though they do contain MSG if that bothers you. However, *ichiban dashi*, the primary stock made from a first infusion of konbu leaf and dried bonito flakes – known as 'number one stock' – and *niban dashi*, or 'number two stock', which is made from cooking on the same ingredients from the *ichiban dashi*, are both so quick and easy to make that there seems little point in not doing so.

ICHIBAN DASHI

There is no Japanese cooking without *dashi*. It is at the very heart of the food culture, a medium in which to cook as well as a standard soup base. Its flavour is as essentially Japanese as Kikkoman soy sauce.

You can buy the konbu in packets of various sizes, but 15-cm squares are fairly standard. The konbu and bonito flakes are not simmered for long periods as one would when making a western stock.

When straining the finished stock you want to pass it through butter muslin but, if you don't have any, use a J-cloth (called kitchen wipes or handi-wipes in the USA). Wash it until it has lost any traces of the manufacturer's 'fragrance' and line the sieve with it. You could also use a drying-up cloth or table napkin.

makes about 2.25 litres (4 pints)
three 15-cm (6-inch) squares of konbu (page 162)
30 g (1 oz) bonito flakes (page 162)

Rinse the konbu under cold water and wipe with a cloth. Put it in a pan with 2.25 litres (4 pints) of cold water and slowly bring to the boil, removing the konbu with tongs as the first bubble breaks the surface. Put the konbu in another pan and reserve for making the *niban dashi*.

Add the bonito flakes to the *dashi*, stir and turn off the heat. Leave to stand untouched until the flakes have settled to the bottom. Wet some butter muslin, wring it out and line a sieve with it before passing the *dashi* into a bowl or clean pan.

NIBAN DASHI

makes about 700 ml (1¼ pints)
blanched konbu and bonito flakes from the Ichiban Dashi (above)
15 g (½ oz) bonito flakes (page 162)

Return the used bonito flakes from the sieve to the pan with the blanched konbu. Pour over 1.1 litres (2 pints) of cold water and bring to a simmer over a moderate heat. Stir in the fresh bonito flakes and turn down the heat to its lowest setting. Simmer for 5 minutes.

Put a sieve lined with a double thickness of damp butter muslin or cloth over a bowl and pour in the *dashi* to drain through. Discard the konbu and bonito.

Return the stock to a clean pan and return to the boil. Turn down the heat and simmer until reduced by one-third.

The stock should be used immediately and, if refrigerated, within two days. It can be frozen but, frankly, when the whole point is the freshness of the flavour and when making it takes only minutes, freezing is more trouble than it is worth.

SHELLFISH AND DASHI WITH STEAMED PRAWN DUMPLINGS

Steamed bread dough makes the best dumplings, because the absence of fat and the process of steaming rather than poaching deliver a lovely light texture and a discernibly different taste. Biting through the spongy exterior into the moist and intriguingly spiced prawn centre is a pleasing experience of taste and textural contrast. These are several miles away from the heavy, suet-based form that people often associate with the dumpling name.

Any raw prawns can be used, the ones sold shell-on giving benefit to the broth. Sichimi is aromatic rather than chilli-hot, which is why I have added a little more heat to the mix with a fresh red chilli.

serves 4
500 g (1 lb 2 oz) unpeeled raw prawns, peeled and deveined
3 spring onions, thinly sliced

1 egg yolk
¼ tsp sichimi pepper mix (page 163)
1 tsp chopped coriander leaves
¼ tsp finely chopped hot red chilli
600 g (1¼ lb) proved Ciabatta dough (page 306)

FOR THE BROTH:
1.1 litres (2 pints) light shellfish broth or fish stock
1 lemon grass stalk, hard outer layers removed and thinly sliced
20 black peppercorns
600 ml (1 pint) Ichiban Dashi (page 30)
1 tbsp Kikkoman soy sauce
100 ml (3½ fl oz) sake
3.5-cm (1½-cm) piece of root ginger, peeled and shaved across into paper-thin slices
16 coriander leaves

The three activities involved in finishing the stock and making the dumplings can be done at the same time and will take about 30 minutes.

Put on a pan of water to boil for steaming.

Put the prawns, spring onions, egg yolk, sichimi, coriander and chilli in a food processor and blitz briefly to a paste. Divide the dough into 8 pieces, forming them into balls on a lightly floured surface. Poke a hole in the centre of each and put a spoonful of the prawn paste in the centre, then pull the dough up and around, and pinch shut.

Put them on plates in 2 steamer baskets, with the pinched edge upwards, cover with a lid and steam over rapidly boiling water for 20–25 minutes.

Make the broth: put the prawn shells and heads in a pan with the shellfish broth or fish stock, bring to the boil and skim. Then add the lemon grass and peppercorns. Lower the heat and simmer for 20 minutes, then strain through a cloth-lined sieve into a clean pan.

Add the *ichiban dashi*, soy sauce, sake and the shavings of ginger. Return to a simmer over the lowest heat for about 5 minutes.

To serve, ladle the broth into warmed bowls, distributing the ginger equally. Add 2 dumplings to each, and 4 whole coriander leaves.

NIBAN DASHI WITH CHICKEN, SPINACH AND TOFU

This is a pretty dish that can also be made substituting large raw prawns for the little mousseline chicken dumplings. The tofu has very little flavour but provides a textural counterpoint to the other ingredients.

serves 4
salt
1.1 litres (2 pints) Niban Dashi (page 31)
500 g (1 lb 2 oz) spinach
1 lemon, preferably organic
250 g (8½ oz) tofu
250 g (8½ oz) chicken breast, skinned
white of 1 egg
¼ tsp sansho pepper (page 163)
¼ tsp caster sugar
about 2 tsp Kikkoman soy sauce
flour for dusting (optional)
8 chive stalks

Put a large pan of salted water on to heat to the boil. Have ready a bowl of iced water. Put the *niban dashi* on to simmer over a low heat. Pick over the spinach, tearing out and discarding large stalks and throwing away or trimming any damaged leaves. Wash the spinach, drain and reserve.

Peel the lemon in a continuous strip and cut this strip into 4. Reserve. Cut the tofu into 8 squares.

Cut the chicken into pieces and put in a food

processor with the egg white, sansho pepper, sugar and soy sauce. Pulse-chop to a purée. Spoon out and divide into eight, form the pieces into balls with damp hands. If too sticky to work with, shape them using a little flour. Reserve on a lightly floured surface.

Blanch the spinach in rapidly boiling water until it starts to wilt, 15–20 seconds only. Using tongs, remove to the iced water for a few seconds to stop further cooking and drain in a colander.

Taste the *dashi*, adding soy sauce to season as you like.

Poach the chicken dumplings in the water in which you have cooked the spinach. They will quickly float to the surface and will be done in 4–5 minutes. Remove with a slotted spoon.

While they are poaching, gently squeeze out excess moisture from the spinach and line 4 warmed bowls with the leaves.

Put the tofu in a blanching basket and dip in the spinach water for 60 seconds to heat through. Put 2 pieces of tofu and 2 chicken dumplings in the middle of each spinach-lined bowl. Put a lemon strip on top, then carefully ladle *dashi* over. Scatter on some tiny pieces of chives. The easiest way is to snip them straight on to the soup with scissors.

CHICKEN AND PAK CHOI IN MUSHROOM BROTH

The chicken is pan-fried and the pak choi and mushrooms blanched separately. All that is required is a decent chicken consommé, some sake and a little mirin to produce a light and well-balanced dish.

When you can't find pak choi, then substitute bok choi, its larger cousin, but you will need to cut it up.

serves 4
salt
1 tsp Sichuan pepper
2 chicken breasts, skin on
2 tsp dark sesame oil
1.1 litres (2 pints) chicken stock
115 g (4 oz) shiitake mushrooms
2 tbsp sake or dry rice wine (page 163)
1 tbsp mirin (page 162)
2 tbsp Pearl River soy sauce
4 baby pak choi, washed

Put a large pan of salted water on to bring to the boil. Grind the Sichuan pepper to a powder.

Brush the chicken breasts with sesame oil and season with a little salt, then rub in the ground pepper.

Put a dry heavy-based frying pan over a low-to-medium heat and lay the chicken in it, skin side downwards. Fry for 6 minutes, then turn and give the other side about 4–5 minutes.

When done, remove to a carving board, skin side up. Leave to stand for 3–4 minutes before carving.

While the chicken is cooking and cooling, bring the stock to a simmer in a pan. Cut the shiitake mushrooms into slices, including the stalks, and add to the stock, together with the sake or rice wine, mirin and soy sauce.

Blanch the pak choi in the boiling water until they just wilt, 2–3 minutes. Drain and put to one side of 4 large warmed soup bowls. Carve the chicken breasts at an angle into 2-cm (3/4-inch) slices and put on the other side. Ladle over the broth.

Finely snip the chives on top before serving.

CHICKEN, SPINACH AND GINGER SOUP

Korean soups tend to be based on clear broths, in this case chicken. It is finished with sesame and chilli oils floated on the surface. My addition to an otherwise mostly traditional recipe is that of freshly squeezed ginger juice and finely shredded ginger, the juice being added just before it is served.

serves 4
7.5-cm (3-inch) piece of root ginger, peeled
2 chicken breasts, skinned
3 tbsp groundnut oil
4 spring onions, shredded
1 hot red chilli, shredded
2 tsp sesame seeds
3 garlic cloves, cut into paper-thin slices
1.5 litres (2¾ pints) chicken stock
2 tbsp Kikkoman soy sauce
450 g (1 lb) spinach, washed and destalked
2 tsp sesame oil
2 tsp chilli oil

Cut half the ginger into thin strips (julienne). Grate the other half into butter muslin over a bowl. Ball the muslin around the pulp and twist the cloth to extract as much juice as possible. Reserve.

Cut the chicken into thin strips. Put the groundnut oil in a wok over a moderate heat. When it shimmers, add the chicken, spring onions, ginger strips, chilli, sesame seeds and garlic. Stir-fry for 2–3 minutes.

Pour in the stock and soy sauce. Bring to the boil, lower the heat and simmer for 20 minutes. Stir in the spinach. As soon as it wilts, turn off the heat and add the ginger juice.

Ladle into deep bowls. Dribble the oils on top and serve immediately.

HOT-AND-SOUR SOUP

Chilli-hot and fragrant rather than vinegar-sour, this is really a winter soup. The inclusion of pork, beancurd, eggs and noodles makes it a substantial dish and one that can be served almost as a meal in itself.

serves 4
60 g (2 oz) dried Chinese mushrooms
1.25 litres (2¼ pints) chicken stock
1 star anise
20 black peppercorns
2 tbsp rice vinegar
2 tbsp Pearl River soy sauce
1 tsp caster sugar
60 g (2 oz) beanthread noodles (page 162)
225 g (8 oz) firm beancurd (tofu)
225 g (8 oz) pork fillet or other lean cut
2 tsp dark sesame oil
2 tsp groundnut oil
1–2 hot red chillies, shredded
1 garlic clove, finely chopped
1 heaped tbsp cornflour
2 eggs

FOR THE GARNISH:
1–1½ tsp dark sesame oil
pepper
2 spring onions, thinly sliced
handful of coriander leaves, coarsely chopped

The day before, soak the dried mushrooms for 20 minutes in 150 ml (¼ pint) of hot water.

Next day, strain through a sieve into the stock in a saucepan. Rinse the mushrooms under cold running water. Remove the caps and reserve, putting the stalks with the stock, together with the star anise and peppercorns. Bring to the boil, skim, lower the heat and simmer for 1 hour. Turn off the heat and leave until the next day.

Next day, strain the stock through a muslin-lined sieve into another saucepan. Bring to a simmer. Add the vinegar, soy sauce and sugar.

Chop the mushroom caps. Soak the noodles in warm water for 5 minutes, then drain and cut them into 12.5-cm (5-inch) lengths. Dice the beancurd. Cut the pork into strips.

Put the sesame and groundnut oils in a wok over a moderate heat. When the oil shimmers, swirl and add the pork and chilli. Stir-fry for 2 minutes, then add the garlic and continue to stir-fry for another minute. Add to the broth.

Stir in the noodles and beancurd. Simmer for 3 minutes. Mix the cornflour to a paste with a little cold water and stir in, continuing to simmer over the lowest heat for a minute or two.

Whisk the eggs. Swirl the soup and pour in the beaten egg in a thin stream. It will set instantly in threads.

Ladle into large warmed soup bowls, dribbling a few drops of sesame oil on top of each and grinding over plenty of pepper. Scatter the spring onions and coriander on top. Serve immediately while still seething-hot.

GARBANZO SOUP WITH HAM AND CHORIZO

This chickpea soup should be flavoured not with any old ham bone, but with one from an air-dried mountain ham, such as Pata Negra or Serrano, which you can buy from a delicatessen. Failing that, a Parma ham bone from an Italian shop will deliver the right kind of flavour. These hams are dry-cured in salt and are intended to be eaten raw and cold which means they are very salty when eaten hot. Before proceeding, cover the bone with cold water and bring to the boil. Throw this water away and rinse the bone under cold running water before proceeding.

To make the soup into a complete meal, add slices of chorizo at the end of cooking just to warm through, but it is still a decent soup without the sausage.

serves 6

300 g (10½ oz) chickpeas, soaked overnight
1 small Serrano, Bayonne or Parma ham bone, desalinated (see above)
2 bay leaves
4 celery stalks with leaves
2 hot red chillies
1.1 litres (2 pints) chicken stock
115 g (4 oz) carrot, peeled and diced
225 g (8 oz) onion, diced
30 g (1 oz) butter
2 garlic cloves, finely chopped
salt and pepper
3 tbsp chopped flat-leaf parsley, plus a handful to garnish
350 g (12 oz) chorizo
extra-virgin olive oil

Bring the chickpeas to the boil in their soaking water and boil hard for a minute or two. Drain, rinse and cover with fresh cold water by 2.5 cm (1 inch), then return to the boil. Add the ham bone, bay leaves, 2 of the celery stalks and the chillies. Turn down the heat and simmer until done, which will take 1–1½ hours. Drain, discarding the bay leaves, celery stalks and chillies, but reserving the ham bone and about 300 ml (½ pint) of the cooking liquid.

Put half the chickpeas in a food processor and purée. Put in a saucepan with the whole chickpeas and add the chicken stock. Reserve.

Dice the remaining celery stalks, the carrot and the onions, and sweat in the butter over a low heat until soft and the onion is translucent, being careful not to brown them. Stir in the garlic and fry gently for 2 minutes, then stir in the chickpeas and reserved cooking liquid. Season with plenty of pepper and bring to a simmer, stirring at regular intervals. Finely chop the celery leaves and parsley and stir in. Bring to the boil, lower the heat and simmer for 10–15 minutes.

Cut and pull any ham from the bone, shredding the meat, and cut the sausage across into 1-cm (½-inch) thick rounds. Taste the soup and season if necessary. Stir the ham and sausage into the soup. Turn up the heat a little and allow the meat to warm through.

Serve in large soup bowls, zig-zagging some extra-virgin olive oil over the surface and scattering on a few whole parsley leaves.

BEEF AND WAKAME IN SHELLFISH BROTH

This is based on a Korean soup but could also be made using *dashi* broth (page 30). The idea of cooking beef in a fishy broth sounds odd, but the result confounds your doubts. If you think of the way fish sauce is used to flavour meat dishes in Southeast Asia, or the way we use anchovies with beef and lamb, then it sounds less odd. Conversely, white firm-fleshed fish, like cod, can be cooked in chicken stock or sauced with a veal-based broth, so perhaps it is just another case of challenging received opinions and getting a result. A little dried wakame turns into an awful lot of seaweed.

serves 4

85 g (3 oz) wakame (page 163)
300 g (10½ oz) fillet of beef
1 tbsp sesame seeds
115 g (4 oz) red onion, diced
1 hot red chilli, shredded
3 tbsp groundnut oil
3 garlic cloves, finely chopped
1.25 litres (2¼ pints) shellfish stock
2 tbsp Kikkoman soy sauce

Reconstitute the wakame by pouring hot water over it and leaving it to soak for 10 minutes. Drain and reserve.

Cut the beef into the thinnest slices you can manage. A razor-sharp knife is obviously important, but chilling the meat in the freezer for 15 minutes to stiffen it also helps. Don't leave it in any longer than that.

Toast the sesame seeds in a dry heavy-based pan over a low heat, stirring until they start to colour. Remove from the heat and reserve.

In a large wok, sweat the onion and chilli in the groundnut oil over a low heat until the onion is soft. Turn up the heat to medium and stir-fry the garlic for a minute.

Pour in the stock and bring to the boil. Lower the heat and simmer for 10 minutes. Stir in the beef, drained wakame and soy sauce. Simmer for 1–2 minutes.

Ladle into deep warmed bowls and scatter the toasted sesame seeds on top.

LAMBS' KIDNEYS AND NOODLES IN BROTH

Briefly cooked kidneys do not, as a rule, feature in Chinese cooking, but since, with the exception of ox kidneys, I do not like them well done, I decided to deconstruct a traditional soup of stewed pigs' kidneys and see what resulted. Here the beancurd and noodles are finished in broth, the lambs' kidneys quickly stir-fried and added to the soup only seconds before it is brought to the table. Veal kidneys could be beneficially substituted for lambs'.

serves 4
400 g (14 oz) lambs' kidneys
1 tbsp rice vinegar
115 g (4 oz) beanthread noodles (page 162)
1.1 litres (2 pints) chicken stock
salt and pepper
1 tbsp cashew nuts
4 spring onions, cut at an angle into 2.5-cm (1-inch) pieces
1 garlic clove, thinly sliced
225 g (8 oz) firm beancurd (tofu), cut into 2-cm (¾-inch) cubes
5-cm (2-inch) piece of root ginger, peeled and cut into julienne strips
3 tbsp dry sherry
2 tbsp Pearl River soy sauce
2 tbsp groundnut oil
handful of coriander leaves, finely chopped

Remove the filmy outer membrane from the kidneys and cut them in half laterally. Using scissors, cut out the central tubes and trim away any fat. Cut the kidneys into bite-sized pieces. Put in a bowl with the rice vinegar, stir to coat and leave to marinate for 20 minutes.

Meanwhile, soak the noodles in warm water for 15–20 minutes. Drain and cut into 7.5-cm (3-inch) lengths and reserve.

Put the stock in a large pan and bring to a simmer.

Drain the kidneys, pat dry with kitchen paper and season generously with salt and pepper.

Put a wok or large heavy-based frying pan over a moderate heat to get hot.

Put the cashews in a small dry pan and toast over the lowest heat until lightly browned.

To the pan of simmering broth, add the noodles, spring onions, garlic, beancurd, ginger, dry sherry and soy sauce.

When the wok or pan is smoking-hot, add the groundnut oil. Swirl, then add the kidneys and stir-fry for 2–3 minutes. Stir into the broth.

Ladle into deep warmed bowls, scatter in the cashews and sprinkle coriander on top. Serve immediately.

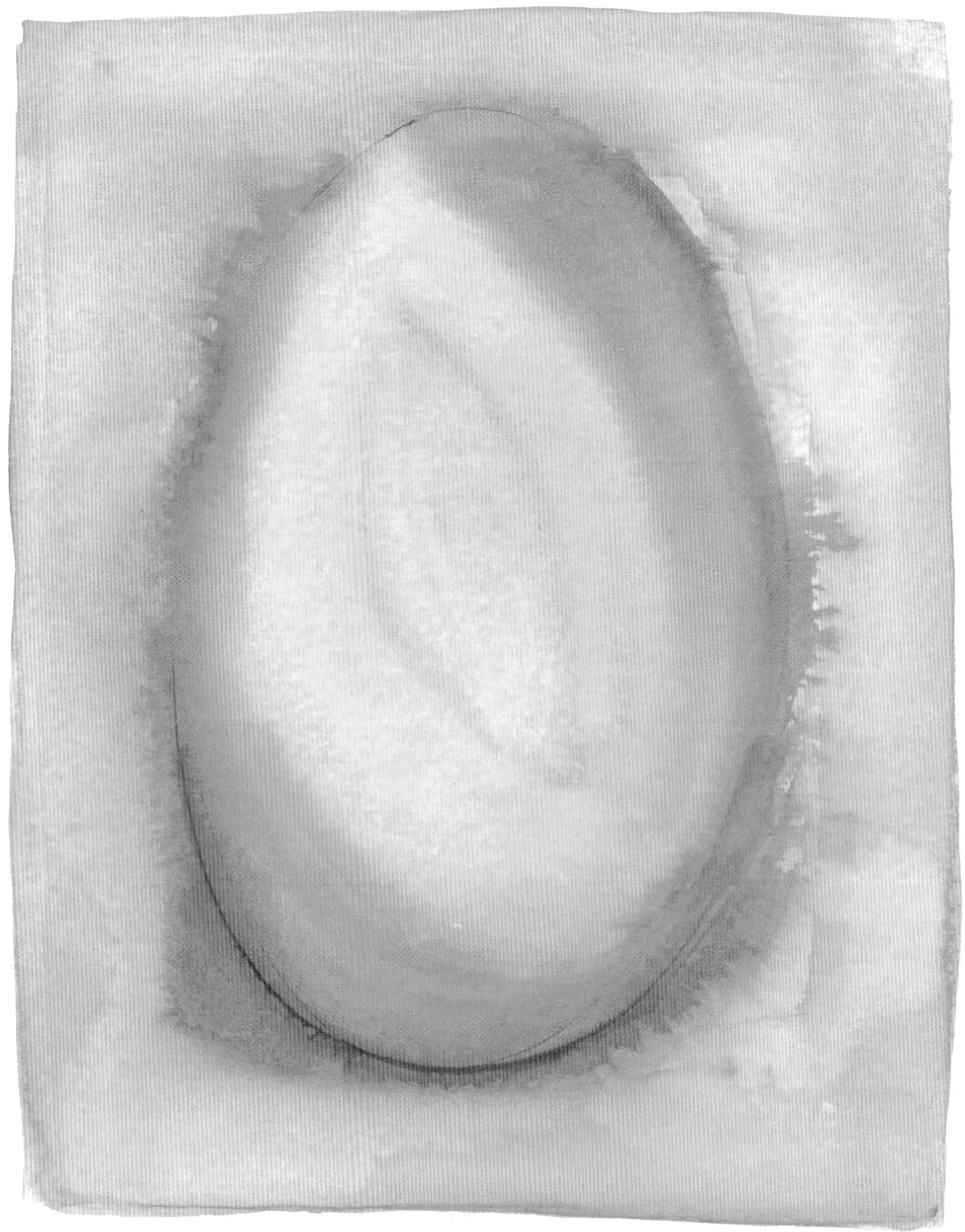

Chapter 2
Australia

An exuberant roller-coaster of a cuisine

There is a very narrow distinguishing line between cooking that can be described as 'fusion food' (which I will take, for the sake of argument, to be a term of approval, implying witty, appropriate and delicious – if sometimes surprising – juxtapositions of ingredients) and 'confusion food', that is cooking which combines inappropriate ingredients from multiple cultural origins, thereby rupturing itself on the plate and the palate and rightly earning its pejorative description.

This is a tricky area, but the danger of getting something wrong is insufficient reason not to try to get it right. It has become rapidly received wisdom that all cooking that is not precisely of one point of origin must be lumped in the confusion camp, a blanket vilification that is as stupid as it is inaccurate, and as blinkered as the failure to understand that an appreciation of local seasonal produce is not invalidated by the all-year-round availability of fresh fruit and vegetables from distant lands. Presumably these new champions of inflexible seasonality spend five months of the year subsisting on root vegetables and salt pork so the excitement of spring's bounties makes them swoon with ecstasy as once their forebears must understandably have done.

I have no desire to eat strawberries at Christmas or asparagus in September, but I revel in much of the produce brought to me from the other side of the world when it is in season there, and quite a lot of these good things now come to us from Australia and New Zealand.

As the world enters another century, it is in Australia more than anywhere else that I find an unparalleled respect and love of seasonality driving the cooking. Much of this, at its best, is expressed through fusion, with dishes emerging from more than one cultural influence yet still recognizably shaped by local produce. The things that make Australian food different in a contemporary sense are taken from the flavours of immigration, most recently from Southeast Asia but, just as significantly, from the Mediterranean.

The latest culture to call attention to itself is, ironically, native Australian, the 'bush tucker' of the Aboriginal diet, with its unique fruits, seeds and nuts. Then there are indigenous meats like kangaroo, emu and crocodile.

In *Fusions*, the book I wrote with Martin Webb about contemporary Australian cooking, I said, 'It is an exuberant roller-coaster of a cuisine, which triumphantly celebrates more highs than lows; a place where, once you understand the rules, it is perfectly all right to break them.'

Once it was Australian chefs who travelled to educate themselves in the kitchens of Europe. Now Australia has restaurants that European chefs want to go and work in, particularly in the nation's twin dining capitals of Sydney and Melbourne, where I ate some of the best food of my life.

This eating revolution is not just about restaurants, for Australians place a happy emphasis on entertaining at home, which (because of the climate) means eating outside for a lot of the year – and, for many people, eating in the kitchen informally. This inextricably links a style of living with a style of eating, something celebrated in one of the world's most influential food magazines, *Vogue Entertaining*, published in Sydney and read internationally – not just read, but copied and imitated.

Good Australian contemporary cooking is identifiable by a certain style, a style well defined and partly led by the magazine which, under Sharyn Storrier Lyneham's editorship, has been massively influential. In a sense, its important pioneering work has been done and, without care, the formula of sharing other people's dinner parties, their life-style (if you will forgive such a gross and shudder-inducing phrase) captured by moody photography, is a formula that can move quickly from mould-breaking innovation to something altogether less attractive.

Fine wine in a Duralex tumbler and a heavy, yet disposable, paper tablecloth as a style statement can easily become self parody. Aspiration is all very well and good, but its relentless promotion in an atmosphere of carefully cultivated and increasingly self-conscious hedonism carries with it a very high gag factor. It is one I discern rearing its ugly head in our own publications about food. As I write, *Food Illustrated*, London's attempt to produce a similar mix of food and style – or food as style – proclaims itself on the cover to be 'the world's most beautiful magazine'. And there I am thinking this is really something one wishes to judge for oneself, not be instructed about. 'I'll be the judge of that,' is a concept that editors lose sight of at their peril.

In these few recipes that follow I have tried to express the feeling of food that you might well eat in Australia. If I have failed to capture that sense of delicious simplicity that characterizes the nation's current love affair with eating well, then that is my fault, not Australia's.

PRAWN AND SWEETCORN PANCAKES WITH SALMON ROE AND CRÈME FRAÎCHE

By chopping raw prawns and incorporating them into the pancakes, the flesh is only just cooked, giving both a better flavour and a lighter texture.

serves 4

4–6 large fresh tiger prawns, peeled and deveined, to give 115 g (4 oz) meat
2 spring onions
1 tbsp chopped coriander leaves, plus more whole leaves for garnish
85 g (3 oz) flour
30 g (1 oz) cornflour
½ tsp salt
150 ml (¼ pint) ice-cold water
2 eggs
60 g (2 oz) fresh or frozen sweetcorn kernels
1 tsp chilli flakes
¼ tsp black pepper
sunflower oil, for greasing the frying pan
5 tbsp crème fraîche
2 limes, quartered lengthwise
4 heaped tsp salmon eggs

Chop the prawns finely. Cut the spring onions across thinly. Mix these with the chopped coriander and reserve.

Sift the flour, cornflour and salt into a bowl. Add the ice-cold water and the eggs, and whisk until the mixture has the consistency of thick cream. Stir in the prawn mixture, corn, chilli flakes and pepper.

Heat a large frying pan over a moderate heat. When hot, wipe with oiled paper and turn down the heat slightly. Use a small ladle or tablespoon to pour in just enough of the batter to make a 7.5-cm (3-inch) pancake. When the bottom is set and lightly coloured with brown veins, turn with a palette knife. Stack wrapped in a cloth in a warm oven while you make the rest of the pancakes.

Put 4 pancakes on each plate, with a spoonful of crème fraîche in the middle and a lime quarter on the side. Put a teaspoon of salmon eggs on top of the cream and finish with a few whole coriander leaves.

GREEN-LIPPED MUSSELS WITH TOMATO SAUCE AND SAFFRON MAYONNAISE

The green-lipped mussels of the southern hemisphere are much larger than those of the north. They are seriously meaty, with an intense flavour that benefits from some assertive saucing. This is a cold dish, with half the mussels covered with a saffron mayonnaise flavoured with the intense juices from the cooking process and the other half with a smooth and garlicky tomato sauce. All the preparation can be done the day before and everything kept refrigerated overnight.

serves 4

16–20 green-lipped mussels
3 shallots
3 garlic cloves
3 tbsp olive oil
300 ml (½ pint) dry white wine
salt and pepper

FOR THE SAFFRON MAYONNAISE:
20–30 saffron threads
2 egg yolks
300 ml (½ pint) olive oil
300 ml (½ pint) sunflower oil
1–2 tbsp white wine vinegar
1 small hot red chilli, finely diced

FOR THE TOMATO SAUCE:
4 tbsp olive oil
115 g (4 oz) onion
2 garlic cloves, finely chopped
450 g (1 lb) canned plum tomatoes, coarsely chopped
1 bay leaf
2 tsp dried oregano

Scrub the mussels and discard any that do not shut when tapped. Finely chop the shallots and garlic.

Put the oil in a large pan over a moderate heat and, when hot but not smoking, throw in the shallots and garlic and cook for 30 seconds, stirring.

Add the wine and some pepper and bring to the boil. Add the mussels, stir to coat, cover with the lid and cook over a high heat for 3–4 minutes, shaking from time to time, when all the mussels should have opened.

Strain through a colander into a saucepan. Reduce this liquid over a high heat to about 3 tablespoons. Off the heat, add the saffron for the mayonnaise to this and leave to soak.

Meanwhile, make the tomato sauce: put the oil in a pan over a low heat and sweat the chopped onion and garlic until soft and translucent. Add the tomatoes, bay leaf and oregano, and season with a little salt and pepper. Simmer for 40 minutes over the lowest heat or until you have a pulp. Discard the bay leaf, transfer to a food processor and blitz briefly to a purée. Allow to cool and then chill until needed.

Make the mayonnaise: in a bowl, add salt and pepper to the egg yolks and whisk in the olive oil, followed by the sunflower oil, working slowly at first to make sure it does not split. As the mayonnaise gets very thick, start to add the mussel and saffron liquor to thin it, interspersed with teaspoons of the vinegar. When all the liquid has been whisked in to all the oil, taste, stir in the chilli and adjust the seasoning as required.

Discard any mussels that have not opened. With a teaspoon, coat each mussel, half with saffron mayonnaise and half with tomato sauce.

Divide between 4 plates and serve with freshly baked Ciabatta (page 306).

CARPACCIO OF YELLOW-FIN TUNA WITH WASABI VINAIGRETTE

The fresher the tuna you use for this carpaccio, the better. Japanese fishmongers offer the finest quality, but at a breathtaking price. However, with the tuna fillet beaten out paper-thin, a little goes a long way.

serves 4
225 g (8 oz) yellow-fin tuna
6 shallots
2 anchovy fillets
2 tsp capers
15 g (½ oz) flat-leaf parsley
15 g (½ oz) coriander leaves
4 chives
oil for deep-frying

FOR THE WASABI VINAIGRETTE:
1 tsp wasabi (page 163)
juice of 1 lemon
2 tsp Kikkoman soy sauce
125 ml (4 fl oz) extra-virgin olive oil
salt and pepper

Slice the tuna as thinly as you can and place the slices between oiled sheets of plastic wrap. Using a rolling pin or mallet, beat the slices gently to a translucent thinness.

To make the wasabi vinaigrette, mix the wasabi with the lemon juice and whisk in the soy sauce and olive oil. Taste and season with salt and pepper. Reserve.

Dice 1 shallot and chop finely with the anchovies, capers, parsley, coriander and chives. Season with salt and pepper. Reserve.

Preheat oil for deep-frying to 190°C (375°F). Shred the remaining shallots and fry until crisp and golden brown. Remove to kitchen paper to drain.

Divide the tuna between 4 plates, spreading a layer on each to cover. Sprinkle the herb mixture evenly over the top. Whisk the dressing and drizzle it over all. Scatter over the crispy shallots and finish with some coarsely ground black pepper.

BROILED SANSHO-PEPPERED SEA BASS WITH SPICED LENTIL PURÉE

Broiling means grilling from above and below simultaneously, an effect that can be achieved with a red-hot dry frying pan used in combination with an overhead grill, a most effective method for cooking fish steaks.

Restaurants, who maintain their ovens at fierce temperatures the domestic oven cannot match, tend to sear both fish and meat aggressively in oil on the hob and finish briefly in the oven. This is to do with getting the food out fast rather than doing something in the best way. Anyway, broiling in the domestic kitchen works as well or better.

Sansho is an aromatic rather than hot Japanese ground spice that can be bought from Oriental markets. It is not really a pepper but the dried berries of the prickly ash.

serves 4

4 sea bass fillets, each about 200 g (7 oz)
2 tbsp olive oil
4 tsp Japanese sansho pepper
small bunch of chives, for garnish

FOR THE SPICED LENTIL PURÉE:

350 g (12 oz) lentils (masoor dal)
2 kaffir lime leaves
225 g (8 oz) onions, finely diced
1 carrot, finely diced
1 celery stalk, finely diced
2 tsp coriander seeds
2 tsp cumin seeds
2 tsp black mustard seeds
2 tsp fenugreek
1 garlic clove, chopped
salt and pepper
300 ml (½ pint) chicken stock
60 g (2 oz) butter, finely diced
handful of flat-leaf parsley, chopped
handful of coriander leaves, chopped
handful of celery leaves, chopped

Prepare the lentils: wash them in a sieve under cold running water. Put into a pan with the lime leaves and cover with water. Add the onion, carrot and celery. Bring to the boil, turn down the heat and simmer for 1 hour or until you can crush a lentil easily.

Meanwhile, toast the spices in a dry pan over a low heat for 2–3 minutes, stirring, until aromatic and then grind to a powder. Reserve.

Remove the lime leaves from the lentils and transfer the lentils to a food processor. Add the garlic with the toasted spice mix. Season with salt and pepper and blitz to a purée, adding chicken stock through the feeder tube to achieve a smooth, spoonable texture.

Return to the rinsed-out pan over a low heat and beat in the butter with a wooden spoon. Stir in the parsley and coriander leaves and cook for 2 minutes. Keep warm.

Heat a heavy frying pan over a moderate heat to smoking-hot and preheat the overhead grill to maximum.

Brush the fish all over with the oil. Season both

sides with salt, then press the sansho pepper into the flesh side only. Lay the fish skin side down in the pan for 60–90 seconds, then transfer the pan to under the grill and cook for a further 2–3 minutes, or until just done. The finish should be moist but not pink.

Stir the celery leaves into the purée. Spoon a mound on each warmed soup plate and lay the fish on top, crisp peppered crust upwards. Snip over a few chives cut into 5-cm (2-inch) lengths.

POTATO, CLAM AND GARLIC WON TON RAVIOLI

Chinese won ton wrappers make great ravioli and it is worth keeping a couple of packets in the freezer to use instead of fresh pasta when pressed for time. The fillings do not have to be remotely Oriental. These are stuffed with a potato and garlic purée studded with clams and served with an onion béchamel. Use a waxy potato for its more pronounced flavour, since a fluffy finish to the mash is not essential here.

serves 4

32 square won ton wrappers, about 7.5-cm (3-inch), which will each take 2–3 tsp of filling
Parmesan cheese, to serve

FOR THE FILLING:
2 tbsp dry white wine
1 tbsp olive oil
500 g (1 lb 2 oz) carpetshell or any other small clams
450 g (1 lb) waxy potatoes, peeled
6 garlic cloves
15 g (½ oz) flat-leaf parsley, chopped
30 g (1 oz) unsalted butter

FOR THE ONION BÉCHAMEL SAUCE:
115 g (4 oz) onions, diced
30 g (1 oz) butter
30 g (1 oz) flour
850 ml (1½ pints) milk
freshly grated nutmeg
1 bay leaf

Start by making the filling: put the white wine and olive oil in a pan over a high heat. When it starts to bubble, add the clams in one go. Shake and toss, then cover with a lid and cook for about 3 minutes, when all the clams should have opened. Drain, reserving the pan juices. When cool enough, shuck, discarding the shells.

Put the potatoes in cold salted water and bring them to the boil. After 10 minutes, coarsely chop 5 of the garlic cloves and add to the pan, then continue cooking until the potatoes are done. Drain, leave to steam dry, then return to the hot pan and mash dry. When smooth, add the remaining garlic clove, finely chopped, the chopped parsley and the butter. Beat to a smooth purée. Finally, stir in the clams.

While the potatoes are cooking, make the béchamel sauce: in a large heavy-based pan over a low heat, sweat the diced onion in the butter until soft. Stir in the flour and cook, stirring, for 2 minutes. Pour in the milk, whisking, then season with salt, pepper and grated nutmeg. Add the bay leaf and clam juices, and simmer gently, stirring from time to time, for 20–30 minutes, until the sauce has reduced by about a third.

Make the ravioli: put a big pan of salted water to heat to the boil. Put 2–3 teaspoons of the filling purée in the middle of 16 won ton wrappers. Brush the edges lightly with water, then lay a second wrapper on top of each and press the edges together hard with your fingers to seal. Trim the edges with scissors, putting them on a lightly floured tray as you go along.

Slide the ravioli into the boiling water. They are done when they float to the surface, about 2–3 minutes. Remove with a slotted spoon, dividing them between 4 large warmed bowls. Spoon over the sauce and scatter on freshly grated Parmesan before serving.

MANGO AND GINGER CHICKEN WITH ROAST MUSTARD POTATOES

Here chicken breasts are marinated with ginger and lemon juice, then brushed with a little puréed mango chutney as they are being pan-fried. Roasting is a good way to treat the older and larger new potato. This recipe does not demand that they be peeled, always a bonus, and they go well with lots of things. The amount of potatoes suggested should serve 6, but they seem to all get eaten by 4 people.

serves 4
7.5-cm (3-inch) piece of root ginger, peeled and diced
juice of 1½ lemons
1 garlic clove
4 chicken breast fillets (with skin)
1 tbsp olive oil
salt and pepper
2 tbsp mango chutney
8 chive stalks, for garnish
1 lemon, quartered, to serve

FOR THE MUSTARD ROAST POTATOES:
4 tbsp olive oil
3 tbsp Dijon mustard
1 tsp chilli flakes
1 tsp dried oregano
1 tsp salt
½ tsp coarsely ground pepper
1 kg (2¼ lb) large new potatoes, quartered lengthwise

Put the ginger in a food processor with the lemon juice and garlic, and blitz to a paste. Spoon this into muslin over a bowl and squeeze out. Put the chicken breasts in a zip-lock bag and add this marinade. Shake to coat and chill overnight.

An hour before you want to cook them, remove the breasts from the refrigerator. Preheat the oven to 200°C (400°F, gas 6).

Prepare the potatoes: mix the oil and other ingredients except the potatoes together in a mixing bowl. Add the potato quarters and turn to coat evenly. Transfer to a gratin dish with the cut faces of potato downwards. Roast for 20 minutes and turn on the other cut face, brushing with the roasting mixture. Turn to sit on the skin after another 20 minutes, brushing again. They should be done in an hour.

Put a heavy frying pan over a low-to-medium heat. Pat the chicken breasts dry and brush with olive oil, then season with salt and pepper. Lay them in the pan, skin side down, and cook for about 8 minutes.

Meanwhile, blitz the mango chutney to a purée in a food processor. When you turn the chicken after 8 minutes, brush the skin side with it. Turn the chicken over again, brushing the other side with the remaining mango purée.

After 2 minutes, turn, give them a final minute and remove to warmed serving plates. Divide the potatoes between the plates and scatter some finely cut chives over them, before serving with a quarter of lemon next to the chicken.

POACHED SALTED DUCK BREAST WITH MANGO

Whole salted duck is a very ancient dish which, in its original Welsh form, was rather heavy-handed in the intensity of the salt cure used to preserve the meat. This version uses only the breasts and a much lighter and more aromatic cure that includes Chinese five-spice powder. The combination of rich duck and clean sweet mango is particularly good. Queensland now produces some of the finest mangoes in the world.

serves 4
2 large duck breasts
2 large ripe mangoes

FOR THE CURE:
4 tbsp sea salt
10 juniper berries
1 tbsp black peppercorns
2 tsp Chinese five-spice powder
2 dried bay leaves

To make the cure: put the salt, spices and aromatics in a coffee grinder and blitz to a powder.

Using a scalpel or very sharp knife and being careful not to cut into the flesh, score the fat of the duck with a crosshatch pattern.

Put half the cure in the bottom of a plastic container and lay the duck breasts in it, skin side down. Cover the top with the remaining powder, cover with a lid and chill for 24 hours.

Rinse the duck, then soak in cold water for 30 minutes.

Bring a pan of water to the boil. Put in the duck breasts, bring back to the boil, then immediately lower the heat and simmer, with only the occasional bubble breaking the surface, for 15 minutes. Remove and leave to cool.

When completely cold, cut across at an angle into very thin slices. Fan these out, overlapping, on 4 cold plates. Cut the mangoes in half, running the blade down either side of the flattish, oval stone. Cut a criss-cross into each half, all the way down to the skin but being careful not to cut through it. This allows you to reverse the flesh out from the skin and slice it off in the cubes defined by your earlier cutting. Arrange these next to the duck and grind black pepper over both.

Options: you could serve the duck with a grapefruit and mint salad with a honey and balsamic vinegar dressing. Alternatively, slices of ripe Comice pear balance the richness of the meat well.

BEEF PIE AND SPLIT PEA PURÉE

The pie floater was once a Sydney street-food institution, and one best eaten when a great deal of beer had been taken on board. The name comes from the way it is served, the pie floating like an island in a sea of split pea purée. This recipe has only a nodding acquaintance with the past, but pays respectful homage to the key ingredients – good-quality minced beef, crisp pastry and creamy split peas.

serves 6
85g (3 oz) pancetta
2 tbsp light olive oil
500 g (1 lb 2 oz) best minced beef (10–15% fat)
225 g (8 oz) onion, diced
2 garlic cloves, chopped
600 ml (1 pint) chicken or beef stock
2 tbsp tomato ketchup
3 tbsp Worcestershire sauce
600 ml (1 pint) beer
600 ml (1 pint) passata
salt and pepper
450 g (1 lb) shortcrust pastry
450 g (1 lb) puff pastry

FOR THE SPLIT PEA PURÉE:
450 (1 lb) split green peas
225 g (½ lb) onions, diced
3 garlic cloves, chopped
1 bay leaf
60 g (2 oz) butter
4 tbsp chopped flat-leaf parsley

FOR THE GLAZE:
1 egg yolk, beaten
1 tbsp cream or milk

Put the split peas for the purée in a sieve and rinse under cold running water. Put in a pan with the onions, garlic and bay leaf. Cover by 3 cm (1¼ inches) with cold water. Bring to the boil, lower the heat and simmer until the peas soften and start to break down, which will take 45–60 minutes depending on how old and dry the peas are. Add more water as necessary to keep them just covered. When done, remove from the heat, discard the bay leaf and reserve in the pan.

Cut the pancetta into matchsticks and fry in olive oil in a heavy flameproof casserole over a low heat until the fat runs. Turn up the heat to moderate and continue to cook for 2–3 minutes, stirring.

Add the minced beef and brown thoroughly. Add the onion, garlic, stock, tomato ketchup and Worcestershire sauce, beer and passata. Season with salt and pepper and bring to the boil. Lower the heat and simmer for 1 hour.

Line a deep 25-cm (10-inch) tart tin with the shortcrust pastry and bake blind in an oven preheated to 200°C (400°F, gas 6). While it is baking, roll out the puff pastry and cut to make a lid. Score the surface with a fine crosshatch of shallow cuts and brush with the beaten egg yolk mixed with the cream or milk.

Fill the pie with the meat and brush the edge with the remaining glaze. Put on the puff pastry lid and bake for 30 minutes, turning the temperature down to 180°C (350°F, gas 4) after 15 minutes.

About 10 minutes before the pie is due to be ready, finish the split pea purée: return the split peas to the heat. When piping hot, beat in the butter with a spoon and stir in the chopped parsley.

Serve wedges of the pie in warmed soup plates on a bed of the purée.

GRILLED VEAL CHOP WITH BUTTER-MASHED BEANS AND CRISP GARLIC

Veal chops look better when they still have the long rib bone attached. This should be scraped scrupulously clean of all fat – a presentational nicety Americans insist on calling 'frenching', a word used in my youth to describe something you would mostly not do in the kitchen. The chops can be cooked on the barbecue or, as here, on a ridged grill pan. If the former, with its attendant vagaries, the beans are very forgiving and can be held until needed. Individual ribs of beef can be cooked in the same way.

serves 4
4 veal chops, rib bone on, each about 250 g (9 oz)
2 lemons, halved, to serve

FOR THE MARINADE:
4 tbsp olive oil
2 tbsp lemon juice
2 garlic cloves, finely chopped

FOR THE BUTTER MASHED BEANS:
450 g (1 lb) dried borlotti beans, soaked overnight
2 bay leaves
2 celery stalks, chopped
1 tsp dried chilli flakes
about 1 tsp salt
2 tsp cumin seeds
½ tsp black peppercorns
4 tbsp olive oil
175 g (6 oz) onions, diced
45 g (1½ oz) unsalted butter
4 garlic cloves, cut into paper-thin slices
handful of flat-leaf parsley, to garnish

Make the marinade: whisk the ingredients together and pour over the chops. Leave at room temperature for 4 hours, turning from time to time.

Bring the beans to the boil, boil hard for 5 minutes and drain. Rinse under cold running water and rinse out the pan, then return the beans to it. Cover with cold water by 2.5 cm (1 inch), bring to the boil, then lower the heat and simmer. Stir in the bay leaves, celery and chilli flakes. Cook until the beans are just done, which will take about 1 hour. Stir in salt to taste at this point, cooking it in for 2–3 minutes. Drain, discarding the bay leaves and celery. This can be done well in advance.

Put the cumin and peppercorns in a dry pan and toast over a low heat for 2–3 minutes, stirring, until aromatic. Grind in a coffee grinder and reserve.

Put 2 tablespoons of the oil in a large heavy-based pan over a low heat and sweat the onions in it until soft. Stir in the ground spices and cook, stirring, for 2–3 minutes. Add the beans, then mash to a coarse purée with a potato masher. Beat in the butter, taste and add a little more salt if necessary. Keep warm.

Sweat the garlic over a low heat until wilted. Turn up the heat to moderate and stir-fry until it starts to brown round the edges. Remove to kitchen paper to drain.

Preheat the grill pan. Wipe the marinade from the veal chops (the garlic will burn and go bitter if left on) and season both sides generously with salt and pepper. Put on the grill pan for 2½ minutes, turning at 2½-minute intervals 4 times so each side has a total of 5 minutes. This is only a guideline because precise timing depends on the thickness. Remove to warmed plates, putting half a lemon on the side.

Spoon the beans into a warmed serving bowl and scatter the stir-fried garlic and a little finely chopped parsley on the top. Offer at the table for people to help themselves. Dress generously with extra-virgin olive oil.

PEPPERED LAMB CUTLETS AND WILD MUSHROOM POTATO CAKES

The lamb can be cooked on a ridged grill pan or on the barbecue. The wild mushrooms are dried and can be a single variety or a mixture. The finished dish is served with a yoghurt relish and deep-fried red onion rings.

serves 4

45 g (1½ oz) dried wild mushrooms
675 g (1½ lb) potatoes
salt and pepper
12 trimmed lamb cutlets
100 ml (3½ fl oz) sunflower oil, plus more for deep-frying
4 shallots, diced
3 tbsp olive oil
225 g (½ lb) red onion, sliced across into thin rings
2 tbsp coarsely crushed peppercorns
handful of flat-leaf parsley, to garnish

FOR THE YOGHURT RELISH:

300 ml (½ pint) thick Greek-style yoghurt
1 hot red chilli (habanero or Scotch bonnet), deseeded and finely chopped
4 spring onions, cut across into thin slices
8 mint leaves, chopped
1 garlic clove, finely chopped

Put the mushrooms to soak in 150 ml (¼ pint) warm water for 30 minutes. Strain through a muslin-lined sieve, reserving the soaking liquid for stock. Rinse the mushrooms under running water briefly to rid them of any twigs or remaining grit. Chop them coarsely.

Boil the peeled potatoes in lightly salted water until done, about 20 minutes. Drain and mash dry. Reserve in a large bowl.

Make the yoghurt relish: stir all the ingredients

together and season with salt and pepper.

Brush the lamb cutlets on both sides with a little of the sunflower oil. Reserve.

Fry the shallots gently in the olive oil until softened, then add the mushrooms and cook for 3–4 minutes.

Add to the mashed potato, season with pepper and work in with a fork, aiming for an even distribution. Mould into 4 balls, then flatten these into thick cakes.

Put half the sunflower oil in a large frying pan and fry the cakes over a low heat. Do not touch or push them round until a crust has formed, 10–12 minutes, then turn them carefully with a spatula. Add the remaining oil and cook for a further 10 minutes.

Preheat oil for deep-frying to 170°C (340°F). Fry the red onion rings until just beginning to crisp up. Reserve in the frying basket. Turn the temperature up to 190°C (375°F).

Preheat a dry ridged grill pan until smoking-hot. Season the cutlets with a little salt and a lot of coarsely crushed peppercorns. Grill for 3 minutes on each side for a pink finish. To achieve a neat crosshatch, lay on the grill at 45 degrees to the ridges. Turn and lay in exactly the same angle. Turn again, this time at 45 degrees in the opposite direction and repeat. Arrange on warmed plates with a potato cake.

While the lamb cutlets are cooking, plunge the onions back in the hot oil for 30–45 seconds to crisp. Remove and drain on kitchen paper. Put a pile of onion on top of each cake and scatter over some whole parsley leaves. Offer the yoghurt relish at the table.

SPICED LAMB SHANK WITH CORIANDER SAUCE

Though not usually a fan of cooked pineapple, its sweetness works well with the spiced lamb.

serves 4

6 garlic cloves, peeled and chopped
large bunch of coriander with stems and roots
4 tsp ground ginger
1 tsp five spice
1 tsp turmeric
2 tsp black peppercorns
salt and pepper
4 lamb shanks, bones scraped
75 ml (3 fl oz) olive oil
170 g/ 6 oz onion, peeled and thinly sliced
600 ml (1 pint) chicken stock
2 tbsp rice vinegar
1 red onion, peeled and diced
2 hot red chillies, shredded
2 x 2 cm (¾ inch) thick slices fresh pineapple

Process to a paste 2 garlic cloves with the coriander stems and roots, the spices and 1½ teaspoons of salt. Rub into the lamb and leave at room temperature for 4 hours.

Brown the shanks all over in 3 tablespoons of oil and reserve.

In a casserole sweat the onions until soft. Add the shanks, the stock and vinegar. Bring to the boil, lower the heat, put on the lid and simmer for 1½ hours or until tender.

Sweat the red onion until soft in 2 tablespoons of oil. Add the remaining garlic, chillies and most of the coriander leaves. Ladle in about 300 ml (½ pint) of the braising liquid from the casserole, season and simmer for 5 minutes, then purée to a sauce in a food processor.

Put the remaining oil in the pan, turn up the heat and fry the pineapple rings for 2 minutes each side. Remove and cut into quarters.

Put a shank on each plate, spooning the sauce around. Add the pineapple pieces and scatter over the remaining coriander leaves. Serve with mashed potatoes.

Chapter 3
The Balkans to the Bosphorus

The smell of the charcoal grill

If this were a culinary gazetteer, then to lump so many countries into one bundle would be a gross impertinence. I mean no offence by it, rather the opposite. The more things I cook from this melting pot, the more certain I am about it. Ethnic loathing, which paints nationalism into dishes that you find cooked with minor variations by an enemy, does not need to colour my selection or my judgement about their similarities. Sectarianism has no role to play at the table.

There is a simplicity about so much of the food from this part of the world that is highly appealing. Yet what you might eat in Corfu is not so dissimilar, as far as I can tell, from much that is eaten across the water in Albania. This is hardly surprising, since you can see it from the eastern beaches of the island. I have had happy times and good food in Corfu, notably in a restaurant the name of which I have forgotten but the name of whose location I have not – The Village of the Dog Catchers. The northernmost and greenest of the Greek islands, and one that has more olive groves than any other, Corfu still shows signs of both Italian and British occupation. Much of the grand architecture of the old town is Italian, while our own legacies in the shape of ginger beer and cricket are suitably quaint. A more recent and shaming export is the British holiday lout who is to be found polluting some of the beach resorts. The once enchanting fishing village of Benitses just south of Kerkyra is now a strip of truly hideous bars and clubs and would be better renamed Benighted. It is a big island though, and the mountainous interior is still little affected. Escape is still possible, though one wishes for a time machine to hop back about 30 years.

Corfu was the 'Prospero's Cell' of Lawrence Durrell, yet it was his younger brother Gerald who branded me with the burning desire to go to Corfu when

I read *My Family and Other Animals* when I was 10 and was to take me to Greece a decade later. Looking again at his vivid memories of life in Corfu in the 1930s, there are constant references to food and wine – and the sharing of them in a beautiful place – that can still make me shut my eyes and open them in some little taverna with the smell of the charcoal grill working its magic, finally something that I could savour alone, even if such an idea once seemed perverse to me. You can still eat well there and probably better than on some of the smaller islands where the visitor's diet can be both basic and repetitive.

The simplicity and minimal preparation and cooking time of much Greek food makes solitary eating a potentially civilized pleasure, though eating too much in isolation remains a miserable business – even if the backdrop is breathtakingly lovely. There are those who eat alone through greed, making of it a private thing, as attractive as self-abuse. Food really only comes alive and is made meaningful in a human context. When you look back on good food, you remember – as Proust did with that bloody orange madeleine dunked in his aunt's cup of lime tisane. The flavour is identical and it then triggers the memory which has nothing to do with the food. It is about friends and places, love and happiness and laughter. The food may have been a catalyst, a central prop or a coincidence. It may have been delicious, but then you may have been hungry when you ate it.

I shall never forget that dinner from a thousand good dinners, when Pippa looked up from the plate and deep into my eyes and smiled that private smile that told me everything I had ever wanted to know or to hear, and the room dimmed around us. Memorable food, of course, even though I cannot remember what it was we ate that day which pleased us so well. It might have been moussaka, a dish which treated with disdain, as one might experience it in Benitses, is a tasteless travesty. Cooked with care and understanding, it becomes one of the world's memorable dishes.

MOUSSAKA WITH DRY-GRILLED AUBERGINE AND PARMESAN CUSTARD

When you cook this meat sauce for a long time the result will be meltingly tender and quite intense, moist but not too runny. Moussaka should always be served warm or at room temperature, never hot from the oven. It may be refrigerated overnight but, if so, warm it through gently in a low oven before serving. It is traditionally made with lamb, but lean minced beef makes a fine alternative.

serves 6–8

1.1 litres (2 pints) chicken stock
60 g (2 oz) dried porcini
115 g (4 oz) pancetta
100 ml (3½ fl oz) olive oil
675 g (1½ lb) minced lamb or beef
225 g (8 oz) onions, diced
175 g (6 oz) carrots, diced
150 ml (¼ pint) dry white wine
2 garlic cloves, finely chopped
1 celery stalk, chopped
1 tsp dried oregano
450 g (1 lb) canned plum tomatoes, puréed
1 bay leaf
3 tbsp Worcestershire sauce
salt and pepper
575 g (1¼ lb) aubergines

FOR THE PARMESAN CUSTARD:
60 g (2 oz) butter
60 g (2 oz) flour
850 ml (1½ pints) milk
1 bay leaf
115 g (4 oz) Parmesan cheese, grated
freshly grated nutmeg
4 eggs, beaten

Heat the chicken stock and put the mushrooms to soak in it off the heat for 20 minutes. Strain through a muslin-lined sieve, reserving the stock. Wash the mushrooms carefully under running water and reserve.

Cut the pancetta into fat matchsticks, then cut these across into dice and fry gently in 2 tablespoons of olive oil until nearly crisp. Using a slotted spoon, remove to a large heavy saucepan.

Brown the meat in the remaining oil and fat and transfer to the saucepan.

Add 2 more tablespoons of the olive oil to the frying pan and sweat the onion and carrot until softened, then put with the beef.

Deglaze the pan with the white wine and pour over the meat and vegetables. Add the reserved chicken stock, garlic, celery, oregano, tomatoes, bay leaf and Worcestershire sauce. Stir, season with pepper (the pancetta is already very salty) and bring to the boil. Lower the heat and simmer gently, covered. Check from time to time, adding water to keep the meat just covered.

After 3 hours, remove the lid and reduce the amount of liquid until you have a thick moist sauce. Taste and adjust the seasoning, if necessary. Remove and discard the bay leaf and celery. The sauce can be made the day before, or will keep refrigerated for a week.

Preheat the oven to 180°C (350°F, gas 4).

Make the Parmesan custard: first make a béchamel sauce by melting the butter over a moderate heat in a heavy-based pan and stirring in the flour over a low heat to make a roux. Stir in the milk and whisk until smooth. Add the bay leaf and simmer for 30 minutes, stirring at regular intervals to prevent burning. Remove the bay leaf and season lightly with salt and pepper. Off the heat, beat in the Parmesan and grated nutmeg to taste, followed by the eggs. Reserve.

While the sauce is cooking, cut the aubergines lengthwise into 2-cm (¾-inch) thick slices. Brush on both sides with the remaining olive oil and dry-fry in a hot pan, turning from time to time. They should take on a dark caramelized colour. Reserve.

To assemble the moussaka, spoon the meat sauce into a suitable ovenproof dish and top with the aubergine. Pour over the Parmesan custard and bake for 30–40 minutes, when the topping will have souffléed slightly and be a dappled golden-brown on top.

Remove and allow to cool to room temperature before serving.

LAMB IN A YOGHURT AND CHEESE CUSTARD

There should be another name for custard when it is savoury, since my first response to the word 'custard' is to think *crème anglaise* and that, in combination with garlic and meat juices, is a less than tempting idea. Putting lamb together with sauces set with eggs is a feature of Greek cooking – think of moussaka – and the Bulgarian *shopski* that follows this recipe is also finished with a savoury custard.

The idea of completing the dish in the bowls in which it will be served comes from Maria Kaneva-Johnson's *The Melting Pot*, a fascinating study of food in the Balkans and the result of 20 years' research. I think it is one of the best cookbooks of recent times, though since it is written in an admirable and educated style you are unlikely to find it on what passes for a popular bookshop shelf.

serves 4
800 g (1¾ lb) lamb neck fillet
1–2 tbsp sunflower oil
2 carrots, quartered
2 celery stalks, chopped
225 g (8 oz) onions, cut into chunks
2 garlic cloves, chopped
1 cinnamon stick
2 bay leaves
salt and pepper
300 ml (½ pint) red wine
rustic bread, to serve

FOR THE CUSTARD:
3 eggs
200 ml (7 fl oz) thick yoghurt
1 tbsp cornflour
60 g (2 oz) grated Parmesan cheese

Cut the lamb into bite-sized chunks, brush with the oil and sear on all sides quickly in a smoking-hot frying pan, transferring to a casserole or saucepan as they are done. Add the vegetables, garlic, cinnamon and bay leaves. Season with salt and plenty of black pepper. Pour over the red wine, then add enough water barely to cover. Bring to the boil, turn down the heat and simmer for 1 hour, or until the meat is meltingly tender. Taste and adjust the seasoning.

Strain the liquid through a colander into a measuring jug. Discard the vegetables, cinnamon and bay leaves. You need 400 ml (14 fl oz) for the custard. If there is less, make up with water; if more, return to the pan and reduce.

Preheat the oven to 180°C (350°F, gas 4). Divide the meat between 4 ovenproof bowls or large cocottes suitable for taking to the table.

Make the custard: whisk the eggs in a bowl, then whisk in the yoghurt. In another bowl, whisk the measured broth into the cornflour, then whisk this into the yoghurt mixture, together with the cheese. Divide between the bowls, place on a baking sheet and put in the oven.

Bake until just set, 25–30 minutes. Remove and allow to cool a little before serving to avoid people burning themselves. Serve with a selection of rustic breads.

SHOPSKI

The Svischtov region on the Danube is one of Bulgaria's most prolific wine-producing areas, with more than one-third of the country's vineyards located in the north of the country. *Shopski* is a braised dish enriched with butter, cooked in two stages and finished with yoghurt. It may be made from lamb, pork or veal and, in Bulgaria, would be cooked in a glazed earthenware pot with a lid. The meat is not traditionally browned before stewing, but the flavour is improved when it is.

serves 4

1 kg (2¼ lb) lamb neck fillet
60 g (2 oz) lard
350 g (12 oz) onions, diced
225 g (8 oz) sweet red peppers, deseeded and diced
2 garlic cloves, thinly sliced
3 hot red chillies, deseeded and finely chopped
115 g (4 oz) unsalted butter
300 ml (½ pint) Cabernet Sauvignon or other full-bodied red wine
500 g (1 lb 2 oz) canned plum tomatoes
1 tbsp paprika
1 tsp dried oregano
2 bay leaves
salt and pepper
15 g (½ oz) flat-leaf parsley
600 ml (1 pint) yoghurt
1 heaped tbsp cornflour
4 egg yolks

Cut the lamb into 5-cm (2-inch) chunks. Put the lard in a heavy-based casserole over a moderate heat and add the lamb when the melted lard shimmers. Brown the meat all over, stirring.

Add the diced onions, red peppers and finely chopped garlic, and fry, stirring, for a minute. Stir in the chillies with the butter. Pour over the red wine and bring to the boil, stirring and scraping. Purée the tomatoes and their can juices in a food processor and pour over. Add the paprika, oregano and bay leaf, and season with salt and pepper. Stir together. Bring to the boil, lower to a simmer, cover with a lid and cook until the lamb is done, 1½–1¾ hours, removing the lid for the last 30 minutes. Taste and adjust the seasoning towards the end of cooking. The dish can be prepared up to this point the day before and this is a good idea because you can then lift off the fat, which will have set in an orange layer on top, before reheating.

Preheat the oven to 220°C (425°F, gas 7).

Finely chop the parsley, stir into the stew and transfer to a gratin dish. Stabilize the yoghurt by mixing the cornflour to a paste with a little water, then stirring this into the yoghurt and bringing it to the boil. Lower the heat and simmer for 10 minutes.

Whisk the egg yolks in a bowl, then whisk in a couple of spoonfuls of the hot yoghurt before returning this mixture to the yoghurt and whisking together. Pour over the meat and bake for 15–20 minutes, until golden brown and set. For regional authenticity, drink a northern Bulgarian Cabernet Sauvignon; otherwise, drink anything.

BEEF GOULASH WITH COTTAGE CHEESE DUMPLINGS

A Hungarian chef told me in no uncertain terms that a goulash is more a soup than a stew. Well, this is more a stew than a soup, but it is served in big soup bowls with lots of sauce. Goulash is frequently made with veal, and a veal stewing cut can be used when following the recipe.

Cook the goulash and make the dumplings a day ahead, refrigerating both overnight. The fat will set in an orange layer on top of the goulash and is easily lifted off with a spoon. Melt this and pour it into a container to use for frying or roasting potatoes.

serves 6
1.35 kg (3 lb) shin of beef
salt and pepper
60 g (2 oz) flour
85 g (3 oz) lard
2 tbsp groundnut or sunflower oil
900 g (2 lb) onions, thinly sliced
2 tbsp paprika
1 tsp dried chilli flakes
150 ml (¼ pint) red wine
6 garlic cloves, cut into paper-thin slices
1 bay leaf
2 celery stalks, chopped
1 tsp dried thyme
1.75 litres (3 pints) beef or chicken stock
handful of flat-leaf parsley

FOR THE COTTAGE CHEESE DUMPLINGS **(makes 12):**
225 g (8 oz) white bread, crusts removed and diced
125 ml (4½ oz) single cream
2 eggs
115 g (4 oz) unsalted butter
150 g (5 oz) cottage cheese
140 g (5 oz) self-raising flour
60 g (2 oz) breadcrumbs

Cut the beef into large cubes, about 5-cm (2-inch). Add salt and pepper to the flour and roll the chunks in it to coat.

Put half the lard and half the oil in a large heavy-based frying pan over a moderate heat. When it shimmers, brown the beef in batches, transferring to a casserole as it is done.

Put the remaining lard and oil in the frying pan, turn down the heat and sweat the onions, stirring at regular intervals, for 20–30 minutes. Turn up the heat to moderate and fry, stirring constantly, until the onions start to caramelize. Add the paprika, the remaining seasoned flour and chilli flakes, lower the heat again and cook together, stirring for 2 minutes. Transfer to the casserole, stirring to mix with the meat.

Turn up the heat under the frying pan and deglaze it with the red wine, scraping the pan thoroughly, and add to the casserole. Stir in the garlic, bay leaf, celery stalks and thyme. Pour over the stock and bring to the boil. Lower the heat and simmer for 1½ hours. Remove a chunk of meat and cut off a piece. Eat it and decide whether it needs further cooking – it should be very tender but not falling apart. Adjust the seasoning at this point, continuing to cook and tasting at 10-minute intervals until done to your liking. Remove and discard the celery and bay leaf. Leave to cool and refrigerate overnight.

Make the dumplings: put the bread in a mixing bowl and pour the cream over it. Leave to stand for 10 minutes.

Separate the eggs. Put the yolks in a second bowl and, using an electric whisk, beat in all but 30 g (1 oz) of the butter until foamy. Add the cottage cheese and whisk in, then fold in the bread-and-cream mixture and season with salt and pepper. Fold in the flour and refrigerate for one hour or overnight.

Lift off the fat from the goulash and heat the goulash to a bare simmer over the lowest heat.

Put a wide shallow pan of lightly salted water on a heat to bring to the boil. Lower the heat to a simmer.

Whisk the egg whites to stiff peaks and fold them into the dumpling mixture. Remove spoonfuls, slide them into the simmering water and cook for 5 minutes.

Melt the remaining butter in a large frying pan over a low heat. Stir in the breadcrumbs and cook until browned. Using a slotted spoon, remove the dumplings to the frying pan and toss gently to coat.

To serve: ladle the goulash into large warmed bowls, put 2 dumplings in each and scatter over a little finely chopped parsley before serving.

PURÉED LAMB SHISH KEBAB

The invaluable food processor – which cannot do the job of a mincer – does precisely what you want it to do here, tearing the ingredients into a purée. The alternative of bashing away with a pestle and mortar is not something I would contemplate.

serves 4

1 tsp cumin seeds
1 tsp coriander seeds
1 tsp chilli flakes
1 tsp black peppercorns
85 g (3 oz) white bread, crusts removed and diced
3 tbsp dry white wine
675 g (1½ lb) minced lamb
85 g (3 oz) onions, diced
1 garlic clove, finely chopped
2 tbsp coriander leaves, chopped
1 tsp salt

Toast the spices in a dry pan over a low heat for 2–3 minutes. Grind and put in a food processor.

Put the bread and wine in a bowl and squeeze together to a pulp. Put this in the processor together with all the other ingredients and blitz for about 4 minutes, stopping from time to time to scrape down the sides. You will have a coherent and malleable mass.

Divide this into 12 balls, rolling them into sausage shapes, shaking on a little flour if too sticky. Slide a metal or soaked wooden skewer through each.

Cook on a barbecue over a moderate heat or on a very hot grill plate, turning frequently, for about 12 minutes or until cooked through.

Serve immediately with Bean Purée (page 311) and *tzadzike* – cucumber in yoghurt with garlic and mint.

KLEFTIKO

Kleftiko, braised lamb shank, is the very essence of Greek home food, and every family will have a view on its proper construction. It can be very basic, with little in the way of spicing, but because of its loose definition is capable of constant reinterpretation. This is why few cookbooks bother to give a recipe for what can be the most delicious of treatments for lamb.

The shank is the bottom portion of the leg, which – with its projecting bone scraped and the meat neatly trimmed – presents nicely as an individual, if substantial, joint.

serves 4

500 g (1 lb 2 oz) canned chopped plum tomatoes
4 lamb shanks, trimmed and bone scraped
salt and pepper
5 tbsp olive oil
500 g (1 lb 2 oz) onions, thinly sliced
4 garlic cloves, finely chopped
300 ml (½ pint) dry white wine
2 tbsp red wine vinegar
2 bay leaves
sprig of rosemary
1 tsp dried oregano
1 tsp turmeric
1 tsp chilli flakes
juice and rind of 1 lemon, cut as one continuous strip
coarsely chopped flat-leaf parsley, to garnish
mashed potatoes or plain boiled rice, to serve

Purée the tomatoes with their can juices in a food processor and reserve.

Trim the meat to make a neat surface at the point where the meat begins. Rub the shanks generously with salt and pepper, then brown thoroughly all over in 3 tablespoons of the olive oil. Put into a casserole or metal saucepan in which they will fit in one layer, standing upright, and for which you have a tight-fitting lid.

Add the remaining olive oil to the browning pan and, over a low heat, sweat the onions until soft and translucent. Add the garlic, turn up the heat and fry for 2 minutes, stirring. Transfer to the casserole, distributing around the shanks.

Over a high heat, deglaze the pan with the wine and vinegar, stirring and scraping, then pour over the lamb. Add the puréed tomatoes, bay leaves, rosemary, oregano, turmeric, chilli flakes, lemon juice and rind. Bring to the boil, cover with a lid and lower the heat to a bare simmer. Check from time to time that it is not drying out, adding a little water if it does. Test the meat is done after 90 minutes. Depending on the size of the shanks it may be; if not, continue cooking until the meat is tender enough to pull easily from the bone. Taste and adjust the seasoning when you judge the meat is done.

Remove the shanks from the casserole and keep them warm on serving plates. Discard the lemon rind, bay leaves and rosemary, then transfer the braising mixture to a food processor. Blitz to a purée and pass through a sieve. Spoon this sauce around the shanks and dress with lots of coarsely chopped flat-leaf parsley. Serve on large warmed soup plates with plain boiled rice or mashed potatoes.

BEEF STIFADO

Stifado is rarely mentioned in cookbooks because, like *kleftiko*, it is essentially domestic fare and every family has its own variation and everybody assumes you know how to make it. Though usually of meat – which may be beef, rabbit or hare – *stifados* of octopus are quite common on the Greek islands. Whatever the main ingredient, all are slowly cooked with small whole onions, wine or wine vinegar, or both. The spicing and herbs will vary and tomatoes or currants are often added, as I have included 'drunken' (brandy-macerated) sultanas. This is quite a sophisticated version with a gentle Middle-Eastern shading.

serves 4

1 kg (2¼ lb) shin of beef
60 g (2 oz) flour
4 tbsp olive oil
600 ml (1 pint) red wine
3 tbsp red wine vinegar
1 tsp sugar
1 tsp salt
½ tsp black pepper
1 tsp dried oregano
½ tsp chilli flakes
½ tsp ground allspice
4 cloves
2 bay leaves
1 cinnamon stick
1 kg (2¼ lb) baby onions
4 garlic cloves
300 ml (½ pint) tomato passata
60 g (2 oz) Drunken Sultanas (page 309)
2–3 tbsp chopped flat-leaf parsley
buttered noodles or boiled potatoes, to serve

Cut the beef into postcard-sized pieces. Dredge with flour and brown in half the olive oil, transferring to a casserole over a moderate heat. Stir in the wine, vinegar, sugar, salt, pepper, oregano, chilli flakes, allspice, cloves, bay leaves and cinnamon stick. Bring to the boil, lower the heat and simmer.

Add the remaining olive oil to the frying pan and sauté the baby onions until they start to brown. Add the chopped garlic and cook with the onions for 2 minutes, then add to the meat and stir in with the

tomato passata. Cover with a lid and simmer for 1½ hours, adding the sultanas after about an hour. Taste and check that the beef is done – it should be moist and tender; if it is still chewy, continue cooking until you are satisfied, but be careful not to overcook. There comes a moment in every stew's life when enough is enough. Cook for too long and all the connective tissue will melt, leaving the meat flaky and dry.

Scatter over the chopped flat-leaf parsley and serve with buttered noodles or boiled potatoes.

FAISINJAN OF DUCK

Faisinjan is a lovely dish that combines pomegranate juice and walnuts in the sauce. It can be made with chicken or lamb or, as here, with duck.

serves 4
200 g (7 oz) walnuts
4 duck legs
seasoned flour
3 tbsp olive oil
30 g (1 oz) unsalted butter
400 g (14 oz) onions, peeled and thinly sliced
2 garlic cloves, peeled and chopped
1 bay leaf
stick of cinnamon
¼ nutmeg, grated
salt and pepper
850 ml (1½ pints) chicken stock
300 ml (½ pint) pomegranate juice
juice of 1 lemon (optional)
handful of fresh coriander

Blitz the walnuts briefly in a food processor and reserve.

Roll the duck legs in seasoned flour, brown all over in the olive oil over a medium heat and transfer to a casserole. Add the butter to the frying pan, lower the heat and sweat the onions until soft. Turn up the heat and fry, stirring continuously until golden brown. Add the walnuts and the garlic and fry, stirring, for 2 minutes. Add to the casserole with the bay leaf, cinnamon, nutmeg, salt and pepper.

Pour over the chicken stock and pomegranate juice. If the juice is quite sweet, also add the juice of a lemon as the sauce should have a distinct, sour backnote. Stir to mix thoroughly and bring to the boil, then lower the heat and simmer for 45 minutes. Test the duck with a skewer, continuing to simmer for a few more minutes if it is not completely tender. It should just be holding to the bone.

Garnish with a handful of coriander leaves and serve with plain boiled Basmati rice or a buttery rice pilaf flavoured and coloured with saffron.

MACARONI WITH A FETA AND CREAM SAUCE

Pasta is eaten a lot in Greece and, unsurprisingly, most often where an Italian influence has been felt. We are accustomed to think of feta as a cheese eaten raw and as the vital sour ingredient in my favourite salad, *horiatiki*. It also makes a pasta sauce when cooked with cream, garlic and parsley.

serves 4
350 g (12 oz) macaroni
salt and pepper
30 g (1 oz) butter
2 garlic cloves, finely chopped
200 ml (7 fl oz) double cream
350 g (12 oz) feta, diced
15 g (½ oz) flat-leaf parsley leaves

1 egg yolk
about 30 g (1 oz) grated Parmesan cheese, to serve

Cook the macaroni in lots of rapidly boiling salted water until *al dente* (use the packet instructions as a guide to timing).

Melt the butter in a pan over the lowest heat and sweat the garlic in it for 2 minutes. Pour in the cream and stir in the feta and parsley. Season with salt and pepper. Cook gently until the cheese melts. Remove from the heat and stir in the egg yolk.

Drain the macaroni and return it to the pan. Pour over the sauce and toss to coat.

Spoon into warmed bowls, scatter grated Parmesan on top and serve at once.

POTATOES CYPRUS-STYLE

Cyprus is one of the great potato-growing environments of the world and is a major exporter. This recipe calls for small – preferably waxy – potatoes. Cyprus potatoes are really quite floury when compared with something like La Ratte, but then so are most potatoes sold as new in the shops.

The potatoes may be small but are not particularly 'new', a word which properly describes immature potatoes without fully formed skins. Whether new in the sense of picked when immature or just small, once the skin forms fully on a potato it should usually be peeled. The greengrocers' trade calls such potatoes 'mids', the next size up 'wares'. The potatoes are parboiled to make the peeling easy and are then baked in olive oil and tomatoes with aromatic herbs. If it is the wrong time of the year to get good plum tomatoes, use canned. This goes well with fish or meat, or is good eaten as a course in its own right, when served with a basket of warm pitta.

serves 4
1 kg (2¼ lb) small potatoes
150 ml (¼ pint) olive oil
450 g (1 lb) onions, thinly sliced
6 garlic cloves, cut into paper-thin slices
2 hot red chillies, finely chopped
450 g (1 lb) ripe plum tomatoes, peeled and quartered
150 ml (¼ pint) dry white wine
20 stoned black olives
1 tsp dried oregano
salt and pepper
coarsely chopped flat-leaf parsley, to garnish

Preheat the oven to 190°C (375°F, gas 5).

Plunge the potatoes into rapidly boiling water for 2–3 minutes. Remove to cold water for a minute, then peel and put in an ovenproof dish into which they will just fit in a single layer.

Put 100 ml (3½ fl oz) of the olive oil in a frying pan and place over a low heat. Sweat the onions until translucent. Stir in the garlic and chillies. Cook, stirring, for 2 minutes.

Blanch the tomatoes in boiling water for 15 seconds, refresh in cold water and skin. Cut them in quarters and strip out and discard the pulp, then add the tomato quarters to the potatoes. Pour over the wine and the rest of the olive oil, then add the olives and the oregano. Season lightly with salt – the olives are salty, so be restrained – and plenty of black pepper.

Put in the oven and bake for 45 minutes, adding a few tablespoons of water if it starts to dry out at any time. Taste, adding more salt if necessary. Cook for another 10 minutes.

Scatter over plenty of coarsely chopped flat-leaf parsley and serve from the dish at the table.

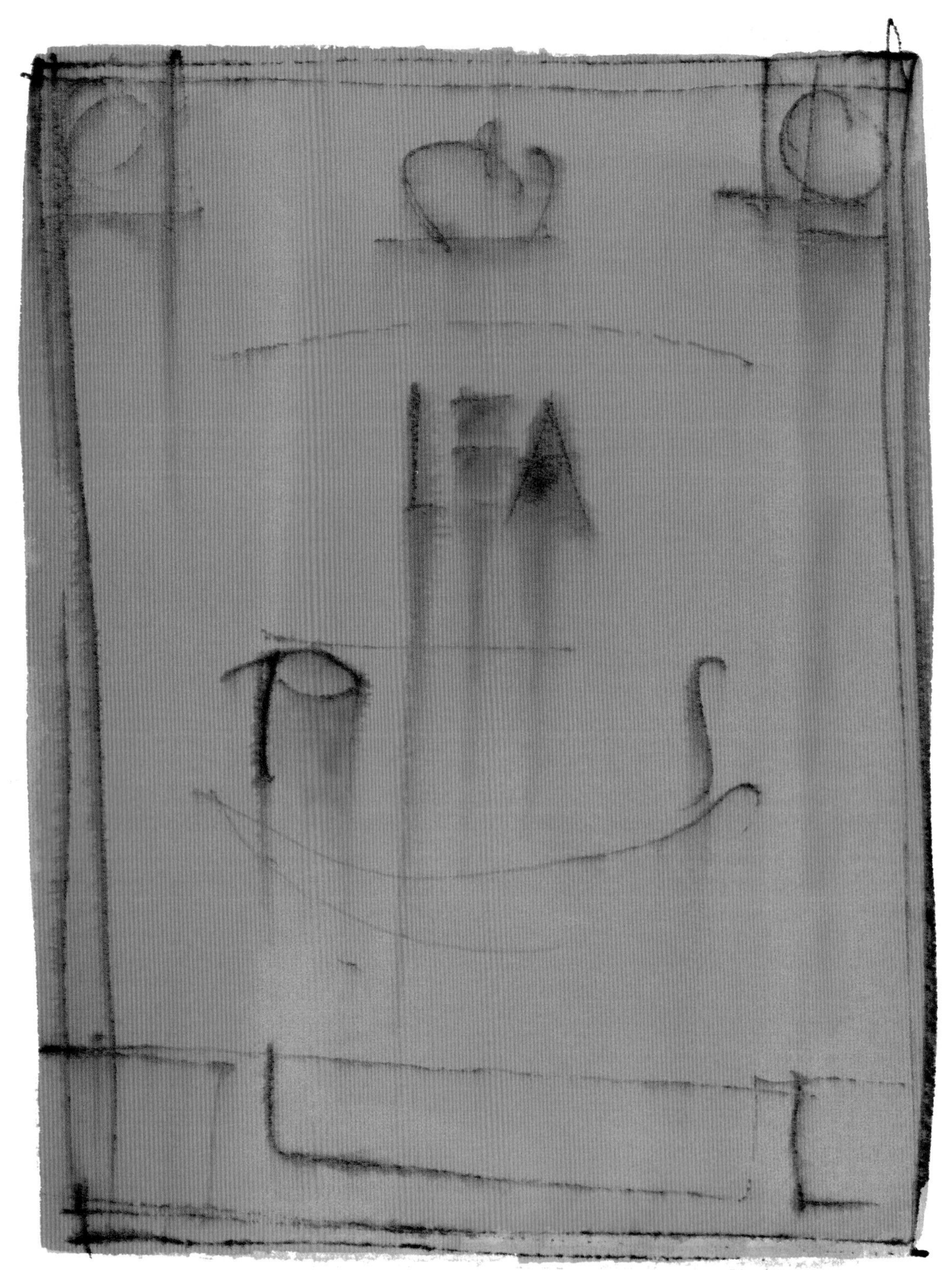

Chapter 4
Britain

A time of profound culinary change

Those who have not visited Britain recently still think that we live off Brown Windsor soup, grisly grey roasts and suet puddings. The imagined smell from millions of kitchens is the dilute mustard gas of over-boiled cabbage. Our cooking is the stuff of jokes in American sitcoms, while old animosities and prejudice die hard – with the French still sneering at the very idea of *La Cuisine Britannique*. Better that you drink the cooking water and throw away the vegetables, ha ha!

For a long time there was a lot of truth in those sneers. Our industrial revolution did massive damage to the way all but the very rich ate. Two world wars did more, and I was born while rationing was still in force. Indeed, my earliest culinary memories have few happy associations, for my parents stayed firmly within the British Isles and we rarely dined out. My mother's cooking shone in some areas – notably, fish pie, curries, oxtail stew and lemon meringue pie – but suffered generally from the then universal domestic practice of overcooking meat, fish and vegetables.

I knew from eating peas straight from the pod in the vegetable garden that green things could be delicious, but recognized early on that something awful was being done to them somewhere between their being picked and coming to the dining table, no longer green but slate-coloured, their texture soapy and malevolent. I had particular nightmares about Sunday lunch which, irrespective of season, involved beef or lamb damaged in a low oven to an even degree of grey and the most grisly vegetables imaginable.

My experience was probably quite typical, and so far removed from British food today that the comparison is almost too extreme to make sense. These are two different worlds, the gulf between them unbridgeable. Food started to change for me only after I left home.

At university I became friends with Alexander Scott-Kilvert, with whom I would often spend weekends at the house of his mother Elisabeth in Suffolk. Elisabeth was a passionate cook, knew Elizabeth David and had many cookbooks. She was American by birth, but had married an Englishman and now, recently divorced, lived in a house with not one but two kitchens. It was she who introduced me to Mrs David's writing, to olive oil and the joy of making mayonnaise by hand in a marble mortar, to shopping for the best ingredients and to eating out.

Here I tasted my first olives, pasta cooked *al dente*, good French cheeses and wine with lunch and dinner. She also introduced me to Robert Carrier, soon to be installed at nearby Hintlesham Hall, and to a fine private cook, Murray Arbeid, the couturier, who lived just down the road with Freddy Fox, the Queen's milliner.

It was during the late Sixties in Suffolk that I first experienced lunches and dinners where the food was discussed with animation by people who knew what they were talking about and good wine was served in copious quantities. It was, in the old-fashioned sense, a gay time. As my confidence and skill grew, I increasingly cooked for Elisabeth's parties. She, more than anybody, opened my eyes to the joys of the kitchen and the enduring pleasures of the table.

There are things we all know to be British – roast beef, pork with crackling, oxtail stew, bacon and eggs, fish pie, fish cakes, rollmops, kippers, hams, kedgeree, treacle tart and steamed puddings – but the extent to which we are convinced that everything we might consider British can only exist in one inflexible state of rightness is very much open to discussion.

Our best artisanal products – for example, smoked salmon, Finnan haddock, bacon, local cured hams like Bradenham or Suffolk, and cheeses such as Caerphilly, Cheddar and Stilton – need neither introduction nor defence. We know precisely how they should be at their best and nobody in their right mind wants to change them. When it comes to cooking with them, however, I believe we have much more leeway to experiment and that we can do so with considerable historical justification. This does not mean culturally inappropriate combinations, and I would hate to find lemon grass in my steak and kidney, but I can roll my beef in coarse black pepper if I want to, or include balsamic vinegar in a stew.

Spices were once standard fare and not thought of as foreign; they later went out of fashion and then had to be rediscovered in ethnic cooking. Locally grown saffron gave Saffron Walden its name. Is garlic something to reject as foreign? It was common here in medieval times and only became unpopular with the Elizabethans. Rocket is another case in point, a favoured and commonly grown leaf in the sixteenth century, currently as fashionable as can be and referred to as rucola or arugula as though it were an Italian gift. John Evelyn, who wrote about rocket's peppery joys 300 years ago, would be amused by this conceit. Bok choi, pak choi and a variety of recently exotic salad leaves are now grown in England on a large scale, as are – perhaps more surprisingly – chillies.

My bread flour comes to me from Marriage's, one of our oldest family millers, but the wheat was grown in Manitoba. Canadian wheat has a 14% protein content and is superior to any produced here, where our climate makes for softer flour. Lea & Perrin's Worcestershire sauce is very British, yet it contains tamarind and anchovies, which patently are not. This is really a *kecap* in the Malay sense, a thin salty sauce used like soy.

The British culinary revolution has embraced the food cultures of the world just as successive waves of immigrants have been reshaping what we eat for hundreds of years. The melting pot food cultures of the USA and Australia are not the dramatic departures of current popular misconception. Historically, we were way ahead of the game. Where would court food have been in the Middle Ages without spices? The impact of the cooking of the Indian subcontinent and of China is scarcely new here, affecting Eliza Acton, Hannah Glasse and Mrs Beeton. French, Italian, Southeast Asian and North African food have opened our eyes wider, with their tremendous variety of flavours, ingredients and cooking styles. As these elements have mixed and crossed, greater creativity has resulted, and we have learned new ways from immigrant examples.

The very spur to Britain's new-found reputation has been an openness to change because we did not, in the main, have a tradition of good food in our homes, like the much vaunted and envied French farmhouse ideal that seized the culinary imagination of M.F.K. Fisher in the Thirties, then Elizabeth David in the Fifties and Sixties. How we learned from them and how we yearned for the sun-splashed tastes they evoked.

With hindsight, one can see that it was the very novelty of the vision that excited us. Having taken those lessons on board, however, we looked about restlessly for more and were able to reach out more readily for new directions and to seize opportunities that consciously broke the rules in a way that French and Spaniards and Italians and Moroccans and Turks have never needed or wanted to do. They have their long-term stability, their enduring benchmarks of excellence. Moorish influences abound throughout the Mediterranean but it was so long ago they are virtually subconscious.

I do not decry the importance or continued relevance of a national *cuisine grand'mère* or *cuisine du terroir*, but I do see their legacy as one of inflexibility and that this ultimately stifles the creative process. Of course, not everybody cooking in France suffers from historic tunnel vision. Not so long ago, the great Bocuse was heard to remark that he was inspired by visits to California, in its way as startling as hearing a commited vegan order a veal chop. Significantly, Bruno Loubet chooses to practise his fusion cooking in London, a location where bold and innovative spicing does not cause shocked inhalations of breath. The presence of chefs like Loubet, Jean-Christophe Novelli, the Roux family, *frères et fils*, Pierre Koffmann and Christian Delteil further reinforces the view that London has become an internationally recognized centre of excellence.

Are those cooking immigrants still French or are they now British? Our chefs are not afraid to mix flavours, to give a new twist to a classic recipe by adding an unusual spice, to appropriate enthusiastically a range of cooking implements from the charcoal grill to the wok. The impact of this revolution is felt throughout the United Kingdom, as I know from my Cookery Doctor correspondents. A question about an exotic ingredient is as likely to come from a reader in Llandudno as it is from one in London. National newspapers, magazines and colour supplements play an educational – as well as motivational – role in this information context. Their coverage creates new needs, and supermarkets respond ever more swiftly to them. It is this process which drives British cooking forward and that gives us so much to be interested in and entertained by.

We are fortunate to be living in a time of profound culinary change and, as we enter a new century, never have the British had so much to celebrate on their plates. Now we can retain that which is excellent and eschew what is bad or mediocre without worrying unnecessarily about whether it is authentic or, indeed, British.

DEEP-FRIED SCALLOPS WITH BACON

This was once a traditional high-tea or supper dish in Yorkshire, and also in Northumberland, though the cost of scallops makes it perhaps more suitable for a lunch or supper dish today. If using the bigger, king scallops, cut them in half and cut off the corals; so for each scallop you have 3 pieces to cook. Queen scallops are fried whole.

If eating this dish for high tea, lots of sliced bread cut from a proper white sandwich loaf should be on the table, a slab of unsalted butter to go with it, and strong tea to drink, though I prefer a dry white Burgundy or that old Yorkshire favourite, champagne.

serves 4

corn or groundnut oil, for deep-frying
2–3 eggs
seasoned flour
fine white breadcrumbs
8 king scallops, corals removed and scallops halved as above, or 24–32 queen scallops
8 slices of lean smoked back bacon
8–12 good sprigs of curly English parsley, to serve

Preheat clean corn or groundnut oil for deep-frying to 190°C (375°F).

Beat 2 of the eggs in a bowl. Put the seasoned flour in a second bowl and the crumbs in a third. Lightly flour the cleaned sliced king scallops or whole queens, dip them in beaten egg, then in the crumbs. Repeat to give a double coating (beating the other egg if needed), and reserve.

Slash the edges of the bacon to stop it curling and grill. When done, turn off the grill but leave the bacon under it to keep warm.

Deep-fry the scallops for 3 minutes and remove to kitchen paper to drain.

Plunge sprigs of curly English parsley briefly into the oil to crisp, then drain on paper.

Serve the scallops and bacon together on warmed plates, with the parsley on one side.

SEARED SALMON AND SMOKED SALMON

The less you do to salmon, the better it tastes. Salmon raw, seared and raw in the middle or cold-smoked all show the fish at its best, and here we combine all these elements. Salmon, when raw or smoked, is very rich so one does not need a large amount for a first course. Few would dispute that the best smoked salmon still comes from Scotland, though Scandinavian countries are now major producers. If buying in a packet, don't be fooled by a bit of tartan. Read the small print and make sure it is Scottish.

Wild salmon is the ultimate choice, but we can now buy very good organically farmed salmon which is raised in pens that are not overcrowded and which are situated in strong currents that make the fish swim. You can always tell by the price. If the salmon is very cheap it will be nasty, flabby and rank-tasting. Buy fillet from the tail end, which will be cheaper than a middle cut. If you can get them, salt-packed capers are preferable to the ones sold in brine. Rinse both in water before use.

serves 4
450 g (1 lb) salmon fillet
115 g (4 oz) smoked salmon
2 tsp wasabi (page 163)
juice of 1 lemon
1 tbsp capers
3 shallots, finely chopped
small bunch of chives, plus 8 chive stalks for garnish
salt and pepper
60 g (2 oz) flour

to serve:
4 slices of white bread, crusts removed
115 ml (¼ pint) sour cream

Run your finger along the pin bone line of the fillets to ensure these have all been removed, then skin the salmon and cut it into small dice. Put into a bowl with the smoked salmon, also diced. Add the wasabi, lemon juice, capers, chopped shallots and chopped chives. Season with a little salt and lots of pepper, then chill for 2–4 hours.

Divide the mixture into 4, shape into cakes and dredge with seasoned flour, shaking off any excess.

Put a large heavy-based frying pan over a moderate heat. When very hot, swirl in the oil and lay in the salmon cakes. Cook them for 1 minute on each side. Remove to kitchen paper and drain.

Toast the bread, put it on plates and sit the cakes on top. Garnish with pieces of chive and put a spoonful of sour cream on the side.

SMOKED HADDOCK PURÉE WITH COURGETTE SLICES IN BATTER

This takes its inspiration from the classic Brandade de Morue. In this variation, smoked haddock fillets are poached briefly before being puréed with potato and garlic in the same way.

serves 4
400 g (14 oz) smoked haddock fillet
600 ml (1 pint) milk
1 bay leaf
115 g (4 oz) mashed potatoes
3 garlic cloves, chopped
2 heaped tbsp flat-leaf parsley leaves
juice of 1 lemon
black pepper
about 250 ml (9 fl oz) extra-virgin olive oil
oil, for deep-frying
1 large courgette (about 350 g / 12 oz)

FOR THE BATTER:
115 g (4 oz) plain flour
pinch of bicarbonate of soda
pinch of salt
1 egg
250 ml (9 fl oz) ice-cold lager

Poach the haddock in gently simmering milk with the bay leaf for 3–4 minutes and drain through a colander, reserving the milk. Pull off the skin from the fish and discard, with any bones.

Put the fish and mashed potatoes into a food processor. Add the garlic, parsley, lemon juice and about 1 teaspoon of freshly milled pepper. Turn the machine on at full speed and slowly pour about 150 ml (¼ pint) of the reserved milk through the feeder tube. Now add the oil in a thin stream, enough to give a thick, scoopable consistency. Adjust the seasoning, if necessary.

Make the batter: sift the flour, bicarbonate of soda and salt into a bowl and reserve. In another bowl, beat the egg to a froth. Continuing to whisk, pour in the lager slowly, then dump the flour into the liquid in one go. Give it a couple of swift turns to incorporate, but do not beat to a smooth batter as this would result in a tough coating when cooked. There should be discernible lumps in it. Leave to stand for 10 minutes.

Preheat oil for deep-frying to 190°C (375°F).

Cut the courgette across into 3-mm (⅛-inch) slices, dip in the batter and deep-fry for 3–4 minutes until crisp. Remove to kitchen paper to drain briefly.

Put 3 pieces of courgette on each plate. Put a tablespoon of brandade on each and top with another courgette slice. Repeat until you have used up the courgettes and purée. Serve while the batter is still crisp.

BROILED SALMON WITH BROAD BEAN AND SMOKED BACON POTATO CAKES

Of course, wild salmon is the best salmon, but a good farmed fish – fed on decent things and penned in clean flowing water – makes good eating. In the absence of a whole fish to judge, price at the fishmonger is usually a good indicator of quality. Very cheap salmon is either nasty or stolen.

serves 4

4 salmon steaks cut from the middle fillet, each about 200 g (7 oz), skin on
2 tbsp olive oil

FOR THE POTATO CAKES:
115 g (4 oz) smoked streaky bacon in a piece
1 kg (2¼ lb) broad beans, shelled
30 g (1 oz) unsalted butter
400 g (14 oz) dry mashed potatoes
3–4 tbsp olive oil

FOR THE HERB AND ANCHOVY BUTTER:
115 g (4 oz) unsalted butter
4 anchovy fillets, drained and finely chopped
1 tbsp finely chopped flat-leaf parsley
1 tbsp finely chopped chives
½ tsp salt
½ tsp pepper

Well ahead, make the herb and anchovy butter: soften the butter in a bowl. Add the anchovy to the butter with the herbs, salt and pepper. Mix together thoroughly with a fork and spoon on to a piece of cling-film or foil. Roll up, screwing the ends tightly to form a compact cylinder. Freeze for at least 1 hour. This can be done well ahead, since it will keep in the freezer without deterioration for up to a month.

Make the potato cakes: cut the bacon into matchsticks and dry-fry over a low heat, stirring regularly until they start to colour. When cool, cut into small dice and reserve.

Shell the beans. Cook in lots of rapidly boiling salted water for about 8 minutes, or until done, the precise time obviously depending on their age and size.

Drain and put in a food processor and pulse-chop to a coarse purée with the butter. Transfer to a mixing bowl, add the mashed potatoes and mix together thoroughly, then mix in the bacon dice and season. Remove, divide into 4 and shape into neat cakes. Flour them lightly, shaking of any excess.

Remove the herb and anchovy butter from the freezer.

Put 2 tablespoons of the olive oil in a heavy-based frying pan over a low heat. When hot, lay in the cakes and fry for 10 minutes without touching them. Turn them and cook the other side for 8–10 minutes, adding a little more oil after turning them over.

Towards the end of cooking, preheat an overhead grill and put a second heavy frying pan over a moderate heat.

Brush the salmon all over with olive oil and season generously on both sides with salt and pepper. As the pan smokes, lay the steaks in skin side down and give them 1–1½ minutes. Transfer the pan to under the grill and grill for 3–4 minutes.

Put a potato cake on each large warmed plate. Remove the steaks carefully with a fish slice to the plates. Cut the butter into 4 discs, put a piece on each steak and serve very hot.

POACHED TURBOT WITH HOLLANDAISE

Once upon a time, when Wheeler's in Old Compton Street was a fine place to eat fish, one of my favourite things in all the world was their poached turbot. This was served simply with hollandaise sauce and boiled new potatoes, and was not garnished – except for a token slice of carrot. It remains one of my most favourite things, though I would no longer choose to eat it in Wheeler's Old Compton Street.

A well-flavoured court-bouillon is all you need to achieve a spectacular result and one puzzles over how anybody could screw it up. When properly cooked, poached turbot is something to share with somebody you love and is truly one of the great dishes of the world.

When buying fish on the bone, allow about 400 g (14 oz) per person; so, for four, buy a whole turbot weighing 1.35–1.8 kg (3–4 lb). Poaching fish is the simplest of all cooking techniques. Follow a few basic rules and you cannot go wrong. Ask the fishmonger for the bones and trimmings. If turbot is unavailable, or the price just too much, brill may be substituted; it is also expensive, but a little less so.

serves 4

4 turbot steaks, skin on, 200–225g (7–8oz) each
buttered boiled new potatoes, to serve

FOR THE COURT-BOUILLON:

1 bottle of sour dry white wine
2 tbsp white wine vinegar
2 carrots, quartered
2 onions, quartered
4 celery stalks, plus their leaves
2 bay leaves
2 lemons, quartered
handful of parsley stalks
1 tbsp black peppercorns
2 tbsp salt

FOR THE HOLLANDAISE:

225 g (8 oz) unsalted butter
2 shallots, finely diced
1 tsp freshly ground black pepper
juice of ½ lemon
1 tbsp white wine vinegar
3 egg yolks

Make the court-bouillon: put all the ingredients into a large, shallow and wide saucepan. Add 3.5 litres (6 pints) of water, put over a moderate heat and bring to a simmer. Simmer for 20 minutes, turn off the heat and allow to cool to room temperature. Taste and adjust the seasoning with more salt, pepper and lemon juice – the liquid should be acid and salty.

Make the hollandaise: put a pan of water to heat and bring to a simmer. Have ready a bowl which can sit over the water. Melt the butter in a small pan over a low heat.

Put the shallots in another pan with the pepper, lemon juice and vinegar. Boil down to about 2 teaspoons of liquid and strain through a fine sieve into the food processor. Add the egg yolks and process for a few seconds to combine. Season with salt and pepper, then, with the machine running at full speed, pour the butter in a thin stream through the feeder tube.

Pour into the bowl set over hot water and whisk until it thickens. Taste and adjust the seasoning if necessary. Turn the heat all the way down and keep the sauce warm.

Slide the fish steaks into the simmering court-bouillon, dark skin side upwards, and poach gently for about 6–8 minutes. They are done when they are opaque and firm to the touch.

Serve with boiled and buttered new potatoes, offering the hollandaise in a sauce boat at the table.

GRILLED MACKEREL FILLETS WITH GOOSEBERRY SAUCE

Gooseberry sauce is a classic British accompaniment to mackerel, its astringent clean taste setting off the rich oily flesh to perfection. Since it is little more than a purée with flavour-enhancing additions that may include lemon juice and chives, it is a good idea to freeze the berries on their own as a purée, which you can then use for other things like tarts, fools or sorbets, or as the fancy takes you.

serves 4

2 large mackerel, filleted
2 tbsp olive oil
salt and pepper
plain boiled new potatoes, to serve

FOR THE GOOSEBERRY SAUCE:
450 g (1 lb) gooseberries
30 g (1 oz) butter
30 g (1 oz) caster sugar
juice of 1 lemon
1 tbsp chopped chives

Detach any remaining element of stalk from the gooseberries and put the berries in a pan with 250 ml (9 fl oz) cold water and the butter. Bring to the boil, immediately lower the heat and simmer gently until the gooseberries are soft. Put them in a food processor and blitz until puréed. Push them through a sieve with a wooden spoon to extract any skins. This can now be held in the fridge for a day or two or frozen.

If proceeding immediately, put the purée into a clean saucepan with the sugar and warm through over a low heat.

Brush the mackerel with olive oil and season with salt and pepper. Lay in a smoking-hot ridged grill pan, skin side down, for 2 minutes. Turn and cook for a further minute.

Add the lemon juice and chives to the sauce just before serving.

Serve the fish with the gooseberry purée and plain boiled new potatoes.

Options: herring, salmon or sardines can be substituted for the mackerel.

POACHED CHICKEN WITH MUSHROOMS IN A SAFFRON SUET CRUST

Generally, when people think of a savoury pudding, they think of beef, and most often of steak and kidney. This one is filled with chicken and mushrooms in a herb velouté sauce, and has a crust flavoured and

streaked with saffron. It is made using only the legs of the chicken, as the breast has a tendency to dry with prolonged cooking, while the flavour of the sauce is given depth by the inclusion of dried wild mushrooms and beer.

serves 4
600 ml (1 pint) chicken stock
30 g (1 oz) dried porcini (ceps)
4 chicken legs
1 bay leaf
30 g (1 oz) flat-leaf parsley, chopped
30 g (1 oz) tarragon, chopped
300 ml (1/2 pint) beer
20 black peppercorns
20 saffron threads
2 tbsp warm water
285 g (10 oz) self-raising flour
150 g (5 oz) suet
115 g (4 oz) pancetta, or bacon, in a piece
30 g (1 oz) butter, plus more for the basin
115 g (4 oz) onions
115 g (4 oz) flat-cap mushrooms, sliced
2 garlic cloves, chopped
30 g (1 oz) plain flour
wilted spinach or blanched Savoy cabbage, to serve

Heat 150 ml (1/4 pint) of the stock and pour over the dried mushrooms, then leave to soak.

Cut through the joint of each chicken leg, separating them into drumstick and thigh. Using a small sharp knife, cut the flesh away from the bone. Slide the knife underneath the bone and cut along its length, detaching it by slicing through next to the cartilaginous ball joint. Discard all skin, cartilage and fat.

Put the bones, bay leaf and parsley and tarragon stalks in the chicken stock. Strain the soaking mushrooms through a sieve, adding this soaking liquid to the stock together with the mushroom stalks, reserving the caps. Add the beer and peppercorns and simmer until reduced by one-third. Reserve.

Soak the saffron in the warm water for about 10 minutes. Make a suet crust by mixing the self-raising flour and the suet in a bowl with 1/2 teaspoon of salt and 1/4 teaspoon of freshly ground black pepper. Add the saffron and its liquid. With a fork, stir in just enough cold water to bind to a sticky dough, then turn out on a heavily floured surface and roll into a ball. Cover with a cloth and leave to rest for 20 minutes.

Divide the dough into 2 pieces, one three times larger than the other, the smaller piece being for the lid.

Cut the pancetta or bacon into matchsticks and fry gently in a dry heavy-based saucepan until just cooked but not brown. Remove with a slotted spoon and reserve.

Add the butter to the pan together with the onions, sliced fresh mushrooms and the reconstituted dried mushrooms, and sweat until the onions are translucent.

Add the garlic, turn up the heat and sauté for a minute. Turn the heat down again and stir in the plain flour. Cook for a minute, then add the stock through a sieve, discarding the solids. Cook, stirring for 20 minutes.

Fold in the chicken pieces, the bacon and the finely chopped parsley and tarragon. Turn off the heat and reserve.

Roll out the larger piece of dough and use to line a buttered 1.5-litre (2 3/4-pint) pudding basin; roll the smaller piece into a disc for the lid. Pour and spoon in the filling to within 5 mm (1/4 inch) of the top. Brush the rim with cold water and put on the lid, then pinch the edges together to seal. Tie a pleated piece of foil on the top – the pleat will allow for expansion – and make a string handle to facilitate lifting the basin out of the hot water.

Sit the pudding on a rack or upside down plate and pour boiling water to come halfway up the basin. Put on a lid and boil for 3 hours, topping up with more boiling water as necessary to compensate for evaporation. Lift out and remove the foil.

Serve straight from the basin, with wilted spinach or blanched Savoy cabbage.

POACHED CHICKEN AND PRUNES

This has interesting parallels with the *escabeches* of Spain and the medieval capon salads of Italy, the chicken being stuffed with prunes and poached in a vinegar-flavoured stock with sugar, mace and cinnamon. It is the kind of thing that would once always have been made with a boiling fowl cooked for hours, but you really get a better result from a free-range bird simmered for only an hour or so. The important thing to ensure depth of flavour is to leave it to cool completely in the poaching liquid, which must then be significantly reduced. Unless the ambient temperature is too high to do so safely, it is better cooked the day before and left in the stock overnight. The best prunes to use are those from California which are stoned and need no preliminary soaking.

serves 4
20 saffron threads
1 tbsp warm water
200 g (7 oz) stoned prunes
115 g (4 oz) fresh white breadcrumbs
45 g (1½ oz) butter, softened
½ tsp freshly grated nutmeg
salt and pepper
115 g (4 oz) onions, diced
3 garlic cloves, chopped
2 tbsp chopped flat-leaf parsley, stalks reserved
1 tbsp chopped tarragon, stalks reserved
2 lemons
1 free-range chicken, about 1.5 kg (3¼ lb)
3 celery stalks
1 cinnamon stick
30 g (1 oz) muscovado sugar
2 bay leaves
1 litre (1¾ pints) chicken stock or more if available
300 ml (½ pint) white wine vinegar
12 no-need-to-soak prunes, halved
4 lemons, quartered, to serve

Soak the saffron in the warm water for 10 minutes.

Coarsely chop the prunes and mix them in a bowl with the breadcrumbs, the saffron and its soaking liquid and the softened butter. Season with the grated nutmeg, salt and pepper, then mix in the onion, garlic, herbs and the grated zest and juice of 1 lemon. Stuff the chicken with this mixture and sew up tightly.

Put the chicken in a saucepan with the celery, cinnamon, sugar and bay leaves. Pour over the stock and the vinegar, and add enough cold water to cover. Bring to the boil, skim, lower the heat, add the peppercorns and simmer gently for 1½ hours. Turn off the heat, cover and leave to cool in the broth. Remove the chicken, take off the skin and cut into neat serving pieces, arranging them on a large serving plate. Return the bones to the broth and spoon the stuffing round the chicken. Return the broth to the boil, lower the heat and simmer for 2 hours.

Pass this stock through a sieve into a clean pan, discarding the aromatics, and reduce at a rapid boil to 300 ml (½ pint). Add the juice of the second lemon. When the reduced stock has cooled to room temperature, put it in the fridge. As soon as it starts to set, spoon it over the chicken and put in the fridge for the stock to set to a jelly. To serve, arrange 12 halved prunes and 4 quartered lemons around the chicken.

JELLIED CHICKEN

Jellied chicken makes an unusual first course, light yet full of intense flavour from the set reduced broth in which the chicken was poached.

serves 6

1 split pig's trotter, well cleaned
1 free-range chicken, about 1.5 kg (3¼ lb)
1.75 litres (3 pints) chicken stock (optional)
1 large onion, halved but unpeeled
2 bay leaves
2 celery stalks
20 black peppercorns
sprig of tarragon or thyme, or 1 tsp dried
3 tbsp Worcestershire sauce
1 tsp salt
150 ml (¼ pint) dry white wine
2 tbsp chopped flat-leaf parsley

to serve:
sourdough toast
diced red onion

Cover the trotter with water and bring to the boil. Boil for 5 minutes, drain and rinse.

Put the chicken in a pan with the blanched trotter and cover with chicken stock, a mixture of stock and water or just cold water. Bring to the boil, skim, lower the temperature and add the onion, bay leaves, celery, peppercorns, tarragon or thyme, Worcestershire sauce and salt. Simmer for 50 minutes.

Leave to cool, remove the chicken and cut the flesh from the carcass, returning the bones to the pan with the trotter and white wine. Simmer for 3–4 hours. Taste and adjust the seasoning, remembering that as this is to be eaten cold it needs more salt than if it was being served hot.

Strain through a fine sieve into a clean pan, discarding the bones and trotter, then boil to reduce to about 600 ml (1 pint).

Cut the chicken into bite-sized pieces, put into a bowl and pour over the poaching liquid, straining through a muslin-lined sieve. Stir in a couple of tablespoons of chopped parsley and refrigerate overnight.

Turn out and cut into slices. Serve with sourdough toast and a bowl of red onion cut in chunks.

PEPPERED FILLET OF BEEF, HORSERADISH CRÈME FRAÎCHE AND ROAST POTATOES

Roast beef does not have to be a five-rib joint to be great, which is just as well since at the time of writing beef on the bone in Britain is illegal in the wake of vile BSE. I hope it is no longer the case when you read this, but if the law continues to insist that bones could give us a spongiform encephalopathy, try this different approach to our favourite Sunday home food.

The whole point of the dish is having the beef virtually raw in the middle. It is suggested you drizzle a tiny amount of truffled oil on the meat just before serving, but this is an optional refinement and not very British. The combination of cold meat and hot potatoes is particularly pleasing. Think of cold roast lamb with a purée of La Ratte. As an alternative to crème fraîche, you could use thick Greek-style yoghurt.

serves 6

900 g (2 lb) châteaubriand steak in a piece
1 tbsp olive oil
salt
1 tbsp black peppercorns
115 g (4 oz) watercress, to serve
2 tbsp truffled oil (optional), to serve

FOR THE HORSERADISH CRÈME FRAÎCHE:
2 tbsp freshly grated horseradish root
1 tbsp lemon juice
¼ tsp caster sugar
1 tsp freshly made Colman's mustard
200ml (7 fl oz) crème fraîche

FOR THE ROAST POTATOES:
5 tbsp olive oil
900 g (2 lb) floury potatoes, cut into 5-cm (2-inch) chunks

Make the horseradish crème fraîche: put the horseradish into a bowl and stir in the lemon juice, caster sugar, mustard and a little salt and pepper. Put the crème fraîche in another bowl, then fold in the horseradish mixture. It should be served chilled, so refrigerate for 1–2 hours before using.

Remove the beef from the fridge about 2 hours before you want to cook it, to bring it to room temperature.

Preheat the oven to 250°C (475°F, gas 9).

Brush the beef all over with olive oil and season with salt. Coarsely crush the black peppercorns (you can do this in a plastic bag with a rolling pin or by briefly pulse-chopping in a coffee grinder). Scatter the pepper in a Swiss roll tin and roll the beef in it.

Heat a dry heavy frying pan until smoking-hot. Using tongs, lay the meat in the pan and sear each plane for 2 minutes. Transfer to the Swiss roll tin and roll to coat with the pepper. Put in a roasting tin, season with salt, and roast for 6 minutes. Remove and leave to cool completely. (This can be done the day before and the beef refrigerated, but if so remove from the fridge an hour or so before carving.)

Lower the oven setting to 220°C (425°F, gas 7). Make the roast potatoes: parboil the potatoes for 5 minutes, drain well and leave to dry with their own residual heat. Put the olive oil in a large bowl with 1 teaspoon of salt and ½ teaspoon of pepper, and toss the potato chunks to coat. Lay in a roasting tin and roast for about 1 hour, turning after 15 minutes and then every 10 minutes until golden brown. Remove and hold for up to an hour if you like. They can be returned to the oven to heat and crisp for 15 minutes before serving.

Serve the meat carved into 5-mm (¼-inch) slices with the crisp roast potatoes and a bunch of watercress, zig-zagging 1 teaspoon of truffled oil over each portion of meat if you like. Offer the horseradish cream in a bowl.

Options: the horseradish cream is equally good with a pork chop or sausages and is excellent with smoked salmon.

SAUSAGE CAKES IN CAUL WITH WINE-STEWED PEARL BARLEY

This dish has multiple cultural antecedents. I reckon the sausage meat and pearl barley can make it British, and everything else that makes it interesting is French.

Grelots are bigger, flatter and altogether hunkier than the spring onions to which they bear a passing resemblance. They are sold to the trade, peeled and trimmed, for several months of the year and it is worth asking your greengrocer if he can supply them. If they are not available, use the much smaller pickling onions instead. Alternatively whole purple shallots may be substituted.

serves 4
1 tsp black peppercorns
½ tsp coriander seeds
½ tsp allspice berries
275 g (10 oz) pork fillet
400 g (14 oz) best sausage meat
2 garlic cloves
3 tbsp port
freshly grated nutmeg
½ tsp salt
4 sheets of caul fat
finely chopped chives, to garnish

FOR THE BARLEY:
175 g (6 oz) onions, diced
3 tbsp olive oil
2 garlic cloves, finely chopped
350 g (12 oz) pearl barley
300 ml (½ pint) red wine
1 bay leaf
12 rosemary leaves, chopped
sprig of thyme or ½ tsp dried thyme
salt and pepper
about 1.25 litres (2 pints) chicken stock

FOR THE ONIONS:
12 grelot onions or 24 pickling onions, peeled
2 tbsp olive oil
30 g (1 oz) unsalted butter
1 tsp brown sugar

The day before, make the sausage cakes: toast the peppercorns, coriander and allspice in a small dry pan over a low heat for 2–3 minutes. Grind to a powder and reserve.

Dice the pork and put through the coarse plate of a mincer or pulse-chop in a food processor. Put in a mixing bowl with the sausage meat, garlic and port. Grate over nutmeg to taste, add the ground spices and the salt. Mix thoroughly with a fork, then work the mixture further with your fingers. Divide into 8 and form the mixture into balls. Wrap each in half a sheet of caul, pressing down gently into a cake. Put on a tray and chill overnight.

Next day, prepare the barley: preheat the oven to 200°C (400°F, gas 6).

In a flameproof casserole, sweat the onion in the olive oil until soft and translucent. Stir in the garlic and cook for 2–3 minutes. Add the pearl barley and red wine. Increase the heat and bring to the boil. Add the bay leaf and herbs, season with salt and pepper, and pour in the chicken stock. Return to the boil, turn down the heat and simmer, stirring, for 45 minutes, adding a little water if it starts to dry out at any time.

After the pearl barley has started cooking, cook the grelot or pickling onions: put them in a gratin dish with the olive oil and butter and put in the oven.

When the pearl barley has been cooking for about 30 minutes, put a heavy-based frying pan over a low to moderate heat. Put the sausage cakes in it before it heats up. The fat from the caul and sausage meat is all you need to fry them. Fry them slowly, turning frequently. They will take about 15 minutes.

As the onions start to colour, scatter the sugar over them and baste with the oil and butter.

Taste the pearl barley and adjust the seasoning as needed.

To serve, divide the pearl barley between 4 warmed soup plates, arrange the sausage cakes and onions on top and scatter over a few finely chopped chives before serving.

VENISON PIE

This treatment will appeal to those who find unadorned venison too strong. The pie element combines both shortcrust and flaky pastries, the base being crisp and short, while the crust is of glazed puff pastry. Have the butcher bone the shoulder for you, but ask for the bones.

serves 6
1 kg (2¼ lb) shoulder of venison
1.1 litres (2 pints) chicken stock
2 bay leaves
3 celery stalks, chopped
small bunch of thyme
115 g (4 oz) pancetta or bacon, cut into matchstick strips
4 tbsp olive oil

225 g (8 oz) onions, diced
2 garlic cloves, chopped
85 g (3 oz) flour
salt and pepper
4 tbsp gin
300 ml (½ pint) dark beer
freshly grated nutmeg
30 g (1 oz) butter
450 g (1 lb) shortcrust pastry
450 g (1 lb) puff pastry
1 egg, beaten

Brown the bones in an oven preheated to 250°C (475°F, gas 9) for 20 minutes. Put the bones in a large pan, cover with the chicken stock, bring to the boil and skim. Turn down the heat and add the bay leaves, celery and thyme. Simmer for 1 hour, then pass through a sieve. Reserve.

Fry the pancetta in half the olive oil over a moderate heat until the fat starts to run and the bacon stiffens. Add the diced onion, lower the heat and fry gently until that is soft and translucent. Add the garlic and cook for 2 minutes. Turn off the heat and reserve.

Cut the venison into bite-sized pieces. Season 60 g (2 oz) of the flour, coat the venison in this and brown it in the remaining olive oil in a heavy flameproof casserole over a medium heat.

Turn the heat down to low, add the onion and bacon and stir to mix. Turn up the heat to full, add the gin and carefully flame, shaking the pan. Add the beer, bring to the boil, then add the reserved stock and season lightly with salt, pepper and nutmeg. Return to the boil, skim, turn down the heat and simmer for 1 hour, or until the meat is just done. Start checking after 60 minutes (venison is lean and will flake if cooked too long).

Pour the stock through a sieve into a pan and reduce to 700 ml (1¼ pints).

In another heavy-based pan, make a roux by melting the butter over a low heat and stirring in the remaining 30 g (1 oz) flour. Cook briefly, stirring, then whisk in the stock and bring to a simmer. Simmer over a low heat, stirring from time to time, for 20 minutes. Taste and adjust the seasoning. Stir the meat into this sauce and reserve. This can be done the day before and refrigerated until you make the pie.

Preheat the oven to 200°C (400°F, gas 6).

Line a deep 25.5-cm (10-inch) tart tin with a detachable base with the shortcrust pastry, making a double thickness round the sides and pulling the pastry above the rim to allow for shrinkage. Line with foil, weight and bake blind for 10 minutes. Remove the weights and foil, and return to the oven for 5 minutes. Remove and leave to cool before filling with the meat.

Roll out the puff pastry lid. Using a scalpel or sharp knife, incise a neat crosshatch pattern on it. Brush the rim of the base with beaten egg yolk. Put on the lid, press down on the rim and cut a small hole in the centre to allow steam to escape. Glaze the top with the remaining yolk and bake for 20 minutes, when the lid will be well risen and golden brown.

Options: You can serve the pie hot or cold; if the former, then serve it with buttery mashed potatoes or new potatoes.

PEPPERED SAUSAGE CAKES IN YORKSHIRE PUDDING

The original toad-in-the-hole used steak or pigeon, not sausages. Here, spicy home-made sausage cakes replace the sausages and the batter is lightened with whisked egg whites. It is important to have at least one-sixth of the sausage mixture as fat, or the cakes will be dry and chewy. If you have a supplier of really excellent pork sausages, then use them – but skin them first.

The most significant factors in achieving a well-risen, crisp-surfaced, airy pudding are the number of eggs, how liquid your batter is and how hot the fat is into which you pour it. This pudding batter has quite a lot of eggs by Yorkshire standards. You can cook the pudding successfully in olive oil, but goose fat will give a better flavour. Serve with spinach tossed in butter until it wilts.

serves 6

225 g (8 oz) loin of pork
225 g (8 oz) fat belly pork
115 g (4 oz) pancetta or bacon in a piece
handful of flat-leaf parsley
handful of coriander leaves
1 tsp salt
1 tsp freeze-dried oregano
½ tsp ground allspice
½ tsp freshly grated nutmeg
1 tsp coarsely crushed black peppercorns
½ tsp chilli flakes
200 g (7 oz) sausage meat
115 g (4 oz) onions, finely chopped
5 tbsp goose fat, or a mixture of olive oil and sunflower oil

FOR THE BATTER:
175 g (6 oz) flour
¼ tsp salt
300 ml (½ pint) milk
150 ml (¼ pint) ice-cold water
2 eggs, beaten, plus whites of 4 eggs

The pork should be very cold before chopping, so refrigerate it for at least 4 hours and preferably overnight. Cut the chilled pork and pancetta or bacon into 2-cm (¾-inch) cubes and put these through the coarse plate of a mincer, or put them into a food processor.

Chop the parsley and coriander leaves coarsely and put with the salt, dried herbs and spices in a food processor. Pulse-chop in 2-second bursts to mince. You don't want a purée, but to have discernible pieces. Transfer to a bowl and add the sausage meat and onion. Mix in thoroughly. Divide into 12 and form into round cakes about 2.5 cm (1 inch) thick.

Make the batter: sift the flour into a mixing bowl with the salt. Mix together the milk and water and whisk with the 2 beaten eggs. Add to the flour in a thin stream, whisking to a smooth batter, and leave to stand for 60 minutes at room temperature.

Preheat the oven to 230°C (450°F, gas 8).

Whisk the egg whites to soft peaks and fold into the batter.

Put the sausage cakes into a metal pan at least 6.5 cm (2½ inches) deep and put into the oven for 5 minutes. Add the goose fat or dripping and return to the oven until smoking-hot, about 5 minutes more. Turn the cakes over, pour the batter over them and bake for 15 minutes, when the pudding will be well risen.

Turn down the oven setting to 200°C (400°F, gas 6) and continue cooking for a further 10 minutes, when you will have a crisp golden crust.

PORK PIE

Pork pies are raised pies, i.e. pies made with a lard-based, hot-water crust pastry which is strong enough to stand alone during baking without the support of a metal mould. A food processor takes the hard work out of making it. When cooled to room temperature the pies are quite robust.

The skill required to make pork pies rests in your ability to make the pastry, a procedure that people can find daunting but which is, in reality, no more difficult than shaping plasticine. The main problem to overcome is the temperature of the pastry while you are shaping it. Because of the lard, it stiffens as it cools and, at a certain point, will become unworkable. It is forgiving stuff and may be warmed until it becomes malleable again several times without detriment to the finished pastry. Until you feel confident, make smaller pies, as large ones like this are more tricky.

serves 6
900 g (2 lb) boneless shoulder of pork, diced
150 g (5 oz) onions, diced
150 ml (¼ pint) dry white wine
salt and pepper
freshly grated nutmeg
1 egg, beaten
150 ml (¼ pint) jellied chicken stock
2 sheets of gelatine

FOR THE HOT-WATER CRUST:
750 g (1¾ lb) plain flour
250 g (9 oz) lard, diced
2 tsp salt
melted butter, for greasing

First make the pastry: sift the flour into a food processor. In a pan, bring 300 ml (½ pint) of water with the diced lard and salt to a rapid boil. With the processor at full speed, carefully pour this mixture in a thin stream down the feeder tube until you have a smooth, elastic dough. When cool enough to handle, transfer to an oiled bowl, cover with a cloth and leave to stand in a warm place for 6–9 minutes.

If the pastry cools too far and becomes unworkable, reform it into a ball, put in a bowl and stand in a warm oven with the door open until it responds to a push with your finger.

Brush the outside of a Kilner-type glass jar with melted butter. Press out about four-fifths of the dough into a round on a non-stick surface. Stand the jar in the middle and shape and pull the dough up round it to a uniform thickness of about 1.5 cm (½ inch). Turn it on its side and roll gently to encourage an even thickness. Recruit help to wrap it round with greaseproof paper, then tie this in place with string. Put in the fridge to set firm, about 30 minutes.

While it is setting, roll out the remaining pastry as a lid. Preheat the oven to 180°C (350°F, gas 5).

To remove the jar, soak a cloth in very hot water, squeeze it out and push it into the jar. After a minute or two the heat will have melted the butter and you should be able to lift the jar out.

Put the diced pork, onion and the wine in a bowl, season with salt, pepper and nutmeg, and turn and work together between your fingers to distribute the seasonings evenly. Brush the pastry edge with water and crimp the lid on top. Push a hole through the centre, brush the top with beaten egg and bake in its paper for 50 minutes.

Remove, carefully cut the strings and take off the paper. Return to the oven, turn up the setting to 190°C

(375°F, gas 5) and continue to cook for 20 minutes. Remove, allow to cool, then refrigerate.

Warm the chicken stock and dissolve the gelatine in it. Using a funnel, pour this liquid through the hole in the lid and return the pie to the fridge to set.

Allow to come to room temperature before serving.

MUTTON PIES

Queen Victoria was passionate about mutton pies, and they were often served with drinks before dinner at Balmoral, and later at Buckingham Palace by George V, another royal fan. This is a late 19th-century recipe, which is rather more elegant than you would generally find today.

Although a few individual bakers and butchers in Scotland still make their own highly seasoned minced mutton pies in a hot-water crust, the numbers are getting smaller. The trade can buy pie shells and fillings, or seasoning mixes, to make pie assembly and baking an easy business – a depressing practice resulting in very poor results.

makes 6

550 g (1 lb 4 oz) lean minced lamb
175 g (6 oz) onions, finely diced
115 g (4 oz) mushrooms, finely diced
sprig of fresh thyme or ½ tsp dried
1 bay leaf
freshly grated nutmeg
salt and pepper
300 ml (½ pint) lamb or chicken stock
300 ml (½ pint) red wine or beer
½ recipe quantity hot-water crust pastry (see above)
butter, for greasing
1 egg, beaten
3 tbsp redcurrant jelly (optional)

In a large saucepan, place the lamb, onions, mushrooms, thyme, bay leaf, nutmeg to taste, 1½ teaspoons salt and 1 teaspoon of black pepper. Add the stock and wine. Bring to the boil, turn down the heat and simmer for 45 minutes, stirring from time to time and adding a little water if it dries out. Strain through a sieve, reserving the remaining cooking liquid and removing the fat from the surface when cold. This can all be done a day ahead.

Preheat the oven to 200°C (400°F, gas 6). Make the hot-water crust pastry as for the pork pie (page 82). Divide into 6, cover with a cloth and leave to cool slightly for 6–9 minutes. The pastry needs to stay warm to be malleable and it is a good idea to put what you are not working with on top of the oven.

Roll out each piece into a 2-cm (¾-inch) thick round. Lightly grease the outside of a small soufflé dish or straight-sided ramekin with butter and stand it in the middle of each round, then mould the pastry up around it. Turn on its side and roll gently to make the sides an even thickness. Sit it on a greased baking tray and lift out the dish. Repeat with the others. Trim the tops level, starting to feel less judgemental about people buying in their pastry shells as you do so.

Fill each shell with the lamb mixture to within 1 cm (½ inch) of the brim, adding a spoonful of the reserved jellied stock. Reform the trimmings into a cylinder, divide into 6 and roll out the lids. Put these on, crimping to make a good seal round the edge. Make a small hole in the middle and brush with egg.

Put in the oven. After 5 minutes, turn it down to 190°C (375°F, gas 5) and continue to cook for a further 25 minutes.

For an authentic Victorian touch, pour a little melted redcurrant jelly through the holes in the tops of the pies when they come out of the oven, and serve hot or at room temperature.

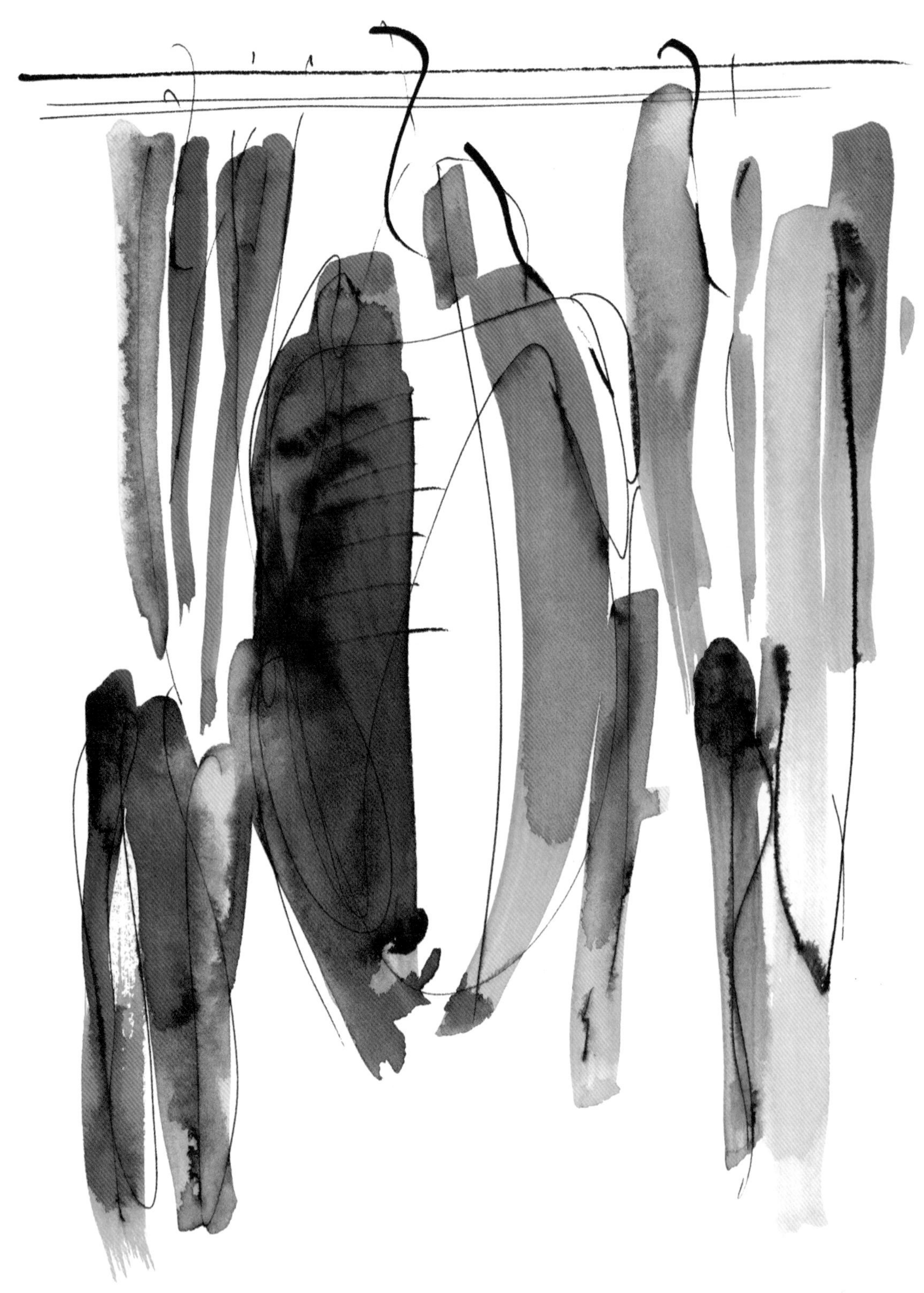

Chapter 5
Chinatown

Our local Chinese village

The first job I ever had was when I was seventeen and working at Harrods, selling men's hats and umbrellas. During that hot summer I ate my first authentic Cantonese food in Limehouse, London's original Chinatown. I loved the gleaming red-brown barbecued pork fillet, steamed whole fish, glossy roast duck and slices of clam in broth, all eaten with tentative chopsticks in spartan cafés in the middle of a dockside wasteland. It bore very little resemblance to what I had previously had in supposedly Chinese restaurants in Edinburgh and Newcastle.

I was taken to these East-End feasts in a Lotus Super 7 by an entertaining young man some 10 years my senior called Stephen, who sold ties. I might today wonder whether he had sexual intentions, but at the time merely thought he was amused by my conversation. He never made any overt moves, though I do recall the odd suggestive look as he tugged on his driving gloves and once or twice a hand might have brushed against my knee instead of the gearshift, but then there never was a lot of room in a Lotus.

By 1970, Chinatown had mostly transferred itself to its present location on and around Gerrard Street, an area largely described by Shaftesbury Avenue to the north and Leicester Square to the south, Charing Cross Road to the east and Wardour Street to the west, right on the edge of Soho. It was in Soho that I met Alastair Little, with whom I started my food-writing career in 1992. We got to know each other during his stint at The Old Compton Wine Bar in 1975. I can take the credit for introducing him to Poon's in Lisle Street, where we ate in an upstairs room that overlooked the free cabaret across the road provided by professional ladies entertaining clients without the benefit of curtains at the window. The premises were unlicensed, but we were allowed to bring in wine and our impromptu dinner parties would extend long into the night.

It was the first place any of us had ever tasted wind-dried food and a range of authentic Cantonese dishes, like stir-fried eel with pork and garlic. The image, one early summer evening, of a cross waiter scampering down the stairs with four live eels gripped by the head in a drying up cloth, their bodies thrashing like snakes on the way to Bill Poon's swift-cleavered dispatch, is vivid – a moment caught in time like a mental Polaroid. Equally memorable, the forceful taste as they were served minutes later, sizzling in sesame oil with whole garlic cloves, a plump and nutty counterpoint to the rich flesh. When I look back on countless meals in so many restaurants, I still remember that day and those flavours with a clarity that is extraordinary.

Since then I have eaten in Chinatowns all over the world, including those of New York, Toronto, San Francisco, Los Angeles – and, in England, Manchester and Leeds. I have never been to China, other than a brief and unscheduled stopover in Hong Kong's Kai Tak airport, which I don't think counts. They are so important, our local Chinese villages, for they bring us real food, most of it here Cantonese, because of the historic British relationship with Hong Kong.

Long before we were introduced to the flavours of Southeast Asia, we had the opportunity to eat good Cantonese food in restaurants where there were more people speaking Cantonese than English, so it was like being abroad without going anywhere, and hard by we had markets, real foreign markets with mysterious foreign ingredients. And, oh, the marvels of how foreign they smelled... not in a nasty way, but in the most fascinating and adventurous way. This was surely another and most desirable reality.

One of the first big Chinese markets to open in London was Loon Fung on Gerrard Street. It remains a great place to shop and is one of the markets to which Chinese people who live outside London come on Sundays, a day when it is best not to try and go for *dim sum* because every table in every restaurant is occupied until late.

TURNIP PASTE

Dim sum – literally 'heavenly delight' but, as literally, snacks eaten with tea – are the dishes served in specialist Chinatown restaurants from 11 am until 5 pm. This is an informal Cantonese way of eating, in which you select what you want from trolleys that are pushed continuously round the dining room. *Dim sum* include many different kinds of dumplings, roast duck and pork, congee rice soup and *lor bak ko* – turnip paste, not an easy thing to pin down.

Help is at hand with this recipe from Diana Ma, the mother of my friend Brian Ma Siy, who also gave me the benefit of her knowledge in the *char siu* recipe on page 98. The turnip paste is made from the foot-long, white Chinese turnips which you buy from Oriental markets.

makes 8 portions
6 Chinese dried mushrooms
300 ml (½ pint) warm water
3 tbsp groundnut oil, plus more for greasing
1 tsp soy sauce
½ tsp sugar
85 g (3 oz) dried shrimp
1.35 kg (3 lb) Chinese turnips (see above)
2 wind-dried sausages, finely chopped
2 strips of wind-dried pork, finely chopped
1 tbsp caster sugar
2 tsp salt
450 g (1 lb) rice flour
2 spring onions, thinly sliced
2 tsp sesame seeds
handful of coriander leaves

The day before: wash the Chinese mushrooms, then soak them in the warm water for 2 hours. Pass through a sieve, reserving the soaking liquid. Rinse the mushrooms to remove any grit and squeeze dry.

Dice them finely, then marinate them in a mixture of 1 tablespoon of the groundnut oil, the soy sauce and sugar for another 2 hours. In another bowl, soak the dried shrimp in cold water for the same length of time.

Peel the turnips, grate them on the medium panel of a box grater and put in a pan. Heat 2 tablespoons of the oil in a wok over a moderate heat and stir-fry the wind-dried sausage for 2–3 minutes, then remove to the pan with the turnip. Repeat with the wind-dried pork, followed by the mushrooms, adding each to the pan. Pour over the reserved soaking liquid and 600 ml (1 pint) of water, stir thoroughly and bring to the boil. Stir in the caster sugar and salt, lower the heat and bubble gently for 15–20 minutes, until the turnip is cooked.

Strain through a sieve, reserving the liquid in a mixing bowl. Stir in the rice flour. The consistency to aim for, Mrs Ma says, is that of wet Polyfilla; so, if it is too dry, add hot water until you get it right.

Oil a 23-cm (9-inch) round cake tin with a depth of 7.5 cm (3 inches) and pour and scrape the mixture into this. Steam, set on a trivet in a large wok with a tight-fitting lid, for 45 minutes.

Stir-fry the spring onions briefly with the sesame seeds and a handful of coriander leaves. Scatter this on top of the turnip paste and continue steaming for another 10 minutes. It is cooked when a chopstick inserted into the middle comes out clean. Remove and leave overnight.

Next day, remove the turnip cake from the tin. Cut it into quarters and then cut these across into slices roughly 5x3.5 cm (2x1½ inches) in size. Just before serving, shallow-fry these in a little groundnut oil for 2–3 minutes on each side.

In *dim sum* restaurants this final frying is done beside the table, giving off the most seductive aroma.

CLOUD EAR SCRAMBLED EGGS AND PANCAKES

Cloud ears are a fungus that grows on trees and they are sold dried in Oriental markets. After rehydration they look rather like a seaweed. Here they are cooked separately from the eggs, only being mixed in just before serving. If you can't buy any cloud ears then you can use porcini or any other dried mushroom in the same way, or substitute fresh shiitake. I use butter and crème fraîche here, foreign ingredients, and cook the scrambled eggs slowly Western-style, so I guess this is really a fusion dish.

Store-bought Chinese pancakes are reviled by Yan-kit So and other purists as having a leathery consistency and tasting of raw flour. I am not sure I would damn them so harshly. Like everything produced commercially you find good and bad. Whether you buy them ready-made or make them yourself, they are steamed to reheat them and the time for which you steam them obviously impacts on how much they taste of raw flour. I find it is beneficial to wipe them with a slightly damp cloth to rid them of excess flour just before putting them in the steamer.

Home-made are superior in taste and texture, though you need to make them a few times to achieve a consistent result. Getting a uniform thickness is important, because thin spots will tear when you try to separate the pancakes, which are initially cooked with two stuck together. I believe that the Chinese method of initially cooking the pancakes in pairs, the two separated with a film of sesame oil, is unique. It is said to produce thinner and more moist pancakes, though I have had good results cooking them individually. As long as you keep the heat down, they should come out all right.

Creamy, soft scrambled eggs are very much a Northern European construction and cooked in the following way could be said to be French. You do not find perfectly scrambled eggs anywhere else in the world, including the USA where they also mostly don't know how to make an omelette. The soft curds of the scrambled eggs may make it less authentically Chinese but are I think an improvement.

serves 6

60 g (2 oz) dried cloud ears
85 g (3 oz) unsalted butter
6 spring onions, thinly sliced
12 eggs
3 tbsp milk
salt and pepper
2 tbsp crème fraîche
4 Chinese chives or 12 chives, finely chopped

FOR THE PANCAKES **(makes about 28)**:
350 ml (12 fl oz) very hot water
425 g (15 oz) plain flour
sesame oil, for brushing
groundnut or corn oil, for the pan

Well ahead, make the pancakes: put the hot water into the bowl of an electric mixer fitted with a dough hook. Switch on at the lowest speed, add the flour and work for 8 minutes, adding teaspoons of cold water after about 3 minutes if the mixture is not holding as an elastic dough. Remove to a lightly floured surface and form into a ball. Cover with a slightly damp cloth and leave to stand for 20–30 minutes.

Divide the rested dough into 2, and roll each piece into cylinders about 35 cm (14 inches) long and 2.5 cm (1 inch) in diameter. Cover one of the rolls and cut the other into 14 pieces about 2.5cm (1 inch) thick.

Take 2 pieces and form them into balls, pushing down with the heel of your hand to make rounds about 5 cm (2 inches) across. Brush one of them lightly with sesame oil, pressing the other on top. On a lightly floured surface, roll the pair out until they have a diameter of about 15 cm (6 inches).

Heat a dry heavy-based frying pan over a low heat. Wipe it with a few drops of groundnut or corn oil on some kitchen paper. Add a pair of pancakes and cook for a minute, or until the bottom is dry and white. Turn and cook the other side, and remove as soon as the surface starts to balloon, gently pulling the pancakes apart. Stack them under a cloth to prevent them drying out, while you cook the rest.

If you can get somebody to help you, with one person rolling and the other cooking, the job is quickly done. Since the pancakes freeze really well, you can make them a week or more in advance. They can be steamed from frozen.

Pour water that has just come off the boil over the cloud ears and leave to stand for 20–30 minutes. Put more water to boil for steaming.

Put 30 g (1 oz) of the butter in a saucepan and place over a low heat. Coarsely chop the drained cloud ears and add these and the spring onions. Stir to coat, cover with a lid and cook for 5 minutes. Take off the lid and continue to cook until any water has evaporated. Keep warm.

Whisk the eggs with the milk. Melt the remaining butter in a heavy-based saucepan and stir in the eggs. Season with salt and pepper and cook over the lowest heat, stirring pretty much continuously to ensure the softest and creamiest curds. This should take at least 20 minutes.

Stop further cooking by whisking in the crème fraîche, then fold in the cloud ear mixture. Spoon into a warmed serving bowl and scatter the chives on top.

Towards the end of the egg cooking time, steam the pancakes gently for 5 minutes or so.

Roll the pancakes into cones and arrange on a warmed serving plate. Take the eggs and pancakes to the table for people to put the two together themselves.

STIR-FRIED RICE WITH EGG AND CRAB

The dish for which leftover long-grain rice was intended, fried rice can be as simple as a mixture of onion and rice or a rather grand concoction including shellfish and meat. What you choose to include is a matter of what is to hand when approaching this as a way of using up leftovers, and then the only thing to avoid is oily fish. A well thought-out fried rice is to be taken seriously and can be really special. Frozen peas are specified deliberately. They do not need to be cooked, just defrosted.

A big wok is the best thing in which to stir-fry, but it works better if you sweat the onions initially in an ordinary frying pan, only adding them to the hot wok when they are soft and already cooked.

serves 4

3.5-cm (1½-inch) piece of root ginger
175 g (6 oz) onions, thinly sliced
5 tbsp groundnut or sunflower oil
3 eggs
salt and pepper
1 hot red chilli, shredded
1 garlic clove
500 g (1 lb 2 oz) cooked long-grain rice (cooked weight)
115 g (4 oz) frozen peas
225 g (8 oz) picked white crab meat
2 spring onions, shredded
1 tbsp soy sauce
handful of coriander leaves, coarsely chopped

Peel the ginger, cut it into paper-thin slices, then cut these across into fine strips.

In a frying pan, sweat the onions in 2 tablespoons of the oil over a low heat, stirring frequently, until soft and translucent. Reserve.

Put 1 tablespoon of the oil in a frying pan over a moderate heat. In a bowl, whisk the eggs with 2 teaspoons of water. Season with salt and pepper and pour into the pan, swirling and tilting to make an even layer. Cook without touching until just set. Slide out on a cutting board and reserve.

Put a large wok over a medium-to-high heat. When smoking-hot, swirl in the remaining oil. Add the onion, ginger, chilli and garlic and stir-fry for a minute, then add the rice and peas. Toss and stir-fry for 2–3 minutes. Remove from the heat and stir in the crab and spring onions.

Mound in deep serving bowls. Cut the omelette into strips and arrange these on top. Zig-zag a little soy sauce on each and scatter over some coriander.

SALT AND PEPPER PRAWNS

A salt-and-pepper coating for deep-frying is almost certainly Chinese in origin, with squid perhaps the most frequently cooked seafood using the technique. Butterflied prawns, heads off but shells on, deep-fry beautifully in the same mixture and are great fun to eat the instant they are cool enough to pick up.

serves 4
1 kg (2¼ lb) large unpeeled raw prawns
oil for deep-frying
2 tsp five-spice powder
2 tsp Sichuan pepper
1½ tsp black peppercorns
3 tbsp salt
225 g (8 oz) flour, sifted
handful of coriander leaves, to serve
lemon quarters, to serve

Remove the heads from the prawns and cut each prawn through the back, pulling out and discarding the intestinal thread. Press down gently to open each prawn out a little. Rinse under cold running water and pat dry.

Preheat oil for deep-frying to 190°C (375°F).

Put the spices and salt in a spice or coffee grinder and grind to a powder. Put the flour in a mixing bowl and mix in the ground spices. Dust the prawns in this mixture, shaking off excess.

Deep-fry the prawn in batches for about 2–3 minutes each batch, taking care you don't put too many in at a time unless you have a professional-standard fryer. Not only will the addition of too many at a time cause the temperature to drop but the evaporating moisture content can cause the oil to boil over.

Remove to kitchen paper to drain briefly and serve at once, scattered with coriander leaves and with quartered lemons to squeeze over as preferred.

PRAWN AND EGG OMELETTE

This is not so much an omelette as a flavoured egg custard that is set in a pan with the prawns and other ingredients in it, a kind of Chinese frittata.

serves 4
6 eggs, plus white of 1 extra egg
1 tbsp dry sherry
2 tsp Pearl River soy sauce
½ tsp caster sugar
½ tbsp sesame oil
pepper
16 raw tiger prawns, peeled and dark intestinal tract removed
½ tbsp groundnut oil
2 spring onions, thinly sliced
1 hot red chilli, shredded

Preheat a hot grill. Beat the eggs and extra egg white with the sherry, soy sauce, sugar and sesame oil. Season with pepper. Shred the prawns.

Put the oil in a 20-cm (8-inch) heavy-based frying pan over a moderate heat. Add the spring onions and chilli, and stir-fry until soft, 2–3 minutes.

Add the shredded prawn and stir in, distributing evenly in the pan. Pour in the egg mixture, shake and turn down the heat to low. When it has set on the base, put under the grill for a minute or 2, until set on top and just starting to fleck with brown.

Slide out on a chopping board and leave for 3–4 minutes before cutting into quarters. Serve warm.

EGG CUSTARD WITH CRAB AND GINGER

Steamed savoury custards are a feature of Northern Chinese cooking, the effect being similar to that of a baked custard, though steaming produces a more silky finish. Unless you have very large steaming baskets, the best thing to use is a wok, which gives you a large volume, making it a very effective steamer and one which does not require a lot of water in the bottom to do the job. You do need to check at regular intervals to make sure it is not boiling dry and, when you top up with water, use boiling water from a kettle. You also want a tight-fitting lid and, if your wok does not have one, you can improvise using metal foil and the lid from a large saucepan.

The combination of crab and eggs is always pleasing, and the flavour of the broth is fragrant with ginger. If you do not have a live crab, then a cooked crab may be used or, as a last resort, white cooked crab meat sold from the chill cabinet may be substituted. Tinned crab in brine is not really acceptable here, and it is better to replace the crab with just-cooked tiger prawns. Steamed custards can also be made with lobster for an even more luxurious result.

serves 4

6 eggs
salt and pepper
250 ml (9 fl oz) shellfish stock or light chicken stock
1 tbsp ginger juice (page 183)
1 tbsp dry sherry
2 tsp finely chopped coriander leaves
2 spring onions, thinly sliced
1/4 tsp finely chopped hot red chilli
275 g (10 oz) white crab meat
steamed rice (page 308) and pancakes (page 179) or Cos lettuce leaves, to serve

Put a rack or a plate upside down in a wok and pour hot water from the kettle to come to a depth of about 5 cm (2 inches).

Whisk the eggs in a bowl which will fit comfortably in the wok, adding 1 teaspoon of salt and 1/2 teaspoon of pepper before gradually whisking in the stock, ginger juice and sherry. Stir in the coriander, spring onions and chilli. Finally, break up the crab meat and gently fold it in.

Place on the rack in the wok. Bring the water to the boil, immediately lowering the heat and putting on the lid. Steam for 25–30 minutes, or until the custard has set.

Serve with steamed rice and pancakes or Cos lettuce leaves.

STEAMED SPICED WHITE FILLETS

You can also use sole, snapper or cod fillets for this dish. If cooked in a Chinese bamboo steamer, it can be served directly from it at the table. You can ask your fishmonger to remove the pin bones, but should still check for any that have been missed by running your finger along the bone line, removing them with a small pair of pliers.

serves 4
450 g (1 lb) white fish fillets, skinned and boned
salt and pepper
4 garlic cloves, coarsely chopped
15 g (1/2 oz) fresh coriander, with roots, well washed and all coarsely chopped
2 purple shallots, coarsely chopped
1 tsp dried chilli flakes
1 tsp ground turmeric
1 egg, beaten
150 ml (1/4 pint) coconut milk
2 tbsp nam pla fish sauce
1 tbsp cornflour
Jasmine Rice (page 308), to serve

Cut the fish fillets into 2.5-cm (1-inch) strips. Scatter with 2 teaspoons of salt and chill for 1 hour.

Remove and rinse under cold running water. Pat dry and return to the fridge until needed.

In a food processor, blitz the garlic, coriander and shallots to a liquid purée with the chilli flakes.

Transfer to a bowl and stir in the turmeric, beaten egg, coconut milk and fish sauce. Grind in about 1/2 teaspoon of pepper and beat to amalgamate all the elements. Stir in the fish strips and turn to coat evenly. Remove to a rack to drain excess moisture, then dust with the cornflour.

Put the fish on a plate on the base of the steamer. Steam for 12–15 minutes. Serve with jasmine rice (page 308).

SWEET-AND-SOUR MONKFISH WITH WIND-DRIED SAUSAGE

Monkfish is a very meaty fish and is treated as such here, being cooked with chicken stock and served with steamed wind-dried sausage. This is a fine combination and very appealing on the plate.

serves 4
4 ripe plum tomatoes
675–700 g (1 1/2–1 lb 9 oz) monkfish tail
300ml (1/2 pint) chicken stock
2 tbsp sake or dry rice wine
1 tbsp rice vinegar
115 g (4 oz) wind-dried sausage
2 tsp cornflour
1 tbsp groundnut oil
1 sweet red pepper, deseeded and diced
3 spring onions, cut at angle into 3-cm (1 1/4-in) pieces
2 garlic cloves, finely chopped
2.5-cm (1-inch) piece of ginger, peeled and cut into fine julienne strips
175 g (6 oz) canned water chestnuts, thinly sliced
1 tbsp tomato ketchup
1 tbsp Pearl River soy sauce
1 tsp caster sugar

Blanch the tomatoes, refresh in cold water and peel. Cut into quarters and strip out the pulp, adding the pulp to the stock mixture.

Skin the monkfish and cut the fillets from the central bone. Chop the bone and skin and put in a small saucepan with the chicken stock, rice wine and vinegar. Bring to the boil, lower the heat and simmer for 20 minutes. Pass through a measuring jug. You want 150 ml (1/4 pint). Pour off any excess. If you have less liquid, top up with water.

Cut the wind-dried sausage at an angle into 5-mm (1/4-inch) slices and steam for 10 minutes. Reserve.

Cut the monkfish into bite-sized chunks. Dice the tomato pieces. Mix the cornflour to a paste with cold water.

Heat a wok over a moderate heat and, when hot, add the oil. As it shimmers, add the pepper dice and spring onion. Stir-fry for a minute. Add the garlic, ginger and water chestnuts, and fry for another minute, then add the reserved fish stock, the ketchup, soy sauce and sugar. As it bubbles, add the cornflour paste, the monkfish pieces and the tomato dice. Stir and toss for 2–3 minutes, when the fish should just be cooked through. Be careful not to overcook as monkfish soon goes chewy.

Serve at once on large warmed plates with steamed rice, scattering the sausage pieces on top.

CRYSTAL CHICKEN

Crystal chicken is the pretty Chinese name for boiled chicken that is always served at room temperature. Poaching delivers a moist result, and the bonus of a well-flavoured stock to use in another dish. You give the bird a Chinese flavour by including appropriate aromatic ingredients in the cooking liquid. If you start with chicken stock rather than water, the flavour will be further enhanced, though this is not essential.

serves 4
8 spring onions
1 free-range chicken, about 1.35 kg (3 lb)
7.5-cm (3-inch) piece of root ginger, thinly sliced
2 lemons, quartered
2 pieces of star anise
12 Sichuan peppercorns
1 cinnamon stick
handful of coriander stalks and scraped roots
1.25 litres (2 pints) chicken stock
125 ml (4 fl oz) rice vinegar
2–3 tbsp Pearl River soy sauce

FOR THE ORANGE AND RADISH SALAD:
3 oranges
16 radishes
8 small shallots
2 tbsp rice vinegar

Shred 4 of the spring onions and put inside the chicken, together with the ginger, quartered lemons, star anise, 6 of the Sichuan peppercorns, the cinnamon and coriander. Put the bird, breast side down, in a pan in which it just fits. Pour in the stock and cold water to cover, add the rice vinegar and bring to the boil. Skim, lower the heat and simmer gently for 30 minutes. Turn the bird breast side up, and cook for a further 15 minutes. Cover with a lid, turn off the heat and leave to cool in the liquid. Remove and drain.

Remove the skin and discard, then pull off the legs and cut them into drumsticks and thighs. Cut and pull the meat from the bones, removing the breasts whole; cut them across at an angle into the thinnest slices you can manage and arrange these overlapping on a large plate. Scatter the shredded dark meat over. Return the carcass, bones and stuffing aromatics to the pan and simmer for 3 hours. This will make beautiful fragrant consommé which you could serve with little dumplings, coriander leaves and some thin matchsticks of ginger as a first course before the crystal chicken and salad. Strain through a sieve, dribble 4 tablespoons of the broth over the chicken, cling-wrap and refrigerate.

Make the salad: peel the skin from the oranges and cut the flesh into segments. Cut the radishes and shallots into paper-thin slices. Toss together in a bowl with the rice vinegar and ¼ teaspoon of salt. Scatter whole coriander leaves over the top.

To serve, trim the remaining 4 spring onions into white and green parts, cutting the white onion across in thin rings and shredding the green parts lengthwise. Distribute both evenly over the chicken. Dress with splashes of soy sauce and serve with the salad.

AROMATIC SOY-BRAISED SQUAB

Squab are the plump, sit-on-their-arse, dovecote pigeons, very tender and very special. You will need one squab per person. Serve them to very special people, because they come with a plump-going-on-fat price tag. Smart butchers sell them plucked, but with their heads still on. These fix you with a beady eye in a rather unsettling manner. Gut the birds before cooking.

serves 4

4 spring onions, cut into 2-cm (3/4-inch) pieces
5-cm (2-inch) piece of root ginger, peeled and thinly sliced
4 star anise
2 cinnamon sticks
30 g (1 oz) muscovado sugar
12 Sichuan peppercorns
850 ml (1½ pints) chicken stock
150 ml (¼ pint) dark Chinese soy sauce
100 ml (3½ fl oz) rice wine
4 squab, each about 450 g (1 lb)

In a pan, put the spring onions, ginger, star anise, cinnamon sticks, sugar and Sichuan peppercorns. Pour over the chicken stock, soy sauce and rice wine. Bring to the boil, lower the heat and simmer for 30 minutes.

Fill a pan large enough to hold the 4 birds with water and bring to a rapid boil. Put in the birds, return to the boil and cook for 5 minutes. Remove to a casserole dish in which they will just fit, then pour the soy stock over the squab. Return to a simmer and cook for 15 minutes. Using tongs, gently turn the birds breast side down. Cover with a lid, turn off the heat and leave for 30 minutes to absorb the flavours from the braising liquid.

Remove and cut off the breasts and legs, then chop all the bird into bite-sized portions. Spoon over a little of the braising liquid (the rest should be strained, then frozen to use again – you can poach chicken or pork in it or, of course, more squab).

CANTONESE ROAST DUCK

When you order a duck from a butcher you can tell him you want it with the neck still on. You can go on to tell him that this is because you want to blow down it, or not. This may be more information than he needs to know. The thing is, you need the neck if you are going to get a really crisp skin because, otherwise, you will not be able to separate it from the layer of subcutaneous fat which is what you have to do prior to cooking. Chinese restaurants use a special compressed-air device, but the rest of us can use a bicycle pump fitted with a football inflator.

The unusual ingredient which helps to get the skin finish right is maltose, a strange thick violet-coloured non-sweet substance that looks like hair gel and sets hard when cold. It is the secret of the burnished glaze you see on Cantonese roast ducks and is sold in Chinese markets in plastic pots. It needs to be warmed by standing the container in near boiling water to make it liquid.

This type of duck is usually served with steamed rice and, sometimes, a green vegetable like bok choi. It is also delicious in pancakes (see page 179) with shredded spring onions, cucumber and hoi sin or plum sauce. This is not a traditional Chinese way of eating duck but we *gwaelo* love it.

serves 4

1 large duck
2 tsp Sichuan pepper
pot of maltose
5 tbsp rice vinegar
200 ml (7 fl oz) chicken stock
4 star anise
1 cinnamon stick
200 ml (7 fl oz) Pearl River soy sauce
steamed rice (page 308), to serve

The day before (you need a second pair of hands for this job... at least, I do): start by pulling out any lumps of fat from the duck's cavity, then give the duck a thorough massage, concentrating on the breasts and legs and kneading and pummelling for 5 minutes. This will start to loosen the skin away from the flesh. Make an incision about halfway down the neck. Now the difficult part: gently insert a sharpening steel or metal chopstick into this cut and carefully push it between the skin and the neck all the way down to the breast and legs, levering the skin outwards so you have an airway. The tricky bit is not puncturing the skin. Tie a piece of string tightly near the top of the neck, leaving a loop to hang it up by. Loop a second piece of string just beyond the cut in a loose granny knot. Rub the inside of the duck with the Sichuan pepper.

Push the football inflator into the incision and under the second string, and pump it up so the skin detaches from the meat, then have somebody pull the granny knot tight as you pull out the pump.

Stand the maltose pot in hot water until it liquefies, then put 200 ml (7 fl oz) of it in a large pan. Add enough water to submerge the duck and the vinegar, bring to the boil and simmer for 5 minutes. Holding the duck by the string, lay it breast side down into the liquid for a minute or two. Pull it up and, holding it upright with the string, baste with a ladle until the skin tightens, then hang up in a dry airy place overnight. If you have a fan to blow cold air at it for 4 hours instead, then so much the better.

Next day: put 150 ml (1/4 pint) of water in a pan with the stock, star anise, cinnamon and soy sauce, and bring to a boil, then lower the heat and simmer for 10 minutes. Leave to cool.

Preheat the oven to 200°C (400°F, gas 6).

Hold the duck neck downwards and have your assistant pour the stock mixture into the cavity, then sew it up or close the cavity with a skewer and tie just below it with string to seal. Place on a rack, breast upwards, and roast for 60 minutes.

Remove and leave on a rack to cool to room temperature. Carve off the breasts and legs. Chop into pieces with a cleaver and serve with steamed rice, spooning over the aromatic liquid from inside the duck as a sauce.

SICHUAN SESAME BEEF

Sichuan, Schezuan or Sechuan food, depending on how you choose to spell it in English, describes the regional food of that northern Chinese province and is characterized by the heavy use of chillies, garlic and aromatic Sichuan pepper. Like all stir-fried dishes, most of the time involved is in the preparation rather than the cooking.

serves 4

500 g (1 lb 2 oz) piece of rump or sirloin steak
3 tbsp sunflower oil
2 tsp sesame seeds
2 garlic cloves, finely chopped
1 tsp dried chilli flakes
1/2 tsp Sichuan pepper
4 spring onions, cut across at an angle into 2-cm (3/4-inch) pieces, to serve
steamed rice (page 308), to serve

FOR THE SESAME MARINADE:

3 tbsp Pearl River soy sauce
1 tbsp rice wine
1 tsp caster sugar
2 tsp sesame oil

Trim any excess fat from the beef and put it on a tray in the freezer for 20 minutes. This firms up the meat and makes it easier to cut into the thinnest slices.

Remove to a board and shave into wafer-thin slices with a razor-sharp knife. Put these in a bowl with the marinade ingredients. Toss to coat, then leave to marinate in the fridge for 1 hour.

Drain the marinated beef through a colander, reserving the marinade.

Heat a wok over a moderate heat until smoking-hot. Add the oil, swirl, then add the sesame seeds and stir-fry for 1 minute. Add the meat, garlic, chilli flakes and Sichuan peppercorns. Toss and stir-fry for 1 minute. Add half the marinade and cook for a minute more.

Remove to a warmed serving plate and scatter over the spring onions. Serve with steamed rice and a blanched green vegetable, such as bok choi.

CRISP PORK WON TON WITH BEANSPROUTS AND DIPPING SAUCE

Won ton wrappers deep-fry to make a light crisp coating around pretty much anything you fancy. You can poach the same won ton and serve in broth for a quite different effect.

serves 4–6

85 g (3 oz) wind-dried sausage
1 tsp coriander seeds
1 tsp cumin seeds
1 tsp black peppercorns
1 tbsp groundnut oil
400 g (14 oz) lean minced pork
½ tsp chilli flakes
115 g (4 oz) onions, finely diced
1 garlic clove, finely chopped
¼ tsp five-spice powder
½ tsp salt
20 won ton wrappers
oil for deep-frying

FOR THE CORIANDER DIPPING SAUCE:
60 g (2 oz) coriander leaves, with stems and roots, well cleaned and trimmed
2 tbsp freshly grated peeled root ginger
2 tbsp rice vinegar
1 hot green chilli, finely chopped
150 ml (¼ pint) thick yoghurt
½ tsp cumin seeds

FOR THE BEANSPROUT STIR-FRY
1 tbsp groundnut oil
1 tbsp sesame oil
5-cm (2-in) piece of root ginger, peeled and cut into julienne strips
2 spring onions, shredded
2 garlic cloves, chopped
225 g (8 oz) beansprouts
1 tbsp Pearl River soy sauce

Slice the sausage thinly and steam for 10 minutes, then chop finely. Reserve.

Toast the coriander and cumin seeds with the peppercorns in a dry pan over a low heat for 3 minutes or until aromatic. Grind to a powder.

Cut off the roots from the coriander to be used in the coriander dipping sauce and finely chop them. Put the oil in a small pan with the chopped roots and ground spices and fry over a low heat, stirring for 2–3 minutes, then put in a food processor with the pork, the sausage, chilli flakes, onions, garlic, five-spice powder and salt. Pulse-chop to a coherent mass. Take out a spoonful, make this into a patty, fry and eat to assess the seasoning. Adjust to taste.

Brush the edges of a won ton wrapper with a little water. Put a heaped teaspoon of the mixture in the middle, draw up two opposite corners and pinch together. Pull up the other two and pinch them together, then pinch the open edges together on both sides. Put on a lightly floured tray, cover with a cloth, and repeat. When all are completed, they can be held in the fridge for 1 hour.

Make the coriander dipping sauce: coarsely chop the coriander leaves and stalks, and put in a food processor with the ginger, rice vinegar and chilli, then blitz to a paste. Stir this into the yoghurt and add salt and pepper to taste. Just before serving, toast the cumin seeds in a dry pan over a low heat for 3 minutes and scatter on the top.

Preheat oil for deep-frying to 190°C (375°F). It is important not to overcrowd the fryer as this will cause the temperature to drop and oil will be absorbed, so cook the won ton in 2 or 3 batches, turning with a slotted spoon to ensure even cooking. They take about 4 minutes. Drain on kitchen paper.

Make the beansprout stir-fry: heat a wok until smoking-hot, then add the oils and swirl, immediately adding the ginger, spring onions and garlic. Add the beansprouts and stir-fry for a minute. Add the soy sauce, toss and remove from the heat.

Divide the won ton between 4 large warmed plates. Mound some beansprouts next to them and place a ramekin of the dipping sauce on each plate.

CHAR SIU

Char siu is one of the world's best ways of roasting pork, delivering a tender and moist result, with a sweet aromatic flavour. It is sliced as it comes hot from the oven and served with anything from steamed rice to stir-fried vegetables and soup noodle dishes. Commercially roasted *char siu* is actually cooked hanging up in the huge round, vertical ovens that are also used for Cantonese roast duck, but you can make a competent version in any domestic oven.

Brian Ma Siy is an architect with whom I have worked on three books. *Cutting Edge*, which was inspired by my time in California, is illustrated only with his watercolour drawings, no gastroporn photographs, and a beautiful book because of his work. Zaha Hadid said of him that he draws like the wind, and he does. He works faster than most photographers and has a slightly unsettling eidetic memory. Put a plate of food in front of him and next day he can draw it with total and detailed recall.

Brian is a fine cook and the toughest critic about food that I know. Some of his passion for food comes from his mother, Diana Ma, who gave me this recipe, which has been handed down in her family for generations. She chooses shoulder of pork for the dish, though you could also use best chump end or neck fillet, which also have the right proportion of fat needed to keep the meat succulent.

Pork was once the meat which supported a year of seasonal cooking. People killed a pig in the autumn – a few parts were eaten immediately, but most were salted or smoked, or both, to provide bacon and salt pork for the rest of the year, and lard with which to cook. Pork today bears little resemblance to that mature meat with its generous distribution of fat. Intensive rearing and a perceived concern about saturated fat has changed the pig for the worse.

You can track down decent pork with difficulty but, if forced to buy from supermarkets, choose the fattier and cheaper cuts on offer, such as belly and shoulder, the latter being the right cut here. If fat is a problem, better not eat this dish, because substituting a leaner cut will only give a disappointing result.

Note that Chinese soy sauce is specified. Mrs Ma deprecates the use of Japanese soy sauce in any Chinese dish as an abomination. If you use the best national product in a national dish, you are not introducing a dissonant note, and it cannot be blamed for any imperfections that may result. Diana also prefers to use Tientsin Rose Liquor, but accepts this is hard to come by in Britain, even in Chinese markets.

serves 4

1 kg (2¼ lb) shoulder of pork
salt and pepper
2 tbsp sunflower oil, plus more for the roasting pan
2 tbsp light Chinese soy sauce
2 tbsp Tientsin Rose Liquor or Shaoxing rice wine
12 red shallots
4 garlic cloves
150 ml (¼ pint) hoisin sauce
3 tbsp runny honey

Cut the pork into strips 5–6 cm (2–2½ inches) wide and put in a dish into which they will just fit in a single layer. Season lightly with salt and pepper, then dribble over the sunflower oil, 1 tablespoon of the soy sauce and the Rose Liquor or rice wine.

Finely chop the shallots and garlic and pound them to a paste. Coat the pork with this paste. Pour over the hoisin sauce, cling-wrap and refrigerate overnight.

Allow the pork to come to room temperature about 1 hour before you start cooking. Preheat the oven to

180°C (350°F, gas 4) – it is better not to use convection, because the sweet and sticky marinade tends to burn with the fan on.

Line a roasting tin with foil and brush it with sunflower oil. Lay the marinated strips on this, not touching. Dribble over 2 tablespoons of the honey and put to roast on a rack in the middle of the oven, turning the pork over after 20 minutes. The marinade will have exuded water but by the end of cooking this will have evaporated, leaving the meat bathed in a lovely sticky glaze.

Turn again after 10 more minutes and baste with the remaining honey, then cook for what should be a final 10 minutes. The exterior should now be slightly charred, the meat within moist but cooked all the way through. If the top does not have the right mahogany-red colour, turn over and give it a final 5 minutes, turning the oven setting up to 200°C (400°F, gas 6) but keeping an eye on it, for this is the point where it can easily burn.

There is no resting period. Remove the *char siu* to a board, chop into bite-sized pieces and serve at once.

PORK CHOPS WITH TANGERINE SICHUAN SAUCE

After brief marination, the chops are slow-fried, the sauce made separately and quickly in a wok. The two meet on the plate, accompanied by fragrant boiled noodles. The chops should be thick-cut and have a nice edging of fat. Very lean chops become dry and tough when cooked slowly. Chinese egg noodles can be bought in bags from Oriental markets, fresh or frozen, and are called *lo mein*.

serves 4
4 thick-cut pork chops
2 tbsp Pearl River soy sauce
1 tbsp sesame oil
juice of 1 lemon
1 tsp dried chilli flakes
½ tsp Sichuan pepper
½ tsp black peppercorns
2 tbsp groundnut oil
handful of coriander leaves, coarsely chopped, to garnish

FOR THE SAUCE:
2 pieces of dried tangerine peel
3-cm (1¼-inch) piece of root ginger, peeled
3 tbsp groundnut oil
3 spring onions
2 garlic cloves, thinly sliced
5 tbsp freshly squeezed orange juice
3 tbsp rice wine or dry sherry
2 tsp sugar
2 tsp cornflour

FOR THE NOODLES:
450 g (1 lb) fresh Chinese egg noodles
salt
4 star anise

Several hours ahead, put the pork chops in a dish into which they will just fit in a single layer. Whisk the soy sauce, sesame oil and lemon juice together and pour over the chops. Leave to marinate at room temperature for 2 hours.

While the chops are marinating, put a saucepan of lightly salted water to heat for the noodles and add the star anise. Bring to the boil, lower the heat and simmer for 30 minutes.

Prepare the aromatics for the sauce: soak the tangerine peel in warm water for about 15 minutes. Drain and shred the peel into a chiffonnade. Cut the ginger into similar thin strips. Reserve.

Toast the chilli flakes, Sichuan pepper and black

peppercorns in a small pan over the lowest heat for 2 minutes. Grind to a powder.

Strain the marinated chops, reserving the marinade, and pat the chops dry. Rub the spice mixture into the chops.

Put a large heavy-based frying pan over a moderate heat. When hot, swirl in the groundnut oil and lay in the chops, immediately turning down the heat to low. Fry gently for 8 minutes and turn, giving the other side about 7 minutes. Remove and keep warm.

Make the sauce: put the wok over high heat until smoking-hot. Add the oil, swirling quickly to coat the sides. Add the spring onions, tangerine strips, ginger and garlic. Cook, stirring, until fragrant, about 10 seconds. Add the reserved marinade, the orange juice and rice wine or sherry and the sugar. As the liquid boils, mix the cornflour with water to a pourable consistency and stir in. As it thickens, turn off the heat.

Bring the star anise water to a rapid boil and cook the noodles for 2–3 minutes, until just done. Drain, discarding the star anise.

Put a chop on each of 4 warmed plates and spoon the sauce over. Mound the noodles neatly beside them and scatter over some coarsely chopped coriander before serving.

CANTONESE RED-COOKED PORK SALAD

Gentle poaching makes even quite lean pork moist and tender, the aromatic spicing of the cooking liquid permeating the meat with a subtle fragrance. The soy stock can be used again, if kept in a covered container in the fridge and reboiled every 3 days, or it may be frozen.

serves 4

1-kg (2¼-lb) piece of boned and tied best end loin of pork (ask your butcher for the bones)
1 Lebanese-type cucumber
6 spring onions
2 tsp chilli oil
2 tsp dark sesame oil
2 lemons, halved, to serve

FOR THE SOY POACHING STOCK:
600 ml (1 pint) soy sauce
300 ml (½ pint) sake
300 ml (½ pint) mirin
5-cm (2-inch) piece of root ginger
300 ml (½ pint) chicken stock
3 garlic cloves
2 tsp chilli flakes
4 pieces of dried orange peel
3 pieces of star anise

The day before, poach the pork: put the soy poaching stock ingredients in a large saucepan and bring to the boil. Lower the heat and simmer gently for 45 minutes. Add the pork and bones to the stock and return to the boil. Skim thoroughly, turn down the heat and then simmer gently for 1¾ hours. Turn off the heat and leave the pork to cool in the stock.

Next day, prepare the salad: cut the cucumber in half lengthwise, scoop out the seeds and cut the flesh into matchstick strips. Slice the spring onions lengthwise into thin strips.

Remove the pork from the liquid and drain well. Carve into the thinnest slices you can manage, slicing downwards through the round, and arrange overlapping on a serving plate.

Scatter the cucumber and spring onions on top. Sieve a little of the soy poaching liquid around the edge of the fanned meat slices. (Pour the remaining stock through a muslin-lined sieve and refrigerate to use again.) Mix the chilli and sesame oils and sprinkle over about a ½ teaspoon of mixed oil per person. Put half a lemon on each plate.

Chapter 6
FRANCE

On ne vie pas à table

If I close my eyes I can smell Provence again, in the white glare of an airless September afternoon, feel the heat and smell the resin from the pines under which we have sought shade as the cicadas scritch-scratch then fall silent around our picnic on the dry brown grass. Never has baguette been crisper-crusted or tomatoes more tomatoey. We have a cold-box but, even so, the rosé rapidly sours as it warms in the glass.

Afterwards we stop at a little graveyard perched askew on the side of a hill and shaped by the bend in the road, baroque tombs crammed close together behind dry-stone walls. We stand silently in this private necropolis of a village. The smell of plastic flowers in the sun is overpowering, sweet and sickly, and the photographs of the dead imprinted on stone plates ask us what business we have there. A luminous green lizard skitters over a tilted mausoleum and vanishes through a crack. We stop at the first bar we see and drink pastis to clear the smell of hot plastic from our heads, a smell I have associated ever since with flimsy mortality.

...I can see the mist, platformed at knee-height over the Dordogne in November, with the great castle of Beynac elevated from the vertical rock-face high above it. After our walk, the mist lifts and we eat at an anonymous riverside restaurant, its flocked wallpaper the rival of any English provincial curry house. It is about to close for the winter and only two other tables are occupied, the atmosphere already frosty. The welcome is scarcely a welcome, more a demonstration of patient resignation. Nobody actually asks what on earth we are doing there so late in the year, but the implication hangs in the air like the fog.

The *boudin noir* baked *en papillote* with apples and a creamy onion tart are delicious and we drink two bottles of an excellent light local claret, the second prompted by the *folies de grandeur* of the enormous cheese chariot in the now empty dining room. As the gleaming dome slides open, the fetor of its contents exhales, corrupt and putrid. The underpinning sour whiff of the room that I had thought to be defective plumbing is now explained. The waiter takes up a position and watches our every move. My wife whispers that it is like eating in a recently vacated lavatory under the eyes of the secret police. I leave the riper examples on my plate and over-tip in the face of madame's disapproval when she presents the bill personally.

...The hotel room in Bordeaux is on a ludicrous scale. The bath is from Brobdingnag and the taps tinkle ineffectively in its Victorian depths. After a lunch of *omelette aux ceps* and buttered roast chicken, there is love in the afternoon. We lie post-coitally on the bed, laughing at the presumption of the ceiling decorations and the demented height of the windows. The perched village, Cordes, is living history in ancient stone spoiled by epicene shops. We drive on through the maize fields and reluctantly don't stop until we reach Toulouse, from where we must fly home in the morning. Cassoulet for dinner, *bien sûr*. We rinse the goose fat from our mouths with hefty Armagnacs, as brown as treacle.

...A late dinner in Belville, so *demi-monde* Paris. *Ici on mange couscous*. We are the only Europeans in the restaurant, strangers in a strange ethnicity, private celebrants at a Moroccan feast. Random postcards from the past.

Is there another harbour in the world as lovely as Honfleur? It is a subject too picturesque for painting, which is why so many have tried to capture it on canvas and failed. No need. Take a bottle of dry Normandy cider and a plate of tiny *crevettes grises*. A sip and a mouthful and it is all there again. It never really went away, only you did.

Love of France can lead to thoughts of living there. How difficult can it be to find a house where so many stand empty, fall in love with it and buy it with British home-owning equity? The Mercedes we collect at Toulouse airport mirrors my complacent hubris. Unfortunately the previous renter had a cheap cigar habit so extreme it has impregnated the car, penetrating every expensive pore in a malevolent fashion. By the time we realize open windows are not even going to put a dent in its awesome proportions we are 40 kilometres on course for Albi, the rolling fields of dwarf sunflowers drawing us inexorably onwards and making the thought of backtracking to get a fresher replacement intolerable. Over lunch of brick-thick *magrets* it ceases to dominate, and we agree that we have exaggerated the smell's offensive dimensions and we laugh with relief. Getting back into the sun-toasted car is like climbing into a cigar's putrid coffin, the stench as strong as skunk road-kill. When we stop to look at a house on the estate agent's list we carry its miasma with us and gradually it pollutes not only the air we breathe but our very mood. As we stand in the courtyard of an entrancing farmhouse with a dramatic view over a valley, the smell obscures its beauty. I look around me and notice for the first time how decrepit the building is and reality rushes in. 'Maybe next year,' says Pippa, only we both know it will never come.

We are always what we have lost. Before you can lose a lot you must first have a lot to lose and I have lost more than most. I have loved France and been in love in France. It is a heady mixture in which food weaves itself into your heart. France holds a special affection for food lovers the world over. They should stamp it in your passport on arrival: *on ne vie pas à table*, or at least, you don't have to in France, where the enjoyment of food and drink continues long past the point when other earthly pleasures have to be put aside. One only has to watch the gusto with which the older members of French families enjoy their food and wine to appreciate the sagacity of that thought. They also ask, what can you do three times a day every day of your life and never get bored? The answer, how very French *bourgeois*, is not to have sex but to eat.

And since we have to eat to live, let us make that necessity a joy. It does not mean eating daily in a Michelin-starred restaurant, for me a ghastly thought. As Elizabeth David titled one of her books, *An Omelette and a Glass of Wine*. Precisely. Or a piece of baguette and a pot of sweet Normandy butter. The best ingredients are not always the most expensive. If you know what you are doing, a bowl of lentils can be made memorable.

We carry with us the folk memories of others. When Mary Frances Fisher documented her French culinary voyage of discovery so beautifully in the 1930s, she gave us the privilege of seeing our contemporary experiences through her eyes, the opportunity to compare and contrast. Elizabeth David in the Fifties and Sixties, Jane Grigson in the Sixties and Seventies, Richard Olney and Anne Willan in the Eighties and Nineties, all have added to our knowledge and our expectations. And Robert Carrier, who first adored France as a young American soldier at the end of the war, has written evocatively about its charms ever since, and he loves it with the same passion today as I write this, fifty years after the start of his affair.

France is the benchmark, the touchstone, the validation and the ultimate expression of the positive role good food plays in a life. It is one of the places I have been happiest and my memories sustain me.

PAN-FRIED AND GRILLED LOBSTER

This produces the best lobster ever. The cooking is in two stages, but is not that difficult. I ate this in a small restaurant across the road from the Deauville fish market, where all the restaurants in the vicinity specialized, logically enough, in seafood. They have a similar situation in and around the fish market in Sydney. I don't think this was ever the case at Billingsgate.

serves 2
1 live lobster, 900 g–1 kg (2–2¼ lb)
2 garlic cloves, finely chopped
2 shallots, diced
60 g (2 oz) unsalted butter
2 tbsp olive oil
3 tbsp brandy
3 tbsp dry white wine
3 tbsp crème fraîche
pepper
bunch of chives, finely chopped

Dispatch and cut open the lobster, reserving the tomalley.

Put the garlic, shallots and butter in a small saucepan over the lowest heat and sweat for 5 minutes. Strain through a sieve into a bowl, reserving the softened garlic and shallots separately.

Preheat a hot grill and put a heavy-based 30-cm (12-inch) frying pan over a moderate heat.

When the pan is smoking-hot, add the oil and swirl to coat the bottom, then immediately lay the lobster in, shell side down, putting the claws on either side, cracked side upwards. Press the lobster halves down with tongs and fry for 3 minutes. Brush the top with the melted butter and transfer to under the grill about 12.5 cm (5 inches) from the heat for 4–5 minutes, brushing a second time with the garlic butter halfway through.

Remove the lobster to a warmed plate. Return the pan over a low-to-medium heat, add the brandy and flame carefully. As the flames die down, add the wine and, as it bubbles, trickle in the remaining melted butter. Whisk in the crème fraîche and the lobster tomalley and season with pepper. Add the finely chopped chives and cook for a minute. Spoon over the lobster and serve at once.

COQUILLES ST-JACQUES

It has become *de rigueur* to serve scallops without a significant sauce, simply brushed with olive oil, seasoned and seared briefly in a hot pan. While this is delicious, the classic French treatment which returns the scallop to the cleaned half shell, bathes it in a cheese béchamel, tops this with a few breadcrumbs and finishes it under the grill, remains one of its finest expressions. It is not a self-conscious exercise in retro cooking, but an excellent example of a French *bourgeois* tradition which has never gone away, only gently receded into the background. It is also a good way of making fewer scallops go further.

While your fishmonger will open and clean scallops for you, it is not difficult to do it yourself, which also means you can refrigerate the scallops for a couple of days without deterioration because, once opened, they should be cooked as soon as possible. Place a scallop on a board with the flat side of the shell upwards. From the side, slide a knife with a flexible blade between the two halves of the shell. They do not have the kind of vice-like grip of an oyster, so this is quite easy to do. You are looking for the muscle, which you sever by following the shape of the top of the shell. Detach the top half.

Cut the scallop away from the muscle which secures it to the base, the flexible blade allowing you to follow the contour of the shell and thereby avoid slicing wastefully into the meat. Remove the scallop, with its surrounding grey skirt. Delicately pull this away from the ivory-coloured meat and red coral then cut the blacker stomach away from the coral and discard. Wash the cylindrical scallop and the coral gently under running water. If there is any of the shell muscle still attached to the base, cut this off and throw it away. If using the shell, scrub it well first.

Scallops need very little cooking before their expensive flesh turns to rubber, the white flesh being more susceptible to toughening than the coral, which is why they are better detached and cooked separately.

To cook the white meat of a king scallop, heat an unoiled heavy frying pan until very hot. Brush the scallops with olive oil and season with salt and pepper. Lay in the pan for 45 seconds, turn and give the other side 30 seconds. You should have a perfect, just cooked scallop, the top and base golden, the flesh white and opaque.

serves 4

8 king scallops or 12 calico or 24 queens
1 tbsp olive oil
45 g (1½ oz) breadcrumbs
30 g (1 oz) unsalted butter

FOR THE MORNAY SAUCE:

45 g (1½ oz) unsalted butter
45 g (1½ oz) flour
150 ml (¼ pint) dry white wine
600 ml (1 pint) fish stock
1 bay leaf
salt and pepper
freshly grated nutmeg
85 g (3 oz) grated Cheddar cheese
5 tbsp double cream

Make the mornay sauce: make a roux by melting the butter in a heavy-based saucepan over a low heat and whisking in the flour. Cook gently for 2–3 minutes. Whisk in the wine followed by the fish stock. Add the bay leaf, bring to the boil, then turn down the heat and simmer, stirring frequently, for 20 minutes. Season with salt and pepper and grate in about ¼ of a nutmeg. Continue cooking, stirring frequently, for a further 10 minutes. Stir in the grated cheese. When incorporated, stir in the cream and keep warm.

Preheat a moderate grill and put a heavy-based frying pan over a medium heat.

Brush the scallops with olive oil and season with salt and pepper. Turn up the heat under the pan to full and, as the pan smokes, lay the scallops in it for 30 seconds, turn and give the other side 20 seconds. If using kings, you should have a slightly underdone scallop, the top and base golden, the flesh white and mostly opaque, but with a slight gelatinous quality in the centre. Remove and slice laterally in 3. If using calicos, slice in 2 and cook for 10 seconds less on each side. Leave queens whole.

Divide between 4 large cleaned scallop shells or put into individual gratin dishes. Spoon the sauce over, sprinkle breadcrumbs on top and dot with butter. Grill for 2–3 minutes, or until the top is nicely gratinéed and seething hot.

Serve with the shells or gratin dishes sitting in the middle of large plates.

COQUILLES ST-JACQUES À LA PROVENÇALE

This is the kind of easy dish to cook that you would eat with pleasure in any one of a hundred small fish restaurants in Nice or Cannes. It is just a quick sauté in butter, with shallots and garlic, and is finished with lots of parsley.

serves 4
12 king scallops
flour, for dusting
salt and pepper
8 red shallots, thinly sliced
2 tbsp olive oil
3 garlic cloves, finely chopped
115 g (4 oz) butter
3 tbsp brandy
large handful of flat-leaf parsley, finely chopped
sliced baguette, to serve

Cut off the corals from the scallops and slice the scallops horizontally into threes. The coral has a different texture from the white flesh and needs a little more cooking. Toss the scallop slices in seasoned flour which has plenty of black pepper in it.

Sweat the shallots in the olive oil over a low heat until soft, then stir in the corals and garlic. Continue cooking for 2 minutes and reserve.

Heat a large heavy-based frying pan until smoking-hot. Add 60 g (2 oz) of the butter and the scallops at the same time and sauté for 2 minutes, allowing the scallops to take a good colour. Add the brandy and carefully flame, shaking the pan until the flames go out.

Stir in the shallots, corals, garlic and parsley, lower the heat and continue cooking for 1 minute. Remove from the heat and swirl in the remaining butter.

Serve at once with a basket of sliced baguette to mop up the juices.

SALMON WITH FENNEL

Wrapping in foil makes baking pieces of fish an easy and effective technique while ensuring a moist result. An airtight seal means the fish cooks in the steam generated from its own juices and the liquid from the wine, fennel and lemon. The fennel lightly perfumes the fish without masking its taste. Baking is suitable for serving salmon either hot or cold.

serves 4
1 large fennel bulb, or 225 g (8 oz), plus its fronds
45 g (1½ oz) unsalted butter
4 salmon steaks, each about 200 g (7 oz)
2 tbsp olive oil
salt and pepper
4 tbsp dry white wine
juice of ½ lemon

Preheat the oven to 200°C (400°F, gas 6). Lay a sheet of foil on a Swiss roll tin.

Dice the fennel in uniform 5-mm (¼-inch) pieces. Melt the butter over a low heat and sweat the fennel, stirring frequently until soft. Reserve.

Brush the salmon all over with olive oil and season both sides generously with salt and pepper. Arrange them on one side of the sheet of foil. Put a sprig of fennel fronds on top of each steak. Put a spoonful of dry white wine and a squeeze of lemon juice on each. Lift over the other half of the foil and crimp the edges together tightly to make a large loose parcel.

Bake for 20 minutes, remove from the oven and leave to cool in the foil.

When cool, open the package and lift the skin away from the side of the steaks with a knife. They should be just cooked, moist and delicately perfumed with aniseed.

STEAMED SALMON WITH A BASTARD SAUCE

Why is *darne de saumon à la Danoise* anything remotely Danish and why is it served with a *sauce bâtarde*? There are some things best left as a mystery in the language and terminology of the French professional kitchen. It is a good combination, whatever you decide to call it.

serves 4
4 salmon steaks, each about 175 g (6 oz)
1 tbsp olive oil
finely chopped chives, to garnish

FOR THE BASTARD SAUCE:
300 ml (½ pint) dry white wine
1 bay leaf
150 g (5 oz) softened unsalted butter
30 g (1 oz) flour
salt and pepper
3 tbsp crème fraîche
2 tsp lemon juice
3 egg yolks
60-g (2-oz) can of anchovy fillets in oil, drained and puréed

Put a pan of water to boil for steaming the fish. If you don't have a steamer, cook the fish on a plate in a wok (page 232). Heat a second pan of water over which to place a bowl, making a double-boiler in which to finish the sauce.

Make the sauce: put the wine in a saucepan with 300 ml (½ pint) of water and the bay leaf, and bring to the boil. Boil hard for 5 minutes. Discard the bay leaf.

In another pan, melt 30 g (1 oz) of the butter and whisk in the flour to make a roux. Cook for a minute, then whisk in the wine and water mixture. Season with salt and pepper and transfer to the bowl over the simmering water.

Whisk in the crème fraîche, followed by the lemon juice, then the egg yolks, one at a time. Cook, stirring frequently, until the egg yolks thicken the sauce further. Whisk in the anchovy purée, followed by the remaining butter, a piece at a time. Keep warm.

Brush the salmon steaks with olive oil and season with salt and pepper. Put on a plate and steam for 5 minutes or until just cooked all the way through.

Put the salmon steaks on large warmed plates and spoon the sauce over. Scatter over the chives and serve with boiled new potatoes.

GRILLED COD WITH MORELS IN A CREAM SAUCE

Morels are the most expensive dried wild mushrooms you can buy. They have a distinctive shape, like a partly unfolded umbrella, and are dark grey in colour, the surface attractively honeycombed. Of all mushrooms they have the most distinctive flavour, retaining more of this individuality when dried than any other variety.

serves 4
45 g (1½ oz) dried morels
150 ml (¼ pint) dry white wine
8 shallots
60 g (2 oz) unsalted butter
1 tbsp olive oil, plus more for brushing
300 ml (½ pint) chicken stock
300 ml (½ pint) double cream
salt and pepper
4 cod steaks cut from a pin-boned fillet, each about 200 g (7 oz), skin on
chopped chives, for garnish

Rinse the morels under running water and put in a bowl. Bring the white wine to a simmer, pour over the morels and leave to soak for 20–30 minutes. Pass the wine through a fine sieve and reserve. Rinse the reconstituted morels briefly and reserve. Slice the shallots very thinly and put with the morels.

Put the butter and olive oil in a heavy-based

saucepan over a low heat and sweat the shallots and morels in this for about 5 minutes.

Turn up the heat and add the wine and the stock. Bubble until it is reduced by half, then stir in the cream. Season with salt and pepper and simmer until the sauce thickens. Turn the heat to its lowest setting and keep warm.

While the sauce is finishing, preheat an overhead grill and put a large heavy frying pan over a moderate heat until smoking-hot.

Brush the fish on both sides with olive oil and season generously with salt and pepper. Lay it skin side down in the smoking pan and sear for 1–1½ minutes.

Transfer the pan to under the grill. Grill for 2–3 minutes, or until the flesh is opaque and just cooked all the way through.

Serve immediately, spooning the morel sauce over and round the fish. Snip a few chives over. Either mashed potatoes or plain boiled long-grain rice go well with the cod and creamy sauce.

TTORO

This sounds more like a Japanese cartoon robot than a French dish, but then it is an old Basque word describing a garlicky fish stew that is red with tomato and spiked with chilli – a chowder of the Spanish border. A little further south, something very like it is called *zarzuela*. It can be very basic, cooked in water and with just one kind of fish. This version is more complex, the execution still simple, but the result just right as a main course for lunch on a summer's day. There are elements of deconstruction: the prawns and mussels being cooked separately and added only at the point of service. I like spicy-hot food, though the Basque use of chilli is never strident. How much heat you add is, as always, a matter of individual preference.

serves 6

400 g (14 oz) monkfish
400 g (14 oz) cod
500 g (1 lb 2 oz) mussels
12 large raw prawns (e.g. tigers), about 500 g (1 lb 2 oz) unpeeled weight
1 celery stalk, halved
16 black peppercorns
2 cloves
2 bay leaves
175 g (6 oz) onions, diced
about 100 ml (3½ fl oz) olive oil
6 garlic cloves, chopped
45 g (1½ oz) flour
325 ml (11 fl oz) dry white wine
300 g (10½ oz) canned chopped plum tomatoes
1 tsp chilli flakes
20 saffron threads
1 tsp oregano
1.5 litres (2½ pints) fish stock, or 650 ml (1¼ pints) light chicken stock and 650 ml (1¼ pints) water
salt and pepper
6 slices of white bread, crusts removed, to serve
bunch of flat-leaf parsley, finely chopped, for garnish

Strip off the skin from the monkfish – it pulls off like a glove. Cut the fillets from either side of the gelatinous central bone. Reserve the fillets and put the skin and bone in a saucepan with the stock. Skin the cod and remove any pin-bones, again reserving the flesh and putting the skin in the stock. Scrub and debeard the mussels, discarding any that fail to close when tapped, and reserve. Pull off the heads from the prawns and add them to the stock, together with the celery, peppercorns, cloves and bay leaves. Bring to the boil, lower the heat and simmer for 20 minutes.

Cut down through the backs of the prawns almost all the way through, leaving the shells on. Remove and discard the intestinal threads. Rinse the prawns in salted water and reserve.

Preheat the oven to 200°C (400°F, gas 6).

Sweat the onion in 2 tablespoons of the olive oil until soft and translucent. Add the garlic, turn up the heat and fry, stirring, for 1 minute. Shake over the flour and stir in like a roux. Stir in 300 ml (½ pint) of the wine, followed by the chopped tomatoes with their liquid, the chilli, saffron and oregano. Pour the stock in through a sieve, discarding the skins, bones and aromatics. Season with salt and pepper and bring to the boil. Lower the heat and simmer, stirring from time to time, for about 20 minutes.

After about 10 minutes, using an appropriate pastry cutter, cut the breads into 6 rounds just big enough to fit the bottoms of the serving bowls. Brush them on both sides generously with olive oil. Lay them on a tray and bake, turning after 5 minutes, until crisp and golden-brown, 8–10 minutes. Keep an eye on them as they are fine one moment, burned and ruined a few seconds later.

In a large shallow pan, put 2 tablespoons of the olive oil and the remaining wine over a high heat. As it bubbles, add the mussels, shaking and tossing for a minute. Put on the lid and cook until they are all opened and cooked, about 4 minutes. Turn off the heat, strain the liquid in the pan into the tomato broth and return the mussels to the still-hot pan to keep warm.

Cut the fish into bite-sized chunks and stir into the tomato broth. Simmer until just done, about 3 minutes.

While the fish is poaching, put 2 tablespoons of the oil in a frying pan over a high heat. When shimmering-hot, throw in the prawns and sauté until just done. They will butterfly open, the blue shells turning pink and red, and the flesh white and opaque. Remove from the pan to avoid overcooking.

Ladle the fish stew into large warmed bowls. Sit a bread croûte in the centre of each. Spoon the mussels on top, finishing with 2 prawns in the centre. Scatter with lots of finely chopped parsley and serve immediately.

GRILLED GREY MULLET WITH FLAMBÉED FENNEL AND HERBS

This may be cooked on a barbecue or under an overhead grill. Since the fish is grilled whole, it helps if you have one of those fish-shaped metal baskets to make turning it easier, though it is not essential. If turning it without the benefit of a basket, slide a fish slice from the tail end lengthwise. If you lift from under the middle you risk the fish breaking. The ideal cleaned weight for the fish is 675–700 g (1½–1 lb 9 oz), just the right size to feed two. A 900-g (2-lb) fish uncleaned should be about right.

If the fishmonger has not done it for you, scale the fish by holding it by the tail and scraping towards the head with a sharp knife (do this over the sink as the scales go everywhere). Snip off the fins and gills using kitchen scissors. Rub the body cavity with salt to get rid of any blood, rinse under the tap and dry with paper towels. Make 2 incisions on both sides of the fish, cutting down to the bone. This will help even cooking.

serves 2
900 g (2 lb) grey mullet, scaled, gutted and cleaned
3–4 tbsp olive oil
1 fennel bulb, plus fronds if possible, diced
4 tbsp flat-leaf parsley, coarsely chopped
4 tbsp Pastis or Pernod
salt and pepper

Preheat the grill. Brush the fish basket, if using, on the inside with olive oil. Season the fish generously inside and out with salt and pepper.

In a small saucepan, sweat the fennel in 2 tablespoons of the olive oil until soft. Stir in the parsley and keep warm.

Grill the fish 15 cm (6 inches) from the flame for 5–6 minutes. As it starts to change colour and the head and tail lift slightly, turn it over (see above). Cook the other side for 4 minutes, checking it is done by pushing a knife tip down to the ribs and gently lifting the flesh away from the bone.

Transfer the fish to a warmed serving dish and spoon the fennel mixture on top.

Heat the Pastis or Pernod in a small saucepan. Pour over the fish and carefully flame, serving as soon as the flames go out.

HERRING ROE POACHED IN OLIVE OIL

I like all kinds of fish eggs from caviar to salmon eggs, sacs of herring and cod roe and, when you can get them, sea bass and tuna roes. They can be brilliant smoked, for example, cod roe in taramasalata and salted and dried roes, like the *botarga* of tuna, are special. All roes are very rich and now that – with the exception of herring roe – all are expensive, it is fortunate that a little goes a long way.

Most herring roes in fish shops have been frozen and it is therefore better to buy them still frozen and defrost them yourself. As they defrost, they will release a lot of milky fluid. You should rinse them under cold running water, handling them carefully as their sacs tear easily, then pat them dry with kitchen paper before cooking.

Herring roes are usually pan-fried, often with a crumb coating. Here they are poached in olive oil and served with a fresh tomato and herb sauce. To work out how much olive oil you need, put the roes in a straight-sided pan into which they will just fit in a single layer. Barely cover them with cold water then drain them, capturing the water in a measuring jug. The volume of olive oil needed is the same. Most of the oil will be used in the accompanying sauce. Any left over should be strained and refrigerated and used for frying fish within a week.

serves 4
500 g (1 lb 2 oz) herring roes, rinsed and dried
salt and pepper
olive oil
2 bay leaves
2 garlic cloves
1 tsp dried chilli flakes
4 pieces of white bread, crusts removed, to serve
finely chopped parsley, to garnish

FOR THE TOMATO AND HERB SAUCE:
4 ripe plum tomatoes
1 hard-boiled egg
4 tbsp flat-leaf parsley leaves, coarsely chopped
1 tbsp chervil
1 tbsp chopped chives
2 tsp Dijon mustard
4 anchovy fillets, drained and chopped
2 tbsp red wine vinegar
1 tbsp capers

First prepare the tomatoes for the sauce: blanch the tomatoes and refresh in cold water. Peel, quarter and strip out and discard the pulp. Dice the tomato strips and reserve.

Dry the roes and season with salt and pepper. Dry the pan and pour in the required amount of olive oil (see above). Add the bay leaves, whole garlic cloves and chilli flakes. Heat at the lowest setting for 10 minutes. Turn up the heat to moderate and carefully lay in the roes. Cook for 2 minutes, then return the heat to its lowest setting and poach for a further 4–5 minutes. Remove the roes to drain on kitchen paper, keeping them warm.

Finish the sauce: remove the garlic from the oil to a food processor. Add the egg yolk, parsley, chervil, chives, mustard, anchovies, salt, pepper and vinegar and pulse-chop to combine.

With the machine running continuously, slowly pour in 150 ml (¼ pint) of the hot oil. Remove to a bowl and taste, adding salt and pepper as needed. Coarsely chop the capers and egg white and stir in with the diced tomato.

Toast the bread and put a piece in the middle of each of 4 large warmed plates.

Divide the drained roes between the toasts and spoon the sauce next to them. Scatter a little finely chopped parsley on the roes.

PAN-FRIED RED MULLET WITH CAPER BUTTER SAUCE

Red mullet, *rouget*, is a small fish with a delicate flavour and a fetching pink skin. The liver is prized by *rouget* know-it-alls, which is why it is never removed during cleaning. The sauce is made in seconds in the pan in which the fish are cooked, and the dish served with a potato cake made from waxy potatoes. The French have always known that waxy potatoes make great mash. If you can, get the oval pale yellow La Ratte, which are the waxiest of all.

The most frequent mistake people make when frying mashed potato cakes is to cook them over too high a heat and to try and move them too soon, both actions causing them to stick and burn.

serves 4

4 red mullet, 225–250 g (8–9 oz), cleaned
60 g (2 oz) seasoned flour
2 tbsp olive oil

FOR THE POTATO CAKES:
675 g (1½ lb) waxy potatoes
salt and pepper
1 tbsp double cream
60 g (2 oz) unsalted butter
freshly grated nutmeg
flour, for dusting
3 tbsp olive oil

FOR THE CAPER BUTTER SAUCE:
60 g (2 oz) unsalted butter
2 tbsp drained capers
4 tsp tarragon vinegar

Boil the potatoes in salted water until done. When cool enough to handle, peel and mash dry with a potato masher. Mash in the cream, then beat in the butter. Season to taste with grated nutmeg, salt and pepper.

Divide into 4 pieces, form into balls, then press down into neat cakes. Flour both sides lightly and shake off any excess.

Put half the olive oil in a heavy-based frying pan over a moderate heat. When hot, immediately turn down the heat to low and lay in the cakes. Fry, without touching, for 8–10 minutes, then turn carefully with a spatula. Add the remaining oil to the pan, dribbling it round the cakes. Give them about 8 minutes more.

While the potato cakes are cooking, coat the red mullet with seasoned flour, shaking off any excess. Put the olive oil in a heavy-based frying pan over a moderate heat and, when it shimmers, lay the fish in it. Fry for 3 minutes, turn and give the other side 3 minutes too, when they should be done with the skin nicely browned.

Put a potato cake and a red mullet on each of 4 large warmed plates.

Make the caper butter sauce: wipe out the pan in which the fish was cooked and add the butter. Swirl it and, as it foams and browns, stir in the capers and vinegar. Immediately remove from the heat and season to taste with salt and pepper. Spoon over the fish and serve at once.

BUTTER-FRIED SLIP SOLE AND CROQUETTE POTATOES

The whole point of croquette potatoes is finding the right thing to eat with them, so they shine. Slip soles or whiting, just coated in seasoned flour and pan-fried in clarified butter, are the sort of thing that fits the bill. This is a good example of comfort food, or food for the grown-up nursery.

serves 4
4 whole slip soles or whiting, skinned
60 g (2 oz) flour
4 tbsp olive oil

FOR THE CROQUETTE POTATOES:
1 kg (2¼ lb) potatoes
salt and pepper
freshly grated nutmeg
85 g (3 oz) unsalted butter
4 egg yolks, plus 2 whole eggs, beaten, for the egg wash
115 g (4 oz) fine breadcrumbs
oil for deep-frying

First prepare the potatoes: boil them in salted water until done, drain, return to the pan over a low heat and mash dry with a potato masher. Season with salt, pepper and grated nutmeg, then beat in the butter. Remove from the heat and beat in the egg yolks.

When the mash is cool enough to handle, form it into 60-g (2-oz) pieces and roll gently into ovals or cylinders on a lightly floured surface. With the egg wash in one bowl and the crumbs in another, coat them in egg, then roll them in the crumbs. Repeat to give a double coating.

Preheat oil for deep-frying to 190°C (375°F).

Dust the fish in seasoned flour. Put over a moderate heat a big heavy-based frying pan into which the fish will fit in a single layer and not touching, or use two pans. When hot, pour in the clarified butter, then lay in the fish. After 2 minutes, turn with a fish slice. Give them another minute or two, then transfer to warmed serving plates.

While the fish are cooking, deep-fry the croquettes until golden-brown. Drain on kitchen paper and serve immediately.

JOHN DORY FILLETS WITH RED WINE BUTTER SAUCE

Butter sauces were first served as delicate accompaniments to poached or grilled fish dishes, but now include stronger flavours and are often served with grilled steaks. Although the flavour base is red wine – *sauce beurre rouge* – this falls into the broader category described as a white butter sauce. It is dependent on the milk solids in the butter for its emulsification and has similarities to hollandaise and béarnaise in that it is essential to reduce the base liquid right down to a syrupy residue before starting to whisk in butter and that the butter you use is really cold. The addition of a spoonful of double cream before starting to add the butter will improve stability, and the inclusion of a little meat jelly at the end will give greater depth to the flavour.

serves 4
8 John Dory fillets (about 90 g/3 oz each)
flour for dusting
salt and pepper
3 tbsp olive oil

FOR THE RED WINE BUTTER SAUCE:
3 shallots, finely chopped
225 g (8 oz) chilled unsalted butter
150 ml (¼ pint) red wine
1 tbsp red wine vinegar
salt and pepper
1 tbsp double cream
2 tbsp jellied chicken or beef stock

Make the red wine butter sauce: sweat the shallots in 30 g (1 oz) of the butter until soft and translucent. Add the red wine and vinegar, then reduce at a rapid boil to about 2 tablespoons. Season lightly with salt and pepper. Lower the heat and whisk in the double cream. Dice the remaining butter and then whisk it in, a few pieces at a time, moving the pan on and off the heat as you do so as too high a heat will cause the sauce to split. Put the jellied stock in another pan. When all the butter is incorporated, pass the thickened sauce through a sieve on to the meat jelly, pressing the shallots with a wooden spoon to extract all their juices before whisking the jelly into the sauce. Taste, adjust the seasoning if necessary and keep warm.

Put a large heavy-based frying pan on a medium heat. Roll the fillets in seasoned flour. Put the oil in the pan and when it shimmers, lay the fillets in skin side down. Fry for 2–3 minutes then turn, using a spatula, and give them another minute. Lift out carefully to warmed plates and spoon the sauce over before serving.

PORK AND CHICKEN RILLETTES

Rillettes are a speciality of the Loire, a classic item of *charcuterie* that is eaten like a pâté with toast. Restaurants always serve *rillettes* with an earthenware pot or glass jar of gherkins and little wooden tongs to help yourself. Because of the slow cooking, a lot of fat is used. This meant in the days before refrigeration that, packed tightly in earthenware crocks and covered with fat to exclude air, *rillettes* would keep through the winter. Now, like *confit*, it is something we eat for its flavour and texture.

Rabbit is often included in *rillettes*, as is goose and sometimes ham. This combination of chicken, pork and bacon is excellent. Any good unsmoked streaky bacon will do, as long as it is in a piece so you can cut it into fat matchsticks.

serves 6
500 g (1 lb 2 oz) belly pork
115 g (4 oz) pancetta, cut into large lardons
85 g (3 oz) lard
freshly grated nutmeg
¼ tsp ground allspice
2 bay leaves
3 chicken breasts
salt and pepper

Cut the pork into 5-cm (2-inch) cubes and put in a plastic box or dish. Scatter over 2 teaspoons of salt and chill overnight.

Rinse the pork in cold running water. Put everything except the chicken in a heavy-based saucepan with ½ teaspoon each of salt and pepper. Add 250 ml (8 fl oz) of water and bring to the boil. Turn the heat to its lowest setting, cover with a lid and poach for 2 hours, stirring from time to time and adding a little boiling water from the kettle if it sticks.

It must not be allowed to boil, just ripple.

Skin the chicken and cut it into strips and stir these in. Cook for another hour, or until all the fat has melted and is clear.

Drain through a sieve, discarding the bay leaves and reserving the fat. Shred the meat. This is traditionally done using 2 forks. Put in a bowl and pour in about half the fat and mix before packing into a sterilized jar.

When cool, refrigerate for at least 24 hours before eating, or for up to a week. It is actually nicer after a week, when the flavours have had a chance to develop.

DUCK CONFIT

Confit, salted goose or duck poached slowly in fat, is best after a couple of weeks, when the flavour will have developed fully. It may be kept much longer and used to be stored in earthenware crocks through the winter in South West France, where the technique originated. The traditional accompaniment is thinly sliced potatoes fried in goose fat with garlic and parsley, which I find *de trop*. It is better with quite dry mashed potatoes, a potato pancake or, of course, as part of the bean dishes of the region, which include *cassoulet* and *garbure* (page 121). A sharp salad of peppery rocket or watercress makes a good contrasting side dish or to follow on. My minor change to the classic recipe is to grind the bay leaves and thyme to a powder. Their flavour is thereby better imparted to the duck and the fat.

makes 4 portions
2 bay leaves
2 tsp dried thyme
6 tbsp sea salt
4 duck legs
1 garlic clove, chopped
about 500 g (1 lb 2 oz) goose fat or lard

At least two days ahead: pull the bay leaves off their stalks. Put them in a coffee grinder with the thyme and blitz to a powder. Reserve.

Scatter half the salt in a dish, then lay the duck portions on top. Rub the garlic all over the duck and lay the duck, skin side down, on top of the salt. Scatter the herb mixture evenly over the duck, then sprinkle over the remaining salt.

Refrigerate for 24 hours, then turn the duck and return to the fridge for a further 12 hours. The salt will have liquefied.

Next day: preheat the oven to 130°C (275°F, gas 1).

Rinse the duck in cold water and pat dry. On the hob, gently melt the fat in a casserole or ovenproof dish into which the duck pieces will just fit in a single layer and, when hot, add the duck. It must be covered; if not, add goose fat or lard until it is.

When just trembling but not boiling, put the dish in the oven and cook for 1½ hours, when the meat will have shrunk a little, the fat starting to shrink away from the flesh while becoming translucent. Push a skewer into it at the thickest point – it should slide in easily; if not, check again after 10 minutes and remove only when satisfied.

Using tongs, transfer the *confit* to a plastic container, then ladle the fat through a fine sieve to cover (being careful not to ladle in any of the meat juices from the bottom of the cooking dishes – add these to your current stock). When cold, put a lid on the container and refrigerate until needed, preferably at least overnight.

To serve, remove the duck from the fat, scraping off as much as you can, then place on a baking tray for an hour to come to room temperature.

Preheat the oven to 200°C (400°F, gas 6). Pour off any melted fat from the tray and roast the *confit*, crisp skin-side down, for 20 minutes, turning it skin side up to serve.

Melt the stored fat from the container and bring to

the boil, then strain back through a sieve into a bowl to keep in the fridge to use again for another *confit*. It can be used three times before it becomes too salty and then is no good for anything.

WINE-BRAISED PHEASANT WITH GREEN LENTILS

My friend Gerry Mordaunt is an excellent shot, the keenness of his eye only slightly less sharp than his passion for the sport. I used to enjoy rough shooting when I lived in Suffolk, but did so in a very small way, doing a hedgerow with my labrador Ruth or taking a bird if she put one up on our walk, but never shooting more than a brace at a time. This was partly because the bitch was a useless retriever and my decision was based as much on my reluctance to play her role as any more admirable motive.

Gerry's shooting is on a grander scale and, as his London neighbour, I am often the recipient of frozen pheasant and partridge, hung, plucked and gutted and ready for the table. Preparing game is an unpleasant chore. Give me a bird frozen before it becomes too high every time, rather than a fresh stinker for which 'gamey' would be an inadequate description.

Both pheasant and partridge freeze well, and will roast perfectly when slowly defrosted, but this French treatment is more appropriate – braised with green lentils and ensuring a succulent finish, even in a rather tired old bird that has come to the end of its freezer life. Perhaps this is an appropriate moment to remind those who have game (or anything else in the meat and fish department) in their freezer that it is not a cold mausoleum. Things still deteriorate when frozen, not to the point of becoming inedible, but certainly in terms of taste and texture. So don your Marigolds and start excavating.

Another good way of cooking frozen game is a salmis. This involves brief, high-temperature roasting followed by slow simmering in a wine-based broth.

serves 4

225 g (8 oz) pancetta or good unsmoked green bacon
4 tbsp olive oil or goose fat
brace of pheasant
225 g (8 oz) onions, diced
175 g (6 oz) carrots, diced
2 garlic cloves, chopped
300 ml (½ pint) red wine
300 ml (½ pint) chicken stock
2 bay leaves
sprig of thyme
1 celery stalk
salt and pepper

FOR THE LENTILS:

350 g (12 oz) green lentils, washed
285 g (10 oz) canned chopped tomatoes
1 whole head of garlic
45 g (1½ oz) butter

FOR THE CARAMELIZED SHALLOTS:

20 red shallots, peeled
2 tbsp olive oil
30 g (1 oz) unsalted butter
1 tsp caster sugar

Preheat the oven to 200°C (400°F, gas 6).

Cut the pancetta or green bacon into fat matchsticks and fry with the olive oil or goose fat over a low heat in a large pan until they start to crisp. Remove with a slotted spoon to an ovenproof casserole just large enough to hold both birds.

Turn up the heat and brown the pheasants one at a time in the fat, transferring them to the casserole when

they have taken a good colour and placing them in breast side down.

Sweat the onion and carrots in the remaining fat until soft. Stir in the garlic, cook for a minute, then add the red wine and chicken stock. Bring to the boil, stirring and scraping the pan. Pour this over the pheasants. Make a bouquet garni by tying the bay leaves and sprig of thyme to the celery, add this and season with salt and pepper. Bring to the boil, cover with a lid and put in the oven, turning the setting down to 190°C (375°F, gas 5) as soon as you close the door. Braise for about 1 hour.

The lentils will take about 40 minutes to cook, so start them when the casserole goes into the oven. In a saucepan, put the green lentils, chopped tomatoes and whole head of garlic with the top cut off. Cover with cold water by 2.5 cm (1 inch) and bring to the boil. Skim, lower the heat, season with pepper and simmer until just done, about 30 minutes. Strain through a sieve and return the lentils to the pan with the butter. Remove the garlic and squeeze out the cooked cloves, which will now be soft and mild-tasting. Chop finely and stir back into the lentils, discarding the skins. Season with salt to taste and keep warm.

Halfway through the lentil cooking time, start to sweat the shallots in the olive oil, stirring from time to time.

Remove the pheasants from the casserole to a chopping board and leave to rest for 10 minutes. Put the casserole over a high heat and reduce the braising liquid by half, then discard the bouquet garni.

Cut off the legs from the birds and separate through the joint into drumsticks and thighs. Remove the breasts whole and cut each in half. Put the lentils on a warmed serving dish and place the pheasant pieces on top. Spoon the reduced braising liquid over.

Turn up the heat under the shallots to high, add the butter, sprinkle with the sugar and fry for 2 minutes, stirring constantly. Spoon over the pheasant and serve at once.

SLOW-FRIED DUCK BREAST WITH GRAPEFRUIT SALAD

Duck breasts, though expensive, are good value. A whole duck has a high bone-to-flesh ratio and, if you cook it so the breast meat is pink, the legs will be inedibly rare. The idea of cooking the breasts of corn-fattened duck – *magrets* in French – almost certainly originally came from the South West of France, where the logic of selling corn-fed duck and geese in their component parts of fresh breast meat and foie gras was self-evident, the salted legs and necks being poached and preserved in fat – *confit* (page 117) – and the carcass used for stock. Two *magrets* will serve 4 people.

Duck breasts are at their best when cooked in a dry frying pan or on a griddle at a relatively low temperature which, after resting, delivers a uniform pink finish and a moist texture. You start them skin side down, and when most of the fat has rendered, turn them to cook for a lesser time on the other side. They are then allowed to rest for 6–8 minutes, before being carved at an angle into slices. The result is a tender meat with a crisp well-flavoured crust. The crust benefits from heavy seasoning, much of which cooks out, leaving a memorable taste and texture, but a flavour which is moderate rather than strident.

Duck, as the Chinese figured out a few thousand years before the rest of us, is actually nicer after roasting or pan-frying if it is served at room temperature rather than hot. It is a rich meat, which benefits from a clean and sharp counterpoint. A salad of rocket or slightly bitter escarole or frisée goes well with duck, as does the tang of citrus. Though scarcely the sort of thing you would be offered with your duck in the Dordogne, this pink grapefruit and mint salad with a light walnut oil vinaigrette is a good partnership, the walnut oil of the dressing another speciality of the South West.

The grapefruit salad can be served as a light first course in its own right, and is also good to have after a rich and heavy main course. Don't use spearmint, a rule that applies to any savoury recipe that calls for fresh mint.

serves 4
2 large duck breasts
salt and pepper
4 large pink grapefruit
8 mint leaves

FOR THE SALAD DRESSING:
¼ tsp salt
1 tbsp red wine vinegar
2 tbsp walnut oil
2 tbsp extra-virgin olive oil
½ tsp pepper

Preheat a heavy dry frying pan or flat griddle over a moderate heat.

Rub lots of coarsely ground pepper and some salt into both the fat and lean sides of the duck breasts. Lay the duck breasts in the pan or on the griddle, fat side down, and immediately lower the heat to low. Fry for about 10 minutes, then turn and give the other side 4–5 minutes. Precise timing will depend on the thickness of the breasts.

Remove to a cutting board, skin side up, and allow to rest for 8 minutes before carving at an angle into thin slices. Arrange to one side of 4 large plates.

Make the salad dressing: whisk the salt into the vinegar until dissolved. Whisk in the walnut and olive oils, then add the pepper.

Cut the peel from the grapefruit with a razor-sharp knife and remove all exterior pith from the flesh. Cut the fruit into segments, removing any pips. Toss the segments in a bowl with the dressing, then spoon on the plates next to the duck. Tear the mint leaves over.

GARBURE

Garbure is a speciality of Bayonne and the surrounding Béarn region that sits on the edge of the Pyrénées. It is a filling bean dish, rich with *confit*, salt pork and goose fat, and has obvious similarities with *cassoulet*, the rib-sticking dish of the Languedoc.

Garbure is cooked in two stages and may be served as two separate dishes, a broth followed by a gratin. Traditionally the gratin is made with the vegetables after they have been cooked to the point of disintegration and has its crust stirred in several times as it bakes. I prefer to make the gratin at the point where the vegetables still have discernible and separate identities, and to serve it as a single dish with a more soupy presentation.

It has become quite a restaurant thing to garnish *garbure* with a slice of seared foie gras – but, really, unless you have somebody with a truly remarkable constitution, this is not a good idea.

serves 6–8
6–8 ribs, a 900 g (2 lb) piece of Petit Salé (page 125)
1 ham hock
275 g (10 oz) dried white beans
400 g (14 oz) small onions, peeled
2 celery stalks, sliced
3 tbsp olive oil
4 garlic cloves, cut into paper-thin slices
½ tsp dried chilli flakes
2 bay leaves
sprig of thyme
3 cloves
20 black peppercorns
400 g (14 oz) small potatoes, peeled
2 leeks, sliced
1 small Savoy cabbage, shredded
salt and pepper

115 g (4 oz) fresh sourdough breadcrumbs
115 g (4 oz) Gruyère cheese
60 g (2 oz) goose or duck fat
3–4 pieces of confit duck leg (page 117)
coarsely chopped parsley, to garnish

The day before: put the *petit salé* and ham hock in a large saucepan, cover with cold water and leave to soak overnight. Soak the beans in another pan.

Next day: bring both pans to the boil, throw away the water and put the *petit salé* and beans in a pot together. Cover with cold water and bring this to the boil. Lower the heat and simmer for 5 minutes. Taste: if it is still very salty, throw the water away and start again with fresh, returning to a simmer.

While this is proceeding, sweat the whole onions and the celery in the olive oil until soft. Stir in the garlic and chilli flakes. Fry gently for a minute, then add to the pork and beans. Tie the bay leaves, thyme, cloves and peppercorns in a piece of muslin to make a bouquet garni and add this. Simmer for 50 minutes, then add the potatoes and leeks. Cook for 15 minutes, then stir in the cabbage. Continue cooking for a final 10 minutes, when the meats should be at the point of coming off the bone. Turn off the heat. Discard the bouquet garni. Taste and season with plenty of pepper and a little salt if needed.

Preheat the oven to 200°C (400°F, gas 6).

Remove the ham from the bone and cut it in thick slices. Cut the *petit salé* into 6 cutlets. Put them and the ham slices in a large ovenproof dish. Use a slotted spoon to ladle the beans and vegetables on top, then ladle over broth to fill to within one bean of the surface. Scatter breadcrumbs on the surface and half the grated cheese. Dot with half the goose fat or, if liquid, zig-zag half of it over the top.

Bake for 15 minutes, then stir the surface crust in. Cover the top with the remaining breadcrumbs, cheese and goose fat, ladle over a few tablespoons of broth and return to the oven for a final 15–20 minutes, when the surface should be nicely gratinéed.

When you put the dish back in the oven for the final baking, cut the *confit* legs into drumstick and thigh portions, lay them skin side down in a frying pan over a low heat and cook until the skin is nicely crisp and golden brown, about 15 minutes.

Spoon the *garbure* into large warmed bowls, putting a piece of *petit salé* in each and dividing the ham equally. Sit a piece of *confit* on top and scatter over coarsely chopped parsley. Put a jug of broth on the table so people can add some more if they like.

CARBONNADE FLAMANDE

Beef stewed in dark beer is about as Belgian as a meat dish can get without speaking Walloon. A carbonnade is characterized as much by its inclusion of masses of caramelized onions as it is by the beer in which it is cooked. To be authentic, you should use a Belgian beer, some of which are now available internationally, like Abbey or Rodenbach, but Carlsberg Special Brew makes a particularly good substitute as it has a powerful sweet flavour that works well with the beef and, of course, the high alcohol content – which makes it, with Tennent's Super, the choice of discerning street debaters – evaporates during cooking.

A carbonnade does not contain garlic, while the inclusion of vinegar and sugar encourages a slightly sweet-and-sour emphasis in the sauce. Typically, both are usually added towards the end of cooking, but I find their impact to the finished dish too obvious, which is why they are included at the beginning here.

serves 4–6
900 g (2 lb) shin of beef
60 g (2 oz) flour

salt and pepper
60 g (2 oz) lard
30 g (1 oz) unsalted butter
675 g (1½ lb) onions, thinly sliced
15 g (½ oz) muscovado sugar
1 litre (1¾ pints) dark beer
600 ml (1 pint) beef or chicken stock
3 tbsp red wine vinegar
2 tsp dried thyme
2 bay leaves
2 celery stalks
finely chopped parsley, to garnish

Cut the beef into 5-cm (2-inch) chunks. Dredge with seasoned flour and reserve. Melt the lard in a heavy-based frying pan and brown the beef all over, doing this in batches and transferring them to a flameproof casserole when done. Shake the remaining flour over the meat and stir over a low heat to brown lightly.

Add the butter to the frying pan and fry the onions in it over a low-to-medium heat, stirring frequently, until they start to colour. At this point, turn up the heat and scatter over the muscovado sugar, stirring continuously until the onions are nicely caramelized, then transfer to the casserole, stirring in to mix evenly with the meat.

Deglaze the frying pan with half the beer, scraping to detach any bits stuck to it. Pour this over the meat and onions together with the remaining beer, the stock and the red wine vinegar. Add the thyme, bay leaves and celery stalks, and season with salt and pepper. Stir and bring to the boil, immediately turning down the heat to a bare simmer. Cook for 1½–2 hours, or until the beef is just tender. Don't over-cook it or the connective tissue which makes shin such a perfect stewing cut will dissolve, leaving the meat dry and flaky.

Taste and adjust the seasoning. Serve with boiled or mashed potatoes and scatter over a little finely chopped parsley.

NECK OF LAMB STEWED IN WHITE WINE WITH GRELOT ONIONS

Neck of lamb on the bone is one of the cheapest stewing cuts and one of the best, the high bone and fat content imparting a mellow flavour to the broth in the way oxtail does. This is one of those easy dishes that is immensely rewarding for the cook as well as those sharing it. The smell, as it slowly simmers on the hob, will make everybody hungry.

The onions of choice are grelots, the fatter, flatter and thicker-based spring onions. Well, technically they are not spring onions, though they look rather like them and have a similar – if stronger – flavour, but you can substitute the latter and get the same kind of effect.

serves 4
60 g (2 oz) flour
2 kg (4½ lb) scrag end neck of lamb
60 g (2 oz) goose fat or lard
800 g (1¾ lb) grelot or spring onions
750 ml (27 fl oz) dry white wine
4 garlic cloves, cut into paper-thin slices
1 bay leaf
salt and pepper
2 tbsp chopped fresh dill or fennel fronds

The day before: flour the lamb pieces, shaking off any excess. Heat the fat in a large frying pan over a moderate heat and, when it is shimmering-hot, brown the meat all over, transferring to a casserole as it is done. Lower the heat under the frying pan.

If using grelots, cut them in quarters; if spring onions, cut into 2.5-cm (1-inch) pieces. Sweat in the fat until soft and transfer to the casserole.

Add 150 ml (1/4 pint) of the wine to the frying pan, turn up the heat and deglaze the pan, scraping with a wooden spoon. Pour and scrape into the casserole.

Pour the remaining wine into the casserole, followed by the garlic and bay leaf, and season with salt and pepper. Add 600 ml (1 pint) of water and bring to the boil. Lower the heat and cover with a lid. Simmer for 1 1/2 hours, or until the meat comes away easily from the bone. Add more water if needed.

Using tongs, remove the lamb to a dish. As soon as it is cool enough to handle, pull the meat off the bones in the largest chunks you can. Discard the bones and bay leaf.

Pour the cooking liquid and vegetables into a large jug or bowl. When cool, refrigerate overnight. Cover the meat and refrigerate also.

Next day: lift off and discard the fat that will have set on top of the broth. Put the broth in a food processor and blitz to chop the vegetables. Pour into a saucepan, add the meat and bring to a simmer. Taste and adjust the seasoning. Stir in the dill or fennel fronds and continue to simmer for 5 minutes.

Serve in large warmed bowls with peeled boiled potatoes.

PEPPERED LAMB LEG STEAKS AND KOHLRABI GRATIN

The French have always appreciated kohlrabi's distinctive flavour, though people had a pretty low opinion of it in Britain, where until recently it was mostly grown as cattle feed. Kohlrabi is not what you would call beautiful – a strange-looking root reminiscent of a purple-and-green-tinted turnip with stalks growing out of it at random, like whiskers on an ancient chin. You want to buy them small because, like turnips, the larger they grow, the woodier and more tasteless they get.

Martin Webb introduced me to the trick of dipping the slices of whatever vegetable you are baking in a gratin into the cream before layering them in the dish. This ensures a more even distribution of the cream and it is less likely to curdle during cooking. Any left over you pour on top.

Lamb leg steaks are an excellent grilling cut, though few restaurants ever offer it. Here, marinated in lemon juice and given a good coating of coarsely ground pepper, they are briefly seared in a grill pan and served pink, just the thing to go with the rich gratin.

serves 6

6 lamb leg steaks, each about 200 g (7 oz)
juice of 1 lemon
2 tbsp olive oil

FOR THE KOHLRABI GRATIN:

30 g (1 oz) butter
400 ml (14 fl oz) single cream
2 garlic cloves, finely chopped
salt and pepper
60 g (2 oz) Pecorino Romano cheese, grated
1 kg (2 1/4 lb) kohlrabi

Put the lamb in a shallow bowl, sprinkle over the lemon juice and leave in a cool place (not the fridge) for about 2 hours.

Cook the gratin: preheat the oven to 200°C (400°F, gas 6). Melt the butter and brush it all over the insides of a 25.5 x 15 x 5-cm (10 x 6 x 2-inch) ovenproof dish. Put the cream in a bowl with the finely chopped garlic, season with 1/2 teaspoon of salt and 1/4 teaspoon of pepper and stir in half the grated Pecorino.

Peel the kohlrabi and cut it in half. With the flat surface downwards, cut it into 3-mm (1/8-inch) thick slices. Put half into the cream and turn to coat. Remove the slices one at a time, allowing excess cream to drip off, and arrange in the dish, overlapping in layers. Repeat with the second batch. Pour any cream left in the bowl over the top, then scatter over the remaining grated cheese.

Bake for about 1 hour, when the surface will have glazed to a golden colour, while the kohlrabi will have cooked all the way through to a creamy finish.

During the last 15 minutes of the cooking of the gratin, preheat a grill pan until smoking-hot. Wipe off the marinade from the lamb steaks, brush with olive oil and season generously with salt and coarsely ground pepper. Cook for 3 minutes on each side and remove to a warmed plate to stand for 5 minutes.

Serve on individual plates with spoonfuls of the gratin. The gratin looks so good, however, I think it is better to take it to the table in its dish, bubbling-hot and golden-brown.

PETIT SALÉ

Dry-salt-cured belly of pork, which includes the spare ribs, is something you hardly ever find outside of France, where it is a staple of every *charcutier*. It is very easy to salt, the only problem you are likely to encounter being the acquisition of saltpetre – potassium nitrate – which you used to be able to buy from any chemist. Its use in the manufacture of IEDs (Improvised Explosive Devices) by terrorists, combined with home-salting being relegated to another era in the domestic kitchen, mean that today's chemist is probably unwilling or unable to prescribe it for your cooking. However, if you talk to any proper butcher he will be able to get you sodium nitrite tablets, which are used by the trade for curing pork and beef, sodium nitrite having no explosive properties but being the active ingredient that colours the meat an attractive pink during pickling.

When you ask for it, however, still do so as saltpetre. Recent correspondence with readers keen to try home-salting suggests that being too accurate is a mistake, since most butchers still refer to potassium nitrite as saltpetre and will deny all knowledge of it by its proper name. Meat can anyway be salted perfectly well without it, but it then emerges from the brine a rather unpalatable grey colour. It tastes the same, but is certainly less appealing to the eye. The other role of nitrite is as an anti-bacterial agent and it is thought to be particularly effective against the deadly nerve toxin, botulism. A grim name for a grim reaper, but nothing to worry about if you follow the basic hygiene precautions outlined below.

Anybody interested in the skills of the *charcutier* should read Jane Grigson's *Charcuterie and French Pork Cookery*. The more cookbooks I read, and on a recent count-up I find I have more than 500, the more I appreciate her insights, her knowledge and the sheer clarity of her prose. I regard her as the best cookery writer that has ever lived, and her legacy of books will be enjoyed and valued as long as there are literate people on this earth who love to cook.

There is little point in pickling a smaller piece of meat than 2–2.25 kg (4½–5 lb). Belly is a cheap cut and, once salted, will keep for two weeks in the fridge. The instant it discolours, acquires a surface foam or smells other than sweet, throw it away.

makes about 2.25 kg (5 lb)
1 tsp dried oregano
5 dried bay leaves
15 g (½ oz) juniper berries
8 allspice berries or 1 tsp ground allspice
1 tsp black peppercorns
6 cloves
500 g (1 lb 2 oz) sea salt
15 g (½ oz) sodium nitrite (or 3 pills)
30 g (1 oz) caster sugar
2.25 kg (5 lb) piece of belly pork, including spare ribs

Put all the herbs and spices in an electric coffee grinder, and blitz to a powder. Mix into the salt with the sugar and sodium nitrite. A good way of doing this is to put the ground aromatics and salt in a food processor and blitz for a minute to combine.

Traditionally, meats were cured in stoneware crocks, but a plastic bucket with a lid is fine. Home-curing of meats must be conducted with scrupulous hygiene precautions if potentially dangerous bacterial contamination is to be avoided. Therefore wipe the washed container, work surface and your hands with a baby-bottle-sterilizing fluid before proceeding.

Put about half the aromatic salt in the bottom of the sterilized bucket. Rub as much of the rest into the meat as you can, working over a tray so you don't waste any of it. Put the meat, skin side up, on top of the salt in the bucket and pour the remaining mixture over it. Put on the lid and leave for 10–14 days in a cool place. A centrally heated room or the kitchen is too warm. Few of us have cool larders any more, but such an environment would be perfect. Otherwise, this is best done from the late autumn through to spring, when finding a cold spot is easier. If it is not actually below freezing, this could be out-of-doors.

Weight the meat with a sterilized weight. Anything will do as long as it is sterile. A plate with a 1-kg (2¼-lb) can of tomatoes, for example (its label removed and the tin and plate washed then wiped with sterilizing fluid), is fine.

Avoid possible contamination during pickling by not taking the lid off the bucket until you reckon it is finished.

Pickling involves an exchange in which the salt is drawn into the meat and the meat juices exude. The resulting solution can be used for another piece of pork if it is first boiled and 225 g (8 oz) salt is added to the brine. The bucket, plate and weight must again be washed and sterilized. If you are not cooking the whole piece immediately, wipe the remainder dry with paper towels and refrigerate.

PETIT SALÉ WITH LENTILS AND BUTTERED CABBAGE

Cut the 2.25-kg (5-lb) piece of salt pork in half, refrigerating half for another meal, or cook the whole piece. Because of the joint's shape, it will take the same time to cook, whatever the weight.

Petit salé is good with lentils, soft polenta (page 146) or mashed potatoes and is an important ingredient in some soups (pages 24 and 29). It is also delicious cold with a chickpea salad or in sandwiches.

Savoy cabbage is a lovely thing. I am sure it was what Michel Eyquem de Montaigne was thinking of when he wrote, 'I want death to find me planting my cabbages, but caring little for it, and even less about the imperfection of my garden.'

serves 4

Petit Salé (page 125)
½ Savoy cabbage, destalked and cut into 4
60 g (2 oz) unsalted butter

FOR THE LENTILS:

150 g (5 oz) onions, diced
2 tbsp olive oil
2 garlic cloves, chopped
350 g (12 oz) green lentils, washed
225 g (8 oz) chopped tinned plum tomatoes
600 ml (1 pint) chicken stock
1 bay leaf
salt and pepper
handful of flat-leaf parsley, finely chopped
extra-virgin olive oil, to dress

Rinse the *petit salé* under cold running water, put it in a large pan and cover by 5 cm (2 inches) with cold water. Bring to the boil, reduce the heat and simmer.

Taste the water after 8–10 minutes and, if it is too salty, throw it away, rinse the pan and repeat with fresh water. Return to the boil, lower the heat and simmer for 35 minutes or a total cooking time of 45 minutes.

The lentils will take about 30 minutes to cook, but may be kept warm for as long as needed or cooked earlier and reheated. Sweat the onions in the oil over a low heat until soft. Stir in the garlic, turn up the heat and cook for 1 minute, then add the lentils, tomatoes, chicken stock and bay leaf. Add just enough water to cover and cook, uncovered, for 20 minutes before seasoning with salt and pepper. Continue cooking until done, then stir in the parsley. Keep warm.

When you remove the pork from the pan, turn up the heat under the pan. When it is boiling rapidly, add the cabbage and cook for 4–5 minutes, using a blanching basket if you have one. Drain, return to a clean pan and add the butter. Season generously with pepper and toss to coat.

Put a mound of lentils and their cooking juices in the middle of 4 soup plates. Dress with a little extra-virgin olive oil. Carve the pork into thin slices and arrange on top. Put the cabbage in a warmed bowl for people to help themselves.

HAM STEAKS WITH PETITS POIS À LA CRÈME

Salty ham and sweet buttery *petits pois à la crème* is a perfect culinary partnership. Also called *petits pois à la Française*, this dish of peas and lettuce stewed in cream is one of the best ways of cooking peas from the pod later in the season. Little Gem lettuces, which are quite bitter as a salad leaf, are shown in a different light when simmered this way in buttery, sugary juices. You can include strips of ham or lardons of bacon, but I would only do so if serving this as a dish in its own right. About 1.35 kg (3 lb) of peas in the pod will produce 450–500 g (1lb–1 lb 2 oz) of shelled peas. The peas need a little sugar because they are quite starchy towards the end of the season. The dish is finished with tangy crème fraîche, though you could substitute double cream.

serves 4

6 spring onions, thinly sliced
115 g (4 oz) unsalted butter
2 Little Gem lettuces
500 g (1 lb 2 oz) shelled peas
1 celery stalk, halved
1 sprig of tarragon (optional)
1½ tsp caster sugar
salt and pepper
2–3 tbsp boiling water
4 ham steaks
150 ml (¼ pint) crème fraîche

Sweat the spring onions in a saucepan with half the butter until soft. Cut the lettuces lengthwise into quarters and lay in the pan with a cut side down. Add the peas, celery and tarragon if you have it. Sprinkle on the sugar and season with salt and pepper. Add a splash of boiling water from the kettle, just 2–3 tablespoons. Turn up the heat and, as soon as the water boils, turn it down to its lowest setting. Cover with a tight-fitting lid (if it is not a good fit, put a piece of foil under it to make it as watertight as possible) and simmer for 15–20 minutes.

Fry the ham steaks in the remaining butter over a low heat, turning once. They take about 15 minutes.

Remove the lid from the peas, turn up the heat and boil away the liquid. Discard the celery and tarragon, and stir in the crème fraîche. Allow this to come to the boil and immediately remove from the heat. Taste and adjust the seasoning. Transfer to a warmed serving bowl for people to help themselves.

MAGIC MUSHROOMS

We all know what mushrooms taste like, but are hard-pressed to describe the flavour. A mushroom tastes like a mushroom, and articulating shades of difference is not easy, short of going into some deranged wine writer's free-associating and babbling about 'gym shoes on hot pavements' and 'creosote', and similar nonsense. Some mushrooms taste more mushroomy than others, an assertion I feel confident everybody accepts and understands. Of course, mushrooms both wild and cultivated have individual and distinctive flavour characteristics, but if one word springs to mind which describes them all, it must be meaty. There is nothing in nature so reminiscent of meat as the mushroom, some – like shiitake – being meatier than others, probably because they are incapable of photosynthesis and so take nutrients directly from organic matter.

The range of cultivated mushrooms available continues to expand, with most large supermarkets offering oyster and shiitake mushrooms as standard, as well as the most common *Agaricus bisporus* which are sold as buttons, the smallest, cups, which are medium size, and flats or open mushrooms, the largest and which have the most pronounced flavour. The best-known wild mushrooms are field or meadow mushrooms which have visual similarities to the cultivated form but a superior flavour.

The most widely available dried wild mushrooms are Italian porcini, the same wild mushroom called *cèpes* in French and ceps in English. If you can't find porcini in your supermarket, then you can buy them in any Italian delicatessen because they are central to so much of that country's cooking and are honoured there dried as much, or more, than in their fresh state. They have an intense flavour, and a little goes a long way, which is just as well, for being gathered by hand in the woods then slowly dried to a fraction of their living weight, they are inevitably expensive, the most expensive being the honeycombed morels of spring.

Dried wild mushrooms available all year round include yellow chanterelles, also known as girolles, blue-tinged wild oysters, grey grisettes and trompettes-des-morts, the inky black and baroque-shaped trumpets of death, known insipidly in English as horns of plenty. They look dramatic, but actually have little flavour. A mixture of assorted French wild mushrooms is often sold by weight as 'forestière mixture', and is good value.

The popularity of wild mushroom gathering has increased hugely in recent times and, given the limited amount of productive woodland in which most of the mushrooms grow, this has caused bad feeling on the part of those old hands who view the new gatherers as interlopers on a private domain. There have not yet been any reports of 'mushroom madness', the bosky equivalent of 'road rage', but presumably it is only a matter of time. It is essential to start picking mushrooms with somebody who can help you identify what is edible and what is toxic. There are some excellent books on the subject, but nothing can substitute for time spent with an expert. As a general rule, never eat any mushrooms you can't be sure of – they could be the last thing you ever eat.

A few dried wild mushrooms reconstituted in warm water may be chopped and added to any recipe using cultivated mushrooms to give a flavour boost. Only the cap is eaten, the stems being too tough, but these are never wasted, making a great addition to chicken or meat stocks and to give vegetable stocks a stronger flavour.

Fresh mushrooms have a high water content. As this is cooked out, the flavour intensifies. Many mushroom recipes call for extreme reductions, but they come down to us from the last century when stronger flavours were predominant. Some of the simplest treatments are the most delicious and one never grows bored of grilled mushrooms on toast, a creamy mushroom omelette or delicate mushroom soup. Fresh ceps need no more than brief frying in olive oil with shallots and parsley, to show at their best.

CHEESE SOUFFLÉ OMELETTE WITH MOREL SAUCE

Morels are the most expensive wild fungus after truffles, beautiful like small furled parasols, their surface marked with interconnected depressions like a honeycomb. As you would expect with such expensive seasonal delicacies, they have a flavour quite different from other wild mushrooms, and a few fresh or dried morels will work their magic in quite large dishes like this omelette.

serves 2
45 g (1½ oz) dried morels
150 ml (¼ pint) warm water
60 g (2 oz) butter
30 g (1 oz) flour
450 ml (¾ pint) milk
salt and pepper
freshly grated nutmeg
60 g (2 oz) Parmesan cheese
2 tbsp chopped flat-leaf parsley
6 eggs
2 tsp groundnut or corn oil
pea-sized knob of butter

Put the morels to soak in the warm water for 20 minutes. Drain and rinse gently. Reserve both the morels and the soaking liquid.

Make a roux by melting half the butter in a heavy-based pan over a gentle heat and stirring in the flour. Cook, stirring, for 1 or 2 minutes, then whisk in the milk, the morels and their soaking liquid. Season with salt, pepper and grated nutmeg. Simmer for 30 minutes over the lowest heat, stirring frequently. Stir in half the grated Parmesan and the parsley. Taste and adjust the seasoning, if necessary, and keep warm.

Preheat a grill and a 23-cm (9-inch) frying pan over a high heat. Don't use a non-stick pan as the fierce heat will damage the surface.

Separate the eggs. Whisk the whites to soft peaks with a pinch of salt. Whisk the yolks with salt and pepper in another bowl. Add a spoonful of the whites to the yolks and stir to lighten before gently folding in the rest.

Wipe the pan with a paper towel moistened with the oil and then add the remaining butter to the pan. Swirl and, as it starts to smoke, pour in the eggs. Turn down the heat to medium and cook for 2 minutes to set the bottom of the omelette, then place the pan under the grill until the omelette soufflés and the top mottles golden brown.

Slide the omelette out flat on a warmed serving dish. Spoon the morel sauce over the middle and scatter with the remaining Parmesan, then fold the omelette over. Gloss the top with the little piece of butter and cut in half to serve.

MUSHROOM TART

A mushroom and shallot tart can be made meaty with shiitake or delicate with cultivated mushrooms. Field mushrooms are perhaps best of all, first fried in butter then suspended in a light savoury custard. The contrast of rich, creamy filling and crisp short pastry is always good news. The pastry mixture is a classic *pâte à foncer*, which is ideal for savoury tarts.

You could serve this tart as a first course or as the main feature of a light lunch, followed perhaps by a rocket or watercress salad and a piece of cheese.

serves 6

350 g (12 oz) mushrooms, sliced
115 g (4 oz) shallots, thinly sliced
60 g (2 oz) unsalted butter
1 garlic clove, finely chopped
4 egg yolks, plus whites of 2 extra eggs
2 tbsp finely chopped flat-leaf parsley
½ tsp salt
½ tsp pepper
freshly grated nutmeg
400 ml (14 fl oz) whipping cream

FOR THE PASTRY:

125 g (4½ oz) butter, chilled
250 g (8½ oz) flour
1 egg
¼ tsp salt
¼ tsp sugar

First make the pastry: remove the butter from the fridge and dice it, then leave to soften for about 30 minutes. Sift the flour on to a work surface and make a well in the centre. Put the butter dice in the well, break in the egg and add the salt and sugar. Rub in gently with your fingertips, pulling in more flour from the outside as you work. When all has been combined, moisten with 2 tablespoons water and knead with the heel of your hand, making 3 turns, when you should have a silky smooth ball of dough. Wrap in cling-film and allow to rest in the fridge for at least 1 hour before using. (The pastry will keep in the fridge for up to a week and also freezes well.)

Preheat the oven to 200°C, (400°F, gas 6).

Roll out the pastry and use to line a 25-cm (10-inch) tart tin with a detachable base. Line with foil, weight and bake blind for 10 minutes. Remove the foil and give it another 5 minutes, when it will have started to brown. Take out as soon as it starts to colour.

While the tart shell is baking, fry the mushrooms and shallots in the butter over a moderate heat for about 10 minutes, stirring and tossing. Add the garlic and cook, stirring, for a further minute or two. Strain through a sieve over a mixing bowl, then spread the mushroom mixture evenly over the pastry base.

Put the egg yolks and whites in the bowl with the pan juices, together with the parsley, salt, pepper and nutmeg, then whisk in the cream. Pour over the mushrooms.

Put into the oven and immediately turn the setting down to 180°C (350°F, gas 4). Bake for 30–35 minutes, when the filling will have risen nicely and be just set to the touch, the surface mottled a rich golden-brown.

Leave it to cool a little, when the surface will have fallen, before removing from the tin. Serve it warm rather than hot.

PAN-FRIED CHICKEN BREAST WITH MUSHROOM AND LEMON SAUCE

Mushroom sauces have been popular since the early eighteenth century, when they tended to be heavy with cream and butter. This rather lighter version is just right for a slow-cooked chicken breast, the mushroom and lemon flavour enhancing rather than masking the delicate meat. When pan-frying chicken breasts, it is better to do so slowly over a low heat, starting skin side down. The result will be more tender and the meat more moist than when cooked at a higher temperature.

serves 4
4 chicken breasts, skin on
4 tbsp olive oil
salt and pepper
1/4 tsp dried chilli flakes
4 ripe plum tomatoes
115 g (4 oz) onions, diced
250 g (8 1/2 oz) mushrooms, diced
juice of 1 lemon
chives, for garnish

Brush the chicken breasts with olive oil and season with salt, pepper and chilli flakes. Lay them, skin side down, in a heavy or non-stick frying pan and cook over a low-to-medium heat for about 8 minutes, when the fat will have rendered, leaving a crisp brown skin. Turn and give them 4 minutes on the other side. The precise cooking time will obviously depend on how hot the pan is and how thick the meat. Press with a finger: the meat should be firm to the touch and spring back when done. Remove to a cutting board and allow to rest for 5 minutes.

Plunge the tomatoes in boiling water for 15 seconds, refresh in cold water and skin. Cut the tomatoes into quarters, strip out and discard the seeds and pulp. Dice the flesh and reserve.

Sweat the diced onion in 2 tablespoons of the olive oil, until soft and translucent. Remove with a slotted spoon and reserve. Add the mushrooms and another tablespoon of olive oil. Turn up the heat and sauté for about 8–10 minutes. Transfer to a food processor with the onion and the lemon juice. Season lightly with salt and pepper and briefly pulse-chop to a purée. Put in a saucepan with the diced tomato and warm through.

Slice the chicken breasts across at an angle into 4 or 5 pieces and put on warmed serving plates. Spoon the sauce over and snip some chives on top with scissors. Serve with buttered new potatoes.

SAVOYARDE POTATOES

Savoyarde is a gratin baked with chicken or veal stock rather than cream. It is flavoured with garlic and enriched with butter and Gruyère cheese. This dish can be the main feature of a single-course lunch or supper, served with ham, bacon or fried eggs – or with cold Petit Salé (page 125), a lovely combination.

serves 4
60 g (2 oz) butter
900 g (2 lb) potatoes, peeled
salt and pepper
freshly grated nutmeg
3 garlic cloves, finely chopped
115 g (4 oz) Gruyère cheese
300–450 ml (1/2–3/4 pint) chicken stock

Preheat the oven to 190°C (375°F, gas 5) and generously butter a shallow gratin dish.

Peel the potatoes and cut them across into paper-thin slices. The easiest way to do this is with a mandolin grater; but if they are a bit thicker it does not matter. Put the slices in a bowl and season with salt, pepper and grated nutmeg. Stir the garlic into the potatoes, then grate the Gruyère into the mixture. Turn to coat as evenly as possible.

Layer the potatoes in the prepared gratin dish. Pour over the stock just to cover the surface. Dot the top generously with butter and bake for 45–60 minutes, when all the ingredients will have amalgamated into a glorious golden, bubbling gratin.

Chapter 7
India & Pakistan

A curry by any other name

Birmingham was where I first enjoyed good Indian food, in a city otherwise limited in its culinary opportunities. Birmingham in 1969 was filled with *folies-de-grandeur* hotels serving a foul Midlands version of steak Diane. Everything appeared to be cooked at the table, with much energetic flambé work by men in nylon dinner jackets with dark-stained armpits. One whiff of those and you could lose your appetite for weeks. The sprawling conurbation was saved by its substantial Indian population, and good curries were only a short stagger from any pub. Nobody then had thought of cooking with a *karahai* or mini-wok and calling it Balti – Bangladeshi for 'bucket' – but generally, while batch-cooking ruled, some of the ethnic food was very good.

I got seriously into cooking with Indian ingredients at home and made friends with a chef from Bombay who allowed me to spend time in his kitchen and taught me about the different masalas which make every dish individual. He took me shopping to spice markets and specialist vegetable suppliers and made me see for the first time how regional his home food really was. I think of those shopping expeditions today when I go to nearby Tooting in South West London, where there is a thriving area of Indian shops and restaurants, many of them Tamil and vegetarian.

We have an astonishing number of Indian restaurants in Britain, more than any other ethnic grouping. Just how authentic most of them are is open to debate but, for sure, the British love their curries. There is even a large and thriving Curry Club, for the anoraks of the food world, which produces a newsletter, organizes curry weekends and seminars, and sells spices and ingredients by mail order. Nico Ladenis, lugubrious Michelin star of French-style *haute cuisine* in one of London's most expensive restaurants, revealed on *Desert Island Discs* that his favourite food was curry and rice. He did not specify quite what he meant by this, but it sounded rather less demanding than his own complex gastronomy.

Curries are still the chosen food to end a lads' drunken night out nationwide, the hotter the better, and consumed with pints of lager, which of course do nothing to ameliorate chilli heat – you need yoghurt or sugar for that. In Sheffield they actually created the hottest curry in the world, called a *tindaloo* or *phal*, for thirsty steel-workers and miners in a part of the city called Tinsley. I imagine the straight faces of the waiters collapsed into laughter when they returned to the kitchen after delivering the dishes of liquid fire to the table.

The only advice I would presume to offer for those falling in love with Indian food is to start using and grinding whole spices and stop thinking about it as curry, a generic catch-all and pretty meaningless unless you use it in a pejorative way to describe a stew flavoured with a commercial mix called curry powder. This being said, in India and Pakistan there is no such thing as a *tindaloo* or a *vindaloo*, just curries with different amounts of chilli. It is everything else in the masalas that distinguishes one curry from another.

The other thing, if you live in a city, is to seek out an Asian market, easier perhaps in Bradford, Leicester or Birmingham – but ask in your favourite restaurant where they do their spice shopping. In such markets you can buy things like curry leaves and besan (powdery, light chickpea flour) that really make all the difference. You can ask advice and there will be restaurants nearby that are frequented by Asians, and where you can conduct an educational eating tour.

CHICKPEA AND LENTIL CURRY WITH IDLI

Idli, or steamed rice cakes, are a staple of southern Indian vegetarian cooking and are usually served with lentil curry, vegetables and fresh chutneys. They are made from soaked and naturally fermented rice and black split peas (*urad dal*), and preparation needs to be started at least 18 hours ahead of the actual cooking. The dal can be bought from Asian grocers. Special trays for steaming *idli* are to be found in Tamil shops, which in London are on Tooting High Road. Since, for most people reading this, however, I might as well have said, 'Pick one up next time you are in Sri Lanka,' cook them in metal egg poachers – unfortunately this will slow down their production, as you can probably only cook about 4 at a time. *Idli* can be made more tasty by including chopped fresh herbs, like coriander or finely diced hot chillies, into the finished batter just before steaming.

serves 6
350 g (12 oz) chickpeas
16 curry leaves or 2 bay leaves
8 ripe plum tomatoes, blanched and peeled
500 g (1 lb 2 oz) canned tomatoes
400 g (14 oz) onions, thinly sliced
4 tbsp sunflower or groundnut oil
3 garlic cloves, thinly sliced
175 g (6 oz) masoor dal (lentils)
30 g (1 oz) butter
225 g (8 oz) courgettes, cut into 1-cm (½-inch) dice
225 g (8 oz) aubergine, cut into 1-cm (½-inch) dice

FOR THE IDLI **(makes 10–12)**:
275 g (10 oz) long-grain rice
175 g (6 oz) black split peas
½ tsp salt
¼ tsp bicarbonate of soda
¼ tsp ground fenugreek
sunflower oil, for greasing the moulds

FOR THE MASALA:
2 tsp cumin seeds
2 tsp coriander seeds
1 tsp black peppercorns
1 tsp fennel seeds
1½ tsp dried chilli flakes
1 walnut-sized piece of asafoetida

FOR THE GARNISH:
5-cm (2-inch) piece of ginger, peeled
300 ml (½ pint) thick yoghurt
handful of coriander leaves, finely chopped

Ideally 2 days ahead: put the rice and black split peas for the *idli* in a large bowl, cover them by 5 cm (2 inches) of cold water and leave to soak overnight.

Next day, make the *idli* batter: drain the rice and split peas through a sieve, reserving the water. Put the rice and split peas into a food processor with the salt, bicarbonate of soda and fenugreek. Blitz to a smooth purée, adding some of the reserved soaking water through the feeder tube, 1 or 2 tablespoons at a time. Transfer to a large bowl, cover with cling-film and leave in a warm place for about 12 hours. Fermentation should occur, which will cause expansion, while the consistency becomes more liquid. Beat this batter smooth with a wooden spoon. You want a consistency like that of double cream; if it is too thick, thin with a little water.

Put the chickpeas to soak in a bowl of cold water overnight.

Next day, bring the chickpeas and their soaking water to the boil and drain, discarding the water. Cover with fresh water, add the curry or bay leaves and bring to the boil. Lower the heat and simmer for 1¼–1½ hours, or until just done. Drain, reserving the cooking liquid.

Make the *idli*: rub 4 moulds (see above) with oil and

pour about 2 tablespoons of batter into each, then steam with the lid on for 10–15 minutes, wrapping in a cloth when done and keeping warm in the lowest oven while you cook the next batch.

At the same time, toast the masala ingredients in a small dry pan over a low heat until aromatic. Grind to a powder and reserve.

Quarter the tomatoes and strip out the pulp, putting the pulp into a food processor. Add the canned tomatoes with their juices and purée. Reserve.

In a large flameproof casserole, sweat the onions in half the oil over a low heat until soft and translucent. Turn up the heat to moderate and fry, stirring, until they start to caramelize. Add the masala powder and garlic. Fry, stirring, for a minute, then pour in 1.75 litres (3 pints) of the reserved chickpea cooking liquid and the tomato purée. Stir in the lentils, add a teaspoon of salt and bring to the boil. Lower the heat and simmer, stirring from time to time, until the lentils collapse, about 30 minutes. Stir in the butter and the chickpeas, and keep warm over the lowest heat.

Prepare the garnish: over a bowl, grate the ginger into a piece of butter muslin, then ball the cloth around the pulp to extract as much juice as you can. Whisk the yoghurt into the ginger juice, then stir in the coriander. Reserve.

Put the remaining oil in a frying pan over a moderate heat. When the oil shimmers, stir-fry the diced courgettes and aubergine for 2–3 minutes. Transfer to the curry and stir in with the tomato pieces. Taste, adding more salt if necessary.

Serve in large soup plates or bowls, with the yoghurt mixture spooned on top and with a basket of *idli*.

YOGHURT AND GARAM MASALA PRAWNS

Yoghurt is a very effective marinade. It tenderizes – in the case of meat – while gentling the spices and permeating any flesh with a subtle flavour. The garam masala is best made in small quantities and used fresh. Stored in a jar, it soon loses its flavour. The prawns can also be cooked on a flat griddle or under an overhead grill.

serves 4

1 kg (2¼ lb) large raw prawns in their shells (16–20)
30 g (1 oz) unsalted butter
pepper
1 lemon, quartered, to serve

FOR THE GARAM MASALA:

¼ tsp cumin seeds
¼ tsp black peppercorns
¼ tsp cardamom seeds
2 cloves

FOR THE MARINADE:

juice of 1 lemon
3 garlic cloves
100 ml (3½ fl oz) plain runny yoghurt
1 tsp ground ginger
½ tsp salt

Several hours ahead, toast the garam masala spices in a dry pan over a low heat for 3–4 minutes, then grind to a powder.

Make the marinade: put 1 teaspoon of the garam masala, the lemon juice and all the other marinade ingredients in a food processor and blitz to a purée.

Peel the prawns (keeping the heads and shells for stock) and put into a bowl with the marinade. Toss to coat evenly, cling-wrap the bowl and refrigerate for at least 1 hour and up to 3.

Light the barbecue about 50 minutes before you plan to cook. Wipe excess marinade from the prawns and thread on 8 presoaked wooden skewers or metal skewers, first pulling the prawns into a straight line so that the skewers run through the whole body. Thread

2–3 prawns per skewer, depending on how many you have.

Melt the butter in a small saucepan. Check that the barbecue is medium-hot (see page 201).

Grill for 2 minutes on each side, brushing frequently with the melted butter.

Grind pepper over the prawns and serve with a quarter of lemon on each plate.

MARINATED SWORDFISH WITH INDIAN SPICES

A firm strong-flavoured fish is needed here, if it is not to be overpowered by the spicing. Swordfish is ideal. Besan is available from Asian markets.

serves 4

675 g (1½ lb) swordfish
6 garlic cloves, chopped
7.5-cm (3-inch) piece of ginger, peeled and chopped
juice of 5 limes
5 tbsp yoghurt
2.5-cm (1-inch) length of cinnamon stick
½ tsp cardamom seeds
2 tsp ground turmeric
¼ tsp ground cloves
1 tsp dried chilli flakes
salt and pepper
4 shallots, chopped
1–2 tbsp sunflower oil
7.5 g (¼ oz) besan (chickpea) flour
handful of chopped coriander leaves. to garnish
steamed jasmine rice, to serve

Light the barbecue. Skin the fish and cut it into 2.5-cm (1-inch) cubes. Pull out and discard any bones. Put the cubes in a bowl.

Put the garlic in a food processor. Add the ginger with the juice of 3 limes. Blitz to a purée, mix with the yoghurt and scrape over the fish, turning and rubbing with your fingers to coat evenly. Refrigerate for 20 minutes.

Scrape the marinade back into the bowl and reserve. Rinse the fish and pat dry. Leave at room temperature for a further 20 minutes.

Toast the cinnamon and cardamom seeds in a dry pan over a low heat for 3–4 minutes. Put into a grinder with the turmeric, cloves, chilli flakes and 1 teaspoon of salt, and grind to a powder.

Put in the food processor with the shallots and remaining lime juice and work to a paste. Mix with the fish and leave for another 20 minutes.

Brush off excess marinade into the bowl with the reserved first marinade and thread the fish on presoaked wooden skewers. Brush with sunflower oil and grind over plenty of coarse black pepper.

Put the mixed marinades in a small pan and bring to the boil, stirring. Mix the besan to a paste with a little water, add to the marinade and simmer for 10 minutes to produce a pourable sauce, thinning with water if too thick.

With the charcoal delivering a medium heat (see page 201), grill the fish for 6–8 minutes, turning frequently. Serve with steamed jasmine rice and the sauce, stirring in a handful of chopped coriander leaves before spooning over the fish.

YOGHURT AND SPICE MARINATED CHICKEN

Yoghurt actually changes the texture of meat, though I have never understood why – presumably something to do with natural enzymes. This mixture may also be used to flavour and tenderize lamb for barbecuing. I rarely shallow-fry in the amount of oil required here, but make an exception in this case because it is the only way to form the crisp spiced crust, something it has in common with American southern fried chicken.

serves 4
1 tsp allspice berries
1/4 teaspoon cardamom seeds
2 cloves
600 ml (1 pint) plain runny yoghurt
4 chicken breasts
1 tbsp cumin seeds
1 tbsp coriander seeds
1 tbsp black peppercorns
salt and pepper
115 g (4 oz) flour
corn or groundnut oil, for frying
2 lemons, halved lengthwise, to serve

The day before: grind the allspice, cardamom seeds and cloves. Mix into the yoghurt.

Cut the chicken breasts in half and put in a bowl. Cover with the yoghurt and refrigerate overnight.

Next day: toast the cumin, coriander and peppercorns in a small pan over a low heat for 2–3 minutes, then grind to a powder.

Put 1 teaspoon of salt in a mixing bowl and add the flour and ground spices, stirring to mix evenly.

Remove the chicken pieces from the yoghurt, wipe them with a cloth and reserve.

Pour oil into a large heavy-based frying pan to a depth of about 2 cm (3/4 inch) and put over a moderate heat. When it shimmers, roll the chicken pieces in the spiced flour mixture, shaking off any excess, and lay them in the pan, skin side down. Do not crowd the pan – the pieces should not touch; if necessary, use 2 pans or cook in batches.

Fry for about 8 minutes before turning, when the skin side should be a deep golden brown. Give it another 7 minutes. The juices should run clear when the chicken is pierced with a carving fork or skewer. If not, a few more minutes will do it.

Remove to kitchen paper and drain briefly. Serve with steamed long-grain rice and put half a lemon on each plate.

LAMB DO PIAZA

The distinctive aspect of *do piaza* is a lot of onions, which give the dish a sweet intensity. How spicy-hot you choose to make it is a matter of personal preference, though it is usually quite mild. The addition of lots of fresh herbs towards the end of cooking delivers a fresh-tasting finish. I doubt that they do this in South-East Pakistan, where *do piaza* – and most of what we think of as Indian food – comes from.

serves 4
1 tbsp cumin seeds
1 kg (2 1/4 lb) lamb neck fillet
1 kg (2 1/4 lb) onions
4 hot green chillies, shredded
5-cm (2-inch) piece of root ginger, peeled and grated
3 garlic cloves, chopped
salt and pepper
2 tsp ground turmeric
4 tbsp groundnut or sunflower oil
30 g (1 oz) coriander leaves and stalks
6 mint leaves
3 tbsp lemon juice
boiled basmati rice, to serve

Toast the cumin seeds gently in a dry pan until aromatic, then grind to a powder.

Trim any excess fat from the lamb and cut it into 5-cm (2-inch) cubes.

Cut the onions in half, then across into thin strips, reserving 225 g (1/2 lb) to fry separately.

Put the lamb and two-thirds of the shredded chillies in a wide, fairly shallow pan or casserole dish and stir together with the ginger, garlic, ground cumin, 1 teaspoon of salt, 1/2 teaspoon of black pepper and the turmeric. Pour over 600 ml (1 pint) of water, bring to the boil, turn down the heat and simmer, covered, for 1 hour.

After it has been cooking for 30 minutes, start frying the reserved onions in the oil over a low heat, stirring from time to time.

When the meat is done, remove the lid, turn up the heat and boil the liquid down to a thick sauce.

Put the coriander leaves and stalks and the mint leaves into a food processor with the remaining shredded chillies, the lemon juice and 2 tablespoons of water. Blitz to a purée, scraping down the sides a couple of times, and stir into the meat. Leave to simmer for 3–4 minutes.

Turn up the heat under the onions and fry, stirring continuously, until crisp and golden brown. Serve the meat with the boiled rice and with the crisp onions scattered over all.

SEEKH KEBABS

The meat should not be too lean or the end result will be dry and chewy. Shoulder is a good cut to have the butcher mince for you, giving something like a 20% fat content. You could also use beef for this essentially Kashmiri treatment.

serves 4

2 tsp coriander seeds
1 tsp cumin seeds
500 g (1 lb 2 oz) minced lamb
5-cm (2-inch) piece of root ginger, peeled and grated
115 g (4 oz) onions, finely diced
3 garlic cloves, finely chopped
handful of coriander leaves, finely chopped
2 tsp ground almonds
4 tsp chickpea flour (besan) or cornflour
juice of 1 lemon
½ tsp salt
2 tbsp yoghurt
2 tbsp sunflower oil, plus more for greasing

to serve:

tomato and onion salad
cucumber, mint and yoghurt chutney
Naan Bread (page 307)

In a small frying pan or heavy-based saucepan, toast the coriander and cumin seeds over a low heat until aromatic. Grind and reserve. Preheat a hot grill or barbecue.

Put the minced lamb into a large bowl with all the other ingredients except the yoghurt and oil. Squeeze and work with your fingers to distribute everything evenly. Do this quite gently; over-compacting will deliver a tougher result.

Oil 8 metal skewers. Divide the meat mixture into 8 and roll into sausages, then thread on to the skewers, moulding into neat cylinders. Whisk the yoghurt and sunflower oil together and brush on the kebabs.

Grill, turning frequently, for about 15 minutes, brushing from time to time. Serve with a tomato and onion salad, some cucumber, mint and yoghurt chutney, and naan bread.

Chapter 8
ITALY

Tennerlo simplice

'Could you pull the car over here, sir?' The customs officer was very polite and, it not being my BMW, I watched with mixed feelings as it was literally taken apart. My drive from Rome had been fast and fun up to this point, and I found that I rather liked the Puccini tapes that were the only music to be had from the glove compartment, my first opera at the speed of sound. The customs leaving Italy had not been a problem. Now, as I was about to enter France, no arias played. 'Not your car, sir?' He gave me a look that spelled many negative things. I watched nervously as a man in a boiler suit unbolted a door sill and stuck a mirror on the end of a wand into the hole, tilting it this way and that. I was by now getting the point of my unscheduled stopover.

This was an unhappy exit from my first time in Italy. I had been working in Cannes – an interview, nothing too arduous – and had been asked by a friend if I fancied picking up a car in Rome and driving it back to London for a friend of his – a banker, he said. 'They'll pay your expenses and you can take your time over it. Bit special,' he said, 'the car. It does 140.' I thought it over long and hard, and five seconds later said yes in a casual, 'well sod it' sort of way. Why not? Next week's not too busy. My pleasure. Next week I was actually unemployed, but no matter.

I flew down from Nice, a 40-minute hop. Fiumecino airport was an experience – more uniformed boys with sub-machine guns than a Bekaa Valley training camp. But Rome, that was something else. First off, it is the most beautiful city on earth. Second, I spent two days walking the seven hills and when I wasn't walking and gawping I was eating Roman food, and that was something else too. That fresh noodles with butter and Parmesan could be a revelation says much about how different then what we thought of as Italian food was from the real thing. I recall a thick veal chop on a big plate with nothing else except half a lemon, followed by a bowl of rocket. I watched what other people ate and imitated them. The atmosphere was urbane and everybody was so cool they made me feel like the country cousin.

Coda alla Romana, oxtail cooked in wine with tomatoes and garlic. Bliss.

Telling myself that I would be back, I picked up the car from an honest-to-God palace filled with paintings that I recognized, and reluctantly set off after a lunch of grilled pink lamb cutlets and potatoes fried with rosemary. Four hours later, I passed the palace going in the other direction, my knuckles white from gripping the wheel against the insanity of the Roman drivers who wanted to kill me. By the time I finally saw a signpost beckoning me north, darkness was falling. I put my foot down and discovered how challenging a two-lane autostrada can be at 120 mph in the dark. I stopped only once before the Swiss border, for petrol and a bowl of pasta at the Italian equivalent of a motorway service station. The petrol, so far as the car was concerned, was no different from the petrol from a British pump. The *spaghetti aglio olio peperoncino*, with which I refuelled, with a flask of Chianti, bore no resemblance that I could identify with food served at any Italian restaurant in London, never mind food served off the M1. And the wine was not wrapped in straw.

In Geneva, the customs men had pretty much reduced the car to its component parts but, so far, had not discovered any heroin. *Nil desperandum*. They started removing the tyres from the wheels. I tasted the garlic from my supper and went to sleep on a bench, wishing I was back in Rome, and slid into a dream of a wolf with tiny twin customs officers in boiler suits suckling on her teats.

SPAGHETTI WITH OLIVE OIL BAKED TOMATOES

The simplest pasta dishes are the best: *aglio olio*, spaghetti with olive oil, chillies and garlic, fresh buttered noodles with lots of grated Parmesan, and macaroni in a perfect cheese sauce, are enduring favourites. Pasta should never be smothered with sauce, and should not automatically be served with grated cheese. This is an absolute rule with fish and shellfish but, unusually, it is not wanted here either, the whole point being the intense tomato flavour. The tomato sauce can be made the day before and refrigerated until needed.

serves 4–6
500 g (1 lb 2 oz) canned plum tomatoes
1 tsp freeze-dried oregano
1 tsp caster sugar
1 tsp dried chilli flakes
5 tbsp olive oil
2 garlic cloves, chopped
2 tsp tomato purée
1 bay leaf
salt and pepper
32 pieces of Olive Oil Tomatoes (page 309)
500 g (1 lb 2 oz) long spaghetti
1 tbsp finely chopped flat-leaf parsley

Purée the canned tomatoes with their liquid, the oregano, sugar and chilli flakes.

Put the oil in a heavy-based saucepan over a low heat and sweat the garlic in it for 2–3 minutes. Turn up the heat and add the tomato purée and bay leaf. Lower the heat so it bubbles gently and reduce, stirring from time to time, until you have a moist paste. Taste and add salt and pepper to taste. Remove from the heat and discard the bay leaf. Stir in the tomato pieces and keep warm.

Bring a large pan of water to the boil. Add 1 tablespoon of salt, then feed in the spaghetti, pushing gently against the side so it coils in as quickly as possible. Bring back to a rapid boil and boil for 8 minutes. Taste a piece – it must be *al dente*, i.e. tender but still with a residual bite. Check every minute until it is, which usually takes 9–12 minutes.

Drain and return immediately to the saucepan. Add the tomato sauce and the parsley and toss to coat. Serve in large warmed bowls.

SPAGHETTI IN RED WINE

This is a pretty showy way of using a bottle of Chianti. It is almost certainly an Italian-American invention – I first ate it in Boston – but belongs here in its inspiration.

serves 4
salt and pepper
3 garlic cloves, cut into paper-thin slices
1 tsp dried chilli flakes
4 tbsp olive oil
1 bottle of Chianti
400 g (14 oz) spaghetti
30 g (1 oz) butter
30 g (1 oz) grated Pecorino Romano cheese

Bring a large pot of lightly salted water to the boil.

Sweat the garlic and chilli in the olive oil in a large shallow saucepan. Add two-thirds of the wine, season with salt and pepper and bring to a simmer.

As the water boils hard, slide in the spaghetti. As it coils and starts to soften, which takes about 3 minutes, drain and add to the wine. Turn up the heat and cook, stirring, adding splashes of wine to prevent the spaghetti drying out as it cooks.

Taste frequently. When it is *al dente*, turn off the heat and add the butter and cheese, tossing to gloss.

Serve at once on large warmed soup plates. It does not need any more cheese.

TAGLIATELLE VERDE WITH DOLCELATTE AND BASIL

The powerful blue cheese is not really cooked at all, but only melted slightly as the sauce is finished, the shredded fresh basil cutting the richness nicely. To accompany it, you want a really bone-dry white wine, almost sour on the finish. A not-too-classic Orvieto fits the bill perfectly.

serves 4
salt and pepper
4 shallots, diced
2 tbsp extra-virgin olive oil
150 ml (1/4 pint) dry white wine
5 tbsp light chicken stock
150 ml (1/4 pint) crème fraîche
about 1/4 of a nutmeg
125 g (4 1/2 oz) Dolcelatte cheese, cut into 1-cm (1/2-inch) dice
10 basil leaves
400 g (14 oz) fresh tagliatelle verde

Bring a large pot of salted water to the boil.

In another wide, shallow saucepan, sweat the shallots in the olive oil over a low heat, until softened. Add the wine and bring to the boil, then boil rapidly until reduced by half. Add the stock and continue to reduce to a syrupy residue.

Whisk in the crème fraîche, immediately turning the heat to low. Simmer, stirring, for 3 minutes. Season lightly with salt and pepper. Grate over the nutmeg and stir in. Turn off the heat and stir in the cheese. Shred 8 of the basil leaves and stir in. Put on a lid and keep warm.

Cook the tagliatelle in the rapidly boiling water for 3 minutes, or until *al dente*. Drain in a colander and add to the sauce, stirring and tossing to coat.

Serve in large warmed soup plates, shredding the remaining basil and scattering it on top.

GORGONZOLA AND CHILLI PASTA

The sauce is made with Italy's strongest flavoured blue cheese, usually too strong when cooked, but you need something with a pronounced flavour if it is not to be overwhelmed by the chilli and pancetta.

serves 4
500 g (1 lb 2 oz) fresh pasta, such as fettuccine
salt

2 medium-hot chillies
115 g (4 oz) pancetta
3 tbsp olive oil
115 g (4 oz) onions, diced
1 garlic clove, chopped
150 ml (¼ pint) chicken stock
115 g (4 oz) ripe Gorgonzola cheese, diced
150 ml (¼ pint) double cream
1 tsp chopped fresh oregano leaves

Put a large pan of salted water to heat for the pasta.

Skewer the chillies and grill them over an open flame, turning until blistered. Put in a heatproof plastic bag to steam for a few minutes, then peel, deseed and cut into 5-mm (¼-inch) dice. Reserve.

Cut the pancetta into 5-mm (¼-inch) dice and fry in the olive oil over a low heat for 10 minutes, stirring from time to time. Add the diced onion and roast chilli, then sweat for about 5 minutes, by which time the bacon should be completely cooked and the onion soft and translucent. Stir in the garlic and cook for 1 minute.

Meanwhile, cook the pasta in rapidly boiling water until just *al dente* (use the package instructions as a rough guide).

Pour the chicken stock into the pancetta pan, increase the heat to moderate and stir in the diced cheese followed by the cream. Cook, whisking until the sauce thickens.

Remove from the heat, stir in the oregano and season to taste with a little salt. Leave to stand for a minute, then toss with the drained pasta.

THREE-CHEESE PECORINO GNOCCHI WITH SPINACH

The inclusion of egg whites in the mixture makes the dumplings very light.

serves 6
1 kg (2¼ lb) floury potatoes, peeled
60 g (2 oz) Pecorino Romano cheese, grated
salt and pepper
grated nutmeg
200 g (7 oz) self-raising flour, plus more for dusting
whites of 2 eggs
1 kg (2¼ lb) spinach, washed and stalks removed if large
60 g (2 oz) Dolcelatte cheese
about 30 g (1 oz) breadcrumbs

FOR THE CHEESE SAUCE:
45 g (1½ oz) unsalted butter, plus more for the gratin dish
45 g (1½ oz) flour
850 ml (1½ pints) milk
150 ml (¼ pint) dry white wine
¼ nutmeg
2 bay leaves
60 g (2 oz) Parmesan cheese, preferably Parmigiano Reggiano, grated

Cut the potatoes into large chunks and boil in salted water until just done. Drain, return to the pan and shake over a low heat until all water has evaporated.

Mash them dry with a potato masher. Beat in the Pecorino with a spoon, then season with salt, pepper and grated nutmeg.

Add the self-raising flour and egg whites. Beat, using an electric whisk, until you have a workable dough. Turn out on a floured surface. Cut into 4 and roll each into cylinders about 2.5 cm (1 inch) in diameter. Cut these across in 2.5-cm (1-inch) wide pieces, then roll gently with the palm of your hand into balls. Cover with a cloth and reserve.

Preheat the oven to 200°C (400°F, gas 6) and butter a gratin dish. Heat a large pan of water to blanch the spinach and which you will then use to poach the dumplings.

Make the sauce: make a roux by melting the butter in a heavy-based pan over a low heat and stirring in the flour with a wooden spoon. Cook gently for 1–2 minutes, then whisk in the milk and wine. Add the grated nutmeg and bay leaves, season with salt and pepper, and bring to the boil. Lower the heat and simmer for 20–30 minutes, stirring at regular intervals. Remove and discard the bay leaves and stir in the grated Parmesan.

Salt the boiling water and blanch the spinach in it for 15–20 seconds only, removing to a bowl of cold water to stop further cooking. Drain and lay half the leaves in the buttered gratin dish.

Drop the gnocchi into the boiling water and cook for 3 minutes, removing with a spider or slotted spoon to sit on top of the spinach in the gratin dish. Spoon over half the sauce, then layer the remaining spinach. Pour over the rest of the sauce. Cut the dolcelatte into small dice and scatter over the top. Scatter on the breadcrumbs and put in the oven until bubbling hot, about 15 minutes.

Serve in large warmed soup bowls.

SOFT BUTTERED POLENTA WITH MUSHROOMS AND MASCARPONE

So-called instant polenta is fine when it has lots of good things beaten into it to enrich it and give it flavour, but it will never be as nice as the real thing and there is a strong argument for trying to make it in the traditional way at least once. Restaurants outside Italy have helped promote the idea that polenta is usually served grilled. In Northern Italy, the home of polenta, grilled polenta made using slices cut from cold set polenta is invariably a way of using up leftovers.

Polenta is made from cornmeal, mostly in the Veneto and Friuli, where it may be served with every meal – including breakfast, when it is not unusual for slices of leftover polenta to be grilled and eaten like toast. Polenta meal is ground from both white and yellow maize and is available in coarse, medium and fine meal. You can buy it in every Italian delicatessen, and some supermarkets offer traditional, slow-cooking polenta as well as the Valsugana instant type. At its most basic it is eaten like a porridge, made with water and lightly salted or with the addition of sugar, but can be very rich and grand.

In *polenta con mascarpone e tartuffi*, for example, smooth hot buttered polenta is poured over cold mascarpone and finished with shavings of white truffle on top. If considerations of finance or season rule the truffle out, a topping of wild mushrooms sautéed in butter is equally appropriate, and you can always add a splash of truffle-flavoured olive oil to finish the dish. And if there are no wild mushrooms either, sliced cultivated flat caps will be fine.

In Italy you can buy polenta pots that are fitted with an electric beater which continuously stirs the porridge for as long as you care to keep it switched on. Since it is essential to keep the stuff moving without a break for about 45 minutes, you immediately understand why instant polenta is so popular. There is no way out of non-stop stirring for, if you pause to relieve aching muscles, the polenta will form lumps or stick and burn round the edges.

serves 4

1.75 litres (3 pints) chicken stock
salt and pepper
225 g (8 oz) stone-ground yellow polenta meal
250 g (9 oz) fresh ceps or field mushrooms, wiped clean and stalks trimmed
85 g (3 oz) unsalted butter
2 garlic cloves, chopped
1 tbsp chopped flat-leaf parsley
4 tbsp mascarpone

Bring the stock to the boil in a large, wide pan. Add 1 teaspoon of salt, then pour in the cornmeal very slowly, while stirring continuously with a wooden spoon. It is essential not to hurry this initial stage or you will end up with lumpy polenta. Turn down the heat and stir continuously for 40–45 minutes. Taste, beating in freshly ground pepper and a little more salt if needed.

Turn off the heat under the polenta and cover with a lid while you quickly fry the sliced mushrooms in two-thirds of the butter. Better still, have somebody else stir while you sauté. When done, add the garlic and parsley to the mushrooms and sauté for a minute more.

Rub 4 large warmed plates with the butter, put a heaped tablespoon of mascarpone in the middle of each and ladle the polenta over. Scatter over the mushrooms and serve at once.

Given the effort involved you may choose to make double the amount of polenta and pour what is left over into a tray and leave it to set. This can then be sliced, brushed with olive oil and cooked on a ridged grill pan or fried, for another meal.

BAKED FENNEL WITH PARMESAN

Finocchio alla Parmigiana – so much more appealing a description than its prosaic translation, baked fennel with Parmesan – is a dish which shows the vegetable to perfection. The fennel bulbs are first blanched in boiling water, then baked in a hot oven with butter and grated Parmesan. The combination of the slightly astringent aniseed flesh of the fennel and the rich buttery cheese is delightful, and will seduce those who have been previously indifferent to fennel's charms.

serves 4
4 fennel bulbs
salt and pepper
60 g (2 oz) unsalted butter
60 g (2 oz) grated Parmesan cheese

Preheat the oven to 200°C (400°F, gas 6).

Trim the fennel bulbs of their tough stalks, bases and outer skins, then cut them in half from top to bottom and boil in lightly salted water for 8–10 minutes. Drain and lay them cut side down in a gratin dish dotted with half the butter. Dot the top with the remaining butter and scatter over the grated cheese.

Bake for 10–15 minutes, or until the dish is seething-hot, with the butter and cheese a bubbling golden brown.

BROAD BEANS WITH MINT AND PANCETTA

Baby broad beans need no cooking – so, if you are fortunate enough to find some, this becomes a superior salad to that made with older beans, which also have to be peeled.

serves 4
1 kg (2¼) broad beans in their shells to produce about 675 g (1¼ lb) shelled weight
4 sprigs of mint
salt and pepper
115 g (4 oz) pancetta in a piece
4 tbsp extra-virgin olive oil
1 tbsp balsamic vinegar
2 tsp Dijon mustard

If cooking older beans: blanch the beans in rapidly boiling water for 2 minutes. Refresh in cold water and peel. Return to the boiling water with 3 sprigs of mint and some salt, and cook for about 8 minutes, or until just done. Drain, discarding the mint.

Cut the pancetta into thin lardon strips. Put

1 tablespoon of the oil in a heavy-based frying pan and sweat the pancetta over a low heat, stirring from time to time, until the fat starts to run and the pancetta starts to darken.

Turn up the heat, add the vinegar and deglaze the pan quickly, then add the beans. If using baby beans, simply add them to the pan at this stage.

Stir and transfer to a serving bowl. Pour over the remaining oil, grind over some pepper and add the mustard. Turn to coat.

Shred 6 mint leaves, scatter over and serve while still warm.

RED SNAPPER IN SPICED POLENTA MEAL

The addition of the chilli flakes and pepper to the crunchy polenta coating delivers a pleasantly tongue-tingling finish.

serves 4

4 red snapper fillets, each about 150–175 g (5–6 oz)
115 g (4 oz) fine polenta meal
1 tsp dried chilli flakes
salt and pepper
2 eggs
3 tbsp clarified butter or olive oil
3 tbsp corn oil
2 leafy organic lemons, halved, to serve

Use tweezers or small pliers to pull out any remaining bones from the fish. Mix the polenta, chilli flakes and freshly ground pepper in a bowl. Beat the eggs with some salt and brush this on both sides of the fillets, then lay them in the polenta mix, pressing it in with your fingertips.

Heat the butter and oil or oil only in a large frying pan and fry the fillets over a moderate heat for 3 minutes on one side and 2 minutes on the other. Drain briefly on paper and serve with halved lemons on each warmed plate.

SPIEDINO OF SALMON AND TUNA WITH CAPONATA

Caponata, a sweet-and-sour cold sauce from Sicily, goes well with meaty tuna and salmon, which are best grilled over a charcoal fire – the slight smokiness this imparts is set off nicely by the complex flavours of the caponata. It can also be served as a relish with cold meats or to top crostini or bruschetta. The amounts given can be halved but, as preparation time is quite lengthy and it keeps well filmed with oil in jars in the fridge, it makes sense to make a larger amount.

serves 4

500 g (1 lb 2 oz) salmon fillet
500 g (1 lb 2 oz) tuna loin
juice of 2 lemons
5 tbsp olive oil
handful of fresh bay leaves
handful of flat-leaf parsley, to garnish

FOR THE CAPONATA (SERVES 8):

400 g (14 oz) ripe plum tomatoes
about 4 tbsp olive oil
400 g (14 oz) onions, diced
225 g (8 oz) stoned green olives, chopped
4 tbsp salt-packed capers, rinsed and drained
1 celery stalk, sliced
45 g (1½ oz) caster sugar
100 ml (3½ fl oz) white wine vinegar
1 kg (2¼ lb) small aubergines
pepper

If grilling the fish on a barbecue, light it and bring to medium-hot (see page 201).

Cut the fish into chunks and put in a bowl with the lemon juice and olive oil. Turn to coat and leave to marinate at room temperature while you make the caponata.

Blanch the tomatoes. Skin, quarter and strip out and discard the pulp. Dice the flesh.

Put half the olive oil in a large heavy-based saucepan over a low heat and sweat the diced onion until soft and translucent. Add the diced tomato and turn up the heat, stirring, for 2–3 minutes. Then add the olives, capers, celery, sugar and vinegar and turn down the heat to low. Simmer gently for 10–15 minutes, stirring at regular intervals, before transferring to a bowl to cool.

Peel the aubergines, cut into cubes and fry in the remaining olive oil over a moderate heat in a non-stick pan, until lightly browned. Stir into the caponata, season and leave to cool.

Skewer the fish on 4 metal skewers, alternating tuna with salmon and threading a fresh bay leaf between the pieces. Grill for 2–3 minutes on each side.

Serve the skewers on large plates with a mound of caponata on the side and whole parsley leaves scattered over.

CHICKEN UNDER BRICKS

In Northern Italy, a brick is the traditional thing used for keeping a spatchcocked spring chicken as flat as a road-kill during pan-frying, a dish called *galletto amburghese*. In Italy, you can buy vacuum-wrapped ready-spatchcocked spring chickens, called *amburghese*, which means 'in the Hamburg style', though why a flattened chicken should be considered Hamburger-ish is a mystery. Flat as a meat patty, I guess. It certainly does not describe the method, nor does it mean – as my friend from Illy Caffè, Marco Arrigo, suggested – an undercover policeman, which is actually *in borghese*, though it is admittedly a more entertaining title.

You will need two large frying pans and two heavy bricks wrapped in foil, unless you know your bricks are very clean.

serves 2
2 spring chickens
4 tbsp olive oil
salt and pepper
4 garlic cloves, finely chopped
1 lemon, halved, to serve

Spatchcock the chickens by cutting out the backbones and trimming out the ribs. Place them on a work surface, cut surface down, and thump the breasts hard with your fist or a cutlet bat to flatten them as much as possible.

Brush all over with olive oil and season generously with salt and pepper. Lay them, skin side down, in the dry pans (see above), place the bricks on top and put over a low heat until the fat starts to run. Increase the heat to moderate and, after 5 minutes, remove the bricks and turn the birds, then replace the weights. Turn again after 5 minutes, but this time scatter the garlic over each bird. Turn down the heat, weight and turn the chickens for the last time, a total cooking time from when the fat starts to run of about 20 minutes.

Serve with the crisp skin side up, accompanied by lemon halves and a rocket salad.

TURKEY SALTIMBOCCA

Saltimbocca is one of the great dishes of the world, a thin veal escalope flavoured with sage and wrapped in Parma ham before being briefly pan-fried. The treatment also works with turkey escalopes cut from the breast and battered out in the same way.

serves 4
8 slices of turkey, each about 45–60 g (1½–2 oz)
pepper
8 sage leaves
8 slices of Parma ham
4 tbsp olive oil
1 garlic clove, finely chopped
100 ml (3½ fl oz) red wine
30 g (1 oz) unsalted butter

to serve:
boiled new potatoes
2 lemons, halved lengthwise
Reggiano Parmigiano cheese
snipped chives

Beat the escalopes out gently between sheets of plastic film to a uniform thickness of 3 mm (⅛ inch), using a cutlet bat, rolling pin or child's wooden hammer. Season with pepper, put a sage leaf on top of each, then put a thin sheet of Parma ham on top and beat softly so it adheres to the veal.

Put the olive oil in a small pan with the garlic and stew over a low heat for 10 minutes. Pass half through a sieve into a frying pan, discarding the garlic.

Over a high heat, fry the 4 saltimbocca for 1 minute on each side in the remaining oil, transferring to a warmed plate. Add the reserved garlic-infused oil and fry the second batch in the same way.

Deglaze the pan with the red wine, swirl in the butter and bubble down to a syrupy residue.

Spoon this over the saltimbocca and serve with boiled new potatoes and lemon halves. To finish, use a potato peeler to shave a few curls of Parmesan and scatter these over the potatoes, together with a few snipped chives.

RISOTTO OF CHICKEN GIZZARDS AND PANCETTA

Hygiene regulations, which have made the sale of the giblets with chickens illegal, have also stimulated their separate supply. This has always been true of chicken livers, but it is now possible to buy cleaned and halved gizzards. After a preliminary long, slow simmering, these emerge plump, tender and delicious, while delivering the additional bonus of an intensely flavoured stock, always the key to a good risotto. The gizzards reduce in size during cooking.

serves 6
675 g (1½ lb) cleaned chicken or duck gizzards
450 g (1 lb) onions
2 celery stalks, chopped
1 bay leaf
300 ml (½ pint) dry white wine
1 litre (1¾ pints) chicken stock
salt and pepper
about 20 saffron threads
115 g (4 oz) pancetta
5 tbsp olive oil
500 g (1 lb 2 oz) Arborio or other risotto rice
2 garlic cloves, chopped
30 g (1 oz) unsalted butter
85 g (3 oz) freshly grated Parmesan, plus more to serve
small bunch of chives, snipped, for garnish

Put the gizzards in a pan with half the onions, topped and tailed and cut in half but with the brown skin left on, the celery, bay leaf and white wine. Cover with the chicken stock and 1 litre (1¾ pints) of cold water and bring to the boil. Skim, lower the heat to a gentle simmer and cook for 2 hours, topping up with more water as necessary.

Strain the stock through a sieve, discarding the

onion, celery and bay leaf. You will need about 1 litre (1¾ pints) of stock, so either reduce to this amount by rapid boiling or top up with water. It is always better to have more than you need, but if you ever find you have run out of stock with the rice still needing further cooking, then use boiling water from the kettle to finish. Taste and adjust the seasoning, keeping in mind that the pancetta and Parmesan are very salty and should provide all the salt that is needed in the finished dish. Keep the stock simmering. In a small bowl, soak the saffron in a few spoonfuls of it.

Cut the pancetta into matchstick strips and the remaining onion into small dice. Put the pancetta in a large heavy pan with the olive oil. Sauté over a medium heat until the fat starts to run. Lower the heat and continue to fry gently for 5 minutes. Add the diced onion and cook, stirring, until the onion is translucent. It must not brown.

Add the rice with the garlic and stir to coat. Start to add the stock, a ladleful at a time, stirring constantly with a wooden spoon and pushing particularly carefully into the edges of the pan where the rice otherwise sticks and burns. Add more stock as soon as the previous addition is absorbed. After 15 minutes, add the gizzards and the saffron with its liquid, continuing to add stock until it is all used up. This will take 20–25 minutes, by which time the rice will have taken on the classic consistency of a risotto, being creamy but with the rice grains still separate. Taste – the rice should give easily to the bite and not be starchy or dry in the middle.

When cooked to your satisfaction, beat in the butter and Parmesan. Taste again, adjusting the seasoning if you think it needs more salt or pepper. Turn off the heat, stir, cover with a lid and leave to stand for 5 minutes.

Serve in warmed soup plates, scattered with snipped chives, offering more grated Parmesan at the table.

QUAILS WITH ORZO

Two quails make a main course, one a starter. These benefit from the flavour of the pancetta, which you should buy from an Italian delicatessen, specifying that it be cut on the thinnest setting (number 1). When sage is unobtainable, put a sprig of rosemary or thyme inside the birds instead.

serves 4

8 quail
8 small dried red chillies
8 sage leaves
60 g (2 oz) butter
2 tbsp olive oil
black pepper
8 paper-thin slices of pancetta
150 ml (¼ pint) red wine

FOR THE ORZO:

500 g (1 lb 2 oz) orzo (pearl barley)
4 tbsp olive oil
450 g (1 lb) onions, thinly sliced
2 garlic cloves, finely chopped
about 150 ml (¼ pint) dry white wine
about 1.1 litres (2 pints) chicken stock
1 tsp freeze-dried oregano
1 bay leaf
salt and pepper
30 g (1 oz) unsalted butter
small bunch of chives, chopped
60 g (2 oz) grated Parmesan cheese

Inside each quail put a chilli, a sage leaf and ½ teaspoon of butter. Brush the birds with olive oil and season heavily with black pepper, then wrap each in a sheet of pancetta. The pancetta is very salty, so no additional salt is needed. Put them in a roasting tin large enough that they are not squeezed together and pour the wine over.

Make the orzo: put the barley in a sieve and rinse thoroughly under cold running water.

Put the olive oil in a heavy-based saucepan or flameproof casserole and sweat the onions over a low heat until soft and translucent. Stir in the garlic, turn up the heat to high and fry, stirring, for a minute. Add the barley, wine and stock. Bring to the boil, lower the heat and stir in the oregano and bay leaf. Season with salt and pepper. Simmer for 45–50 minutes, stirring at regular intervals and adding more wine or stock if it starts to dry out or stick at any point.

Preheat the oven to 230°C (450°F, gas 8). Roast the quail for 15 minutes. Remove and leave to stand for 5 minutes.

Stir the remaining butter into the orzo together with the finely chopped chives. Spoon this on warmed soup plates and scatter over the grated Parmesan. Sit 2 quail on top and spoon over the pan juices. Serve immediately.

STRACOTTO

This lovely slow-cooked braise of beef could be served with noodles, mashed potatoes or soft polenta as here. The addition of anchovies is not traditional and may be excluded. It does not, however, impart a fishy taste, but rather enriches the sauce, while giving the dish most of the salt it needs.

serves 4–6

115 g (4 oz) piece of pancetta
3 tbsp light olive oil
1.25 kg (2 lb 10 oz) piece of rolled, tied brisket
225 g (8 oz) onions, diced
115 g (4 oz) carrots, diced
2 celery stalks, thinly sliced
3 garlic cloves
1 bottle of dry white wine
1.1 litres (2 pints) chicken stock
100 ml (3½ fl oz) white wine vinegar
2 bay leaves
20 black peppercorns
10 juniper berries
60 g (2 oz) canned anchovies in oil
salt and pepper
1 packet (375 g/13 oz) of Valsugana-type (instant) polenta
85 g (3 oz) mascarpone cheese
30 g (1 oz) grated Parmesan cheese
10–12 chive stalks, chopped, for garnish

Cut the pancetta into fat matchsticks and fry over a low heat in the olive oil in a flameproof casserole until soft. Remove with a slotted spoon and reserve.

Turn up the heat and brown the brisket all over, remove and reserve.

Lower the heat. Add the onion, carrots, celery and garlic, and sweat until soft but not coloured. Return the beef and pancetta to the pan and pour over the wine, stock and vinegar. Bring to the boil and skim, then lower the heat to a simmer. Add the bay leaves, peppercorns and juniper berries and cook uncovered for 1½ hours. Test that it is done by piercing to the centre with a skewer, continuing to simmer for a while longer if there is any resistance. Remove the meat to a board and leave to stand for 10 minutes before carving.

While it is resting, finish the sauce by pushing the remaining cooking liquid and vegetables through a sieve with the back of a wooden spoon into a saucepan. Finely chop the anchovies and add with the oil from the tin. Bring to the boil, lower the heat and simmer for 5 minutes. Taste, adding more salt and pepper if needed.

At the same time, make the polenta following the packet instructions. When smooth, beat in the cheeses and season to taste.

Cut the brisket into thick slices. Pile the polenta in the middle of a warmed serving dish and arrange the slices around it, then spoon the sauce over the meat. Chop the chives and scatter over all.

RACK OF LAMB WITH ARTICHOKE POLENTA

The rack should be well trimmed. There is a trend of going too far and removing all the fat, which is a mistake. Ideally it goes into the oven with just enough fat to lubricate the meat as it cooks, but only sufficient for this purpose, so that it has rendered completely by the time it comes out of the oven. Trim the fat cover back to a depth of about 2 mm (1/12 inch) for 16 minutes' high-temperature cooking. Since, on this occasion, we are sealing the rack in a pan before it goes in the oven it may be trimmed even more.

The artichokes for this dish are the baby ones which are briefly available before the choke forms. You can also use the ones preserved in jars called *carciofi alla Romana*, or substitute peeled cooked Jerusalem artichokes for a different effect.

serves 4

2 racks of lamb, each with about 6 chops
4 tbsp olive oil
2 garlic cloves
7.5 g (1/4 oz) tarragon leaves
1 tsp balsamic vinegar
85 g (3 oz) flaked almonds
7.5 g (1/4 oz) flat-leaf parsley
8 chive stalks, for garnish

FOR THE GREEN CHILLI BUTTER:
2 medium-hot green chillies
115 g (4 oz) unsalted butter, softened
1 tsp salt
1/2 tsp black pepper

FOR THE ARTICHOKE POLENTA:
20 baby artichokes
1 packet (375g/13oz) of Valsugana-type (instant) polenta
60 g (2 oz) mascarpone
60 g (2 oz) Pecorino Romano cheese, grated
small bunch of chives, chopped

Make the chilli butter the day before or further in advance (it freezes for a month without deteriorating): cut the chillies in half and strip out the seeds and discard. Chop the chillies as finely as you can and put in a bowl with the softened butter and the salt and pepper. Beat with a fork to mix evenly. Spoon out on a rectangle of foil and roll up into a neat cylinder. Twist

at both ends to tighten like a Christmas cracker. Chill until needed.

Remove the lamb racks from the fridge an hour before you want to start cooking. Preheat the oven to 250°C (475°F, gas 9).

Prepare the artichokes for the polenta: if using fresh artichokes, blanch them in rapidly boiling salted water for 8–10 minutes. Refresh in cold water and reserve. If using bottled, drain and rinse under cold running water.

Heat a sauté pan until smoking hot, add half the olive oil, swirl and then seal the lamb on all sides, starting fat side down. Remove the lamb and allow to cool until you can handle it.

Finely chop the garlic and tarragon together and mix with the remaining olive oil, the vinegar, salt and pepper in a bowl. Put the nuts and parsley in a food processor and blitz to a crumb. Reserve.

Brush the lamb with the garlic mixture, then press to coat with the ground nuts. Roast on a rack for 10 minutes. Remove and allow to rest for 6–8 minutes.

As the lamb goes into the oven, make the polenta: bring 1.5 litres (3 pints) salted water to a rolling boil. Pour in the polenta and cook, stirring, until it forms a coherent mass and comes away from the sides of the pan. Beat in the cheeses and chopped chives and stir in the artichokes. Season with salt and pepper.

Spoon the artichoke polenta into the centres of 4 soup plates. Carve the racks into cutlets, arranging 3 on each pile of polenta. Put a disc of chilli butter in the middle of each and garnish with the whole chives.

BOLLITO MISTO

You don't get a more basic name for a dish than 'boiled meats', though the reality is grand and captivating rather than ordinary and dull. Amongst the most superior home food to share with friends, it features at least four kinds of meat and sausage and, because of their collective contributions to its flavour, the poaching broth becomes its heart and soul rather than a by-product.

In Lombardy and Piedmont – both areas which claim the dish as their own – there are restaurants which make a feature of *bollito misto* and always have it on the menu. This must be boring for whoever has to cook it every day, but it is the customers who benefit and that is what so many restaurants forget about. It is a bonus to be able to say, 'Let's meet at so-and-so for a *bollito misto* the Sunday after next' in the same way that I can go to Tae Ka Lok, my favourite roast meat place in Gerrard Street, for duck and rice any time because I know it will be on the menu 365 days a year.

Bollito misto is an ideal thing to cook for lots of people, since the scale makes no difference to the preparation time. Anyway, it actually benefits from using large pieces of meat which, after carving, are presented at the table for people to help themselves, along with boiled potatoes and carrots and a sharp-tasting *salsa verde* to cut the richness of the more fatty ingredients. Freshly grated horseradish also goes well with the meats, as do English and Dijon mustards and Mostarda di Cremona, sweet mustard candied fruits – the traditional regional accompaniment.

The cotechino sausages are very fatty and gelatinous. Most of the ones you buy in foil packs are pre-cooked and only need to be simmered in their packs for 20 minutes. In the event of you having an uncooked sausage, this needs to be pricked all over to stop it bursting and will need about 1 hour's poaching. Inclusion of wine in the dish is not obligatory, but after the lengthy cooking and given the amount of liquid involved, I find it benefits the broth. You need a very large pan. Dividing everything between two pans is one way out, but it is not as satisfactory.

serves 10
2 pig's trotters, split
4 large onions, quartered
1 whole head of celery, with its leaves
1 kg (2¼ lb) shin of beef, tied in a round joint
1 bottle of red wine
2.25 litres (4 pints) well-flavoured chicken stock
30 black peppercorns
5 cloves
10 allspice berries
4 bay leaves
salt and pepper
1 kg (2¼ lb) veal brisket
1.35 kg (3 lb) pickled ox tongue
2 free-range chickens, each about 1.35 kg (3 lb)
2 cotechino sausages, each about 300 g (10½ oz)

FOR THE VEGETABLES:
10 potatoes, peeled
10 carrots, peeled
10 onions
10 small leeks

to serve:
Salsa Verde (page 309)
Mostarda de Cremona
horseradish root
freshly made English mustard
Dijon mustard

Blanch the trotters by covering them in cold water and bringing it to the boil. Boil for 5 minutes, then dump in the sink. Run cold water over them and give them a scrub.

Transfer to your giant pot with the 4 large quartered onions and the outer stalks and base of the celery. Add the beef and pour over the wine and stock. If necessary, add more water to cover. Bring to the boil and skim.

Lower the heat and add the peppercorns, cloves, allspice berries and bay leaves tied together in a piece of butter muslin to make a bouquet garni. Salt lightly and simmer for 30 minutes, skimming from time to time.

Add the veal brisket and ox tongue, adding more water if necessary to cover, and continue to simmer for 1 hour.

Add the chickens, again adding more water if necessary to cover, and give it another 1¼ hours, when everything should be cooked – a total of 2 hours 45 minutes from when the liquid was returned to a simmer after the beef was put in.

Bring another pan of lightly salted water to the boil. In this you are going to cook both the sausages and the vegetables. Follow the pack instructions for the cotechino. This will enable you to calculate when to put in the pan the potatoes, celery heart, carrots, onions and leeks, which will take about 20 minutes. When making your calculations, factor in a 15-minute standing time for the meats before carving.

Turn the oven on low and put the largest serving dish you have in it to warm. Drain the tongue, leave to cool for 10 minutes, then cut off the rough outer skin. This is easy to do while it is still fairly hot, but more difficult if you allow it to cool down too much. Carve in thin slices.

Carve as much of the chickens and other meats in thicker slices as you think appropriate. Leftover meats are all delicious cold, so there will be no waste.

Lift out the cooked vegetables with a wire scoop, transferring them to a pan with a ladle of broth. Cut open the cotechino wrappers and lots of watery fat will gush out. Throw this away and carve the sausages in thick slices.

Using a blanching basket, dip each batch of meat into the stock to reheat it, layering the slices of different meats to make an attractive presentation on the warmed serving dish.

Drain the vegetables and mound them in the centre, scattering a little chopped parsley on the vegetables only. Taste the stock and adjust the seasoning if necessary. Ladle over a little of it and bring a jug of it to the table for people to add as they like.

Put the salsa verde, Mostarda de Cremona, grated horseradish and Dijon and English mustards on the table, putting each in several dishes or bowls so everybody can reach what they want. Large warmed soup plates are the best things from which to eat *bollito misto* and Barolo is the very thing to drink with it. *Buono gusto!*

FRIED RABBIT WITH POLENTA CHIPS

Rabbit is very lean, which is why so many recipes sauce it heavily. Because of the high bone-to-meat ratio it's a tricky thing to cook, as it must be done all the way to the bone.

Nobody wants to eat rare rabbit, but even a few minutes too long and it will go dry and chewy. I have eaten deep-fried rabbit in Mexico, but do not recommend this for people who do not have cavernous deep-fryers. Come to think of it, I do not recommend it, period. A sauté is a classic treatment and it is also possible to shallow-fry slowly if you do not have the heat too high under the pan. It is also possible to barbecue rabbit, again with the proviso that the grill is not too hot.

Ask the butcher to prepare the rabbit, which he will do by first cutting it into three joints – the front legs, the saddle and the rear legs. Have him cut the saddle through the spine into two, then separate the hind and front legs to give you six pieces. The front legs have so little on them, use them for stock, along with the head, if you can bear to look at it.

serves 2–4

1 tsp black peppercorns
1 tsp dried chilli flakes
1 tsp salt
1 tsp oregano
85 g (3 oz) polenta
1 rabbit, about 800–900 g (1¾–2 lb)
2 eggs, beaten
100 ml (3½ fl oz) corn or groundnut oil
2 lemons, halved, to serve

FOR THE POLENTA CHIPS:
1 packet (375g/13oz) of Valsugana-type (instant) polenta
60 g (2 oz) grated Parmesan cheese
salt and pepper
oil, for deep-frying

Make the polenta chips: make up the polenta according to package instructions, stir in the cheese and season with salt and pepper. Pour into a tray to set. When set, cut it into fat chips. This can be done a day ahead.

Preheat oil for deep-frying to 190°C (375°F).

Grind the peppercorns, chilli flakes, salt and oregano to a powder. Mix with the polenta meal and put in a large bowl. Brush the rabbit with the beaten eggs and toss in the seasoned polenta mix.

Put the oil in a very large frying pan, or 2 smaller frying pans, and place over a low-to-medium heat. When hot, lay the rabbit pieces in, flesh side down. Leave for 5 minutes before turning. After giving the other side 5 minutes, turn again, giving them about another 3–6 minutes, a total of 13–16 minutes. Remove to kitchen paper on a warmed plate to drain.

Fry the polenta chips until crisp and golden, about 4 minutes, putting them into the oil a few at a time as they otherwise have a tendency to stick together. Drain on kitchen paper.

Put a piece of rabbit and a mound of chips on each warmed plate with a half of lemon. Finger bowls of lemony hot water are a good idea.

SPICED SAUSAGE CAKES WITH GRAPES AND VERJUICE

In Umbria, coarse-cut sausages are sometimes served with fried grapes – *salsicce all'uva* – an odd-sounding combination, but actually delicious. If you have a good local Italian delicatessen that makes its own sausages, then use them; if not, these home-made sausage cakes make a good alternative. Have your butcher mince the pork and back fat for you.

More places are now stocking verjuice, which is made from crushed and strained unripe grapes and has been used for cooking since medieval times. These days it is produced with a particular market in mind, but used to be how wine-makers used up grapes in cold wet summers, when the fruit did not achieve a high enough sugar content to make good wine. Now it tends to be made from the sediment left over after the young wine is first racked.

The verjuice is not acidic, like vinegar, having a sherry-like quality with a relatively high alcohol content of 10.5%. If you can't get any, then substitute balsamic vinegar in this dish, though they are not generally interchangeable.

serves 4

675 g (1½ lb) white seedless grapes
2 tbsp verjuice or 1 tbsp balsamic vinegar

FOR THE SAUSAGE CAKES:

675 g (1½ lb) shoulder of pork
60 g (2 oz) pork back fat
1 tsp caster sugar
1 tsp dried chilli flakes
1 tsp freeze-dried oregano
2 tbsp red wine
salt and pepper
4 sheets of caul fat

A day or 2 ahead: mix all the sausage ingredients except the caul fat together in a bowl and season with about 1½ teaspoons of salt and ½ teaspoon of coarsely ground pepper, then mix thoroughly with a fork. Remove a spoonful of the mixture, shape it into a small patty and fry over a moderate heat. Eat this and then adjust the seasoning if it needs it.

Divide the mixture into 8 balls. Wrap these in caul, flattening them into neat cakes. Put on a tray and chill for 24–48 hours, to allow the flavours to develop.

When you want to cook, remove the sausage cakes from the fridge to come to room temperature. Put them in a dry cold heavy-based or non-stick frying pan and turn on the heat to moderate. Cook for about 8 minutes, turn and give them 6–7 minutes on the other side. Remove and keep warm.

Turn up the heat to high and add the grapes. Stir-fry until they start to collapse, then add the verjuice or vinegar and shake.

Serve the grapes in warm soup plates, with 2 sausage cakes on top.

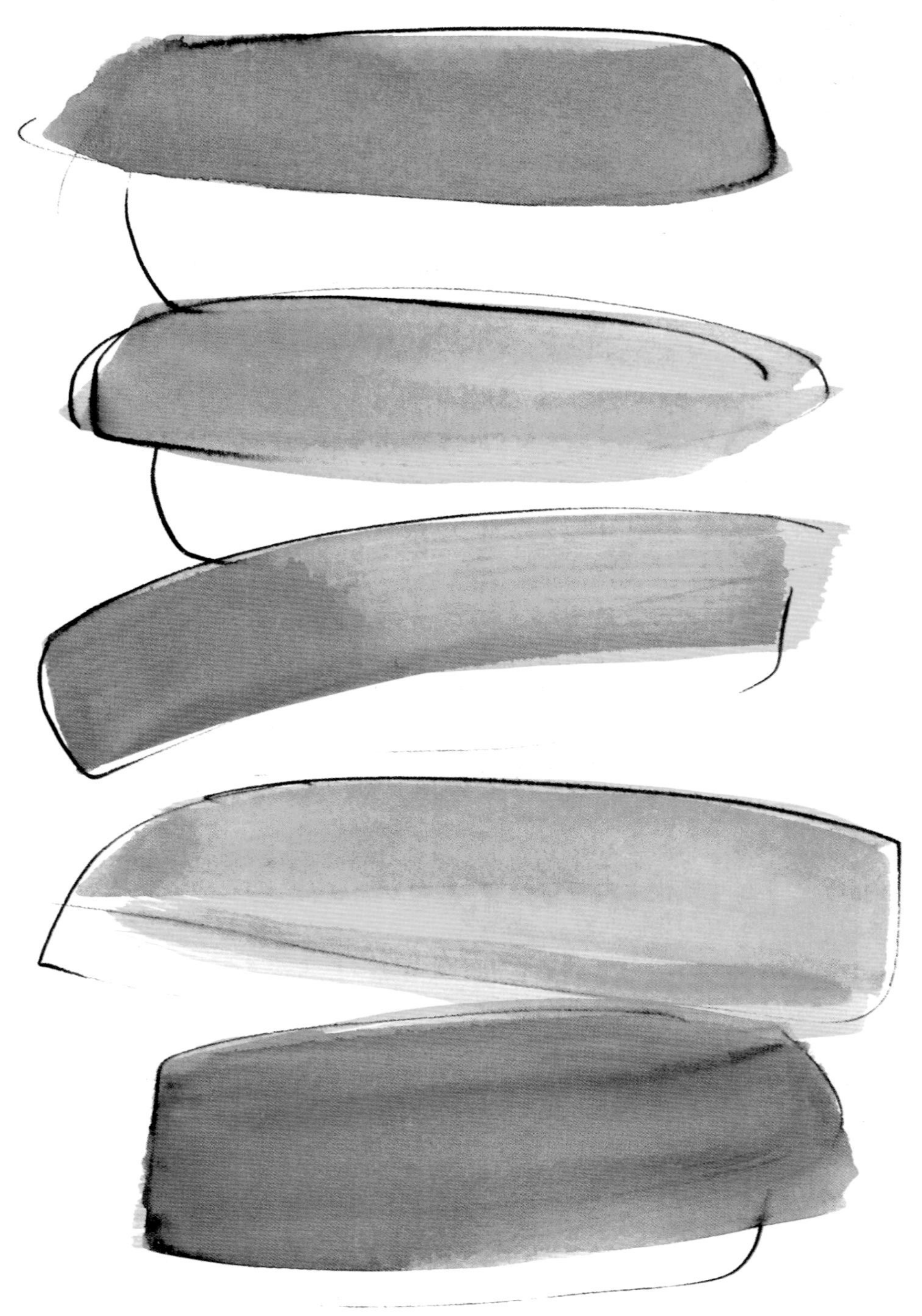

Chapter 9
JAPAN

Ofukuro no aji

I went to Japan several times when I was in my twenties. I fell in love with it on many different levels and in many different ways, and I fell in love with a beautiful Tokyo girl who spoke very little English but sang 'Strumming my fate with his fingers' in the roof bar of the New Otani Hotel, sounding like Dionne Warwick only much sexier. I spoke almost no Japanese, but we got along famously. She collapsed in giggles in the most delightful way, and at the most surprising moments, and it was only much later that I learned this meant she was not so much amused as embarrassed.

It is said that as a visitor, or even a long-term immigrant, one experiences Japanese culture as a series of revelations. It is like unpeeling the layers of an onion, for every time you think you have grasped something, another skin splits to reveal a deeper level that is an even greater mystery, and with it the realization that you have understood nothing.

A Japanese life exists for the observer in tableaux that make sense on the surface, frequently things of breathtaking beauty and style, but things that the *geijin* can appreciate only as the impressionable and gauche art student assesses a complex post-Impressionist painting, eager to understand but unable to penetrate beneath its most obvious planes and primary colours. We are unlikely to graduate in our Japanese studies and are thus condemned to be spectators even in our most enthusiastic participation. The tea ceremony staged for tourists is not the tea ceremony conducted alone, or for an honoured guest, or for a lover.

That which is inside remains veiled, intriguing and lovely, but essentially mysterious. It is the difference between a Westerner doing karate as a series of defensive and attacking movements – as street-fighting techniques – and a Japanese living within *bushido*, which may be crudely translated as 'the way of the warrior', the martial arts, a philosophy of life and honour. A *samurai* would arrange flowers, paint, write haiku, lose himself in the private tea ceremony and kill without compunction or mercy.

The interweaving of seemingly disparate elements is seamless, for its moral coda dances to a different beat. The steps are not at all the awkward ethical fandango of a Western soldier, who, if he does arrange flowers or say prayers, puts such things in a separate compartment of his mind and distances them from the killing fields – 'Other Men's Flowers', General Wavell called his collection of favourite poems. There have always been hard men in every culture, who knitted, did needlepoint or wrote blank verse – and went to war. But the difference in perception between East and West of that apparently similar mixture of bathos and barbarity, of visual aesthetics and violence, is profound, and I would not know where or how to begin to define the chasm in a meaningful way. I would just end up spinning platitudes, comparing and contrasting, as we had to do in our essays at school and, I guess, owning up to not knowing myself.

The historic Japanese experience is a complex filling within a dazzling visual container, and a Judaeo-Christian starting point is not the best lever to open it. I had to decide whether I wanted to try and become Japanese, or to leave well alone. I did not want to be on the outside looking in, but on the inside looking out. In the end, it was another thing I did not want passionately enough or was not capable of doing. With that recognition my decision was to step back, shutting the door on all but the food and my memories.

If I shut my eyes, I can stand again on a wooded hill in Hakkone and look at Fuji. Or sit in a Ginza bar and eat yakitori chicken and drink copious amounts of warm sake, my flask refilled again and again from a giant Gekkeikan bottle bobbing in a hot water bath. Or contemplate a bowl of shining *dashi* with slices of perfect matsutake mushroom. It is asymmetrical and fluid, while the flavours are clearly defined. Nothing is smudged, either on the palate or when eating with the eyes. The two are in harmony, and the way food looks on the plate or in the bowl comes from understanding the natural relationship between what something looks like and its taste. Even at ease with my pleasure, however, I know that I am forever a tourist.

Yoshio Tsuchiya's writing in *The Japanese Art of Food Arrangement* is in the purest Japanese terms, but his thoughts have a broader relevance, and are for us all to take on board: 'The presentation of Japanese food was traditionally impressionistic, with no firm rules. The only guidelines were to be absolutely natural; to use ingredients in season; to balance foods and vessels so that neither dominated the other; and to execute the arrangements swiftly, making them easy to eat and dismantle with chopsticks. The way food is arranged in a dish can bring the dish to life or as easily kill it. Success requires both a love of food and an eye for beauty.'

He urges cooks not to alter the natural shape of things and not to move or reshape the food once it is in place. Elaborate cutting or forcing something into a shape gives 'an impression of uncleanliness'. Tsuchiya communicates directly with my heart when he says: 'The sort of arrangement which collapses when one piece is removed is taboo.' And yes, a thousand times yes: 'Inedible garnishes such as leaves and flowers should be avoided. The food can and should speak for itself.' The Japanese art of food arrangement, he concludes, is neither precious nor inscrutable, '...but a way of greatly multiplying one's pleasure in the simple, creative, and universal act of preparing food.'

I will always be an outsider, but I can still eat delicious Japanese things whenever I want to, and I don't have to go to a Japanese restaurant to do so. In fact when I leave my desk today I am going to eat tuna sashimi with wasabi – Japanese green horseradish – and, with the next bite, freshly made English mustard for contrast. (Colman's English mustard is hugely popular in Japan.) I will cut my tuna with a scalpel-sharp sashimi knife and arrange the slices at an angle so that their rectangles sit easily with the lines of the plain rectangular plate against which the deep red of the fish will blush and glow. There are pleasures in these quick and simple rituals. I will have five pieces, because sashimi is always presented in groups of three, five or seven slices, the uneven numbers preferred to even numbers by Japanese – yang rather than yin – and, if I think about it, a reflection of the five elements which, of course, I never think about. I will conclude my solitary meal with a bowl of steamed Japanese rice and some pickled pink ginger that I made a week ago. I will eat with chopsticks, the wooden, disposable kind. I will drink chilled sake with the tuna, and I will finish at the table with a cup of green tea. Then, if I want to and if the weather is fine, I can take a Marc de Bourgogne in the garden, a segue into another culture and another place.

Getting inside the food of another country is a game which can be played dead straight or tongue-in-cheek. Either course is valid if what you cook and eat is delicious, and what I really object to is some old Nippon hand, by which I mean a *geijin* who claims to know best, being sniffy about it and ticking me off for my lack of authenticity. Frankly, my dear...

Home food in Japanese is called *ofukuro no aji* – mother's cooking. Some things are the same the whole world over. And some mothers cook well, while other mothers would be better not cooking at all.

SOME JAPANESE INGREDIENTS

Some of the store-cupboard ingredients you need, such as rice vinegar, are now sold in supermarkets, but you will have to make a special trip to a Japanese market for essentials like konbu and wakame seaweeds and sansho and sichimi peppers. The only danger is that Japanese packaging is so beautiful, you will find yourself filling your trolley with all kinds of fascinating but mysterious things which, being labelled only in Japanese and you being too shy to ask what they are, will remain mysterious and unwrapped features of your dry goods shelves for the foreseeable future. The recipes which follow don't call for too many unusual ingredients, but to cook Japanese style, you need:

Beanthread noodles (*harusame*)
Looking like spun glass, *harusame* are made from mung beans. They require no cooking. You just pour boiling water over them and leave them to soak for 5 minutes.

Bonito flakes
Bonito is a line-caught fish somewhere between a tuna and a large mackerel. It is filleted as soon after it is caught as possible and then air-dried into blocks called *katsuoboshi*. While every Japanese restaurant shaves its *katsuoboshi* using a special tool rather like a mandoline grater attached to a wooden box, the home cook uses *hana-katsuo*, packets of bonito flakes. They are brilliant sprinkled on top of hot spinach or bitter greens like Swiss chard, or the Asian brassicas like bok choi and pak choi.

Konbu
Konbu is a kelp with long flat leaves sold trimmed and dried in 15-cm (6-inch) squares; it is the second ingredient in *dashi*, basic soup stock.

Mirin
This sweet rice wine is used for cooking, not drinking. It keeps well, so buy a big bottle, transferring it to smaller screw-top bottles for storage. I use tonic bottles.

Miso
Miso is made from fermented soya beans and crops up in many dishes as well as soups. Its flavour, colour and constitution vary depending on whether the beans were fermented on their own – *mame-miso* – or with malted barley or rice.

Nori
Nori is a type of laver seaweed that is widely cultivated in Japan and is similar to the greeny-black Welsh laver found clinging to rocks in the Bristol Channel at low tide, though they are treated differently and have a different flavour. After processing and drying, nori presents as wafer-thin, almost translucent, purple-green sheets. Briefly grilled, these are delicious to eat as a nibble with drinks or crumbled over rice, but nori's main use in the Japanese kitchen is as a wrapper for vinegared rice when making sushi. It can also be deep-fried. Nori-wrapped sushi – *makizushi* – is traditionally rolled using a special bamboo mat called a *sudare*, but you can use a clean kitchen tea towel to achieve the same effect.

Rice
Japanese rice is round and short-grained, and cooks to a sticky finish. It is always steamed. I use an electric rice steamer, a simple and inexpensive piece of kit that cooks any kind of rice perfectly and then keeps it warm and in perfect condition for up to 4 hours. I could not imagine going back to boiling water on the hob – the time, the fuss, the occupation of precious burner space.

Rice vinegar
Mitsukan, one of the biggest vinegar producers in Japan, has invested heavily in marketing rice vinegars in the West. They make interesting alternatives to wine and cider vinegars in western dishes and *escabeche*.

Sake
This is the traditional dry rice wine that is traditionally drunk warm, though it is becoming fashionable to drink some of the finer examples chilled. It is extensively used in cooking, often in conjunction with mirin.

Sansho
Called a pepper, this is actually the ground seed of the prickly ash.

Shiitake
These cultivated dark meaty mushrooms are now sold fresh by most supermarkets.

Shoyu (soy sauce)
The best-known and arguably the finest type of this ubiquitous, entrancing, salty dark sauce made from fermented soya beans is Kikkoman. Japanese soy sauce differs from Chinese in being fermented with wheat. Civilized life would be impossible without it.

Sichimi (*togarishi*) pepper mix
Sichimi is sold in small glass jars and is expensive. It is a red spice mixture that includes ground chilli flakes, sansho pepper, sesame seeds, toasted nori and dried orange peel.

Soba
These buckwheat noodles are a Japanese passion.

Tofu
Tofu is beancurd, a high-protein processed food made from soya beans which comes in a variety of consistencies, from custard-soft to firm, depending on how much water it contains. With the growth of vegetarianism, consumption has increased dramatically in the west, though it has been eaten in China and Japan for nearly 2,000 years. It has virtually no taste, but provides a blank canvas on which to paint flavour colours, which it readily absorbs. It may be eaten uncooked, but grills and fries well. You can buy it in packs from the supermarket chill cabinet, usually of 500 g.

Udon
These thick wheat noodles are invariably eaten with *dashi* flavoured with soy sauce.

Wakame
This is a seaweed that is rich in calcium and dietary fibre but, despite this ominously healthy fact, tastes great. It is sold dried in packets and is simply reconstituted in water before being dressed, usually with a vinegary dressing, to balance its pleasant, mildly iodine flavour (page 166), or it is served in soup (page 36).

Wasabi
What we buy as wasabi in powder and tubes is our kind of dried horseradish dyed green and contains Colman's mustard with no guarantee that it is the Japanese kind. When mixed with water to form a paste it makes a hotter-than-the-hottest-mustard condiment and always accompanies sushi and sashimi. I also use it to spike commercial English horseradish sauce when I can't buy fresh roots. Richard Hosking, in his exemplary *A Dictionary of Japanese Food*, says the real thing only grows wild in the purest mountain streams and he is very dismissive of commercial wasabi. I, with my coarse palate, love the stuff. Check it out with sausages instead of mustard or with rare beef to be seduced by its fiery charms.

TATAKI OF TUNA LOIN

Much of the best line-caught tuna taken around the world goes straight to Tokyo's central fish market after being prepared *ikajimi*-style. This is a highly skilled procedure where the tuna is bled through the heart arteries and gutted through the gills, to avoid rupturing intestines which – to a refined Japanese palate – taints the belly flesh, the most highly prized cut for sashimi. Within minutes of being caught, the prepared fish are put into ice slurry and are flown to Tokyo as soon after landing as possible.

Fresh tuna is best eaten raw or very rare. Getting hold of tuna fresh enough to be eaten uncooked is getting easier, the global boom in sushi bars triggering an interest in preparing and eating it at home. Demand stimulates supply. Absolute freshness is essential, as tuna deteriorates rapidly. Temperature fluctuation accelerates deterioration, so when you buy it take it home in a cool bag and, as soon as you can, trim the fillet of any black or bloody bits and generally tidy it up with a very sharp knife before brushing with a neutral oil, cling-wrapping and refrigerating it. The flesh discolours rapidly when exposed to the air. The sooner you eat it after purchase the better and certainly this should be the same day.

Tataki, the process of searing the outside but leaving the tuna raw in the middle, is my favourite way of eating tuna. This is also an excellent way of cooking salmon, and even fillet of beef. Tuna is rich, so you need no more than 115 g (4 oz) per person for a first course, though you need to allow 175 g (6 oz) bought weight when buying untrimmed loin, to allow for skin and trimmings. The shape of the untrimmed loin is that of a rectangle topped by a triangle, with thick black skin at the base of the rectangle.

First trim away blackened or bloody parts and discard. You then cut away the skin. It will not pull like the skin of a flat fish. Next, you cut the triangular top off to produce as neat a block of flesh as you can. This you cut in half lengthwise to produce two neat blocks with four flat planes on each. The triangular piece may be cooked in the same way as these blocks, though it will obviously not present in the same way when sliced.

Start by heating a dry heavy frying pan or griddle over a moderate heat until smoking-hot. Brush the fillet with a neutral oil and season all over generously with salt and pepper. Sear for 15–20 seconds on each plane, turning and holding in place with tongs. Plunge into ice-cold water to stop the cooking process and immediately pat dry with kitchen paper.

Cut into 2-cm (¾-inch) thick slices and serve with soy sauce, wasabi and English mustard in separate small dishes for each person. The Japanese use disposable chopsticks, which you can buy cheaply at Japanese food shops.

MACKEREL WITH VINEGAR AND DIPPING SAUCE

The Japanese revere mackerel in a way that we never have. Until I ate it raw for the first time I never greatly cared for it either, or thought it merited more than a passing glance unless it was lightly smoked. In all the ways it was served to me, it had seemed so worthy, rather oily and heavy – the taste too strong, almost overpowering.

Here it is lightly salted overnight in the fridge and then only briefly marinated, so it is still raw. The sweet-and-sour vinegar dressing is good with the succulent dark flesh, neatly tempering its richness. It has obvious similarities with South American *escabeches* (page 216). Mitsukan rice vinegars are now widely available in the West. Although an accompaniment here, *namasu* is also served as a salad in its own right.

Mackerel is strongly flavoured, with a taste that gets stronger for every hour after it is killed. It should be gutted as soon as you buy it. When choosing your fish, look out for brilliant colouring and shining silver in the skin. Ask your fishmonger to clean, scale and fillet it for you, but to leave the skin on.

serves 4 as first course, 2 as main course

675 g (1½ lb) mackerel
4 tsp salt
5 tbsp rice vinegar
150 ml (¼ pint) hot water
2 tsp sugar

FOR THE NAMASU:

225 g (8 oz) daikon radish, peeled
1 carrot, about 5.5 cm (2¼ inches) long, peeled
300 ml (½ pint) iced water
2 tsp salt
7.5 g (¼ oz) katsuoboshi (bonito flakes, page 162)
3 tsp rice vinegar
1 tsp caster sugar

FOR THE DIPPING SAUCE:

2 tbsp rice vinegar
2 tbsp Niban Dashi (page 31)
1 tbsp Kikkoman soy sauce
1 tbsp caster sugar
¼ tsp salt

to serve:

3.5-cm (1½-inch) piece of root ginger, peeled
handful of flat-leaf parsley

The day before: remove any obvious bones from the fish with tweezers. Sprinkle half the salt into a shallow glass or earthenware dish and lay the fillets on it, skin side up. Sprinkle the remaining salt on top and cling-wrap. Refrigerate overnight.

Next day: take the fillets out of the dish and wipe with kitchen paper. Wash out the dish and return the fillets to it, skin side down. Return to the fridge until needed.

About 2 hours before you want to eat, make the *namasu*: shred the daikon using the shredder on a food processor or *benriner* (Japanese mandolin with special shredding attachment). Shred the carrot in the same way. Put in a bowl with the iced water which has had the salt dissolved in it and leave to soak for 1 hour.

Meanwhile, toast the bonito flakes in a dry pan over the lowest heat, stirring constantly, for 2–3 minutes. Grind to a powder and reserve. Squeeze the daikon and carrot dry and put in a bowl with the vinegar, sugar and powdered bonito. Toss to coat.

Make the dipping sauce: put the vinegar, *dashi*, soy sauce, sugar and salt in a pan and bring to the boil, immediately removing from the heat. Leave to cool to room temperature.

Mix the rice vinegar for the fish with the hot water and dissolve the sugar in it, then pour this over the mackerel. Leave to stand for 20 minutes.

Remove from the vinegar dressing and dry with more paper towel. Cut the fillets at an angle into 1-cm (½-inch) slices and arrange in neat rows on 4 cold plates, skin side up. Put a pile of *namasu* beside the fish. Grate the ginger and arrange it in mounds on the other side of the fish. Finish with parsley.

WAKAME AND CRAB SALAD

A salad of wakame (page 163) and cucumber is called *osu no mono* in Japanese. Authentically, the salad would also contain *shirasuboshi*, which are dried tiny fish. As these are not so easy to obtain, you can substitute shredded crab meat instead.

serves 4
85 g (3 oz) wakame
1 tbsp rice vinegar
½ cucumber
salt
5 tbsp rice vinegar
30 g (1 oz) caster sugar
1 tsp Kikkoman soy sauce
225 g (8 oz) white crab meat
2.5-cm (1-inch) piece of root ginger, peeled

Pour boiling water over the wakame, then immediately immerse it in cold water as this helps to keep its vivid green colour. Leave to stand in the water for 10 minutes, then drain. Put in a bowl, sprinkle over the rice vinegar and toss to coat.

Slice the cucumber thinly on a mandoline grater, put the slices in a colander and sprinkle with salt. Leave for 5 minutes, then squeeze out excess water.

In another bowl, mix the rice vinegar, sugar and soy sauce until the sugar dissolves.

Put the wakame, cucumber and crab in a serving bowl, pour over the rice vinegar dressing and toss to coat.

Cut the ginger across into paper-thin slices, then cut these into julienne and scatter over the top.

SUSHI

Sushi bars are the most popular form of Japanese restaurant in the west and what they serve has encouraged us to believe that sushi always contains raw fish and seaweed. This is a misconception. Small pieces of raw fish are often included, but the only constants are Japanese short-grained rice and rice vinegar, the sushi usually being served at room temperature. Other standard ingredients include egg, tofu, mushrooms, shellfish, fish eggs, wasabi and pickled vegetables.

Bite-sized pieces of rice squeezed gently into rectangular or ball shapes and topped with something are called *nigirizushi*. When rolled in a nori wrapper they are called *makizushi*. There really is no point in listing dozens of different recipes, since they are all variations on the same theme. An obvious example would be to substitute mackerel or tuna for the salmon in the following recipe – which should be used as a template for all *makizushi*.

SALMON SUSHI

A perfect *makizushi*... for those who do not like raw fish, the sushi can be made with smoked salmon.

serves 4
250 g (9 oz) short-grain rice
2 tbsp sake or dry sherry
1½ tbsp rice vinegar
2 tsp caster sugar
½ tsp salt
4 sheets of nori
225 g (½ lb) salmon fillet
3 tsp wasabi

Wash the rice in cold running water until the water runs clear. Cook the rice in a rice steamer, following the manufacturer's instructions but including the *sake* or sherry in the specified amount of liquid. Alternatively, put the rice in a pan with 350 ml (12 fl oz) cold water and the sake or sherry and bring to the boil, put on a tight-fitting lid, reduce to the lowest heat and steam for 12 minutes. Turn off the heat and leave undisturbed for 10 minutes. This matters because, if you take the lid off to take a look, you will let out moisture as steam which should otherwise be in the rice.

When the time is up, stir the rice thoroughly with a wooden spoon to separate the grains. Transfer to a bowl. Mix the rice vinegar with the sugar and salt and stir this into the rice, then cover with a damp cloth.

One at a time, put the sheets of nori under the grill for a few seconds, or run them over a gas flame, or lay them briefly on a very hot griddle. This subtly changes the flavour and makes the seaweed less chewy.

Cut the salmon into thin strips. Mix the wasabi powder with water to produce a brushable paste. Lay a *sudare* or a tea towel on the table and put a sheet of nori on top. Leaving a 5-cm (2-inch) strip of nori clear on the side nearest to you, spoon about one-eighth of the rice in a neat line across its remaining full width. Lay strips of salmon along the top and brush with wasabi. Spoon the same amount of rice on top. Fold the strip of nori closest to you over the rice and roll into a neat cylinder. Transfer to a damp tea towel and roll over so the join is underneath. Leave for 10 minutes so the moisture is distributed through the nori. Repeat until you have used up all the ingredients.

Unwrap each cylinder and cut across into 3.5-cm (1½-inch) thick rounds. Present on plates, cut side up.

CHICKEN YAKITORI

Chicken yakitori, a fast food eaten in specialist restaurants, consists of skewered grilled chicken basted with a sweet barbecue sauce to give a lovely glossy finish. Because of the basting sauce's high sugar content, it is easy to burn, so it is important not to have the barbecue or grill plate too hot and to turn the skewers frequently. For an authentic finishing touch, dust with a little sichimi and sansho peppers before serving.

serves 4

500 g (1 lb 2 oz) boneless chicken thigh and breast meat
6–8 spring onions
3 tbsp mirin
3 tbsp Kikkoman soy sauce
3 tbsp sake
1 tsp sugar
sichimi and sansho peppers

Cut the chicken into neat pieces and thread on 12 presoaked bamboo skewers, interspersing each piece with quarter of a spring onion threaded crosswise.

In a bowl, mix the mirin, soy sauce, sake and sugar, stirring until the sugar dissolves.

Grill for 2 minutes on each side, then start to brush on the glaze, turning every 30 seconds and brushing the top each time, for a further 6–8 minutes, when the chicken should be just cooked through, with the surface burnished to a mahogany red glaze. Dust with a little sichimi and sansho pepper before serving.

GRILLED EEL

Trust me, you will not want to kill and skin the eels yourself, so have your fishmonger do the business for you with two large eels, which you also want filleted. This should give you enough for 4 portions, as eel flesh is very rich. You want to cook them as soon as possible after you get them home.

serves 4

2 eels, each about 1 kg (2¼ lb), skinned and filleted
5 tbsp Kikkoman soy sauce
4 tbsp mirin
2 tbsp sake or dry sherry
1 tsp caster sugar
sansho pepper

First, cut the eel fillets into 10-cm (4-inch) lengths, lay them flat on a work surface and thread the pieces on 4 bamboo skewers, pushing these through from one side. Put into a steamer and steam for 5 minutes.

While they are steaming, make a basting liquid by mixing the soy sauce with the mirin, sake or sherry and the sugar.

Preheat an overhead grill or flat grilling pan and grill the eel for 2 minutes on each side. Brush with the basting liquid and cook for a further 3 minutes, turning and brushing every minute.

Season with sansho pepper just before bringing to the table. Serve with steamed Japanese rice (page 308) and drink warm sake or cold Japanese beer with it.

TEMPURA

Though it is now considered uniquely Japanese, tempura – the deep-frying of prawns and vegetables in batter – is thought to have been introduced to Japan as a technique in the second half of the sixteenth century by the Portuguese, who had themselves acquired the practice of deep-frying from Marrano Jews, the sect believed to be the first to cook coated fish in olive oil. Just when that might have been is not known, though it was certainly commonplace by the fifteenth century. (It was this same group, according to Claudia Roden's painstakingly researched and fascinating *The Book of Jewish Food*, who introduced fried fish to the East End of London. This was always sold and eaten cold, but was the obvious precursor of fish and chips). The

Portuguese batters and crumb coatings were probably a bit crude compared to the sophisticated and feather-light crisp batter of today's tempura.

If you want to eat the very best tempura you go to specialist restaurants where you sit at a bar and the chef fries the food in front of you, putting it into individual bamboo baskets lined with absorbent paper after an initial brief draining, and within seconds of it being taken from the oil. The batter is so delicate it does not stay crisp for long, so this is what you should try to do at home, deep-frying and serving your tempura in small batches at the kitchen table. Frying tempura for large numbers is asking for trouble.

Here I suggest three batter mixtures: the first uses self-raising flour, which I think works best of all. Mark Edwards, chef at the Metropolitan Hotel's Nobu restaurant in London, adds a little potato flour to his mix for the extra crunch it imparts. Or you could add a pinch of bicarbonate of soda to plain flour. A really great flour for batter is the Chinese Green Dragon brand – a self-raising flour – which you can buy in Oriental markets. Experiment to find the one you like best.

Flour is always sifted, then added to the liquid in one go, and is rapidly stirred in with chopsticks. When the water is icy-cold, strain it through a colander or sieve into a measuring jug to get the required volume, then transfer this to a large cold mixing bowl with the yolk or yolks or whole egg as specified. Whisk to mix before dumping in the flour, stirring together with chopsticks. The finished batter should still have discernible traces of flour and little lumps in it. Whisk it to a smooth batter and you will end up with too solid a coating, more like an English fish-and-chip-shop batter than the airy cocoon of crispness that is the tempura ideal.

Buy the largest raw prawns you can and serve 3 or 4 per person. Alternatively, you could fry strips of white fish fillets – for example, pieces of boned skate, sole, cod or haddock taken off the skin. Whitebait, oysters, scallops and squid are also delicious in *tempura* batter. For the vegetables, green beans, mushroom caps, sweet peppers, asparagus and spring onions would be an appropriate selection, though it is sensibly a choice made of what is best and seasonal.

Tempura is served with a light dipping sauce and grated daikon, and is followed by steamed rice and pickles. Once you have your ingredients prepared, all you need is clean hot oil and, most importantly, the right batter, which is made only minutes before it is used, so first prepare the food for frying.

serves 4

flour, for coating
oil, for deep-frying
1 green pepper, deseeded and cut lengthwise into 1-cm (½-inch) strips
1 red pepper, deseeded and cut lengthwise into 1-cm (½-inch) strips
16 French beans
caps from 8 button mushrooms
8 spring onions, cut in half lengthwise
8 asparagus spears
12 large raw prawns, peeled and butterflied, leaving the tails on
115 g (4 oz) grated daikon, to serve
Pickled Ginger (page 173), to serve (optional)

FOR THE DIPPING SAUCE (SOBA TSUYU):

5 tbsp mirin
2 tsp caster sugar
250 ml (9 fl oz) Niban Dashi (page 31)
5 tbsp Kikkoman soy sauce

FOR THE FIRST BATTER:

2 egg yolks
350 ml (12 fl oz) iced water
225 g (8 oz) self-raising flour, sifted

FOR THE SECOND BATTER:
1 large egg
175 ml (6 fl oz) iced water
125 g (4½ oz) plain flour, sifted

FOR THE THIRD BATTER:
1 egg
250 ml (8 fl oz) plain flour (i.e. a volume measurement), sifted
250 ml (8 fl oz) iced water

To make the dipping sauce: bring the mirin to the boil with the sugar. Remove from the heat and stir in the *dashi* and soy sauce. Serve still warm, in small bowls or saucers for each person.

Make one of the batters as described above. Preheat the oil for deep-frying to 190°C (375°F).

Put the vegetables in a bowl with some flour and toss well to coat, then dip the individual pieces in the batter and fry for 2 minutes, turning once. Cook one vegetable at a time and do not overcrowd the pan or the oil's temperature will drop, causing the batter to absorb oil and become greasy. In between batches, skim out any pieces of batter left behind and discard. Left in the oil for too long they will burn and taint it. Remove the cooked pieces to kitchen paper, serving immediately for people to eat with chopsticks. Fry the prawns last.

People add grated daikon to their dipping sauce as individual preference dictates. Pickled ginger is a nice pickle to have with the steamed sticky rice with which you finish your meal.

SHABU-SHABU

Shabu-shabu is so easy yet so good. It is a twentieth-century dish, probably post-World War II, because beef is a recent addition to the Japanese diet. A well-flavoured pot of simmering broth is put over a flame at the table for guests to cook their chosen ingredients as they like. After cooking and eating the solids, you drink the broth. The poaching part demands the skilful use of chopsticks, but is the greatest of fun – a Japanese variant on the fondue party, and you could use a fondue pot to do the job. Otherwise you will need a hot plate on which to put the broth pot.

serves 6
450 g (1 lb) sirloin, fillet or rib-eye steak
12 raw tiger prawns
225 g (8 oz) spinach
2.25 litres (4 pints) chicken stock
3 tbsp rice wine vinegar
4 small carrots
5-cm (2-inch) piece of root ginger, peeled
6 spring onions
1 sachet of dashi-no-moto (page 30)
4 tbsp Kikkoman soy sauce
2 chicken breasts
6 shiitake mushrooms
225 g (8 oz) beansprouts

to serve:
steamed rice
Pickled Ginger (page 173)

Put the steak in the freezer for 20 minutes to firm up so that it will slice thinly more readily. Peel and devein the prawns, leaving on the tails. Wrap the heads and shells in a piece of butter muslin. Wash the spinach, stripping out any thick stems and damaged leaves.

Put the stock in a saucepan on the hob, add the rice vinegar and the bag of prawn heads and shells.

Cut the carrots lengthwise into wafer-thin slices (a potato peeler makes this easy). Cut the ginger into similarly sized slices and cut the spring onions at an angle into 2.5-cm (1-inch) pieces. Add all of these to the stock. Bring to the boil, lower the heat and simmer for 10 minutes.

Discard the bag of prawn trimmings and stir in the *dashi* and soy sauce. Pour into the serving pot, which will go on the hot-plate or flame on the table.

Select a large serving plate on which to present the raw ingredients. Skin the chicken and cut it into strips. Cut the steak into paper-thin slices and quarter the mushrooms. Arrange with the other ingredients.

Serve with steamed rice and pickled ginger. Drink sake throughout, or until people fall over.

MUNG BEANSPROUTS AND GINGER WITH GREEN MISO DRESSING

The vivid green of the miso-based dressing comes from puréed spinach. The ginger brings sweetness and heat, a nice combination with the clean, delicate flavour of the beansprouts.

serves 4
225 g (8 oz) beansprouts
5-cm (2-inch) piece of root ginger, peeled

FOR THE GREEN MISO DRESSING:
salt
225 g (8 oz) spinach
115 g (4 oz) white miso paste
15 g (½ oz) caster sugar
150 ml (¼ pint) sake
1 egg yolk
iced water, for cooling

First prepare the dressing: bring a large pan of salted water to the boil, blanch the spinach in this for 1 minute, drain and transfer to a food processor without refreshing in cold water. Purée and reserve.

Put the miso, sugar and sake in a pan and bring to the boil, stirring. Lower the heat and simmer to a paste, stirring frequently to prevent sticking and burning. This will take about 15 minutes.

Remove from the heat and beat in an egg yolk, followed by the spinach purée. Immediately place the pan in iced water to cool the dressing rapidly.

Cut the ginger lengthwise into thin slices, then cut these into thin julienne strips.

When the dressing is quite cold, put the beansprouts in a mixing bowl. Toss to coat with the dressing and mound in 4 bowls. Scatter the ginger on top to finish.

PICKLED GINGER

Ideally, prepare this a week in advance.

serves 12
125 ml (4 fl oz) Japanese rice vinegar
45 g (1½ oz) caster sugar
30 g (1 oz) table salt
150 g (5 oz) root ginger, peeled and cut into paper-thin slices
1 small slice of beetroot

Bring the rice vinegar and sugar to boil in a small saucepan. Remove from the heat and leave to cool.

In a second saucepan, bring 375 ml (13 fl oz) water to the boil with the table salt. Blanch the ginger in this for 2 minutes, drain (reserving the brine) and leave to cool.

Put the ginger and beetroot in a sterilized jar, pour in brine to cover, seal with a tight-fitting lid and refrigerate for a week before eating.

Chapter 10
Korea

Neither China nor Japan

The films I have seen of Korea show a rather lovely country, lush from its heavy rainfall and at odds with the grim images of military confrontation on its border with North Korea. It was in Tokyo I first encountered Korean cooking in a bulgogi restaurant, the Japanese love of beef creating the perfect commercial opportunity in a country not always noted for its admiration of all things Korean. There was something about the flavours of the dishes we tried that instantly appealed – strong, distinctive yet well balanced. It was that indefinable something which you either embrace enthusiastically or reject out of hand. You will not find many Chinese who are complimentary about Korean cooking, partly I suspect because of historic prejudice and partly because much of the cooking is an interesting hybrid that shows the influence of centuries of colonial domination by China and Japan. If you are rooted culturally in either of those countries xenophobic considerations preclude its ready acceptance. Returning to London without the benefit of routing via Seoul to check out the real thing, I found that somebody had thoughtfully anticipated my new taste fix by opening a restaurant called Kaya in Dean Street, Soho. The manager was a Mrs Park, the Scottish wife of the Korean owner whom one never saw as he spent much time abroad on business. Mrs Park had an unusual front of house sales technique whenever I asked to try something new. 'Well, I wouldn't eat it personally,' she would say in the dismissive accent of Miss Jean Brodie. 'I think it's disgusting.'

Without wishing to give an impression of a limited cuisine, which it most certainly is not, Korean food is in part defined by its two most popular dishes, bulgogi and kimchee, the former being marinated barbecued beef usually grilled at the table and the latter a rather fierce pickle usually of salted cabbage fermented with plenty of garlic, ginger, chilli and fish. The word ubiquitous is sufficiently tempting to find regular application in cookbooks and this is one where its use is irresistible since kimchee is literally eaten at every meal, including breakfast, an option I can resist.

KIMCHEE

Kimchee, fermented Chinese cabbage and garlic pickle, is a Korean national institution served with every and any meal from breakfast to dinner. It is still produced there in huge amounts, but can be made easily on a small scale. There are many recipes for the pickle which contain fish. Fish sauce substitutes for whole fish in this recipe, and has the same effect without making it at all fishy tasting. A tablespoon or two of the pickling liquid may be added to soups. After fermentation, kimchee will keep for a month in the fridge.

serves 8 (makes 2.25 litres/4 pints)

1 kg (2¼ lb) Chinese cabbage (also called Chinese leaves)
450 g (1 lb) daikon radish, peeled
3 tbsp salt
7.5-cm (3-inch) piece of root ginger, peeled
8 garlic cloves
6 spring onions
4 tbsp fish sauce
1 tbsp hot chilli powder
2 tsp caster sugar

Cut the Chinese cabbage in half lengthwise and then across into 5-cm (2-inch) sections. Peel the daikon, cut it in half lengthwise, then across into 5-mm (¼-inch) thick slices. Put into a bowl.

Dissolve the salt in 1.75 litres (3 pints) of cold water and pour this brine over the vegetables. Cover the top with a cloth and leave at room temperature overnight.

Finely chop the ginger and garlic and thinly slice the spring onions. Put in a bowl with the fish sauce, chilli powder and sugar, mixing together with a spoon. Remove the vegetables from the water with tongs or a slotted spoon and add to this spice and aromatic mixture, turning to coat evenly. Don't throw away the brine!

Pack the vegetables into a 2.25-litre (2-quart) jar, leaving a 3-cm (1¼-inch) space at the top, and add the reserved brine to cover. Don't put on the lid, but cover with a cloth – the pickle needs air to ferment. Leave at room temperature for 3 days, then taste a piece. If it is sour enough to your taste it is ready, but the precise time will depend on the ambient temperature. The warmer it is, the quicker it works.

To serve 4, remove about a cupful and put it in a bowl on the table for people to help themselves.

DU BU

A perception of Korean food being beef-based is inaccurate. Meat only entered the diet significantly in the 1950s, while beancurd has been central to Korean cooking for more than 2,000 years. Beancurd is called *du bu* in Korean, and both the custard-like fresh curd and firmer curd are ubiquitous, the former being eaten chilled with a cold soy-based dressing as here, the latter being stewed and stir-fried. Treatments like this are also popular in Japan. The silkier and finer-textured the beancurd, the better the dish.

serves 4

350 g (12 oz) soft beancurd
2 shallots
2 spring onions
3 tbsp Kikkoman soy sauce
1 tbsp sesame oil
1 tbsp rice vinegar
1 tsp caster sugar
ice cubes, to serve

Slice the beancurd into 1-cm (½-inch) slices and arrange in overlapping circles on the bases of 4 deep bowls.

Slice the shallots and spring onions across as thinly as you can and scatter them over the beancurd.

Whisk the remaining ingredients together until the sugar is dissolved and the dressing is homogenized. With a teaspoon, dribble this on top.

Put 2 or 3 ice cubes in each bowl and serve at once.

DU BU BOKUM

Why does this sound like a private-eye in a 'B' movie? The crisp shallots contrast nicely with the just-cooked courgettes and lightly fried marinated beancurd.

serves 4

2 tbsp sesame oil
2 tsp caster sugar
4 tbsp soy sauce
2 garlic cloves, cut into paper-thin slices
675 g (1½ lb) firm beancurd (tofu)
5 tbsp groundnut oil
225 g (8 oz) shallots, thinly sliced
400 g (14 oz) courgettes
4 spring onions, cut at an angle into 2.5-cm (1-inch) pieces

Whisk the sesame oil, sugar and soy sauce together in a bowl. Whisk in the garlic.

Cut the beancurd into 2.5-cm (1-inch) cubes and put to marinate in the mixture for 30 minutes.

Put 3 tablespoons of the oil in a large frying pan or wok over a low heat and stir in the shallots. Sweat, stirring frequently, for 20 minutes, or until they just start to colour. Turn up the heat and stir-fry until crisp and caramelized. Transfer to kitchen paper to drain and reserve.

Cut the courgettes in half lengthwise and, if large, in half again, then cut into 2.5-cm (1-inch) batons.

In a second frying pan or wok, put 2 tablespoons of oil over a moderate heat. As the oil shimmers, add the courgettes and stir-fry quickly for 2–3 minutes until just done. They should retain some bite. Remove with a slotted spoon and reserve.

Strain the beancurd and garlic through a sieve, reserving the marinade. Pat the curd dry with kitchen paper.

Add a little more oil to the pan in which you cooked the courgettes and fry the beancurd, garlic and spring onions for 2–3 minutes. Add the reserved sauce and return the courgettes to the pan for 30 seconds, stirring and tossing to warm through and combine.

Divide between 4 warmed deep bowls and scatter the crisp shallots on top. Serve immediately.

EGG PANCAKE WITH PRAWNS, SPRING ONION AND CHILLI

Thick pancakes with different fillings cooked into them are popular in Korea and Japan. There are, indeed, special restaurants that feature them, rather like pizzerias offering pizzas as the main event, though they have nothing in common on the plate with an Italian pizza. Cooked in a 15-cm (6-inch) crêpe or omelette pan, the following will make four *pajon*, as they are called. The use of self-raising flour is not authentic, but delivers nicely raised light pancakes.

makes 4

1 garlic clove
salt
1 egg
2 tsp sesame oil
½ tsp sansho pepper (page 163)
200 g (7 oz) self-raising flour, sifted
4 spring onions
8 raw tiger prawns, shelled and deveined
1 hot red chilli, cut into tiny dice
2 tbsp groundnut oil

FOR THE VINEGAR DIPPING SAUCE:
2 tsp sesame seeds
1 tsp dried chilli flakes
2.5-cm (1-inch) piece of root ginger, peeled
100 ml (3½ fl oz) Kikkoman soy sauce
2½ tbsp rice vinegar

Make the dipping sauce: toast the sesame seeds and chilli flakes in a small dry pan over a low heat for 2–3 minutes, stirring, until the sesame starts to colour. Grind to a powder and put in a bowl. Grate the ginger finely into the bowl, then whisk together with the soy sauce and vinegar. Leave to stand at room temperature.

Crush the garlic and chop and scrape to a paste with ½ teaspoon of salt. Whisk the egg, the garlic, sesame oil and 300 ml (½ pint) of cold water in a bowl. Season with the sansho pepper, add the flour and whisk to a smooth batter. Leave to stand at room temperature for 45 minutes.

Cut the spring onions in half, then shred them lengthwise. Dice the prawns. Mix the prawns, spring onions and chilli together and divide into 4.

Put the pan over a low-to-medium heat and, when hot, add ½ tablespoon of the oil. Tilt and swirl the pan to distribute the oil and scatter over one-quarter of the prawn mixture. Wait 30 seconds then pour over one-quarter of the batter and turn the heat down to low. Put a lid or tray on top of the pan and cook for 4 minutes. Turn the pancake with a spatula and cook the other side for 3–4 minutes, again covering the pan.

Remove to a warmed plate in a low oven while you cook the rest in the same way, each time turning the heat up a little before you begin, turning it down again in the same way.

To serve, cut the pancakes into quarters. Whisk the sauce before dividing between 4 individual ramekins, placing these in the middle of warmed serving plates and arranging the pancake quarters round them. Eat with chopsticks.

KUJOLPAN

Kujolpan is perfect food for entertaining. It is a first course comprising nine separate elements, one of them being plain pancakes. All but the pancakes are traditionally served in ornate lacquered boxes, though these are obviously not essential. People take a pancake, fill it with their chosen filling, roll it and eat it before moving on to the next. One taste sensation follows another, the contrast as pleasing as the sharing.

The pancakes can be made well in advance, either the day before or frozen. I often cheat and use Chinese pancakes bought ready-made from the market. Otherwise you need to make a daunting number of pancakes. How many you allow per person is a vexing question. If everybody is to try everything, then you need eight pancakes each. The Chinese pancakes are not large, so this would be by no means excessive.
All the fillings serve 4.

FOR THE PANCAKES (**makes 16**):
250 g (9 oz) plain flour, sifted
salt and pepper
1 tbsp groundnut oil, plus more to grease pan

FOR THE BEANSPROUT AND GINGER FILLING:
5-cm (2-inch) piece of root ginger, peeled
1 garlic clove
2 tsp sesame oil
150 g (5 oz) beansprouts
2 tsp Kikkoman soy sauce
pepper

FOR THE CUCUMBER AND RED ONION FILLING:
1 cucumber
1 red onion
1 tbsp groundnut oil
1 tbsp toasted whole sesame seeds

FOR THE OMELETTE FILLING:
salt and pepper
4 eggs
1 tsp sugar
groundnut oil

FOR THE BEEF FILLING:
400 g (14 oz) rib-eye steak
pepper
4 shallots
2 garlic cloves
3 tbsp groundnut oil
2 tsp sesame seeds, toasted and ground
1 hot red chilli, shredded
1 tbsp Kikkoman soy sauce

FOR THE MUSHROOM FILLING:
2 tbsp groundnut oil
1 tbsp sesame oil
1 garlic clove, finely chopped
8 shiitake mushrooms, wiped and thinly sliced
2 tsp Kikkoman soy sauce
12 chives, thinly chopped

FOR THE PRAWN FILLING:
2.5-cm (1-inch) piece of root ginger, peeled
2 tbsp groundnut oil
2 spring onions, thinly sliced
½ tsp dried chilli flakes
12 tiger prawns, shelled and deveined
2 tsp rice vinegar

FOR THE STIR-FRIED MINCED PORK FILLING:
115 g (4 oz) Kimchee (page 176)
8 shallots
1 garlic clove
3 tbsp groundnut oil
400 g (14 oz) minced pork
4 spring onions
2 tbsp Kikkoman soy sauce
2 tbsp sake (page 163)
2 tbsp mirin (page 162)

Make the pancakes: put the flour in a mixing bowl and season with salt and pepper. Add the oil, then whisk in 400 ml (14 fl oz) water until you have a smooth batter like single cream. Leave to stand for 30 minutes.

Heat a crêpe pan over a low-to-medium heat. When hot, wipe with oil-soaked kitchen paper and start cooking the pancakes, stacking them when done. Wipe out the pan with oiled paper at regular intervals while making the pancakes.

To make the beansprout and ginger filling: cut the ginger into thin strips and chop the garlic finely. Put the oil in a wok over a moderate heat. When it shimmers, add the garlic and ginger and stir-fry for a minute. Add the beansprouts and soy sauce, and stir-fry for another minute. Mound in a warmed bowl and grind over lots of pepper.

To make the cucumber and red onion filling: cut the cucumber into 5-cm (2-inch) batons. Thinly slice the onion. Put the oil in a wok over a medium heat. When it shimmers, add the cucumber and onion together, turn up the heat and stir-fry, tossing for a minute or two until very hot. Mound the mixture on a warmed serving dish, scattering the toasted whole sesame seeds on top.

To make the omelette filling: heat a 30-cm (12-inch) flat-based frying pan over a moderate heat. Season the eggs in a bowl, add the sugar and 1 tablespoon of water. Beat for a minute. Film the base of the pan with oil and pour in the eggs, swirling to coat evenly. Lower the heat a little and cook until just set. Slide out on to a cutting board and leave to cool. Cut into strips and pile these on a serving plate, grinding some pepper on top.

To make the beef filling: cut the beef into strips and grind over plenty of pepper. Slice the shallots thinly and cut the garlic cloves into paper-thin slices. Heat the oil in a wok over a high heat until it shimmers. As it starts to smoke, add the shallots, sesame seeds and chilli, and stir-fry for a minute. Add the beef and stir-fry for another 2 minutes. Add the soy sauce and toss to coat. Transfer to a warmed serving dish.

To make the mushroom filling: put the groundnut oil in a wok over a moderate heat. When it shimmers, add the sesame oil and garlic. Stir-fry for a few seconds, then add the mushrooms and stir-fry for 2–3 minutes. Add the soy sauce and toss to coat. Mound on a serving dish and scatter over the chives.

To make the prawn filling: grate the ginger finely and reserve. Put the oil in a wok over a medium-to-high heat. When it shimmers, add the spring onions and chilli flakes, and stir-fry for a minute. Add the prawns and stir-fry for 2 minutes, or until just cooked through. Add the ginger and vinegar and toss. Transfer to a warmed serving dish.

To make the stir-fried minced pork filling: rinse the kimchee, chop and reserve. Thinly slice the shallots and chop the garlic. Put a wok over a moderate heat. Add the oil and swirl, then turn up the heat and add the pork. Stir-fry for 2–3 minutes. Add all the remaining ingredients and stir-fry for a further 4–5 minutes. Turn out onto a warmed serving plate.

Reheat the pancakes briefly in a steamer before serving. Present them in bamboo steamers around the table, putting all the fillings in the middle of the table for people to fill their pancakes as they like.

GRILLED BEEF WITH BUCKWHEAT NOODLES AND KIMCHEE

Koreans share with the Japanese an appreciation of beef over pork or lamb, which are not eaten to the same extent or with the same enthusiasm. You can increase the amount of steak if you like, but really 115 g (4 oz) a head is masses in combination with the noodles and broth.

serves 4

1.1 litres (2 pints) clear beef or chicken broth
1 hot red chilli, shredded
salt and pepper
350 g (12 oz) buckwheat noodles
1 tbsp sesame oil
2 tsp Kikkoman soy sauce
2 rib-eye steaks, each about 225 g (8 oz)
1 tbsp groundnut oil
4 spring onions
4–6 tbsp Kimchee (page 176)
Chinese garlic chives

Bring a large pan of water to the boil. Bring the stock to simmer in another pan with the chilli. Put a dry ridged grill pan to heat to smoking-hot.

Salt the boiling water and cook the noodles for 8–10 minutes. Drain, return to the pan with the 2 teaspoons of the sesame oil and the soy sauce, and toss to coat.

While the noodles are cooking, brush the steaks with the groundnut oil, then season heavily with salt and pepper. Give the steaks 2–3 minutes a side on the grill pan, turning 4 times. Cooking time depends on how thick they are and how rare you like them. Leave to rest on a carving board for 4–5 minutes before slicing.

Cut the spring onions at an angle into 4. Brush the onion pieces with the remaining sesame oil and toss in the ridged grill pan for a minute until they wilt.

Mound the noodles in 4 deep warmed bowls, ladling the broth over. Cut the steaks at an angle into thick slices and arrange the slices on the noodles, then put a spoonful of kimchee in the centre.

Scatter a few thinly sliced rings of garlic chive over all and serve at once.

BULGOGI

There is a Korean cooking device called a *bulgogi* or *pulgogi*, a domed metal grill on which marinated slices of beef are cooked at the table. The original heat source for this device was red-hot charcoal. When I have eaten bulgogi in Korean restaurants, the 'grill' is never hot enough, because you can't bring red-hot charcoal to the table so, consequently, the metal dome gets cooler and cooler and the meat sticks and goes tough. Health and safety regulations forbid lit charcoal outside the kitchen and the fumes would, in any case, poison the diners. Bulgogi is best grilled on a barbecue outside.

The beef is sliced before it is marinated in a soy-sauce-based liquid. It is therefore important not to leave the meat in the marinade for more than 45–50 minutes, or it will become inedibly salty.

serves 4

800 g (1¾ lb) rib-eye or sirloin steak
4 garlic cloves, finely chopped
1 tsp dried chilli flakes
3 tbsp Kikkoman soy sauce
2 tbsp mirin (page 162)
2 tbsp sake (page 163)
1 tbsp sesame oil
coarsely ground black pepper
8 spring onions
1 tbsp crushed toasted sesame seeds
steamed rice (page 308), to serve
Kimchee (page 176), to serve

Chill the beef in the freezer for 15–20 minutes, then cut at an angle into 5-mm (¼-inch) slices.

In a bowl, mix the garlic and chilli, then add the liquid ingredients and whisk vigorously. Lay the beef slices in a single layer in large roasting tin and pour the marinade over.

After 45 minutes, drain the beef and wipe with a cloth. Reserve at room temperature.

Preheat the barbecue (page 201) – it should be very hot.

Grind pepper generously over both sides of the beef slices, then grill for 45 seconds on each side, removing to a warmed serving plate.

Toss the spring onions on the barbecue until they wilt and scatter them over the beef with the sesame seeds.

Serve at once with steamed rice and kimchee.

BARBECUED CHILLI AND SESAME BEEF SHORT RIBS

Short ribs are taken from the upper section of the ribs. You can marinate steaks and cook them in the same way during periods of government interdiction of the selling of beef on the bone.

serves 4

1.5 kg (3¼ lb) short-cut ribs of beef in 7.5-cm (3-inch) pieces
7.5-cm (3-inch) piece of root ginger, peeled
2 garlic cloves
2 tbsp Kikkoman soy sauce
2 tbsp mirin (page 162)
1 tbsp sesame oil
1 tsp dried chilli flakes
1 tsp coarsely ground pepper
1 tbsp crushed toasted sesame seeds
steamed rice (page 308), to serve
Kimchee (page 176), to serve

Score the meat in a 2-cm (¾-inch) diamond cross-hatch, cutting to a uniform depth of 5 mm (¼ inch), and put on a tray in a single layer.

Grate the ginger into a piece of butter muslin set over a bowl. Ball and tighten the cloth to squeeze out as much juice as possible.

Crush the garlic and chop to a paste. Add to the ginger juice with the soy sauce, mirin, sesame oil and chilli. Whisk and pour over the meat, turning to coat evenly. Cover and refrigerate overnight.

Remove from the fridge 2 hours before cooking, turning the meat over when it comes from the fridge. Preheat the barbecue to medium-hot (page 201).

Wipe the marinade from the meat, pouring the remaining marinade into a bowl. Grind plenty of pepper over the beef. Grill 12.5 cm (5 inches) from the coals, turning after 5 minutes and brushing with the marinade every couple of minutes. The meat should be completely cooked, which will take about 20–25 minutes in total. Scatter with the sesame seeds and serve with steamed rice and kimchee.

TWAEJIGOGIKIMCHEEBOKUM

The first recipe to have an e-mail address for its name, this is an excellent stir-fried pork dish which includes kimchee in the cooking rather than as a cold relish.

serves 4
450 g (1 lb) lean boneless pork
6 spring onions, green parts removed and reserved
2 tbsp Kikkoman soy sauce
2 hot red chillies, cut in thin strips
1 tbsp sesame oil
1 tbsp toasted sesame seeds
2 garlic cloves, peeled and finely chopped
pepper
2 tbsp sunflower or groundnut oil
170 g (6 oz) Kimchee (page 176)
1 tbsp oyster sauce
1 tsp caster sugar

Cut the pork into fat matchsticks and put in a bowl. Thinly slice the white parts of the spring onions and add to the pork with the soy sauce, chillies, sesame oil, the sesame seeds and garlic. Season generously with pepper and leave to marinate for 1 hour.

Squeeze out the moisture from the kimchee, slice thinly and reserve.

Preheat a wok or large frying pan until smoking hot. Add the sunflower oil and, as it shimmers, the pork mixture, then stir-fry for 5 minutes. Add the kimchee, oyster sauce, sugar and 300 ml (½ pint) of water. Bring to the boil, lower the heat and simmer for 10 minutes.

Serve with steamed rice (page 308), scattering thinly sliced green onion on top.

Chapter 11
Mexico

The world's first fusion kitchen

None of the world's unique and wonderful cuisines has been as bastardized and abused as that of Mexico. The food called Mexican in the majority of restaurants outside that country is a joke literally in bad taste, looking like brown slurry, greasy, ill-spiced and badly executed. Yet some of the dishes I have eaten in Mexico were enthralling, complex, subtle and rewarding.

Our culinary debt to Mexico is, of course, huge in terms of ingredients and produce alone. From chillies to squash, from avocados to tomatoes, tomatillos and chocolate, cooking would be a lot less interesting without Mexican ingredients. Historically Mexico was for hundreds of years a Spanish colony, as was California, which was nominally governed from Mexico – the cooking which grew out of it, the world's first fusion kitchen. Spaniards embraced local produce, such as turkeys, beans, corn, tomatoes, potatoes, guavas, chillies and chocolate, while introducing beef, pork and chickens. With hindsight it is not difficult to decide who got the most out of the deal.

Of all indigenous produce, nothing was as important as corn. It remains at the centre of Mexican food, and tortillas are its heart. The name *tortilla* was the Spanish one given by the *conquistadores* to the flat corn pancakes that were part of the staple diet of the native Indians in Mexico, as they remain for the population as a whole to this day.

Tortilla dough is made with dried white field corn – *posole* or *pozole* before the kernels are ground (page 191) – which is starchy and not at all sweet. This is first brought to the boil in water with slaked lime, simmered for 15 minutes and then left to soak overnight. It is then washed under running water, while being rubbed to rid it of the yellow hulls until only the white kernels remain. These are ground while still wet and then mixed with more water to give a smooth soft dough.

Travelling outside the cities, you may still see cooks in small cafés with open kitchens making tortillas in the traditional way, which involves patting them out between the palms of the hands in a seamless process that produces perfect, uniformly thin rounds. It looks easy until you try to do it and find it quite impossible. Tortilla presses, round hinged metal plates with a handle to apply leverage, provide a simple solution to our lack of dexterity, and you can now buy them quite cheaply in many kitchen shops. Tortillas are eaten in many different forms – as bread, as wrappers for hot fillings and also deep-fried to make crisp chips for scooping up salsas and dips like guacamole and refried beans.

In Mexico and the south-western states of America, few people make tortillas because they can be bought cheaply from *tortillerias* (the factories which produce them) where, should they wish to make some at home, they can also buy masa, fresh tortilla dough. If no *tortilleria* is nearby, then every supermarket has a huge range of both corn and wheatflour tortillas made fresh every day. It is still early times for mass-produced tortillas in the UK, so an ability to make them yourself is an advantage. Quaker brand masa harina – dried cornmeal – is now quite widely available here and, if you can't find it locally, you can buy it mail order from Made in America (01249 447608), a useful supplier of otherwise hard-to-find US staples. Mexican spices and ingredients can be bought by mail order from The Cool Chile Company (0870 9021145).

The finished dough is not easy to work with since it has none of the elasticity of a yeast dough. You want to achieve a consistency which is soft but not sticky, a bit like Plasticine or Play-doh. When you do get this right, it irritatingly dries out and becomes unusable very quickly. If this happens, return it to the mixer and work some more, adding water a tablespoon at a time until it feels malleable again. Mexican cooks may not need to use mixers to do the job, but it really is a lot easier for novices.

CORN TORTILLAS

makes about 15
600 ml (1 pint) hot water
500 g (1 lb 2 oz) masa harina (see above)

Pour the hot water into the bowl of an electric mixer. You want it to be hot to the touch – about 70°C (160°F). Turn on the dough hook, add the masa harina and work at slow speed until you have a soft but not too sticky dough. If it is too wet, add a little more masa harina. Remove, cling-wrap and leave to rest for 20–30 minutes at room temperature.

Divide into 15 balls, keeping them covered with a damp cloth. Put a square of flexible plastic slightly larger than the tortilla press (see above) on the bottom half and position one of the dough balls in the middle. Lay a second square on top and close the press, applying pressure. The resulting tortilla should be about 12.5–15 cm (5–6) inches in diameter and the thickness of a 50p coin. If it breaks when you unpeel the top sheet, the dough is too dry; if it sticks, you have either pressed it too hard or the dough is too wet.

Cook in an ungreased hot dry frying pan for about 30–40 seconds on each side, when the bread should puff up a little while the second side is cooking and be speckled brown. Wrap in a cloth and leave for 15 minutes before serving.

WHEATFLOUR TORTILLAS

Wheatflour tortillas are eaten mainly in the north of Mexico and in the USA. They are much easier to make than corn tortillas – a food processor or electric mixer makes the dough child's play – but perfect results will only come from practice. Knowing how hot the frying pan or griddle should be is also a matter of trial and error. It needs to be hot enough so a tortilla starts to bubble within 3 seconds of it hitting the pan.

Authentic wheatflour tortillas have lard in them, but a mixture of lard and corn oil actually produces the best results. Duck or goose fat, while scarcely traditional, also make delicious tortillas. The dough can be made the day before, cling-wrapped and kept in the fridge. If using it that day, first allow it to rest, covered with a slightly dampened cloth, for 1 hour before rolling. Separated by sheets of greaseproof paper, they also freeze well, raw or cooked.

makes 12
about 175 ml (6 fl oz) hand-warm water
2 tbsp lard, or duck or goose fat
3 tbsp corn oil
1 tsp salt
350 g (12 oz) strong white flour, plus more for dusting

Put the water, lard or other fat, oil and salt into the bowl of an electric mixer with the water and process at full speed, pouring the flour in gradually until the dough balls and starts to pull away from the sides. If it is too dry, add more water a tablespoon at a time, continuing to work until you have a smooth, elastic dough.

Turn out on a floured surface and divide into 12 pieces. Roll these into balls, put them on a plate, cling-wrap and leave to rest for 45 minutes.

Heat a dry heavy frying pan or flat griddle over a moderate heat. On a lightly floured surface, roll out a ball of dough, rotating, rolling and turning until you have a 17.5-cm (7-inch) circle. Dust with more flour if it sticks.

Place the tortilla on the hot metal and within

seconds the surface will start to bubble. Turn after about 30 seconds, when the under surface will have brown blisters on it. Cook for another 30–45 seconds, remove and wrap loosely in a thick cloth to keep warm. Do not overcook or the tortilla will go crisp and brittle. Repeat with the rest of the dough balls.

You can reheat fresh tortillas wrapped in a slightly dampened cloth which, in turn, has been surrounded with foil, in an oven at 130°C (275°F, gas 1), or turn them briefly in a hot pan.

NACHOS WITH BLACK BEAN PURÉE AND CHEESE

In Mexico, bean purées are described as refried. In fact, refried beans are neither fried nor actually refried, but boiled and mashed to a purée with fat over a low heat. Traditionally this means lard, but here the beans are beaten with olive oil and goose or duck fat. Nachos are quartered corn tortillas deep-fried, then baked briefly with cheese and a little chilli. The bean purée is added by people as they like. A hot tomato salsa is optional but a nice addition.

serves 6

450 g (1 lb) black beans, soaked overnight
2 celery stalks, coarsely chopped
2 bay leaves
225 g (8 oz) onions, diced
125 ml (4 fl oz) extra-virgin olive oil
4 garlic cloves, finely chopped
1 hot red chilli, shredded
salt and pepper
juice of 1 lemon
2 tbsp finely chopped flat-leaf parsley
about 2 tbsp duck or goose fat
4 spring onions, shredded
guacamole, to serve

FOR THE NACHOS:
corn oil, for deep-frying
9 Corn Tortillas (page 186)
115 g (4 oz) Cheddar cheese
2 green chillies, shredded
handful of coriander leaves, chopped

The day before: put the beans to soak in cold water overnight.

Next day: bring the beans to the boil and boil hard for 10 minutes. Drain, return to the pan and cover by 2.5 cm (1 inch) with fresh water. Bring back to the boil. Add the celery and bay leaves, lower the heat and simmer until done, about 1 hour. Discard the celery and bay leaves. Drain and reserve.

Preheat the oven to 200°C (400°F, gas 6). Preheat oil for deep-frying the nachos to 190°C (375°F).

Sweat the onions in 2 tablespoons of the olive oil in a pan, until soft and translucent. Stir in the garlic with the diced chilli. Cook stirring for 2 minutes, then add the beans. Season with salt and pepper and mash thoroughly with a potato masher. Return to the heat, add the lemon juice and finely chopped parsley and mash in the goose or duck fat. The purée should be stiff enough to scoop, but quite moist. Mash in more fat if you think the mixture is too dry. Taste, adjust the seasoning and keep warm.

Make the nachos: cut the tortillas into quarters and deep-fry until crisp, about 3 minutes. Drain on kitchen paper and reserve.

Grate the Cheddar and mix with the shredded green chilli. Put a spoonful on each tortilla quarter and lay them on baking trays. Put in the oven, removing as soon as the cheese melts.

Arrange on a large serving dish, scatter over the finely chopped coriander. Mound the remaining bean purée in a large warmed bowl and zig-zag the remaining olive oil on top. Finish by scattering the shredded spring onion over. Put a bowl of corn chips and a bowl of guacamole on the table.

POACHED PRAWN AND RED BEAN SALAD

This is to be made when really small fresh ears of corn are available. Barbecue them over a moderate heat or cook them on a ridged grill plate for 8–10 minutes, turning frequently.

A lot of effort goes into making the court-bouillon, but this pays big dividends in terms of the way the prawns taste. The liquid is too salty to use for anything else, but may be strained and frozen to use again for poaching any shellfish. If using defrosted prawns, don't refreeze.

serves 4
1 kg (2¼ lb) tiger prawns
30 g (1 oz) coriander leaves
30 g (1 oz) flat-leaf parsley
2 bay leaves
300 ml (½ pint) dry white wine
4 tbsp white wine vinegar
salt
1 tbsp coriander seeds
1 tsp black peppercorns
1 tsp dried chilli flakes
2 lemons
Corn Tortillas (page 186), to serve

FOR THE RED BEAN SALAD:
1 tsp cumin seeds
1 tsp coriander seeds
350 g (12 oz) red kidney beans, soaked overnight
1 tsp ground cinnamon
2 bay leaves
juice of 1 lime
4 tbsp extra-virgin olive oil, plus more for dressing
4 ripe plum tomatoes, blanched and peeled
2 fresh corn ears, husked
2 hot red chillies, blackened on the grill and shredded
115 g (4 oz) red onion, cut into chunks
1 sweet red pepper, roasted and peeled, then chopped

Prepare the beans for the salad: toast the cumin and coriander seeds in a dry frying pan until aromatic, then grind to a powder. Bring the beans to the boil and boil hard for 10 minutes. Drain and return to a clean pan. Cover with water by 2.5 cm (1 inch) and bring back to the boil. Add the ground spices, cinnamon and bay leaves, then lower the heat to a gentle bubble. Cook for 1 hour or until the beans are tender. Salt the water for the last 10 minutes of cooking only. Drain, discarding the cinnamon and bay leaves. Put the beans in a mixing bowl and toss to coat with the lime juice and olive oil. Reserve.

Prepare the tomatoes for the salad: quarter the tomatoes, stripping out the pulp. Put the pulp in a large saucepan.

Remove the heads and shells from the prawns and put them in the saucepan. Butterfly the prawns, removing the intestinal threads. Refrigerate.

Remove the leaves from the coriander and parsley and reserve. Put the stalks of both in the pan. Add the bay leaves, white wine and vinegar with 1.1 litres (2 pints) of water. Bring to the boil and bubble briskly for 20 minutes.

Pass through a colander into another pan. Add 4 tablespoons of salt, the coriander seeds, peppercorns and chilli flakes. Add the juice of the lemons and their skins. Bring to the boil, lower the heat and simmer for 30 minutes.

Have ready a bowl of well-salted iced water. Turn up the heat under the court-bouillon and, as the water bubbles, add the prawns. Immediately turn off the heat and stir. Leave for 3 minutes then drain, putting the prawns in the iced water. Leave for 1 minute, then drain and reserve.

Finish the salad: grill the corn for 8–10 minutes. It will be marked by the grill. As soon as it is cool enough to handle, cut the kernels from the husk and stir them into the beans.

Stir in the chillies and onion chunks. Taste, seasoning with plenty of coarsely milled pepper and a little more salt if needed. Stir in the whole leaves of coriander and parsley. Refrigerate for 2–3 hours to allow the flavours to develop.

To serve, spoon the salad on plates, putting 4 pieces of tomato on each. Arrange the prawns on top. Zig-zag a little more extra-virgin olive oil on top and serve with a basket of warm corn tortillas.

RED SNAPPER AL MOJO DE AJO

If you sweat it rather than fry it, garlic can be slow-cooked in a pan to give a sweet and nutty flavour. Too much heat and it burns and goes bitter. In this classic Mexican pan sauce, the number of cloves sounds as if it will overpower the snapper, but it doesn't.

serves 4

60 g (2 oz) unsalted butter
4 tbsp olive oil
10 large garlic cloves, cut into paper-thin slices
4 red snapper fillets, each 175–200 g (6–7 oz), skin on
1 tsp dried chilli flakes
salt and pepper
flour, for dusting
juice of 1 lemon
1 tbsp finely chopped coriander
plain rice or Wheatflour Tortillas (page 186), to serve

Put the butter and olive oil in a large heavy-based frying pan and place over the lowest heat. Sweat the garlic in this for 8–10 minutes, stopping as soon as it starts to colour. Pour through a sieve into a bowl and leave to drain.

With a razor-sharp knife, cut a cross-hatch into the snapper skin. Rub the chilli flakes into the cuts, then dredge in seasoned flour.

Turn up the heat under the frying pan to moderate, pour the oil and butter back into the pan and fry the fish, skin side down, for 2 minutes. Turn carefully, lower the heat a little and cook for a further 2–3 minutes. Transfer to warmed plates, skin side up.

Return the garlic to the pan, add the lemon juice and the finely chopped coriander. Stir, bubble briefly and spoon over and round the fish.

Serve with plain rice for a main course or on its own with a basket of wheatflour tortillas as a first course.

SPICED CHICKEN WITH CHICKPEA FRITTERS AND SALSA CRUDA

Chickpea flour is to be found most easily in Asian grocers, where it is called besan. Cooked with water to a thick paste, it is spiked with chilli and flavoured with herbs, before being left to cool and set. It is then pan-fried as one would a piece of set polenta, or can be deep-fried as chips. You can make this base with cornmeal if you prefer, spicing and flavouring it in the same way. You can substitute beef for chicken here. Rib-eye, with its tracery of fat, is a good cut for stir-frying.

serves 4

3 tsp cumin seeds
¼ tsp black peppercorns
1 sweet yellow pepper
1 hot fresh green chilli
4 chicken breasts, skinned
3 tbsp olive oil
115 g (4 oz) onions, diced
2 tbsp Tequila
2 garlic cloves, chopped
115 ml (¼ pint) crème fraîche
bunch of chives
Salsa Cruda (page 197), to serve

FOR THE CHICKPEA FRITTERS:
salt and pepper
1 tbsp olive oil, plus more for greasing
250 g (9 oz) chickpea flour
30 g (1 oz) Parmesan cheese, grated
30 g (1 oz) finely chopped coriander
1 tsp dried chilli flakes
1 egg, beaten
corn oil, for frying

First make the chickpea fritters: bring 1 litre (1¾ pints) lightly salted water to boil. Add the olive oil, flour, cheese, coriander, chilli flakes and ½ teaspoon of coarsely ground black pepper. Stir vigorously with a wooden spoon and, when smooth, lower the heat and simmer for about 20 minutes, stirring slowly but, I'm afraid, continuously. Like real polenta it quickly sticks tenaciously and burns, particularly round the edges. Remove from the heat and beat in the egg.

Brush a shallow flat dish or Swiss roll tin with olive oil and pour and scrape the paste out into it, smoothing it flat with a spatula. Leave to cool.

Toast the cumin seeds and peppercorns in a pan over a low heat until they give off a strong aroma. Grind to a powder and reserve.

Deseed the pepper and the chilli, cut the pepper into strips and shred the chilli. Cut the chicken into strips.

Put 2 tablespoons of the oil in a large frying pan and fry the pepper strips, chilli and onion until soft. Add the garlic and cook for 1 minute. Remove everything to a tray or bowl and reserve.

Add the remaining olive oil to the pan. Turn up the heat to moderate and sauté the chicken for 2–3 minutes. Add the cumin and pepper mix and salt, and toss to coat, stirring for a minute. Add the Tequila and flame carefully, shaking the pan.

When the flames go out, add the crème fraîche, stirring and shaking to mix everything together. Turn down the heat to its lowest setting and keep warm.

In a second frying pan over a low-to-medium heat, put corn oil to a depth of 1 cm (½ inch). With a pastry cutter, cut out 4 rounds from the chickpea paste. Fry it in the oil for 3 minutes on each side, when it will be golden-brown and crisp. Remove to paper towels and drain.

Put a chickpea croûte on each warmed plate and divide the chicken between them, mounding it on top of the croûtes and spooning the sauce around them. Scatter on chopped chives and serve immediately.

PORK AND POZOLE STEW

Pozole is dried field corn kernels. After soaking in water, it is slowly simmered and acquires a unique texture as the kernels burst and release their starch.

Even after lengthy cooking, it remains a little chewy. *Pozole* can be cooked without meat as part of a vegetable stew or as a side dish to be served instead of beans. You can produce *pozole* by leaving husked sweetcorn cobs in a warm place to dry for a couple of weeks. After cutting from the cobs, the kernels will not need a preliminary soaking.

serves 6

175 g (6 oz) dried pozole
1 kg (2¼ lb) pork shoulder
115 g (4 oz) coriander leaves, with stems and roots
1 cinnamon stick
1 bay leaf
3 dried hot red chillies
4 garlic cloves
500 ml (18 fl oz) dark beer
2 tsp dried oregano
175 g (6 oz) onions, diced
2 tbsp corn oil
4 mild fresh green chillies
225 g (8 oz) courgettes, cut into chunks
250 g (8½ oz) hard white cabbage, shredded, to serve

FOR THE SALSA:

2 garlic cloves, chopped
1 habanero chilli
4 spring onions, sliced
2 avocados
salt and pepper
5 limes
3 tbsp olive oil

The day before: rinse the *pozole* and soak overnight in water in a saucepan.

Next day: cut the pork into bite-sized chunks. Tie the coriander stalks and roots with the cinnamon, bay leaf and dried chillies as a bouquet garni. Cut the garlic cloves into paper-thin slices.

Bring the pan of soaking *pozole* to the boil, drain and return to the pan with the pork. Add the beer and 1.5 litres (2¾ pints) of water. Add the bouquet garni and oregano, bring to the boil, reduce the heat and simmer.

In another pan, sweat the onions in the oil until soft, then stir in the garlic and cook gently for 2 minutes. Stir this into the stew, return to a simmer and cover with a lid.

Grill the fresh green chillies, turning frequently, until they are blackened and blistered all over. Remove them to a zip-lock bag and leave to steam for 10 minutes. Peel and shred.

Make the salsa: coarsely chop the coriander leaves and put in a bowl with the garlic, habanero, spring onions and 1 of the avocados, peeled, stoned and cut into dice. Season with salt and pepper, add the juice of 1 lime and toss with a little olive oil.

When the *pozole* kernels begin to burst, season with salt and pepper to taste. The stew is ready when the corn is no longer tough and chewy, but still has some residual bite, and most of the kernels have burst. Add the courgettes and cook for a few minutes more, until just done. Taste, and adjust seasoning.

Peel and stone the second avocado, cut it into slices and put the slices in a bowl with a squeeze of lime juice. Cut the remaining limes into quarters and put these on a plate. Put the salsa and shredded cabbage in separate bowls for people to help themselves.

BLACK BEAN PURÉE WITH PORK ALBONDIGAS

With the addition of more liquid, the purée becomes a soup. The texture you want is that of a creamy mashed potato. *Quesa fresca* is a mild-tasting, slightly sour fresh cheese; feta is a good substitute.

serves 6

350 g (12 oz) black beans, soaked overnight
400 g (1 lb) canned plum tomatoes
300 ml (½ pint) chicken stock
150 ml (¼ pint) sour white wine
2 tbsp sherry vinegar
2 habanero chillies, shredded
2 celery stalks, plus their leaves
2 bay leaves
salt and pepper
225 g (8 oz) onion
5 tbsp extra-virgin olive oil
2 garlic cloves
115 g (4 oz) quesa fresca or feta cheese
30 g (1 oz) unsalted butter
warm Wheatflour Tortillas (page 186), to serve

FOR THE ALBONDIGAS:
2 tsp cumin seeds
1 teaspoon dried chilli flakes
450 g (1 lb) minced pork
1 slice of white bread, crusts removed
3–4 tbsp dry white wine
1 tbsp finely chopped chives
1 tbsp finely chopped coriander
1 garlic clove, finely chopped
white of 1 egg
flour, for dusting
4 tbsp corn oil

Bring the beans to the boil and boil hard for 10 minutes. Drain and rinse under cold running water. Return the beans to the pan.

Purée the tomatoes in a processor with their liquid and add to the pan with the chicken stock, wine and vinegar, topping up with cold water if necessary to cover the beans completely. Add the chillies, celery stalks, bay leaves and 1 teaspoon of coarsely ground black pepper. Bring to the boil, lower the heat and simmer for 1 hour or until the beans are done. Add salt only towards the end of cooking or the beans' skins will toughen. Discard the celery and bay leaves.

Dice the onion and sweat in the olive oil until soft and translucent. Finely chop the garlic and stir that in. Increase the heat and fry, stirring continuously, for a minute or 2. Transfer to a food processor.

Drain the beans, reserving the cooking liquid. Transfer the beans to the processor with the cheese and blitz, adding the reserved liquid gradually through the feeder tube until you have a smooth, spoonable purée. Return this to a saucepan over a low heat and whisk in the butter.

Make the *albondigas*: toast the cumin seeds and chilli flakes in a dry pan over a low heat for 2–3 minutes, stirring. Grind to a powder in a coffee grinder and put in a mixing bowl with the minced pork. Soak the bread in wine, squeeze dry and add to the bowl together with the chopped herbs and garlic. Add the egg white and mix with a fork to a coherent mass. Season with salt and pepper and mash through thoroughly to distribute evenly. Make a small patty and fry it in a hot pan and eat it to judge the seasoning, adjusting as you like.

On a floured surface, roll the mixture into balls about the size of walnuts, put these on a lightly floured tray or plate and reserve.

Film the base of a large frying pan with the corn oil and put over a medium heat. As it shimmers, add the *albondigas* and fry for 6–8 minutes, turning frequently, until golden brown all over and cooked all the way through.

Spoon the purée into large warmed bowls, arrange the *albondigas* on top and scatter over some coarsely chopped celery leaves. Serve with a basket of warm wheat tortillas.

A tart green tomatillo salsa makes a refreshing side dish. Make as for the salsa cruda on page 196, substituting tomatillos for tomatoes.

CHILES RELLENOS

Chiles rellenos – stuffed deep-fried chillies – is an authentic Mexican dish, though their popularity in New Mexico and Texas has led people to think that they are another of the hybrid forms dubbed TexMex. A more typical TexMex dish would be *chile con carne*, something made in the USA from beef with complex seasoning but based on the original simple Mexican stew of pork and chillies from which it takes its name.

The right chillies to use are the green poblano or the Californian Anaheim, both large enough to stuff and mild enough not to cause consternation and hand-flapping in front of the mouth on the part of those not used to spicy food. They may be stuffed either with cheese or with picadillo – spiced pork – though you could also make the meat sauce with beef. A bean purée spiked with plenty of chilli could also be substituted. To make cheese *chiles rellenos*, proceed in the same way but use a strong Cheddar cut into fat matchsticks which will just fit into the chillies.

A Mexican dark beer such as Dos Equis is suggested, but any well-flavoured lager will do.

serves 4
8 large mild chillies
3 eggs
about 115 g (4 oz) cornmeal (polenta)
oil for deep-frying

FOR THE PICADILLO:
1 tbsp ground cumin seeds
500 g (1 lb 2 oz) lean boneless pork
2 tbsp corn oil or 60 g (2 oz) lard
175 g (6 oz) onion, finely diced
2 garlic cloves, chopped
500 g (1 lb 2 oz) canned chopped tomatoes
300 ml (½ pint) Mexican dark beer
1 tsp salt
1 tbsp slivered almonds
1 tbsp raisins

FOR THE SAUCE:
500 g (1 lb 2 oz) canned chopped tomatoes
115 g (4 oz) onions, finely chopped
1 garlic clove, finely chopped
2 tbsp olive oil
1 tsp oregano
salt and pepper
½ tsp sugar

Prepare the picadillo stuffing: toast the cumin seeds in a dry pan over a low heat for 2–3 minutes, grind to a powder and reserve.

Cut the pork into pieces the size of the nail on your little finger. It is a characteristic of Mexican meat sauces that they are rarely minced. Fry the pieces in the corn oil or lard until browned, then add the onion and continue to cook, stirring, until the onions soften.

Add the garlic and cumin, and fry for a minute, stirring, then add the chopped tomatoes with their juice, the beer and 1 teaspoon of salt. Bring to the boil, lower the heat and simmer, stirring from time to time, for 1 hour.

Add the slivered almonds and raisins and cook for a further 10 minutes, when almost all the liquid should have evaporated. Leave to cool.

While the picadillo is cooking, make a simple tomato sauce by bubbling down the chopped tomatoes with their liquid, the onion, garlic, olive oil, oregano, ½ teaspoon each of salt, pepper and sugar. When well reduced, blitz to a purée in a processor, return to the pan and reserve.

Spear the chillies with a skewer and turn them over am open flame until the skin blisters and chars. If you only have electricity, char them under a very hot grill, turning frequently. Transfer to a zip-lock bag or plastic container with a lid and leave to steam for 10 minutes before peeling them. Do not remove the stems.

Make an incision down one side of each chilli to within 5 mm (1/4 inch) of each end, being careful only to cut through one side. Strip out the seeds and discard. Fill the chillies with the picadillo sauce but no liquid.

Separate the eggs. Season the yolks and beat to a froth in one bowl; whisk the whites with a little salt to soft peaks in another. Fold these into the yolks.

Put half the cornmeal in a wide shallow dish. Holding the chillies by their stems, dip in the egg, then roll in the cornmeal to coat.

Heat oil for deep-frying to 190°C (375°F). Deep-fry the stuffed chillies for about 4 minutes, when the coating will be crisp and golden-brown. Drain on kitchen paper and serve at once with a spoonful of the tomato sauce on the side.

ACHIOTE PORK CHOPS WITH RECADO ROJO AND SALSA CRUDA

Achiote seeds, also called anatto, colour foods brick-red and are used to make seasoning pastes called *recado*. Different chillies have distinctly different flavours and habanero, as well as being the hottest Mexican chilli, has a fruit taste and smell that is quite lemony. Not as fruity as a scotch bonnet perhaps, but a good chilli to use for its taste as well as for its fire.

When trying a chilli to assess how hot it is, touch your tongue to a tiny piece. This is the only way you can judge. Capsaicin, the fiery part of the chilli's chemical makeup, is held in highest concentrations in the placenta – the white fibre in which the seeds are embedded. Including this therefore gives a hotter result. The seeds themselves are not really hot by comparison, so include them or leave them out, it will not make any but a cosmetic difference.

serves 6

6 pork chump chops from the hind loin
30 g (1 oz) lard
steamed rice, to serve
Wheatflour Tortillas (page 186), to serve

FOR THE RECADO ROJO:

2 garlic cloves
1/4 tsp salt
2 tsp achiote seeds
1/2 tsp dried oregano
2 cloves
2-cm (3/4-inch) piece of cinnamon
1/2 tsp coriander seeds
1/2 tsp coarsely ground pepper
1 tbsp olive oil
1 tbsp red wine vinegar

FOR THE SALSA CRUDA:

4 habanero chilli
1/2 tbsp corn oil
6 ripe plum tomatoes, blanched and peeled
3 1/2 tbsp orange juice
1 tbsp red wine vinegar
1/2 tsp salt
115 g (4 oz) red onion, diced
4 mint leaves

A day ahead, make the *recado rojo*: smash the garlic and chop to a paste with the salt. Put into a mixing bowl. Put the remaining solid flavouring ingredients in a grinder and grind to a powder. Add to the garlic and mix to a paste with the oil and vinegar. Transfer to a clean jar and refrigerate for 24 hours.

Next day, make the salsa: heat a heavy-based frying pan until smoking-hot. Brush the chillies with the oil and toss them in the pan until they blister. Remove to a zip-lock bag and leave to steam for 10 minutes, then peel and put in a food processor with all the other ingredients except the onion and mint. Blitz to a smooth purée and push through a sieve. Leave to stand for 1 hour before eating but use within 4 hours, as it loses its freshness and becomes watery if left too long.

Slash the fat of the chops round the edges at intervals. Rub the *recado* into both sides of the chops. Leave to marinate for 1–2 hours.

Heat a heavy-based frying pan over a low-to-medium heat. When hot, add the lard. When it shimmers, lay the chops in the pan. Fry slowly, turning after 8 minutes. Cook until done around the bone, a total of 15–16 minutes. Remove to warmed plates.

Finish the salsa by shredding the mint and stir it into the salsa with the diced onion. Spoon some next to the chops and put the rest in a bowl for people to help themselves. Serve with steamed rice and a basket of warm wheatflour tortillas.

SPICED BEEF AND BEET SALAD

The beef is cooked rare and left to cool before being sliced and added to the salad. With the red beets and onion, this makes a pretty salad, but add the grapefruit right at the end or it will be stained by the beet juices.

serves 4

1 tsp coriander seeds
½ tsp cumin seeds
½ tsp black peppercorns
1 clove
1 tbsp olive oil
2 rib-eye steaks, each about 225 g (8 oz)
½ tsp salt
500 g (1 lb 2 oz) small beetroot, boiled and peeled
4 spring onions
115 g (4 oz) red onion
1 habanero or scotch bonnet, shredded
2 pink grapefruit
handful of coriander
warm Wheatflour Tortillas (page 186), to serve

FOR THE DRESSING:
1 tbsp lime juice
1 tbsp orange juice
1 tsp runny honey
4 tbsp extra-virgin olive oil
salt and pepper

Toast the coriander and cumin seeds, the peppercorns and the clove in a small pan over a low heat for 2–3 minutes. Grind to a coarse powder. Mix this to a paste with the olive oil and rub it into both sides of the steaks. Leave to marinate at room temperature for 2 hours.

Put a ridged grill pan over a high heat until smoking-hot. Wipe excess spice paste off the steaks, season with salt and grill for 3 minutes on each side. Remove to a board and leave to cool to room temperature.

Cut the beetroot into 2-cm (¾-inch) cubes. Cut the spring onions at an angle into 2-cm (¾-inch) pieces. Cut the red onion into 2-cm (¾-inch) chunks. Put them in a salad bowl with the finely shredded chilli.

Put the dressing ingredients in a jar and shake vigorously to combine.

Cut the beef into strips and add to the salad. Pour over the dressing and toss. Peel the grapefruit and cut into segments, discarding any pips. Arrange on top.

Coarsely chop the coriander and scatter on top before serving with a basket of warm wheatflour tortillas.

Chapter 12
North Africa & the Middle East

Just the best barbecue ever

The smell of lamb grilling over charcoal is an instant call to the table. It is one of the most appetizing smells of the summer barbecue and will transport you immediately in your mind to a Greek taverna or a myriad other destinations throughout North Africa and the Middle East. I have eaten great food in Morocco and Tunisia but, surprisingly, one of the most memorable dishes of barbecued lamb I ever ate was in Saudi Arabia – in the equivalent of a transport café.

Returning hungry from an afternoon scuba-diving over a Red Sea coral reef to go back to work – afternoons were free-time, because of the heat, so offices reopen in a rather ghastly fashion after early-evening prayers – my host, from the esteemed company Zagzoog and Matbouli, and known privately to me as Zigzag and Ratballs, suddenly slammed on the brakes of the Cadillac and swung violently off the Mecca–Medina road, ploughing to a halt outside a scruffy and windowless building. The driving in that part of the world 20 years ago was insane and dangerous, and any trip in a car was straight terror from start to finish. I looked round to see what we had hit. 'This you like,' Samir said, grinning and pointing towards the building which, on closer inspection, looked like a public lavatory. Saudi cottaging? I wondered. How to explain that this was not my inclination. 'Barbecue, yes. You like barbecue? Come on.' Samir waddled rapidly ahead, his love handles see-sawing visibly through his voluminous, dazzling-white *tob*. I followed with marked reluctance. The food so far had been indescribably vile and this looked less than salubrious.

Inside, the lavatory turned out to be pretty much hollow, the exterior walls concealing little more than a courtyard with awnings. The place was filthy, but good smells were coming from the kitchen area, where smoke seeped out in a grey haze from a long serving hatch set in another wall. Samir did some aggressive shouting and we were immediately seated on a greasy rug on the floor, other customers being bundled unceremoniously out of the way to make space for these obvious VIPs. 'You eat chicken. You eat lamb. You eat rice.' The last time this had been said to me was at a seven sheep engagement party, the number of whole sheep served determining how impressively the father of the bride had pushed the boat out, and the experience had been less than enchanting. This was gloriously different and we ate gluttonously and with our hands, just the best barbecue ever.

The lamb was served in three ways. The first cut in large hunks and speared on big metal skewers. Though streaked almost black on the outside, it was sweet and tender within, just a faint pink round the metal and tasting of lemon and cumin. It had probably been marinated in yoghurt, because it was very tender. Then there were slices carved off a whole leg, cooked well-done and, I would guess, marinated with lemon juice, rosemary and lots of pepper, or a little chilli. The third was lamb steaks with a more aromatic spicing. We tried them all. The chickens were served whole on big battered tin trays, crisp of skin and juicy. They had been seasoned with nothing but salt and pepper and were a little chewy, but their flavour was superb.

The rice was a triumph, yellow and fragrant with turmeric, and sweet with plump raisins and slivered almonds. There were big, puffy flat breads, very white with charred blistering on the surface. It was the best meal I ate in four long teetotal, abstinent weeks, maybe one of the best meals I ever ate. It cried out a bit for a glass of wine, and would have benefited from a girl to discuss its pros and cons with afterwards, but that was – in that country – quite out of the question. I lay back, no longer bothered by the greasy rug and wiping my mouth with the back of my hand. 'Good, yes, good?' I nodded. 'Bloody good, thank you.' And, as one does when unable to communicate one's full appreciation in Arabic, gave him a big thumbs-up.

As steamed rice is central to the cooking of Southeast Asia and the Far East, so pilaff is the most frequently served rice dish of the Middle East. It has executional similarities to risotto, since the rice is first fried with onion and spices to flavour it, before being cooked in water or stock. The rice, though, is long-grain and the finish is usually less rich than a buttery risotto. It can have butter beaten into it before serving and is often coloured with saffron or turmeric. The inclusion of raisins and nuts is also typical.

ON THE GRILL – BOUCAIN, BARBACOA, BARBECUE

How hot a charcoal fire should be to grill different foods can only be judged with experience. You stick your hand over the fire, palm downwards, and after doing it a few times you learn to relate what you feel to grill performance. This, in turn, leads to consistent results, though however skilled you become there will always be the weather to mess you about and make life difficult. A strong wind will make coals burn faster and hotter, while the temperature also affects the barbecue's performance. The weather may not be an issue in Perth, Australia, but it is in Perth, Scotland.

There are things you should do every time you light a charcoal barbecue, wood fires being a separate issue. Throw away the ashes, then clean the grill with a wire brush. Buy the best quality charcoal you can because value can only be judged by performance. Cheap charcoal is usually a false economy, since it does not burn as hot and, having achieved its maximum temperature, does not sustain it for as long. A heavy bag is not a good sign and suggests the inclusion of a filler like sand. The best charcoal is the lightest.

When building the fire, make a double layer of charcoal extending beyond the cooking area by 7.5 cm (3½ inches). This gives you the right amount of fuel. Build the pieces into a rough cone before lighting them. As they burn, they collapse, spreading out to the right area relative to the grill space. The barbecue should be ready to cook about 30–45 minutes after being lit. The precise time will depend on how good the charcoal is and what the weather is like. When ready, during daylight the charcoal will be grey with a powdery appearance while at night it gives off a red glow. At this point, hold your hand about 7.5 cm (3½ inches) above the grill rack. If you have to snatch it away at once, it is almost certainly too hot for doing anything but searing meat or fish steaks to be cooked rare. It is too hot for chicken, lamb or whole fish, because the food will burn on the surface before the inside is done. When you can leave your hand above the heat for 4–5 seconds, then you have achieved the temperature described in the recipes as 'medium-hot'.

YOGHURT MARINATED SKEWERED LEG OF LAMB

Yoghurt marinades are widely used throughout North Africa and the Middle East for their tenderizing effect. Boning a leg is tricky, so have your butcher do it. You want him to give you a roughly rectangular piece of meat about 5–7.5 cm (2–3 inches) thick, a good shape for cooking on the grill in one piece, or to cut up and skewer.

serves 6
1.8 kg (4 lb) boned leg of lamb
juice of 4 lemons
salt and coarsely ground pepper
3 tsp cumin seeds
1 tsp coriander seeds
1 tsp black peppercorns
2 cloves
7.5-cm (3-inch) piece of cinnamon stick
600 ml (1 pint) thick yoghurt
18 fresh bay leaves

The day before: cut the boned leg into 3 strips and then cut these across to make 12 long strips in total. Lay them in a dish into which they will just fit in a single layer. Pour over the lemon juice and scatter over 1 teaspoon of salt. Cover and refrigerate for 24 hours.

Toast the spices in a small pan over a low heat for

2–3 minutes. Grind to a powder and put in a mixing bowl, then whisk in the yoghurt. Remove the meat from the dish and put in the bowl with the yoghurt and turn and rub it between your fingers. Push the meat chunks down so they are covered and cling-wrap the top. Return to the fridge for a further 24 hours.

Next day, remove the meat from the fridge at least 2 hours before you want to cook. Light the barbecue an hour before you cook to obtain maximum heat.

Brush the marinade off the meat and thread the strips lengthwise on 6 skewers, with a fresh bay leaf between each piece and at either end. Season with salt and coarsely ground pepper, and lay on the grill, salt side downwards, about 15 cm (6 inches) above the coals. Leave to cook untouched for 7–8 minutes. Season the upper surface before turning and cooking for 7 minutes. Remove and leave to rest in a warm place for 10 minutes before serving.

WHOLE BARBECUED LEG OF LAMB

serves 6

1.8 kg (4 lb) leg of lamb
about 5 tbsp olive oil
salt and pepper
juice of 3 lemons
6 garlic cloves, peeled
2 tsp dried chilli flakes
big sprig of rosemary

Preheat the barbecue to very hot.

Brush the lamb all over with some of the olive oil and season generously with salt and pepper. On the very hot barbecue, sear it quickly on all sides, then remove and put on a big double layer of foil. Squeeze the lemon juice on it. Smash the garlic with the flat of a heavy knife and rub into the meat, then dribble on 3–4 tablespoons of olive oil. Sprinkle over the dried chilli flakes and the rosemary leaves. Wrap loosely in the foil, crimping it closed. It must not be too tightly wrapped or hot air cannot circulate around the meat.

Move the grill to 20 cm (8 inches) away from the fire and put the package on it. Cook, turning from time to time. Add more charcoal after 1 hour and again after the second hour, cooking for a total of 3 hours. The lamb should now be cooked all the way through. Remove from the grill and leave to rest for 15 minutes before unwrapping and carving.

BARBECUED SPICED LAMB STEAKS

serves 6

6 lamb leg steaks, each about 250 g (9 oz)
2 garlic cloves
salt and pepper
5 tbsp olive oil
3 tbsp red wine vinegar
1 tsp cumin seeds
1 tsp coriander seeds
2 cloves
1 tsp dried chilli flakes
Naan Bread (page 307), to serve
3 lemons, halved lengthwise, to serve

Put the steaks in a shallow dish. Smash the garlic then chop to a paste with a little salt, and rub into both sides of the steaks. Grind over plenty of coarsely milled pepper and lay them in a dish into which they will just fit in a single layer. Spoon over the oil and vinegar. Leave to marinate for 4 hours at room temperature.

Preheat the grill to medium-hot. Toast the spices for 2–3 minutes in a dry pan over a low heat until aromatic, then grind to a powder.

Wipe most of the marinade from the lamb and roll in this spice powder. Lay on the grill and give the steaks 5 minutes on each side. Remove to a plate and allow to rest for 5 minutes.

Serve with naan bread and lemon halves on each plate.

LAMB AND QUINCE TAGINE

Quince is rarely eaten in savoury dishes, though it goes well in spicy meat stews like this where it needs no sugar to sweeten it, yet still delivers an intriguing and slightly perfumed flavour. Tagines take their name from the terracotta pots in which they are cooked; shallow and thick, and glazed only on the inside, they have conical lids like Pierrots' hats. Casseroles may not be as appealing to present at the table, but they cook tagines just as well. The wine is a bit iffy on the authenticity front, so think of this as a *Pied-noir* dish, but none of which is fried.

serves 4
900 g (2 lb) lamb neck fillet
300 ml (½ pint) dry white wine
2 tsp ground turmeric
1½ tsp cumin seeds
1 tsp coriander seeds
1 tsp dried chilli flakes
½ tsp fenugreek
1 cinnamon stick
juice and zest of 1 orange
300 ml (½ pint) chicken stock
225 g (8 oz) onions, thinly sliced
1 garlic clove, cut into paper-thin slices
salt and pepper
2 large quince, about 675 g (1½ lb)

to serve:
steamed long-grain rice
slivered pistachios
caramelized onions

Cut the lamb into large chunks, put in a bowl and pour over the wine. Marinate overnight in the fridge.

Next day, transfer the lamb and marinade to a tagine or casserole.

Toast all the spices except the cinnamon in a dry pan for 2–3 minutes, then grind to a powder. Add to the tagine with all the other ingredients except the quince. Stir to mix thoroughly and bring to the boil. Lower the heat and simmer for 45 minutes.

Peel the quince, quarter them and cut out and discard the hard core and seeds. Stir the quince quarters into the tagine and cook for another 45 minutes. Taste and adjust the seasoning. Discard the cinnamon.

Serve with steamed long-grain rice which has had slivered pistachios and caramelized onions stirred into it.

SPICED LAMB STEW WITH RHUBARB

Rhubarb is one of those oddities, a sour leafy vegetable the stems of which are eaten sugared in puddings. It has always been thought to be good for you as a natural laxative, although an effective purgative is scarcely the sales-line for a rehabilitation campaign, but it was one of its most admired attributes in ancient Greece, then in the Roman Empire and latterly throughout Northern Europe.

Stewed rhubarb was often served as the healthy part of a great British breakfast, until people felt they could live happily without its laxative contribution and took more generally to cereals in the 1950s, the higher-fibre varieties enjoying similar benign digestive properties in the public imagination.

Only the young pink stalks of rhubarb should be eaten, older and thicker bright red stalks being excessively stringy and very acidic even when treated with lots of sugar.

In this dish, where the rhubarb is added only towards the end of cooking, it strikes an intriguing, slightly sour note, which nobody will recognize as rhubarb. Well, somebody might, but hopefully in the nicest possible way.

serves 4
2 tsp cumin seeds
½ tsp black peppercorns
900 g (2 lb) lamb neck fillet
4 tbsp groundnut oil
350 g (12 oz) onions, thinly sliced
2 garlic cloves
1 tsp ground turmeric
salt
2 hot red chillies, finely chopped
4 tbsp white wine vinegar
1.75 litres (3 pints) chicken stock
1 bay leaf
8 mint leaves
400 g (14 oz) young rhubarb
30 g (1 oz) butter
150 ml (¼ pint) thick yoghurt
3 tbsp finely chopped flat-leaf parsley, plus more whole leaves for garnish
plain boiled long-grain rice, to serve

Toast the cumin seeds and peppercorns in a dry pan over a low heat until aromatic. Grind to a powder and reserve.

Cut the lamb fillet into 4 equal pieces and brown in a little very hot oil. Remove to a pan or casserole.

Fry the onions in the oil that remains in the pan, adding a little more if needed, lowering the heat and sweating until soft and translucent. Add the chopped garlic cloves, the ground cumin and pepper, the turmeric and ½–1 teaspoon of salt. Stir in and continue frying for 2 minutes, before adding the chilli, white wine vinegar, chicken stock and bay leaf. Bring to the boil, lower the heat and simmer for 1 hour.

Finely chop the mint leaves and stir in after 15 minutes. Cut the rhubarb into 2.5-cm (1-inch) pieces and add to the pot. Continue simmering for 15–20 minutes, when both the lamb and the rhubarb should be perfectly cooked. Remove all the solids with a slotted spoon and reserve.

Skim the remaining liquid, turn up the heat and reduce to about 700 ml (1¼ pints). Whisk in the butter, followed by the yoghurt and finely chopped parsley. Taste and add a little more salt and some pepper if necessary.

Return the other ingredients to the pan and warm through over the lowest heat. If the temperature is too high, the yoghurt will split. Serve with plain boiled long-grain rice and with whole leaves of flat-leaf parsley liberally scattered over.

NECK OF LAMB AND CHICKPEA T'FINA WITH SPICED MEATBALL

If this seems rather a lot of lamb, the ratio of bone to meat in scrag end is high. It is an inexpensive cut and delivers a really good broth during cooking. Ask your butcher to chop and saw it into pieces.

serves 6
350 g (12 oz) chickpeas, soaked overnight
225 g (8 oz) onions, diced
2 celery stalks, sliced
225 g (8 oz) carrots, peeled and diced
3 tbsp olive oil
1.8 kg (4 lb) scrag end neck of lamb, cut into pieces (see above)
1 cinnamon stick
1 head of garlic
2 bay leaves
3 tbsp red wine vinegar
1 tsp dried chilli flakes
2 tsp ground turmeric

1 tsp coriander seeds
½ tsp ground black pepper
handful of flat-leaf parsley, coarsely chopped, to serve

FOR THE MEATBALL:
½ tsp cumin seeds
2.5-cm (1-inch) piece of cinnamon
¼ tsp dried chilli flakes
¼ tsp black peppercorns
3 cloves
115 g (4 oz) white bread, crusts removed
350 g (12 oz) minced lamb
1 tbsp flat-leaf parsley, finely chopped
2 garlic cloves, chopped
2 eggs
¼ tsp salt

Make the meatball: toast the spices gently in a dry pan until aromatic, grind to a powder and reserve.

Moisten the bread with water and squeeze dry. Put this and all the other ingredients including the spices in a mixing bowl and work together with a fork. Form into a ball and tie in butter muslin. Reserve.

Bring the chickpeas to the boil and throw the water away.

Sweat the onions, celery and carrot in the oil in a large flameproof casserole until soft. Stir in the spices and fry for a minute, stirring. Turn off the heat.

In a frying pan, brown the lamb in the oil over a high heat, transferring it to the casserole as it is done. When the base is covered with a layer of meat, ladle over half of the chickpeas. Put in the cinnamon, the head of garlic and bay leaves, then the rest of the meat. Add the remaining chickpeas and the vinegar, then cover with cold water. Bring to the boil and skim. Stir in the spices and pepper, turn down the heat and simmer for 1 hour.

Add the meatball, pushing it down as far as you can. Cook for another hour, turning the meatball after 30 minutes. Taste and add salt as needed.

Remove the meatball and discard the cinnamon stick and bay leaves. Cut off the top of the garlic and squeeze and scrape out the soft garlic flesh, returning this to the casserole and stirring in.

Unwrap the meatball and cut in slices. Ladle the chickpeas and some of the broth into a large serving bowl, then arrange the lamb on top. Lay the slices of meatball around the sides and scatter lots of coarsely chopped flat-leaf parsley over all. Serve at the table in warmed bowls.

TURMERIC PILAF WITH RAISINS AND FLAKED ALMONDS

serves 6
175 g (6 oz) onions, thinly sliced
4 tbsp olive oil
350 g (12 oz) long-grain rice
½ tsp ground black pepper
¼ tsp ground allspice
700 ml (1¼ pints) chicken stock
1 cinnamon stick
2 tbsp raisins
6 whole cardamom pods
1 bay leaf
salt
60 g (2 oz) unsalted butter
30 g (1 oz) toasted flaked almonds

Sweat the onions in the oil over a low heat until soft and translucent.

Turn up the heat, add the rice and ground spices, and stir to mix and coat. Pour over the stock and add the cinnamon, raisins, cardamom, bay leaf and ½ teaspoon of salt. Bring to the boil, lower the heat to a simmer, cover with a lid and cook for 15–18 minutes,

until the stock is absorbed and the rice is fluffy and tender.

Before serving, discard the bay leaf and cinnamon, and stir in the butter. Scatter the flaked almonds on top. Pilaf is served hot or at room temperature.

DEEP-FRIED BEEF MEATBALLS WITH CHICKPEAS AND COURGETTES

This is really a fusion between France and Algeria, the so-called *Pied-noir* cuisine. The technique of egging and crumbing the meatballs and deep-frying them rather than shallow-frying adds a pleasing textural counterpoint that is absent from the traditional one-pot, oven-baked treatment.

serves 4

250 g (9 oz) chickpeas, soaked overnight
1 onion
4 cloves
2 bay leaves
300 g (10½ oz) canned chopped tomatoes
¼ tsp dried oregano
675 g (1½ lb) courgettes
2 tbsp olive oil
2 garlic cloves, thinly sliced

FOR THE MEATBALLS:
100 g (3½ oz) white bread, crusts removed
500 g (1 lb 2 oz) minced beef
1 garlic clove, finely chopped
1 tbsp chopped flat-leaf parsley, plus a few more whole leaves for garnish
¼ tsp ground allspice
¼ tsp ground cinnamon
¼ tsp dried chilli flakes
¼ tsp ground black pepper
salt
2 eggs, beaten
85 g (3 oz) fine dry breadcrumbs
oil for deep-frying

Bring the chickpeas to the boil, throw away the water and cover with fresh. Add the onion stuck with the cloves and the bay leaves. Return to the boil, lower the heat and simmer for 1½ hours or until done.

Take out the onion, discarding the cloves, and put it in a food processor with the tomatoes and their liquid and the oregano. Blitz to a purée and reserve.

Make the meatballs: moisten the bread with water and squeeze dry. Put in a bowl with all the other meatball ingredients except the eggs and breadcrumbs, and work together evenly with a fork. Divide into 4 and roll into balls. Roll in the beaten egg, then toss in crumbs to coat. Repeat to give a double thickness of coating and reserve.

Preheat oil for deep-frying to 190°C (375°F).

Cut the courgettes in quarters lengthwise. Put them in a saucepan with the olive oil and garlic over a moderate heat. Cover with a lid and cook for 2 minutes.

Pour over the tomato and onion purée. Drain the chickpeas, discard the bay leaves and stir in. Taste, adjusting the seasoning if necessary, and keep warm over the lowest heat.

Deep-fry the meatballs in batches for 4–5 minutes each. Remove and drain on paper towels.

Ladle the chickpea and courgette mixture into warmed bowls. Cut the meatballs in quarters and arrange on top. Garnish with a few parsley leaves before serving.

CHICKEN STEWED WITH BERBER RED SPICE PASTE

This is another *Pied-noir* dish, the red wine an instant give-away of the French influence. Aromatic and spice-hot, Berber red pepper paste is a good way to enliven soups, stews and fried dishes. It is a useful addition to the flavouring armoury, along with harissa – which it resembles – piri-piri and jerk seasoning.

serves 4

4 chicken leg joints
juice of 2½ lemons
60 g (2 oz) flour
5 tbsp groundnut or sunflower oil
350 g (12 oz) onions, thinly sliced
4 garlic cloves, finely chopped
1 teaspoon ground fenugreek
3 tbsp Berber red pepper paste (see below)
300 ml (½ pint) sour red wine
freshly grated nutmeg
5-cm (2-inch) piece of root ginger, peeled and cut into julienne strips
4 hard-boiled eggs, shelled
salt and pepper
couscous or boiled long-grain rice, to serve
finely chopped parsley, to finish
cooked chickpeas, to serve

FOR THE BERBER RED PEPPER PASTE **(makes 285g / 10 oz):**

1 tsp cardamom seeds
1 tsp allspice berries
¼ nutmeg
4 cloves
2.5-cm (1-inch) piece of cinnamon
5 tbsp groundnut or sunflower oil
60 g (2 oz) onion, diced
4 garlic cloves, finely diced
1 tsp ground ginger
1 tsp ground fenugreek
100 g (3½ oz) paprika
45 g/ (1½ oz) chilli powder
30 g (1 oz) salt
1 tbsp wine vinegar

First make the Berber red pepper paste: in a small pan over a low heat, toast the cardamom and allspice berries for 2–3 minutes. Put in a grinder with the nutmeg, cloves and cinnamon, and grind to a powder.

Put the oil in a medium-sized sauté pan over a low heat and sweat the onion until soft and translucent. Add the garlic and cook for a minute, then add all the spices and the salt, and cook together for another minute.

Transfer to a food processor or blender with the vinegar and blitz to a paste. Add water, a tablespoon at a time, through the feeder tube, scraping down the sides a couple of times, until you have a thick, spoonable consistency.

Pack in a sterilized jar and refrigerate when cold. It will keep for a month or longer if you ensure the surface is always filmed with oil and you use a clean spoon to remove it.

To make the stew: cut the chicken pieces into

drumsticks and thighs. Rub them with a teaspoon of salt and put them in a zip-lock bag with the lemon juice. Marinate for 1 hour at room temperature, shaking and turning a couple of times.

Remove from the bag, reserving the juice, and pat dry. Roll in the flour to coat, shaking off any excess. Put 3 tablespoons of the oil in a casserole over a low-to-medium heat. When shimmering-hot, add the chicken and brown all over. Remove to kitchen paper to drain and reserve.

Add 2 more tablespoons of the oil and sweat the onions until soft and translucent. Stir in the garlic and spices. Add 2 tablespoons of the Berber red pepper paste, turn up the heat and sauté for 2 minutes.

Pour in the wine and 1.1 litres (2 pints) of water, and bring to the boil. Boil for about 5 minutes.

Add the chicken pieces, grate in about 1/4 of a nutmeg, lower the heat and simmer for 30 minutes. Stir in the reserved marinade, lemon juice, ginger and eggs. Taste and adjust the seasoning, if necessary, and simmer gently for a final 5 minutes.

Put 1 drumstick and 1 thigh in each of 4 large warmed bowls, divide the sauce between them and serve with couscous or boiled long-grain rice. Scatter over finely chopped parsley and put a bowl of cooked chickpeas on the table for people to help themselves.

CHICKEN AND OLIVE EMSHEL

Emshel is only one of a number of Moroccan dishes that combine chicken (*djej*) with green olives and salt-preserved lemons. There are different kinds of green olives, however, and for *emshel* these should be the ripe, lightly brined sort which are almost browny-purple, like the Greek Kalamata. I like sour tastes, but you can use less lemon juice if preferred. Stoning olives is a bit of a bore unless you have a special implement to do the job.

serves 4

1 chicken, about 1.5 kg (3 1/4 lb)
4 tbsp sunflower or groundnut oil
1/2 tsp cumin seeds
1/2 tsp black peppercorns
4 garlic cloves, smashed and chopped
2 tsp paprika
1/4 tsp dried chilli flakes
salt
1 kg (2 1/4 lb) onions, coarsely grated
450 ml (1 1/4 pint) chicken stock
30 g (1 oz) chopped coriander leaves, plus some more whole leaves for garnish
30 g (1 oz) chopped flat-leaf parsley, plus some more whole leaves for garnish
2 preserved lemons (page 209)
225 g (8 oz) Kalamata-style green olives, stoned
about 20 saffron threads
5-cm (2-inch) piece of root ginger, peeled
juice of 2 fresh lemons

Joint a chicken into breast, leg and thigh pieces, halving the breasts. (Use the carcass for stock.) Heat 2 tablespoons of the oil in a non-stick pan. Place the chicken pieces, skin side down, in the pan and fry gently until the skin is brown and crisp.

Toast the cumin seeds and peppercorns gently in a dry pan until aromatic. Grind to a powder and mix with the garlic, the remaining oil, paprika, chilli flakes and 1/2 teaspoon of salt. Rub this into the chicken. Cling-wrap and refrigerate overnight.

Put the chicken with its marinade in a casserole and cover with the grated onions and the onion juice generated during grating, the chicken stock, chopped coriander and parsley. Bring to the boil, lower the heat and simmer for 20 minutes, turning the chicken with tongs from time to time.

Rinse the preserved lemons, cut into quarters, then strip out and discard the pulp. Add the lemon quarters with the olives, saffron threads and grated ginger. Stir in and continue to cook for 5–10 minutes.

Remove the chicken to a warmed serving plate, reduce the sauce at a rapid boil to about 350 ml (12 fl oz). Stir in the lemon juice and pour over the chicken. Scatter over some whole parsley and coriander leaves before serving.

PRESERVED LEMONS

Preserved lemons are one of the defining tastes of North African cooking. They are very easy to prepare, but you need to start pickling them at least a month before you eat them. If you can't get organic lemons, wash the skins in warm soapy water, scrubbing gently with a brush to remove the chemical-impregnated wax that coats most commercially produced citrus fruit.

5–6 organic lemons, plus juice of 4 more lemons
85 g (3 oz) sea salt
½ tsp black peppercorns
½ tsp cumin seeds
2 bay leaves

Scrub the lemons then, cutting downwards lengthwise, quarter them, stopping the cuts about 1 cm (½ inch) from the base. Press sea salt into the cut surfaces and re-form the fruit.

Put 1–2 tablespoons of salt into the base of a sterilized preserving jar and pack the lemons in, scattering over more salt as you go and adding the peppercorns, cumin seeds and bay leaves to distribute their flavours evenly. Press down to squeeze out the juice, then pour over freshly squeezed lemon juice to cover and seal tightly.

Leave at room temperature for 1 month, shaking the jar daily. They will keep for months and the lemon brine can be reused for second, and even third, batches.

BASS ROASTED WITH YEMENI HOT SAUCE

Presenting a whole fish at the table always looks special. It can be served still very hot from the oven or at room temperature. A small cod responds equally well to this treatment. Follow the fish with a tomato, olive and red onion salad dressed with lemon juice and olive oil.

serves 4
1 whole sea bass, 900 g–1 kg (2–2¼ lb), scaled and gutted
150 ml (¼ pint) olive oil
2 tsp dried chilli flakes
2 tsp cumin seeds
1 tsp paprika
1 tsp coriander seeds
1 tsp ground turmeric
½ tsp ground fenugreek
½ tsp black peppercorns
4 shallots
4 garlic cloves
handful of celery leaves
juice of 3 limes
flat-leaf parsley, to garnish

Preheat the oven to 250°C (475°F, gas 9) and brush with a little olive oil a gratin dish into which the fish will just fit. Carefully cut a crosshatch into one side of the fish.

Toast the spices in a small dry pan over a low heat for 3 minutes. Grind to a powder with 1 teaspoon of salt.

Coarsely chop the shallots and garlic. Put in the food processor with the ground spices, celery leaves

(reserving some for garnish), olive oil and the juice of 2 limes. Blitz to a paste and spread half of it over the fish.

Roast for 5 minutes, turn down the oven setting to 200°C (400°F, gas 6) and cook for 15 minutes. Remove, spread over the rest of the sauce and return to the oven for a final 10 minutes, a total cooking time of 30 minutes.

Serve straight from the gratin dish, with the reserved celery leaves sprinkled over and with the remaining lime juice squeezed over.

FATTOUSH

Bread salads are found throughout the Mediterranean countries. The Italian version, for example, is called panzanella. The main difference between them is in the type of bread used. In North Africa and the Middle East, this is a flat type like khoubiz or pitta, the inclusion of toasted yeast-raised white breads becoming more typical in Italy, Spain and Portugal. Indeed, the ingredients are pretty much the same as for gazpacho, the chilled Spanish soup of tomatoes, cucumbers and sweet pepper, though the effect is very different.

Although bread salads are traditionally a way of using up stale bread, they are actually nicer made with fresh bread toasted on a ridged grill pan, which chars the bread with stripes and adds to the flavour. Care must be taken when grilling that this is not too heavy-handed. The emphasis is on lightly charred, not burnt – which would make the salad taste bitter.

The time you leave the bread to soften after mixing it with the other ingredients is also crucial, but not something one can specify in a recipe because there are too many variables. You have to keep tasting until the texture is right for you. You may want to add a little more lemon juice or olive oil, or even a few drops of water.

You can make the salad a one-dish meal by including grilled or poached prawns, or pieces of cold roast chicken. The balance of the dish may be altered by including capers, garlic or anchovies as liked.

serves 4
1 red pepper
4 pitta breads
6 ripe plum tomatoes
salt and pepper
2 tbsp lemon juice
225 g (8 oz) cucumber
1 celery stalk
1 large red onion
8 stoned black olives
150 ml (¼ pint) extra-virgin olive oil
12 basil or mint leaves

Preheat a ridged grill pan until smoking-hot. Cut the red pepper in half, discarding the stalks and seeds, and lay it on the grill, turning when nicely striped and beginning to wilt and giving the other side 2–3 minutes. Reserve.

Grill the pitta breads, turning after a few seconds only. Reserve.

Dice the plum tomatoes roughly, without peeling or deseeding. Put in a large bowl and mash with a fork to extract the maximum amount of juice. Season to taste with salt and pepper and add the lemon juice.

Cut the grilled pitta into 2.5-cm (1-inch) squares and add to the bowl. Cut the cucumber, pepper, celery and red onion into 1-cm (½-inch) dice. Add the chopped black olives and toss thoroughly. Leave for 15 minutes before tasting.

The fattoush is ready to serve when the bread is fairly soft, but retains some crisp bits. When satisfied, pour over the olive oil and stir. Taste and adjust the seasoning. Tear the basil or mint leaves and scatter over before serving.

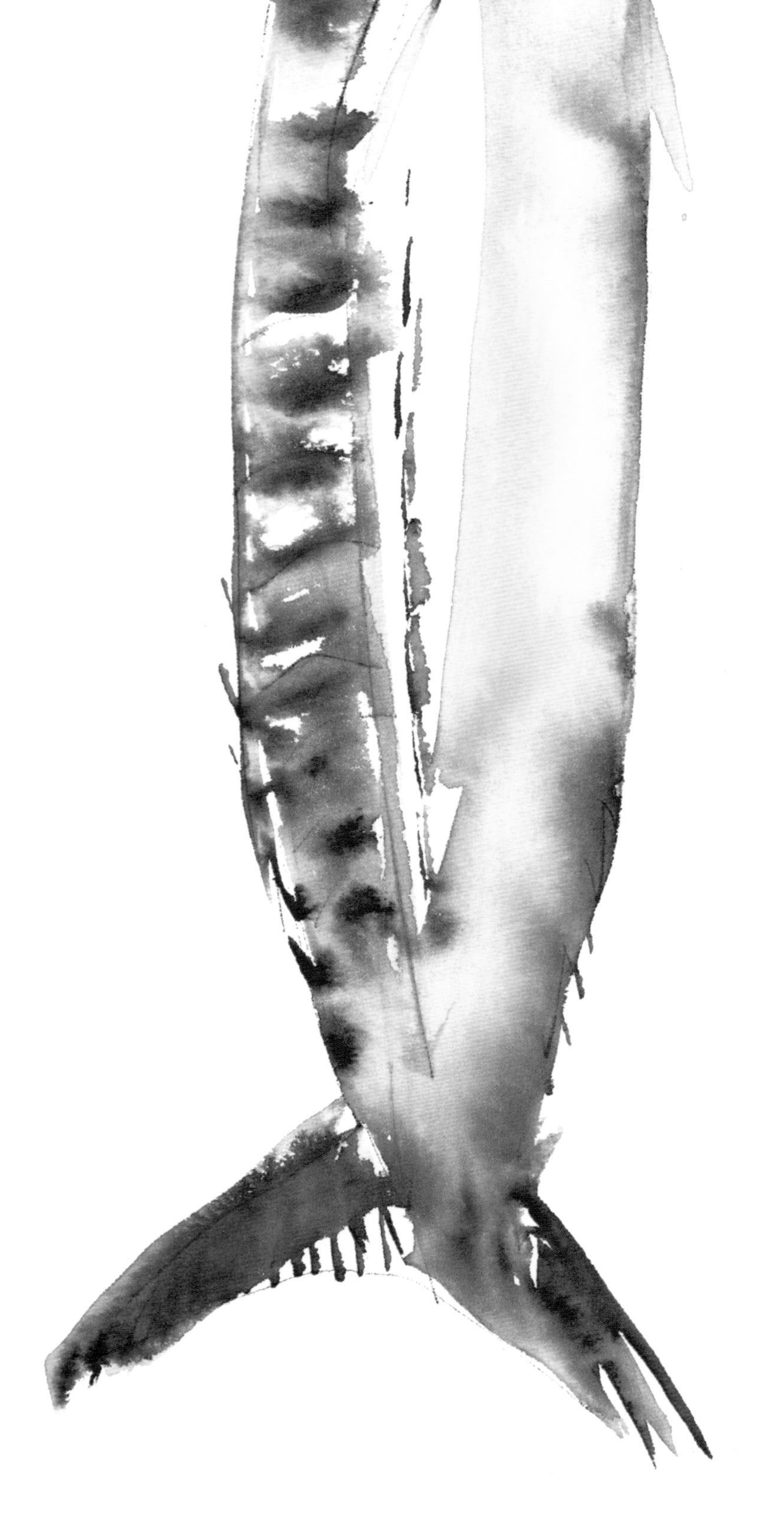

Chapter 13
SOUTH AMERICA

So hot it's cool

The purpose of a cookbook is, in part, to stimulate vicarious pleasure, taking us to places inside our heads where we have never been and where we may never go. It is unlikely, now, that I will ever travel through the vastness of South America, which I regret. Another one to add to the list. The recipes which follow are therefore based entirely on my reading and some television programmes I watched in America, as well as a couple of visits to restaurants in New York, where South American cooking is now very hot – so hot it's cool. If there is one book of the many I have read that stands out, then it is Felipe Rojas-Lombardi's *The Art of South American Cooking*. His is a seriously good cookbook, with more ideas between the covers than most, and I recommend it highly.

I have been drawn most particularly to the *ceviches* – raw citrus-marinated seafood – the *escabeches* – vinegar-flavoured dishes which have strong Mediterranean/Arab influences – and to the great one-pot dishes that include *feijoada* and *puchero*. These last epitomize generosity and sharing, two of the key ingredients in any good home food. Complex in construction and lengthy in execution, they offer exciting opportunities to put new and delicious things on the table. Many mix different meats with beans, the new and old worlds meeting harmoniously in a dish. They are ideal for entertaining on a large scale, since they make the least demands on the cook after the guests have arrived.

There seems little doubt that in the first decade of the new century, more chefs will turn to the countries of South America for inspiration. This is the last continent to be explored by cooks eager for ideas and new flavours that can find wide application. I therefore offer these few recipes that I have cooked and modified with this thought very much in mind.

CEVICHE

Ceviche is a citrus-based marinade used to 'cook' fish and shellfish, its acid action changing the texture of the flesh from an obviously raw state to an opaque firmness. Since the fish is not cooked with heat, it is essential that it be absolutely fresh. Come to think of it, there is no situation where it is desirable to eat fish that is not absolutely fresh, but when it is raw the time between the fish being killed and you eating it is critical. In an ideal world you would be killing the fish on your chopping board but this is perhaps fresher than most cooks would want. If the tuna only smells of the sea, it is fine.

Ceviche can be made with any kind of fish or shellfish, though it must first be sliced very thinly or cut into cubes no larger than 1 cm (½ inch), as for this typically Pacific Coast treatment.

TUNA LOIN CEVICHE

serves 4
450 g (1 lb) tuna loin fillet
250 ml (9 fl oz) fresh lime juice
3½ tbsp olive oil
1 garlic clove, finely chopped
450 g (1 lb) ripe plum tomatoes
115 g (4 oz) onions, finely diced
7.5 g (¼ oz) chopped coriander leaves
1 hot red chilli, finely chopped
¼ tsp salt
¼ tsp pepper

to serve:
corn chips
green olives
lime wedges

Dice the fish with a razor-sharp knife, put it in a glass or porcelain dish and cover with the lime juice. Leave to marinate at room temperature for 2–2¼ hours.

Put the olive oil and garlic in a small pan over a low heat and sweat for 5 minutes. Leave to cool.

Blanch and skin the tomatoes, cut into quarters and strip out the pulp and discard. Put the pieces of tomato flesh into a glass serving bowl with the onion, coriander, chilli, salt and pepper. Pour over the olive oil through a sieve, discarding the garlic.

Rinse the fish under cold running water for 2–3 minutes, drain well and add to the tomato mixture. Toss together and refrigerate for 30 minutes.

Serve with corn chips, green olives and lime wedges.

OCTOPUS CEVICHE WITH CUCUMBER AND GINGER

You rarely see octopus in the fishmonger's but, if you ask, he will get you some from the market. Well, that's the theory. You want only the tentacles, so have the fishmonger remove the head and guts for you – an unpleasant chore. Octopus tentacles rapidly cook to a rubbery texture and then need lengthy cooking before they become tender again. Here they are cooked for just a minute, the lemon juice marinade completing the job. Somebody told me recently that the octopus is a very intelligent, sensitive and loving creature, and as bright as Eddie, the Jack Russell on *Frazier*. I hope this was a lie.

serves 4
500 g (1 lb 2 oz) fresh octopus tentacles
salt
1 hot red chilli, finely diced
5 tbsp lemon juice
1 cucumber
5-cm (2-inch) piece of root ginger, peeled and grated

Wash the octopus tentacles in cold water and allow to drain. Bring a large saucepan of salted water to the boil. Wearing rubber gloves, clean the tentacles by rubbing with salt in a bowl for 5 minutes. Rinse thoroughly under running water.

When the water in the pan is boiling hard, using tongs dip a tentacle in and hold it under the water for 20 seconds. Lift out, wait 5 seconds, then put it back in for a further 20 seconds. Lift out, hold for 5 seconds and repeat for the third and last time – a technique known as scaring. It will now have curled and stiffened. Cook the other tentacles in the same way.

When cool enough to handle, cut across at an angle to produce scalloped slices 1 cm (½ inch) thick, leaving the curled tips intact.

Put the slices and tips in a bowl. Add a little salt, the chilli and the lemon juice, and leave to marinate at room temperature for 1–1½ hours, turning from time to time with a spoon.

Cut the cucumbers across, preferably on a mandolin, to achieve the thinnest slices possible. Place in a bowl with 1 teaspoon of salt and 200 ml (7 fl oz) cold water, and leave for 5–10 minutes. Drain, then dry on kitchen paper.

Put the cucumber slices in another bowl with the octopus and grated ginger. Toss together and serve heaped in small bowls.

ESCABECHE

In an *escabeche*, cooked fish, shellfish, fowl or meat is marinated in a vinegar-flavoured liquid. Originally this was an ancient Arab technique, used for preservation – vinegar being an excellent anti-bacterial agent – and it came to South America via Spain. Strong similarities with a classic medieval Italian chicken salad also exist, where the poached flesh is shredded while still warm then left to cool in a sweet-and-sour vinegar-based marinade, precisely the technique at the heart of all *escabeches*, whatever the principal ingredient.

Today, *escabeche* uses vinegar for its flavour more than for its preservative properties, often in conjunction with sugar or dried fruit and giving a sweet-and-sour effect. The common use of prunes, figs and dates makes me think of the tagines of North Africa, while the frequent inclusion of nuts is an obvious Moorish reference. Spicing the raw primary ingredient with turmeric, achiote and dried sweet peppers – paprika – is typical.

Since the vinegar is the defining ingredient, its quality is obviously a key determinant in the success of every *escabeche*. Any good wine vinegar will do, while balsamic, cider and sherry and rice vinegars provide opportunities to modify the flavour. You can further experiment with flavoured vinegars.

Escabeche is usually served with small sweetcorn cobs cut across into thin slices, black olives and small cubes of sour fresh cheese like feta.

ESCABECHE OF SALMON

The high natural oil content of salmon makes it a suitable candidate for cooking and marinating in a liquid based on red wine. The wine can be any soured, leftover wine.

serves 4

4 salmon steaks, each about 225 g (8 oz), cut across the whole fish and containing the backbone
600 ml (1 pint) red wine vinegar
600 ml (1 pint) red wine
4 spring onions, sliced
4 bay leaves
1 tsp dried chilli flakes
4 sprigs of thyme
20 black peppercorns
6 garlic cloves
100 ml (3½ fl oz) corn oil

60 g (2 oz) flour
salt and pepper
60 g (2 oz) raisins
30 g (1 oz) slivered almonds
3 tbsp olive oil
handful of coriander leaves

Select a wide, shallow pan in which the salmon steaks will fit in a single layer without touching. In this, put the vinegar, red wine, spring onions, bay leaves, chilli flakes, thyme, peppercorns and 1.1 litres (2 pints) water. Bring to the boil, lower the heat and simmer for 20 minutes.

While this simmers, cut the garlic into paper-thin slices and fry gently in the corn oil until they just start to colour, then transfer to the simmering liquid with a slotted spoon.

Season the flour and coat the salmon steaks with it. Turn up the heat under the oil and brown the salmon all over. Transfer to the simmering liquid and increase the heat. The salmon should be completely immersed; if it is not, add water to cover. As soon as it starts to bubble, turn off the heat and cover with a lid.

Leave to stand at room temperature for 2–3 hours before removing the salmon to a serving plate.

Just before taking to the table, fry the raisins and almonds in the olive oil over a low heat until the almonds start to colour. Spoon them over the fish, scatter on some coriander leaves and serve immediately.

ESCABECHE OF PRAWNS

The prawns must not be overcooked by the marinade, which is therefore applied only briefly – and not too hot – to add a sweet-and-sour finish. Buy the largest frozen prawns you can, in a 1-kg pack (about 16). Leave them to defrost overnight in a cold place. The slower the defrosting process, the more succulent the prawns will be when cooked.

Why specify frozen rather than fresh tiger prawns? Well, they mostly come from Thailand, and that means air-freight for the fresh variety and almost certainly some temperature fluctuation between their leaving the cleaning tanks and reaching your local fishmonger 5,000 or so miles later... and even very good fishmongers are not going to throw away tiger prawns if they are not sold after their first day in the shop. Temperature fluctuation accelerates decomposition. The prawn frozen from life into death is very often in better shape after defrosting than the supposedly 'fresh' prawn, but you do have to defrost them slowly. An overnight stay in the fridge before exposing them to room temperature helps.

When buying frozen prawns, always buy them in a block and defrost them yourself. After defrosting, peeling and deveining, a quick rinse in icy salty water before cooking has a freshening effect. I don't know why, but it does.

serves 4
1 kg (2¼ lb) frozen tiger prawns, defrosted
salt and pepper
1 tsp chilli flakes
3 tsp paprika
4 garlic cloves, cut into paper-thin slices
5 tbsp light olive oil
600 ml (1 pint) champagne vinegar
4 lime leaves
1 tsp caster sugar
handful of parsley, coarsely chopped

to serve:
2 Little Gem lettuces
115 g (4 oz) feta cheese, cubed
12 Kalamata olives

When the prawns are fully defrosted, pull off the heads and set them aside to make stock for another dish. Cut carefully through the centre line of the back, but not all the way through. Remove the intestinal threads and gently push the prawns down on the cutting board, cut side downwards, to flatten. Put them into a bowl of heavily salted water and rub gently between your fingers, then rinse under cold running water and leave to drain or pat dry with kitchen paper.

Put 1 teaspoon each of salt and coarsely ground pepper, the chilli flakes and paprika in a bowl and toss the prawns in the mixture to coat evenly.

Over a low heat and in a large frying pan or wok, sweat the garlic in the oil until it just starts to turn a pale golden colour. Using a slotted spoon, remove to drain on a paper towel and reserve.

Turn up the heat and, as soon as the oil starts to smoke, throw in the prawns and sauté, stirring and tossing to ensure even cooking. This will take about 2 minutes, no more, when the prawns will have butterflied open, the shells now pink with darker lateral stripes and the flesh white and opaque. Remove to a bowl with a slotted spoon.

Pour the vinegar into the pan and deglaze it, stirring and scraping. Add the lime leaves and sugar. Bring to the boil, lower the heat and simmer for 10 minutes, then remove from the heat and allow to cool to room temperature. Pour over the prawns.

To serve, cut each lettuce into quarters lengthwise, put 2 on each plate with some cheese and olives on top. Arrange the prawns next to the lettuce. Spoon a little of the marinade over and round the lettuce, scattering on the crisped garlic and chopped parsley.

SWORDFISH SMOTHERED IN ONIONS AND SWEET PEPPERS

Swordfish is rich and meaty and, like tuna, this makes it a suitable candidate for brief grilling at a very high heat. Cooking masses of onions over the lowest heat, down to the point where they have a sweet intensity, provides us with the basis for the smother. This is a different technique to what is inaccurately referred to as an onion *confit*, where a higher heat produces an unappetizing dark brown slurry. Only when the onions have softened are they fried, and then only to the point where they acquire a golden shading.

The steaks need to be at least 3.5 cm (1½ inches) thick or they will defy your best efforts to keep them rare. This will translate to about 210–225 g (7½–8 oz).

serves 4

1 kg (2¼ lb) onions
100 ml (3½ fl oz) olive oil
½ tsp dried oregano
60 g (2 oz) pancetta, diced
2 hot red chillies, shredded
3 garlic cloves, finely chopped
1 tbsp lemon juice
5-cm (2-inch) piece of root ginger, peeled
4 swordfish steaks, each about 210–225 g (7½–8 oz)
salt and pepper
16 Olive Oil Tomato quarters (page 309)
2 red peppers, roasted, peeled and cut in strips
handful of coriander leaves

Slice the onions across as thinly as possible. You could use a mandolin. Put them in a large heavy-based pan or flameproof casserole dish with 4 tablespoons of the olive oil and cook over the lowest possible heat for about 40 minutes, stirring at regular intervals. The object is to extract as much water as you can, without the sugar in the onions caramelizing too quickly. When they have softened and become translucent, stir in the oregano and turn off the heat.

Fry the pancetta gently in 1 tablespoon of the oil until it starts to brown. Add the chilli and continue cooking until softened, then add the garlic. Turn up the heat and fry, stirring, for 30 seconds. Deglaze the pan with the lemon juice and add to the onions.

Grate the ginger into a piece of butter muslin over a bowl. Ball the muslin and twist the material to squeeze out as much juice as you can. Discard the pulp, but reserve the ginger juice.

Preheat a ridged grill pan. Brush the swordfish steaks with the remaining oil and season generously with salt and pepper. Cook, turning 4 times and giving each surface 15 seconds each time, a total cooking time of 1 minute. Put on a warmed serving plate and reserve.

In a small pan, warm the tomato quarters in their oil over a low heat.

Turn the heat back on to moderate under the onions and stir-fry until the onions take a pale golden colour. Stir in the pepper strips, turn off the heat and allow to stand for 1 minute.

To serve, put the swordfish steaks in the middle of 4 warmed plates. Spoon the ginger juice over the fish, then mound the onion mixture on top. Scatter over a few coarsely chopped coriander leaves and serve at once.

CLAMS AND MUSSELS MARISCADA

Mariscada describes any dish that combines different shellfish, which may either be steamed or sautéed, the difference between one dish and another mostly defined by the vegetables included. These are cooked separately here, and combined with the shellfish only at the point of service.

serves 4

500 g (1 lb 2 oz) onions, thinly sliced
5 tbsp olive oil
500 g (1 lb 2 oz) canned plum tomatoes
½ tsp caster sugar
1 tsp thyme leaves or ½ tsp dried oregano
salt and pepper
2 garlic cloves, finely chopped
1 tsp dried chilli flakes
150 ml (¼ pint) dry white wine
1 kg (2¼ lb) mussels, cleaned
500 g (1 lb 2 oz) carpetshell clams, scrubbed
handful of finely chopped flat-leaf parsley

Sweat the onions in 3 tablespoons of the olive oil in a large heavy-based saucepan or casserole over the lowest heat, until soft and translucent, taking care not to allow them to brown.

Purée the tomatoes and their juices in a food processor with the sugar and thyme or oregano. Season with ½ teaspoon of pepper and salt to taste.

Pour over the onions and stir to mix evenly. Turn up the heat and bring to the boil. Lower the heat and simmer for 10 minutes.

Put the remaining oil in a large shallow saucepan over a moderate heat and, when it shimmers, add the garlic and chilli flakes. Fry for 30 seconds, stirring, then pour in the wine and bring to the boil. Boil for a minute, then add the mussels and clams. Shake and turn with a spoon. Cover with a lid and cook until all the shells have opened, about 3 minutes.

Strain the shellfish through a colander over the tomato and onion mixture, stirring this in.

Ladle the tomato and onion mixture on to warmed soup plates and divide the shellfish on top. Scatter the parsley over all. Serve with a basket of bread.

SQUID WITH CHILLI AND CACHACA

Cachaca is the rough cane spirit of Brazil, some of which comes in serious-looking brown bottles, the label illustrated with a dramatic red scorpion, more entertaining than a government health warning and after a couple of glasses you get the point. *Caipirina – cachaca*, crushed limes, sugar and ice – is a fine

cocktail for a summer's day when you have nothing else to do. Having acquired a taste for it, leave a splash to flame the pan in this simple treatment for squid and to anoint the grilled pineapple on page 291.

serves 4
225 g (8 oz) canned chopped plum tomatoes
3 tbsp olive oil
2 hot red chillies, shredded
115 g (4 oz) shallots, thinly sliced
3 garlic cloves, finely chopped
1 tsp paprika
4 tbsp cachaca or cooking brandy
1 tsp caster sugar
juice and zest of 1 lime
1 kg (2¼ lb) cleaned squid, crosshatched and cut into strips
handful of coriander leaves, finely chopped, plus some whole leaves for garnish
salt and pepper

In a food processor, purée the canned tomatoes with their juices and reserve. If you have really ripe fresh tomatoes, then use them instead.

Put the oil in a big frying pan over a moderate heat. Stir-fry the chilli and shallots, until the shallots are soft and starting to take a little colour, then add the garlic and paprika. Fry for another minute, then add the *cachaca* or brandy, shake and flame carefully.

When the flames die down, add the tomatoes, sugar, lime juice and lime zest. Bubble for a minute or two, stirring. Taste and season accordingly.

Stir in the squid and cook, stirring, until the flesh is opaque and the strips have curled over, about 2 minutes.

Stir in the chopped coriander and serve on large warmed soup plates with the whole coriander leaves scattered on top. All it needs to go with it is decent bread. Something light like a ciabatta (page 306) is appropriate or perhaps warm wheatflour tortillas.

CAIPIRINA

Was ever a drink easier to make? It means 'little peasant girl', though one puzzles over how it got the name.

serves 1
1 lime, quartered
1 tbsp caster sugar
5 tbsp cachaca
ice cubes

Mash the lime quarters in a highball glass with a wooden pestle to extract as much juice as you can.

Add the sugar and *cachaca*. Fill to the top with ice cubes and stir well.

QUINOA

You may have wondered what health-food enthusiasts were going on about when they extolled the virtues of 'keenwa'. Quinoa is a South American relative of spinach that originated in the Peruvian Andes. It is a high-protein savoury grain, rather like cracked wheat, which has a distinctive nutty taste and, when grown on, is also eaten as a leaf vegetable. Until recently it was sold mainly through health-food shops, but is now acquiring a wider popularity in fashionable restaurants. In their natural state the seeds have a very bitter coating, but this is removed during processing, so the quinoa you buy is ready to cook. About 125 g (4½ oz) of raw quinoa makes a serving.

serves 4
500 g (1 lb 2 oz) quinoa
1 tsp salt

Put the quinoa in a sieve and run cold water through it until the water runs clear. Put the quinoa in a pan with 2 litres (3½ pints) of cold water and the salt, and bring to the boil, stirring occasionally. As it boils, lower the heat and simmer until all the grains are translucent, 10–12 minutes. Drain, put in a bowl and stir vigorously with a fork.

Quinoa is always boiled in this way and may be eaten immediately, needing only a little butter, salt and pepper, like mashed potatoes. Alternatively, it may be incorporated into soups, stews, salads and even puddings.

MUSSELS WITH QUINOA AND NEW POTATOES

This is a soupy stew that is best made with real new potatoes – that is, immature potatoes on which the skin has not fully formed – rather than small potatoes. When new potatoes are not available, the small potatoes should be peeled... a bore.

serves 6

1 tsp coriander seeds
½ tsp cumin seeds
450 g (1 lb) new potatoes, scrubbed
salt and pepper
225 g (8 oz) prepared quinoa (see previous recipe)
150 g (5 oz) fresh or frozen corn kernels
600 ml (1 pint) shellfish stock, fish stock, light chicken broth or water
3 tbsp olive oil
115 g (4 oz) purple shallots, thinly sliced
2 garlic cloves, thinly sliced
1 tsp dried chilli flakes
150 ml (¼ pint) dry white wine
2 kg (2¼ lb) mussels, cleaned and any that remain open discarded
30 g (1 oz) flat-leaf parsley, plus a few whole leaves to finish

Toast the coriander and cumin seeds in a dry pan over a low heat for 2–3 minutes until aromatic. Grind to a powder and reserve.

Cook the potatoes in rapidly boiling salted water for 10–15 minutes, or until just done. (The time obviously depends on the size of the potatoes and something like a small Jersey Royal may only take 8 minutes.) Plunge into cold water to stop further cooking, drain and reserve.

If using fresh corn, boil briefly in unsalted water until just done. Refresh in cold water, drain and reserve.

Put the potatoes, prepared quinoa and stock in a large saucepan. Bring to the boil, lower the heat and stir together. Leave to simmer gently.

Put the olive oil in a pan large enough to cook the mussels in one go. If you do not have one large enough, or a big wok with a lid, then you will need to cook them in 2 batches, halving the oil, spices, wine, shallots and garlic when you do so.

Stir the shallots and garlic into the oil and sweat for a minute. Add the ground spices and chilli flakes. Fry, stirring, for a minute then add the wine. Turn up the heat and, when bubbling fiercely, add the mussels. Shake and turn, then cover with a lid and cook until they have all opened, probably – with this many mussels and depending on the size and shape of the pan – about 5 minutes.

Drain the mussels through a colander, stirring the cooking liquid into the stew. Taste and season with salt and pepper. Stir in the corn and simmer for a minute. Stir in the chopped parsley.

Ladle the stew into large warmed soup bowls or soup plates. Ladle the mussels on top and scatter over the reserved leaves of parsley. If preferred, the mussels may be shucked.

CHICKEN AND YELLOW SQUASH STEW WITH APRICOTS

Yellow squashes crop up in so many dishes throughout Central and South America, and people are starting to use them more internationally as they realize that smaller varieties bear only a passing resemblance to the giant pumpkins that we connect with Hallowe'en lanterns and overly sweet pumpkin pie.

The sweetness of the apricots is cut with vinegar and the bacon gives it a gentle, smoky flavour. You can serve it as a one-dish meal or think of it in smaller portions as a soup.

serves 4 as a main course, 6 as a soup
about 85 g (3 oz) coriander, including roots and stems
2 tsp coriander seeds
1 tsp cumin seeds
1 tsp black peppercorns
115 g (4 oz) piece of smoked bacon
3 tbsp corn oil
1 tsp dried chilli flakes
2 tsp ground turmeric
1 chicken, about 1.35 kg (3½ lb)
500 g (1 lb 2 oz) whole unpeeled onions
1 head of garlic
2 celery stalks, cut into pieces
2 bay leaves
1 cinnamon stick
150 ml (¼ pint) sherry vinegar
salt
1 large butternut squash, about 675 g (1½ lb)
12 no-soak apricots

Scrub the coriander roots and chop them and the stems coarsely. Toast the coriander and cumin seeds and the peppercorns in a dry pan over a low heat until aromatic, then grind to a powder and reserve.

Cut the bacon into fat matchsticks. In a large pan, fry them in the corn oil until browned, then stir in the ground toasted spices, the chilli flakes and turmeric. Fry, stirring, for a minute.

Add the chicken, breast side down, the unpeeled onions, the whole head of garlic, the celery cut in pieces, the bay leaves, the coriander roots and stems, and the cinnamon stick. Pour over cold water to cover, add the vinegar and about 1½ teaspoons of salt. Turn up the heat and bring to the boil. Skim, turn down the heat and simmer for 40 minutes. Turn the chicken breast-side up and continue poaching until done, about another 20 minutes.

Remove the chicken to a carving board and take out the solids with a slotted spoon. Discard the bay leaves and cinnamon and return the bacon to the broth.

As soon as they are cool enough to handle, peel the onions, discarding the skins. Cut across the top of the garlic and squeeze out the cloves. Put these, the onions, coriander roots and stems and celery in a food processor and blitz to a purée. Return this to the broth.

Cut the flesh of the squash into chunks and add to the broth with the apricots. Simmer until the squash is cooked and the apricots are plump, 15–20 minutes.

Towards the end of cooking, cut and pull the flesh from the chicken, shred and add to the pot.

To serve, ladle into deep warmed bowls and scatter over coarsely chopped coriander leaves.

SQUAB WITH BABY FENNEL AND CORN CAZUELA

Cazuela is a Chilean casseroled meat and vegetable soup-stew, but I have cooked this as the vegetable element, roasting the spiced squab separately and only combining the two as they go to the table. This is a good way of making very expensive squab go a bit further. The flesh of squab is both rich and delicate, and should always be served pink – if not the blood-rare that is unpalatably fashionable as I write. Charlie Trotter actually serves squab carpaccio and the thought of eating pigeon raw is even less appealing.

serves 4
500 g (1 lb 2 oz) waxy potatoes
5 tbsp olive oil
4 garlic cloves, cut into paper-thin slices
2 hot green chillies
1 kg (2¼ lb) small fennel bulbs
500 g (1 lb 2 oz) canned chopped tomatoes
300 ml (½ pint) dry white wine
1 tsp dried oregano
salt and pepper
2 large squab, each about 500 g (1 lb 2 oz)
175 g (6 oz) frozen corn kernels
small bunch of chives, chopped, for garnish

FOR THE DRY RUB:
1 tsp cumin seeds
1 tsp black peppercorns
1 tsp dried chilli flakes
½ tsp salt

Preheat the oven to 250°C (475°F, gas 9). Peel the potatoes and cut them into bite-sized chunks.

Put 3 tablespoons of the olive oil in a casserole over a low heat. Fry the garlic, stirring, until just starting to colour. Cut the chillies across in thin strips and stir in with their seeds. Add the fennel and potato chunks, the tomatoes with their juices, the white wine, and the oregano. Season with salt and pepper and stir to coat everything. Pour over 300 ml (½ pint) water, bring to the boil, lower the heat and simmer until the fennel and potato are just cooked and most of the liquid has evaporated, 20–30 minutes (the same time, more or less, as the squab, which need to be roasted for 20 minutes and rested for 10).

Make the dry rub: toast the ingredients in a dry pan over a low heat until aromatic and grind to a powder.

Brush the squab with the remaining olive oil and rub them all over with the ground mixture. Put them in a roasting tin, breast side down, and roast for 10 minutes. Turn breast side up for 10 minutes, then remove and allow to rest for 10 minutes.

Carve off the legs and breasts whole, then cut the breasts across into halves. Stir the corn into the vegetable stew and heat through.

Ladle the vegetables on to warmed soup plates, arranging a breast half and a leg on top of each. Scatter over finely chopped chives before serving.

CRUZADO

Cruzado is the Venezuelan equivalent of a *pot-au-feu*, of a New England boiled dinner, of *bollito misto* (page 154). It is principally of beef and may, rather oddly, include shellfish, though I think the combination of beef, bacon and chicken works best. Shin of beef is a favoured cut because of its connective tissue, which permits slow cooking to a meltingly tender finish without drying out, but brisket or any stewing cut is fine. You will need, though, to choose a cut that can be tied and cooked in one piece so you can slice it for serving.

The vegetables you add are also a movable feast and may include potatoes, turnips and cabbage. Here we combine young carrots, tiny onions and small sweetcorn cobs. The broth is enriched with beer, spiked with chilli and flavoured with coriander and celery. You really need coriander roots as well as stems for the bouquet garni.

The overall flavour will be more intense if the meats are cooked in a well-flavoured chicken or beef stock, but shin produces a fine stock when cooked in water alone, which is why it is called 'gravy beef' in the USA.

A similar dish in Ecuador and Columbia is called sancocho, a Peruvian soup-stew called sancochado follows the same lines and all have similarities to the Argentine *puchero*. *Cruzado* is a fine dish to cook and eat on a large scale, and you can make it go further by including more vegetables. Any meat left over can be used to make sandwiches, or cut in strips and used instead of steaks in the beet salad on page 197.

This recipe suggests browning the meat – which is neither essential nor traditional – and caramelizing the onions, which are usually just boiled. Both modifications give colour and a richer flavour to the finished dish.

serves 8

1.35 kg (3 lb) piece of shin of beef, tied in a round
salt and pepper
4 tbsp corn oil
1.35 kg (3 lb) chicken
1 kg (2¼ lb) piece of boiling bacon
1.1 litres (2 pints) dark beer
about 4.5 litres (8 pints) stock or stock and water
24 button onions, peeled
3 tbsp olive oil
1 tsp caster sugar
24 baby sweetcorn
24 new potatoes, peeled
8 small carrots, peeled
handful of coriander leaves, to garnish

FOR THE BOUQUET GARNI:
4 hot red chillies
3 leafy celery stalks
2 bay leaves
bunch of scrubbed coriander, stems and roots
20 black peppercorns

to serve:
Piri-piri Sauce (page 309) or Encona pepper sauce
Cornbread (page 307)

First make the bouquet garni: split the chillies and wrap with the other bouquet ingredients in butter muslin, then tie securely with string.

Rub the beef with coarsely milled pepper. Heat the corn oil until smoking-hot and brown the beef all over, before putting it in a pot which is big enough to hold it, the chicken and the bacon.

Pour over the beer and cover with stock or stock and water. This may take as much as 4.5 litres (8 pints). Bring to the boil. Skim, add the bouquet garni, season with salt (about 2 teaspoons initially) and simmer for 1½ hours.

Add the chicken and bacon, topping up with water if necessary to keep them all submerged, and cook for another hour. Check that everything is cooked. When satisfied, turn off the heat and remove the chicken to a carving board.

About 35 minutes before the meats have finished

cooking, put on a big pan of water to heat to the boil and, in a heavy frying pan over a low heat, slowly fry the onions in the olive oil until caramelized, which will take 20–30 minutes. Just before they are done, sprinkle over the sugar and stir to coat evenly.

Plunge the corn into the boiling water for 2 minutes, refresh in cold water and reserve. Salt the water and cook the potatoes and carrots, which will take about 15 minutes.

As soon as the chicken is cool enough to handle, cut and pull off the meat, transferring it to a warm plate and discarding the skin. Remove the beef and chicken and return the chicken bones to the pan, turning the heat back on to bring the broth to a simmer. The bacon will have contributed its salt, but you are cooking a lot of meat and liquid and, if underseasoned, they will be insipid. Taste and add salt now if you think it needs it.

To serve: slice the beef and bacon. Arrange alternate slices of beef, bacon and chicken overlapping in warmed deep bowls. Apportion the potatoes, carrots and onions. Plunge the corn into the simmering stock for 30 seconds, then drain well and add to the bowls. Ladle over the broth and scatter coriander leaves on top.

Put some chilli sauce on the table and the cornbread will go well to mop up the juices.

(You will have quite a lot of good broth left over. Continue simmering it with the chicken bones for 2 hours. Strain into a clean pan, reduce at a rapid boil and freeze in an ice tray to use in other dishes).

FEIJOADA

While people think of *feijoada* as Portuguese, it originated in Brazil, where it is a dish of celebration. It is an early example of a fusion stew, mixing the local black beans with the pork and sausages first brought by the Portuguese and Spanish to South America in the 15th and 16th centuries.

In Portugal, it is most frequently cooked in the north-eastern part of the country and is based on large dried white beans of the lima type, and has a higher percentage of cured meats to fresh. Because *feijoada* is very much a family dish rather than a restaurant fare, the recipe varies widely in the balance of fresh pork to cured. However, it always includes blood sausage (*morcilla*) and pig's ear, snout, trotter and tail, which give the finished dish its authentic rich, gelatinous quality. These may seem difficult to come by, but a good old-fashioned butcher will supply them for pennies. The *morcilla* won't be easy to get here, so substitute any spicy black pudding.

Like a cassoulet, *feijoada* is best made in large quantities and, with this Brazilian-style version, the lengthy preparation is most easily done over 2 days. In Brazil, *feijoada* would typically be accompanied by some blanched kale and a salad of oranges and red onions.

serves 8–10
900 g (2 lb) black beans
salt and pepper
pig's snout, tail, ear and trotter (see above)
3 ham hocks, about 450 g (1 lb) each
3.5 litres (6 pints) chicken stock
2 bay leaves
2 hot chillies
675 g (1½ lb) onions, thinly sliced
2 tbsp groundnut or corn oil
4 garlic cloves, chopped
125 ml (4 fl oz) dry sherry
400 g (14 oz) morcilla or other blood sausage
bunch of coriander
¼ tsp dried chilli flakes
handful of flat-leaf parsley

The day before: rinse the beans, cover with lots of cold water and leave to soak overnight. Scatter salt over the trotter, ear, snout and tail, and refrigerate overnight.

Next day, rinse the pig parts, cutting the snout into 2.5-cm (1-inch) cubes, and put in a large pan with the ham hocks. Cover with the stock, add the bay leaves and whole chillies, and bring to the boil. Skim, then lower the heat and simmer for about 2 hours.

Remove the hocks and reserve. Cut the ear into thin slices, add them to the stock and continue to simmer for a further 40 minutes.

Use a sieve to remove the meat and bones. Discard the bones, chillies and bay leaves, reserving the meat.

Turn up the heat and reduce the broth to about 1.1 litres (2 pints). Return the reserved meat to the broth and remove from the heat.

Drain the beans, cover with cold water, bring to the boil and boil hard for 5 minutes. Drain, rinse and return to the pan. Cover with fresh water, bring to the boil, lower the heat and simmer for 1–1½ hours, or until just done.

In a large casserole and over a medium heat, fry the onions in the oil. When they start to brown, stir in the garlic then pour over the dry sherry.

Peel off the skin from the sausage and cut it into large dice. Add to the pan with the broth together with the pork meat and pour the bean cooking liquid over, reserving the beans. Add a bunch of coriander stalks tied with a piece of string, bring to the boil, lower the heat and simmer for 30 minutes.

Remove and discard the coriander stalks and stir in the beans, chilli flakes, the ham hocks and the tail, cut into pieces. Continue simmering gently for a final 20–30 minutes, adding a little water if it starts drying out. During this last phase, taste for seasoning – it is unlikely to need salt, but add some pepper.

Serve straight from the casserole in large soup bowls, scattering over some whole leaves of flat-leaf parsley and coriander.

LOCRO

Versions of this vegetable stew appear in many forms throughout South America. This Argentinian version mixes butternut squash with peas, tomatoes, corn and whole mild chillies, and is served with boiled long-grain rice. As a contrast, whole small onions are caramelized and served separately. They take about 15 minutes less time to cook than the stew.

serves 4

2 kg (4½ lb) butternut squash (peeled weight)
450 g (1 lb) onions, sliced into rings
100 ml (3½ fl oz) olive oil
3–4 garlic cloves, chopped
225 g (8 oz) canned chopped tomatoes
8 mild green chillies
1 tsp dried oregano
salt and pepper
2 tsp toasted cumin seeds
225 g (8 oz) frozen sweetcorn
225 g (8 oz) frozen peas
15 g (½ oz) chopped coriander leaves
1 ear of fresh young corn (optional), for garnish

FOR THE CARAMELIZED ONIONS:

60 g (2 oz) unsalted butter
450 g (1 lb) baby onions, peeled
½ tsp salt
¼ tsp pepper
15 g (½ oz) muscovado sugar
2 tbsp wine vinegar

Cut the skin from the squash and remove the seeds. Discard the seeds and skin and cut the flesh into 5-cm (2-inch cubes). Reserve.

Over a moderate heat, fry the onions in the oil, stirring constantly, until they start to brown, about 5

minutes. Add the garlic and cook, stirring, for 1 minute.

Add the squash, the chopped tomatoes with their juices, the whole chillies, oregano, salt and pepper. When the liquid boils, turn down the heat and simmer, stirring from time to time, for about 20–25 minutes, or until the squash is just done. If it shows signs of drying out, add a little water.

While the squash is cooking, cook the onions for caramelization: melt the butter in a wide shallow saucepan. Add the onions, season with salt and pepper, then stir gently to coat with a wooden spoon. Cook over a low heat for about 20 minutes, shaking at regular intervals to prevent them sticking. Scatter over the brown sugar and add the vinegar when the sugar dissolves into the butter and the colour begins to turn to golden brown. Swirl the pan until the onions are nicely glazed.

While the onions are glazing, if you are preparing the optional corn garnish, bring a pan of water to the boil. About 5 minutes before the stew is due to be done, cook the corn cob for about 3 minutes. Cut across into slices each about 2 kernels thick.

To complete the *locro*, stir in the toasted cumin seeds and the frozen corn kernels and peas, then simmer for 2–3 minutes more. Remove from the heat and stir in the chopped coriander. Ladle into bowls, add a spoonful of onions and place a corn ring on top.

CORN AND SWEETCORN

Corn, which in this country used to describe any grain, now has the American meaning of maize. Sweetcorn and corn are both maize, although maize is generally used to describe the original starchy field corn that is the staple diet of much of South and Central America from where it originated. Most corn outside South and Central America is grown for animal feed, though corn porridge is popular in the Southern United States, where it is called hominy or grits, while polenta is now considered rather smart food. Ironic since it was once exclusively the food of the poor in Northern Italy, where its staple role in the diet led to mineral deficiency conditions like rickets.

Sweetcorn is a variety with a high sugar content and was developed quite recently. It tends to be grown in colder climates and in this century we have seen the development of sweetcorn which will even grow in our miserable climate. Sweetcorn's sweetness is transitory, as sugar converts rapidly to starch – the reverse of what happens to potatoes. In an ideal world, it is picked, cooked and eaten within the hour, though this is a luxury denied to most of us. Having said that, corn that comes from the other side of the world can still be very good even after a few days. It is all a matter of compromise and reality.

When selecting sweetcorn, pull part of the husk away and press the kernels, which should be small, milky and firm to the touch. If not cooking them immediately, put them in an airtight bag or wrap them in a damp cloth and refrigerate.

Most people overcook corn, which when young and fresh takes only about 3–5 minutes in rapidly boiling water. Overcooking mushes the kernels and toughens the skin. Never salt the water in which you cook corn, as this has the unwanted effect of toughening the skin, just as it does with beans. Do not remove the husks until just before cooking the corn. Do it while the water is coming to the boil.

Another way of cooking corn is to steam it on a bed of husks, a good means of enhancing the flavour. As you strip the husks from the ears, pile them in a wide pan. Pour in an inch or so of water and bring to the boil. Lay the corn on top, cover tightly with a lid and steam for 5–7 minutes. In South America, just-cooked young corn cobs are often cut into slices about 2 kernels thick and these rings are added to a dish as a garnish.

Chapter 14
Southeast Asia

A wake-up call to palates everywhere

For the past ten years the influence of the food of Southeast Asia on cooks the world over has been huge, the ingredients and flavours sounding a wake-up call to palates everywhere. In Britain, as I write, Thai food is the fastest-growing area in terms of perceived desirability, particularly amongst the young and upwardly mobile. Thai food concessions are attaching themselves to pubs, as they first did in Australia, and it is increasingly the style of food for fashionable cocktail bars. A bowl of noodles fragrant with Southeast Asian spices and fired-up with chilli is quick to prepare, easy to eat and, on the whole, inexpensive.

The popularity of a certain kind of food and a particular way of eating reflects social change as much as fashion. Southeast Asian cooking expanded its popular base in the same way that Indian and Chinese food first achieved cross-cultural success – at a grass-roots level. They did not so much cascade down from isolated privilege in expensive restaurants as, say, French food did, but rather percolated out and up from the communities that first gave shelter to the immigrant populations. Thus the first Chinatowns were around the docks and some of the first Southeast Asian restaurants were often English greasy-spoon cafés during the day, converting by some surreal effect into places of taste explosion and exciting culinary exploration with the coming of night.

The cultures of Southeast Asia – of Burma, Laos, Thailand, Vietnam, Cambodia and the myriad islands of Indonesia – have never been significantly industrialized. Food in this part of the world has never been polarized by class in quite the way it has in Britain. People may often not have enough to eat, but here poverty does not manifest itself, as it does in the West, with a complete loss of an ability to cook. Food is honoured, central to social intercourse and emblematic of hospitality. We have no equivalent of rice in the sense of food as a symbol of life.

Of course, one does not need to ponder on such weighty themes before being able to enjoy eating the food which has developed partly from them. Anybody and everybody can fall in love with the tastes and textures of Southeast Asia. Not everything is chilli-hot and even those dishes which authentically should be very hot can be moderated as a concession to a sensitive palate. Pungent dipping sauces and fiery chilli relishes, like sambals, provide the opportunity to add layers of heat at the table. These are feasts for all seasons and all men, for you can pick and choose and make of them what you will.

Since few Southeast Asian homes have ovens, this is mostly food that is fried in a wok, grilled over charcoal or steamed. Woks are now pretty standard in British and American kitchens, but I am always surprised by television chefs who choose to cook with woks not much larger than soup bowls, thereby totally missing the point. A large surface area is needed to fry quickly and efficiently, and overcrowding food in a wok mitigates this effect by lowering the temperature and thus the heat being transferred to the food, as well as generating unwanted steam.

Buy large woks cheaply from Chinese markets, but bear in mind that it is a pretty pointless exercise to buy any traditional round-bottomed wok if you do not have the right kind of gas jet to burn underneath it. Woks do not work with electric rings, Agas and halogen hobs, and you will often be better off using a large heavy-based frying pan in preference to a wok when stir-frying. What we call barbecues are also, of course, charcoal grills. When weather or time makes barbecuing impractical, heavy grill pans can be substituted for things like satay. If you plan to grill things on bamboo skewers frequently, then invest in a flat heavy grill, more a griddle really. Le Creuset have one which sits across two burners and has only barely raised ridges, making it less suitable for steaks but ideal for skewered meat or fish. Ridged grill pans with high sides make it difficult or impossible to cook with skewers. Steamers can be fashioned from existing equipment, though (as I have noted more than once) the bamboo baskets for steaming that are standard kit throughout the East are cheap and immensely useful, being not only a practical item with which to cook but also an aesthetically pleasing form from which to serve.

If you are going to make curry pastes you should really have a pestle and mortar, though acceptable pastes can be made with a food processor. The large heavy cleaver is used throughout the Far East for pretty much everything, from shredding vegetables to chopping through bones. Excellent examples can be bought relatively cheaply from Chinese markets.

SOME SOUTHEAST ASIAN INGREDIENTS

As with all foods relating to an area, the cooking of Southeast Asia is defined by its ingredients. Herbs like coriander, Vietnamese mint and Thai basil are used by the handful to finish dishes rather than garnish them. Sweet is as important as sour in balancing dishes, and palm sugar and coconut milk both play a part here, sourness mainly coming from lime juice and tamarind. Rice is served at almost every meal while noodles, though common enough, are essentially an imported Chinese ingredient. The rice tends to be of the glutinous type, invariably steamed. The recipes which follow don't call for too many unusual ingredients, but you will need:

Beancurd (tofu)
Made from soya beans, this high-protein soft material like a custard comes in different degrees of firmness. It scarcely tastes of anything, but absorbs flavours readily, making it a blank canvas on which the cook may paint.

Belacan
Shrimp paste can be bought fresh or dried and compressed in cakes from specialist shops. Made from partially decomposed salted shrimps, it has a pungent odour (to put it mildly), particularly the fresh variety, but fortunately this smell vanishes during cooking. Dried shrimp paste is stronger in flavour than fresh. Belacan is usually first dry-roasted before use. The easiest way of doing this is to wrap the amount you need in foil and put it under a grill for a few minutes.

Bok choi
With its dark leaves and crisp white stems, this is used extensively, as is its smaller cousin, pak choi. It should be lightly cooked as you would spinach. Choi sum is a smaller variant with green stems, sometimes sold in yellow flower.

Ceun chai or Thai celery
Greener and leafier than the European variety, this also has a stronger flavour. When substituting European-style celery, use only the leaves and inner stalks.

Chillies
There are so many varieties of chilli that there is nothing one can say about them short of writing the book. They are so central to Southeast Asian cooking that it is odd to think that they originated in South America. The hottest varieties are the smallest. There is a tiny Thai green chilli with a distinctive pin-like stem which is, whatever Scoville units say to the contrary, the hottest chilli I have ever come across – including the Scotch bonnet.

Coconut milk and cream
The coconut is central to the cultures of Southeast Asian countries, where virtually every part of the palmyra palm is used. Coconut milk is one of the most important elements in Asian cooking and is used in both savoury and sweet dishes. This is not the clear, sweet liquid you find inside coconuts, but the extract of fresh, shredded coconut flesh achieved by soaking it in boiling water. You can now buy coconut milk and thick coconut cream in cans and packets. These are excellent – and among the most fattening substances on earth.

Daun kesum
This herb resembles spearmint in appearance but not in taste, and it has no substitute.

Fish cake
Sold ready-cooked in rolls by Chinese and Vietnamese shops, this is made from the puréed flesh of different kinds of fish.

Fish sauce

More than any other ingredient, fish sauce is the flavour which differentiates so many dishes, where it replaces salt. Like soy sauce, it is used as a table condiment, but it is also much used in cooking. The most common fish sauces are Thai nam pla and Vietnamese nuoc mam. Made in the same way from small sea fish and squid fermented with sea salt, they are to all intents and purposes indistinguishable. The taste is hard to describe and fortunately not anything like its smell.

Galangal

This looks similar to ginger, but has a harder and smoother skin that does not need to be peeled. With a flavour that is more earthy than ginger, it is hotter on the tongue and has a resinous smell.

Holy basil

Also called Thai basil, its purple-tinged leaf with a strong aniseed note is a very different thing from the Mediterranean herb used in pesto, and the two are not interchangeable.

Kaffir lime leaves

These are uniquely flavoured, perfumed really, and you cannot make a green curry paste without them. They are a thick, shiny and dark green, and look as if two leaves have stuck themselves together while growing. It is actually illegal to import fresh lime leaves into any EU country, a piece of bureaucratic nonsense to do with a perceived risk of diseased leaves infecting our citrus groves. Next time you sight one of our endangered lemon orchards, let me know. I find that you can buy them without any difficulty. Freeze-dried lime leaves are not the same thing.

Lemon grass

Another important ingredient, now fortunately quite common here, even in our supermarkets. Unless the stalks are left whole and removed at the end of cooking, the woody outer leaves should first be removed and discarded.

STEAMED SCALLOPS WITH GINGER AND SPICED VEGETABLE SALAD

Steamed on a bed of ginger, the scallops are sliced and served with a spiced vegetable salad which should include Thai basil. Although Mediterranean basil is not the same thing at all, on this occasion it may be substituted. The salad should be served at room temperature after a period in the fridge to allow the flavours to develop. Kecap manis is a deep dark and thick Malay soy sauce sweetened with palm sugar.

serves 4

7.5-cm (3-inch) piece of root ginger, peeled
8 large scallops
1 tsp sesame oil
8 Thai purple basil leaves, for garnish
coriander leaves, for garnish

FOR THE SPICED VEGETABLE SALAD:

225 g (8 oz) okra
¼ tsp caster sugar
4 plum tomatoes, quartered and pulp discarded
½ tsp cumin seeds
½ tsp black mustard seeds
¼ tsp fenugreek seeds
¼ tsp caraway seeds
¼ tsp peppercorns
2 tbsp sunflower oil
2 tsp sesame oil
3-cm (1¼-inch) piece of root ginger, peeled and cut into matchsticks
1 red onion, cut into chunks

2 garlic cloves, chopped
salt
1 tbsp kecap manis or soy sauce
225 g (8 oz) baby cucumbers, quartered lengthwise
4 spring onions, cut at an angle into 2.5-cm (1-inch) pieces

First prepare the salad: put the okra in iced water. Scatter the sugar over the tomato and reserve. Roast the spices in a dry pan over a low heat for 3–4 minutes, stirring, until aromatic. Grind to a powder and reserve.

Heat the sunflower and sesame oils in a large frying pan. Add the ginger, the onion chunks and the spice mixture. Sweat over the lowest heat until you can smell all these aromatic ingredients, then stir in the garlic and cook for 2 minutes.

Drain the okra and add to the pan. Turn up the heat to high and stir-fry for 2–3 minutes. Add the tomato, season with a pinch of salt and continue to stir-fry for 1 minute. Stir in the soy sauce and remove from the heat.

Transfer to a serving dish and leave to cool to room temperature, then chill for 2 hours. Remove to a serving bowl and add the remaining ingredients.

Bring a saucepan of water for your steamer to the boil.

Shred the ginger and put on a plate. If the scallops are large, cut them across into 3, leaving the corals whole, then brush with the sesame oil and sit on top of the ginger. Sprinkle with a little salt and steam for 5 minutes or until just done, opaque white all the way through. Check one by slicing into it laterally and lifting up the flap.

Divide the salad between 4 deep bowls. Arrange the scallops on top with the steamed ginger and, just before serving, tear the basil and scatter over all with some whole coriander leaves. Thai purple basil dries rapidly so buy and use the same day.

SOFT-SHELL CRABS WITH PENANG CURRIED VEGETABLES

Soft-shell crabs have long been popular in the USA and are now gaining popularity around the world. They take very little cooking and are rich, so two make a generous helping. Penang curry powder is aromatic rather than hot and complements the delicate crabs well.

serves 4
4 pak choi
675 g (1½ lb) new potatoes
1 lemon grass stalk, thinly sliced
1 star anise
2 tsp cumin seeds
1 tsp cardamom seeds
1 tsp black peppercorns
1 tbsp Penang curry powder or other fragrant mild curry powder
225 g (8 oz) onions
150 ml (¼ pint) sunflower or groundnut oil
2 garlic cloves, chopped
juice of 1 lemon
7.5-cm (3-inch) piece of root ginger, peeled and grated
8 soft-shell crabs
75 g (3 oz) flour
salt and pepper
2 tsp dried chilli flakes
whole coriander leaves, for garnish

Blanch the pak choi in rapidly boiling salted water for 2 minutes. Refresh in iced water, drain and reserve.

Parboil the potatoes with the lemon grass and the star anise for 15–20 minutes, until just done. Refresh in the cold water, drain and reserve.

Toast the cumin and cardamom seeds with the peppercorns in a dry pan over a low heat for 2–3 minutes, stirring, until aromatic. Then grind to a powder and mix with the curry powder. Reserve.

Cut the onions in half, then cut these across into thin slices. Sweat in 2 tablespoons of the oil until soft and translucent. Add the garlic to the onions, stir in and cook for 2 minutes. Stir in the spice powder and cook for 2–3 minutes. Cut the potatoes in half lengthwise and stir these in with the pak choi. Lower the heat as far as possible, stir in the lemon juice and grated ginger. Keep hot.

Put the remaining oil in a large pan over a moderate heat. Roll the crabs in seasoned flour which has had the chilli flakes mixed into it and fry for about 3 minutes on each side.

Put a pak choi in the centre of each plate, spooning the potatoes around. Place 2 crabs on top of the pak choi and garnish with lots of whole coriander leaves.

THAI FISH CAKES WITH CABBAGE SALAD AND NUOC CHAM

These may be steamed or fried since they are not the potato-based sort, being made of puréed fish. If you flour them lightly, they shallow-fry well. The inclusion of the egg white is not authentic but delivers a lighter cake which holds together better.

Nuoc cham is a chilli-hot lime-based Vietnamese dipping sauce that is as easy to make as vinaigrette. You decide precisely how hot you want to make it, but it really should be quite fiery. If you do not have any shrimp paste, then include 2 teaspoons of fish sauce instead.

serves 4

550 g (1¼ lb) cod fillet, skinned and any pin bones removed
1 lemon grass stalk
1 shallot
handful of coriander
1 hot green chilli
1 tsp turmeric
1 tsp salt
white of 1 egg
flour, for dusting
groundnut or sunflower oil, for frying (optional)

FOR THE NUOC CHAM:
3 hot red chillies, cut into tiny dice
3 garlic cloves, finely chopped
juice of 5 limes
3 tbsp fish sauce
1 tsp sugar
2 tbsp shredded carrot

FOR THE CABBAGE SALAD:
350 g (12 oz) white cabbage
1 red onion, cut in rings
2 red shallots, shredded
1–2 hot red chillies, shredded
2 tbsp coarsely chopped coriander leaves
2 tsp belachan (shrimp paste), grilled (see page 233)
juice of 1 lime
1 tbsp groundnut or sunflower oil
salt and pepper

Cut the cod into chunks and put them in a food processor.

Peel off the thick outer leaf of the lemon grass stalk, top and tail it and cut across into the thinnest rings possible. Finely chop the shallot, coriander and chilli. Add all of these to the fish, together with the turmeric, salt and egg white. Blitz to a smooth purée, scraping down the sides 2 or 3 times. Transfer to a bowl, cling-wrap the top and refrigerate for at least 2 hours or overnight.

Meanwhile, make the *nuoc cham*: put the chillies in a bowl with the garlic. Cover with the lime juice and

leave to marinate for 30 minutes. Add the fish sauce, sugar and shredded carrot. Mix together and leave for at least 10 minutes before using. (It will keep in the fridge for a week without deterioration.)

Using a tablespoon to give the right amount, form the chilled fish mixture into 12 balls and then flatten these into cakes on a lightly floured surface. Shake off any excess and either steam on plates for 12–15 minutes or shallow-fry in oil over a low-to-medium heat for about 3 minutes on both sides, until golden brown.

Make the cabbage salad: cut the stalk out of the cabbage and discard it, then cut the cabbage across into thin slices. Pull them apart and put in a salad bowl with all the other ingredients. Season with salt and pepper and toss. Serve the *nuoc cham* in little bowls, mounding the cabbage salad on one side of a serving platter and the fish cakes on the other.

STEAMED COD WITH COCONUT AND CHILLI

You could also use a cheaper fish, like coley, or anything firm and whiteish. If cooked in a Chinese bamboo steamer, it can be served directly from it at the table. You can ask your fishmonger to remove the pin bones, but should still check for any that may have been missed by running your finger along the bone line, removing them with a small pair of pliers. If you can't find pandanus leaves then substitute fresh fig leaves, which also impart a similar flavour. Sounds daft, but it's true.

serves 4

450 g (1 lb) white fish fillets, skinned and any pin bones removed
salt and pepper
4 garlic cloves
15 g (½ oz) coriander, with stems and roots
2 purple shallots
1 tsp dried chilli flakes
1 tsp ground turmeric
1 egg
150 ml (¼ pint) coconut milk (page 233)
2 tbsp nam pla fish sauce
1 tbsp cornflour
2 fresh pandanus leaves or large fig leaves
Jasmine Rice (page 308), to serve

Cut the fish fillets into 2.5-cm (1-inch) strips. Scatter with 1 teaspoon of salt and refrigerate for 1 hour. Remove and rinse under cold running water. Pat dry and return to the fridge until needed.

Coarsely chop the garlic, coriander and shallots. In a food processor, blitz these to a liquid purée with the chilli flakes. Transfer to a bowl and stir in the turmeric, the beaten egg, coconut milk and fish sauce. Grind in about ½ teaspoon of pepper and beat to amalgamate all the elements. Stir in the fish strips and turn to coat evenly. Remove to a rack to drain excess moisture, then dust with the cornflour.

Lay the leaves on the base of the steamer and place the fish on top. Steam for 12–15 minutes, until firm and opaque. Serve with jasmine rice.

THAI GREEN CURRY WITH FISH

Cod is obviously not an Asian fish, but it is ideal for inclusion in a curry. Added right towards the end of cooking, its firm, plump flesh holds up well and will present as coherent pieces. You can substitute any white fish fillets. Monkfish is a good choice, if rather expensive, as are large raw prawns. The cabbage salad on page 236 could follow this dish.

When properly made with a pestle and mortar, a true curry paste results, which will keep for a long

time in an airtight container. A processor, by comparison, produces a wet purée which does not keep so well and has too much water in it to fry. Sweating the paste with oil to drive off the water prior to using it is therefore a good thing to do. Packed in jars and filmed with oil, fresh processor-made paste will keep in the fridge for a month. It may also be frozen in ice-cube trays and stored in the freezer in zip-lock bags.

Finding a manufactured food product which is really authentic is rare. The Thai green curry paste imported and marketed in Britain by Merchant Gourmet is one such rarity. It is expensive, but you will be hard-pressed to make it any better, so a couple of sachets in the storecupboard is a good idea.

There is no single recipe for a curry paste, and you can change the balance and emphasis by adding more or less of a given ingredient. Obviously, the amount of hot chilli can be varied to taste.

serves 4

175 g (6 oz) red shallots, thinly sliced
2 tbsp groundnut or sunflower oil
300 ml (½ pint) coconut milk
800 g (1¾ lb) cod fillet, skinned and pin bones removed
steamed Jasmine Rice (page 308), to serve
handful of whole coriander leaves

FOR THE GREEN CURRY PASTE (**makes about 225g / 8 oz**):

2 tsp cumin seeds
2 tsp coriander seeds
1 tsp black peppercorns
10 hot green chillies, chopped
3 long mild green chillies, chopped
10 red shallots, chopped
10-cm (4-inch) piece of galangal, peeled and grated
3 lemon grass stalks, tough outer leaves removed and chopped
115 g (4 oz) coriander, including stems and roots
60 g (2 oz) Thai basil
5 garlic cloves, chopped
4 tsp belachan (shrimp paste)
8 kaffir lime leaves, chopped
2 tbsp sunflower or groundnut oil
fish sauce

First make the curry paste: in a dry pan and over a low heat, toast the cumin and coriander seeds with the peppercorns for 2–3 minutes, until aromatic. Grind to a powder in a coffee grinder and put into a food processor with the chopped chillies, complete with their seed membranes, and all the remaining ingredients except the oil. Blitz, adding 1–2 tablespoons of the oil through the feeder tube and stopping from time to time to scrape down the sides, until you have a thick purée.

Put this purée in a dry frying pan over a low-to-medium heat and cook, stirring constantly, until you have driven off most of the water and you are left with an oily, dry paste.

Store in a sterilized jar in the fridge filmed with oil, where it will keep for weeks, using 1–2 tablespoons per 4 servings with the other curry ingredients.

In a wide shallow pan, wok or frying pan over a moderate heat, stir-fry the shallots in the oil until they start to soften, but do not allow to colour. Add 1–2 tablespoons of the curry paste and continue stir-frying for a minute, before adding 300 ml (½ pint) of water and the coconut milk. Bring to the boil, lower the heat and simmer for 10 minutes.

Taste and add fish sauce to season instead of salt, then stir in the fish and continue to simmer until just cooked, about 3 minutes.

Serve in deep warmed bowls, with steamed jasmine rice and scattered with whole coriander leaves.

GRILLED SNAPPER WITH TAMARIND BROTH AND BELACAN

The overhead grill is not something you find in Southeast Asia and, while sometimes barbecued, fish is most often fried. Here it is seared quickly in a dry pan and finished under a hot grill for a lighter effect, then served in a tamarind and belacan broth with steamed jasmine rice and deep-fried red onion rings. This broth goes well with any grilled firm-fleshed white fish, especially monkfish, halibut or cod.

serves 4

30 g (1 oz) fresh belacan (shrimp paste), or 15 g (½ oz) dried
3 tbsp groundnut or sunflower oil, plus more for deep-frying
3 lemon grass stalks, thinly sliced
6 spring onions, thinly sliced
2 hot red chillies, chopped
4 garlic cloves, thinly sliced
30 g (1 oz) coriander, with stems and roots
1.1 litres (2 pints) tamarind water (page 20)
about 60 g (2 oz) palm or muscovado sugar
175 g (6 oz) red onions, sliced into thin rounds
4 boneless steaks of white fish, skin on, each about 200g (7 oz)
½ tsp cracked pepper
2 tbsp fish sauce
1 tbsp Pearl River soy sauce
Jasmine Rice (page 308), to serve

If using dried belacan, prepare as described on page 233.

Put 2 tablespoons of the oil in a pan over a moderate heat. When shimmering-hot, add the belacan and stir for 2 minutes, lowering the heat when it sizzles. Then fry gently for 20 minutes, stirring from time to time. Add the lemon grass, spring onions, chillies, garlic and the coriander stems and roots, finely chopped. Turn up the heat to moderate and fry, stirring, for 2 minutes. Pour over the tamarind water, add the sugar and bring to the boil. Lower the heat and simmer for 15 minutes, then strain through a sieve into a clean pan, discarding the solids. Taste, adding more sugar if it is too sour, and keep warm over the lowest heat.

Preheat oil for deep-frying to 170°C (335°F). Fry the red onion until almost done and remove, leaving in the basket. Increase the oil temperature to 190°C (375°F). You will plunge them back in again for a minute to crisp only just before serving.

Preheat the grill and put a frying pan large enough to accommodate the fish steaks without touching over a moderate heat until smoking-hot. Brush the fish on both sides with the remaining oil and season with plenty of cracked pepper (all the salt you need will come from the belacan, fish sauce and soy sauce). Lay the fish in the pan, skin side down, and cook for 1 minute. Then transfer to under the grill for about 4 minutes, when the flesh will be opaque and firm to the touch.

Stir the fish sauce and soy sauce into the broth. Carefully transfer the fish to large warmed bowls, skin side up. Ladle over the broth and scatter over the coriander leaves.

Plunge the red onions back into the oil to crisp, removing to kitchen paper for 30 seconds to drain. Serve the rice and onions separately.

SINGAPORE PRAWN AND CHICKEN NOODLES

This dish is based on fried curried rice stick noodles, the word 'Singapore' in this context implying inclusion of spices usually found in an Indian curry and not necessarily a Singapore provenance. Once you have gathered the elements together and soaked the noodles, its preparation takes less than 5 minutes.

Rather than use a commercial curry powder, make your own from freshly roasted whole spices, thereby lifting a very good dish to a much higher plane. If you don't have a Cantonese roast meat take-away nearby, leave the cooked pork out or substitute *char siu* (page 98).

serves 4
225 g (8 oz) rice stick noodles
4 eggs
1 tbsp dark sesame oil
salt and pepper
5 tbsp sunflower oil
115 g (4 oz) skinned chicken breast fillet
1 tbsp fish sauce
225 g (8 oz) peeled raw tiger prawns
1 habanero or Scotch bonnet chilli, deseeded and thinly sliced
1 sweet red pepper, deseeded and thinly sliced
5-cm (2-inch) piece of root ginger, peeled and cut into tiny matchstick strips
2 garlic cloves, cut into paper-thin slices
5 tbsp chicken stock
115 g (4 oz) Cantonese roast pork fillet (optional)
8 spring onions, shredded
115 g (4 oz) beansprouts
3 tbsp Kikkoman soy sauce
coriander leaves, for garnish

FOR THE CURRY POWDER:
1 tsp coriander seeds
½ tsp cumin seeds
½ tsp black peppercorns
½ tsp black mustard seeds
½ tsp fennel seeds
½ tsp ground fenugreek
½ tsp ground turmeric

First make the curry powder: put all the spices in a dry heavy pan over a low heat and toast, stirring, for 3–4 minutes until aromatic. Grind to a powder and reserve.

Pour boiling water over the noodles and leave to stand for 3 minutes. Drain in a colander and leave for 45 minutes before use.

Put a 25-cm (10-inch) frying pan over a moderate heat. In a bowl, whisk the eggs with the sesame oil, 1 teaspoon of the curry powder and ½ teaspoon of salt. Brush the pan with sunflower oil, pour in the eggs and quickly, with the back of a fork, turn the eggs with a circular movement in the middle, then tilt the pan to spread the eggs and make a flat omelette that coheres but is still moist. Remove to a cutting board and reserve.

Cut the chicken into 5-mm (¼-inch) slices, then cut these into matchsticks. Put a tablespoon of the oil in the same pan and stir-fry the strips until just done, which will only take 60–90 seconds. Remove to a bowl with the fish sauce, toss and reserve. Butterfly the prawns, put another tablespoon of oil in the pan and stir-fry quickly. Add to the chicken, toss and reserve.

Put another tablespoon of the oil in a large wok over a moderate heat. When smoking-hot, add the chilli, red pepper, ginger and garlic, and stir-fry. As they start to soften, add the remaining curry powder. Toss and stir in, cooking for about 60 seconds.

Add the stock and bubble until it has evaporated, then add the pork (if using it), the shredded spring onions, the noodles and beansprouts, tossing to combine. Add the prawns and chicken and toss until hot.

Add the soy sauce and serve immediately in deep warmed bowls. Slice the omelette into 2.5-cm (1-inch) strips and arrange on top, finishing with whole coriander leaves and a turn or two of the peppermill.

VIETNAMESE FIVE-SPICE CHICKEN

Five-spice powder is a mixture of star anise, cinnamon, cloves, Sichuan pepper and fennel seeds. This is rubbed into the bird, which is then marinated in rice wine and soy sauce before being grilled then deep-fried. The two-stage cooking is quite common in Southeast Asia, where few homes have ovens, but it is much easier to just roast the chicken and this also produces a much less fatty dish.

serves 4

1 chicken, about 1.5 kg (3¼ lb)
1 tbsp five-spice powder
Cos lettuce leaves, to serve
mint leaves, to serve

FOR THE MARINADE:

2 spring onions, thinly sliced
3 garlic cloves, finely chopped
5 tbsp soy sauce
3 tbsp rice wine or dry sherry
3 tbsp sesame oil
2 tsp brown sugar

FOR THE DIPPING SAUCE:

5 tbsp Vietnamese fish sauce
2 tbsp fresh lime juice
1 hot red chilli, thinly sliced

The day before: put the spring onions and garlic in a bowl with the soy sauce, rice wine or sherry, sesame oil and brown sugar. Mix to dissolve the sugar.

Spatchcock the chicken by cutting down and through both sides of the backbone. Rub it all over with the five-spice powder. Lay the bird in a tray big enough for it to lie opened out and pour over the marinade. Refrigerate for 24 hours, turning the other way up halfway through.

Next day: preheat the oven to 220°C (425°F, gas 7). Put the chicken, skin side down, on a rack over a tin. Roast for 15 minutes, then turn skin side up. Brush with the marinade, turn down the oven to 190°C (375°F, gas 5) and roast for another 15 minutes. Turn again, brushing with marinade, and give it another 15 minutes. Turn for the last time, brush the skin and give it a final 15 minutes – an hour in total. Remove and allow to rest for 15 minutes before jointing, then chop into bite-sized pieces through the bones. Mix the dipping sauce ingredients together in a bowl.

Serve with crisp lettuce leaves, mint leaves and the dipping sauce.

MUNG BEANS WITH CHICKEN AND PRAWNS

Mung beans, so often eaten when sprouted, are here cooked whole. Chicken and prawns are a natural partnership, and the sambal makes an appropriate spicy side dish. Lard is a traditional Thai cooking medium – even for chicken and prawns – and is used here for the added flavour it imparts.

serves 4

225 g (8 oz) mung beans
4 chicken breasts
1 tbsp groundnut oil
1 tsp five-spice powder
1 tsp dried chilli flakes
30 g (1 oz) lard
8 spring onions, shredded
5-cm (2-inch) piece of galangal
2 garlic cloves
12 tiger prawns, heads removed and butterflied in their shells
2 tbsp nam pla fish sauce
8 Thai basil leaves, coarsely chopped, for garnish
Hot Chilli and Garlic Sambal (page 246), to serve

Cover the mung beans with water and bring to the boil. Turn off the heat and leave to stand for 1 hour.

Pour away the water, cover with fresh water and

return to the boil. Turn down the heat and simmer for 45 minutes.

Brush the chicken breasts with groundnut oil, then rub the five-spice powder and chilli flakes into the chicken. Lay the breast in a frying pan, skin side down, over a low-to-medium heat and cook for 6 minutes. Turn, giving the other side 4 minutes. Remove to a board and, after 5 minutes, cut across at an angle into thick slices. Reserve.

Drain the beans and reserve.

In a wok over a moderate heat, melt the lard and, when shimmering-hot, add the spring onions, galangal and garlic. Stir-fry for a minute, then add the prawns and cook until just done. Add the fish sauce, followed by the beans and the chicken, tossing all together.

Ladle into large warmed bowls and scatter over the coarsely chopped Thai basil, giving people small individual bowls of sambal.

RED CURRIED CHICKEN

Although made in the same way as green (page 240), red curry paste has different characteristics and is hotter. The paste forms the basis for many curries, though chicken and beef are my favourites.

serves 4
4 chicken legs
225 g (8 oz) onions, thinly sliced
2 tbsp groundnut or sunflower oil
300 ml (½ pint) coconut milk
salt
steamed Jasmine Rice (page 308), to serve
handful of whole coriander leaves, for garnish

FOR THE RED CURRY PASTE (**makes about 200 g / 7 oz**):
10 hot red chillies
2 tsp cumin seeds
2 tsp coriander seeds
2 tsp peppercorns
3 lemon grass stalks, tough outer leaves removed and sliced
10-cm (4-inch) piece of galangal, grated
handful of coriander stems and roots, chopped
5 garlic cloves, chopped
8 kaffir lime leaves, chopped
4 tsp belachan (shrimp paste), grilled in foil for 5 minutes
3 tbsp groundnut or sunflower oil

First make the curry paste: put all the ingredients except the oil in a food processor and blitz to a purée, scraping down the sides at regular intervals and dribbling a little oil through the feeder tube as required.

Fry the purée in 2 tablespoons of the oil over a low-to-medium heat to drive off excess liquid. Store the paste, filmed with oil, in a screw-top jar in the fridge.

Cut through the joints of the chicken legs to divide them into drumsticks and thighs. Reserve.

In a wok or other appropriate large pan, stir-fry the onion in the oil until it starts to brown. Add 2 tablespoons of the curry paste and continue to fry for a minute, before adding the coconut milk and 300–400 ml (½ pint–14 fl oz) of water. Stir in the chicken pieces and bring to the boil. Season with a little salt, turn down the heat and simmer for about 45 minutes, or until the meat pulls easily from the bone. Taste and adjust the seasoning.

Serve with steamed jasmine rice and scattered with whole coriander leaves.

NASI GORENG

Nasi goreng – literally 'rice fried' – is a one-dish meal for an informal party. A special fried rice is the central feature, but much of the fun comes from the wide range of side dishes, which typically include hot chillies, onion and tomato salad, cucumbers, rolled omelettes, hot chilli and garlic sambal, crisp deep-fried shallots, hard-boiled eggs, prawn wafers, peanuts and bananas. These are presented in small dishes at the table for people to add to their fried rice as they choose.

This is one of the best-known Indonesian dishes outside the Far East, along with beef *rendang*, *satay ayam* and the complicated salad, *gado-gado*. Holland's long colonial involvement in the 13,000 islands they called the Dutch East Indies has left a legacy of Sumatran, Javanese and Balinese restaurants in Amsterdam, where *nasi goreng* is the basis of that Dutch Sunday lunch institution, the *rijksstaffel* – rice table.

Prepare as many side dishes as you fancy, but include rolled omelettes, chilli sambal and crisped shallots. These last can be bought from Oriental stores ready-to-serve – they are really good and save a lot of time when you are in a hurry. One of the biggest manufacturers and consumers of crisped shallots are the Danes. Go figure, because I can't.

serves 6
400 g (14 oz) long-grain rice
2 tsp belachan (shrimp paste)
4 chicken breast fillets
4 tbsp groundnut oil
salt and pepper
½ tsp dried chilli flakes
4 shallots, chopped
18 large peeled raw prawns
handful of whole coriander leaves

FOR THE CRISP SHALLOTS:
500 g (1 lb 2 oz) purple shallots
corn or groundnut oil, for frying

FOR THE ROLLED OMELETTES:
4 eggs
salt
1 tsp caster sugar
groundnut oil, for frying

Wash and steam the rice as described on page 308. Drain, then spread out on a dish, fluff with a fork and leave to cool.

Wrap the belachan in foil and put it under the grill for 3–5 minutes or put the packet in a dry frying pan over a low heat, turning occasionally, for 8–10 minutes. It will give off an aroma which we will be genteel and call 'pungent'.

To make the crisp shallots, cut them in half lengthwise, then across into the thinnest strips. The quickest way is to deep-fry them, but this taints the oil, precluding its use for anything else but onions. A large wok is a good solution, though until you have fried shallots a couple of times, it is advisable to use a thermometer to gauge the temperature. Put in corn or groundnut oil to a depth of 5 cm (2 inches) and heat to 190°C (375°F). Put in half the shallots, which will bring the temperature down, and stir-fry for a minute or so, then lower the heat. Fry, stirring continuously until they take a uniform mahogany colour. It is quite tricky to judge the precise point when they are crisp and ready to drain because, within seconds, you can take them too far and they become burned and bitter. Remove to kitchen paper to drain, put in more oil and fry the second batch. If not using immediately, put them in a screw-top jar with some kitchen paper in the bottom.

Make the omelettes: break 2 of the eggs into a bowl with half an eggshell of cold water, ½ teaspoon each of salt and caster sugar. Whisk vigorously. Heat a 20-cm (8-inch) frying pan – not an omelette pan. Wipe with groundnut oil and set over a moderate heat. Pour in the eggs, swirling and tilting to achieve an even depth. As soon as the bottom has set, turn the omelette over and give the other side a few seconds to set before turning out. Repeat with another 2 eggs. When they have cooled slightly, roll them up and cut across into

5-mm (¼-inch) strips. Reserve.

Brush the chicken breasts with groundnut oil and season with salt, pepper and half the chilli flakes. Dry-fry 2 of the chicken breasts over a low-to-medium heat, starting skin side down. Depending on thickness, they will take about 8 minutes on the first side and 6 on the other. Leave to stand for 10 minutes before cutting across into strips.

Make a frying paste by putting the shallots, remaining chilli flakes, grilled belachan (shrimp paste) and the remaining groundnut oil in a food processor and blitzing. Put this paste in a large wok over a medium heat and fry until all the liquid has evaporated, then add the peeled raw prawns. Stir-fry, tossing, for 1 minute, then add the cooked rice and chicken and continue stir-frying for about 4 minutes, when the rice will be heated through.

Serve immediately, scattered with whole coriander leaves and with as many side dishes as you like.

SKIRT STEAK WITH COCONUT AND SPINACH

Skirt steak is usually cooked only briefly or it toughens, requiring lengthy cooking before it goes tender again. This takes the longer option.

serves 4

675 g (1½ lb) skirt steak
30 g (1 oz) palm or muscovado sugar
2 tbsp nam pla fish sauce
1 litre (1¾ pints) coconut milk
6 shallots, coarsely chopped
2 hot red chillies, coarsely chopped
4 garlic cloves
1 lemon grass stalk, coarsely chopped
60 g (2 oz) dry-roast peanuts, shelled
3 tbsp sunflower oil
salt
350 g (12 oz) pak choi
small bunch of Chinese chives, snipped, for garnish

Cut the steak into strips and put in a pan with the sugar and fish sauce. Cover with the coconut milk and 300 ml (½ pint) of water. Bring to the boil, lower the heat to a simmer and cook for 1 hour, or until the beef is tender. Do not overcook or the meat will become dry and flaky. Strain through a sieve into a clean pan, reserving the beef.

Reduce the cooking liquid by half over a moderate heat. While it is reducing, put the shallots, chillies, garlic and lemon grass in a food processor with the shelled peanuts, 1 tablespoon of the sunflower oil and 1 teaspoon of salt. Blitz to a paste. Bring a pan of salted water to the boil for the pak choi.

Fry the paste in the remaining oil over a moderate heat, stirring, for 2 minutes. Lower the heat to a minimum and continue to fry, stirring from time to time, for 10 minutes.

Add the cooked beef and pour over the coconut sauce. Bring to the boil, lower the heat and simmer for 2 minutes.

Blanch the pak choi for 30–45 seconds in the rapidly boiling salted water and drain in a colander. Press gently to remove excess water.

Put on a warmed serving dish. Spoon the beef and sauce on top. Scatter over snipped Chinese chives and serve immediately.

HOT CHILLI AND GARLIC SAMBAL

This can be made well in advance, since it will keep in a jar in the fridge for weeks. You can make it in much larger quantities using roughly the same proportions. There is no need to discard the chilli seeds or seed placenta.

serves 6–8
10 large mild red chillies
15 hot red chillies
8 garlic cloves
4 tsp shrimp paste (belachan)
100 ml (3½ fl oz) groundnut oil
2 tsp salt

Cut the chillies in half lengthwise, then across into the thinnest strips you can manage. Finely chop the garlic.

Grill the belachan (see page 233).

Put the oil in a wok or high-sided frying pan over a moderate heat and, when shimmering-hot, add the chilli strips, garlic and toasted belachan. Stir-fry for 3 minutes.

Stir in the salt and immediately remove from the heat.

When cool, serve in small bowls at the table or transfer to a sterilized jar, filmed with oil, and refrigerate until needed.

RED PORK AND CELERY SALAD

Any cooked pork can be used for this dish but I like the slow-simmered Cantonese red cooked pork on page 101. The celery should be Thai but any leafy celery will do, the leaves being the defining ingredient.

serve 4
1 head of leafy celery, outer stalks discarded
285 g / 12 oz cooked pork, cut in matchsticks
1 hot red chilli, shredded
8 red shallots, cut in quarters
juice of 2 limes
1 tablespoon fish sauce
2 tsp caster sugar
115 g/ 4 oz onion, thinly sliced
2 tbsp sunflower or groundnut oil

Cut the celery into 2.5 cm (1 inch) pieces. Put in a bowl with the pork, chilli and shallots. Add the lime juice, fish sauce and sugar and toss. Refrigerate for 1–2 hours.

Sweat the onions with the oil over a low heat until soft. Turn up the heat to medium and stir-fry until caramelized. Transfer to kitchen paper to drain and crisp.

Transfer the chilled salad to a serving plate. Scatter over the crisp onion. Shred the celery leaves and cover the salad with them.

Chapter 15
Spain & Portugal

Much more than paella

Not only are these not the same place, but the cooking differs regionally as well as nationally, though there are significant similarities. The food traditions are ancient and may be directly compared to those of France and Italy, being as complex and sophisticated in their restaurant expressions, but sharing the same joy of a more accessible and universal cooking. This is based on a farmhouse kitchen rooted in historic continuity and born of an obsession with the quality and freshness of ingredients, as well as the seasonal nature of its dishes.

Portugal and Spain are both major holiday destinations, a fact which has given rise to perceptions of their cooking that may be erroneous, since tourism involves giving people what they want and that usually means a modification or an evolution that is not always desirable. Paella is one example of a dish that has been blown up to give it a party gloss, and *zarzuela* is another. As Colman Andrews wrote in *Catalan Cuisine*, after eating a complicated fish stew so described by American friends in their restaurant in Hollywood as *zarzuela a la Port Lligat*: '... I doubt sincerely that *zarzuela* – which literally means a kind of light opera or variety show and which in the food sense is an elaborate, touristy sort of neo-bouillabaisse found mostly in pricey restaurants – has ever, in fact, been served in the tiny Costa Brava cove of Portligat.'

Both countries have remarkable produce and Spain is, amongst other things, the world's largest producer of fine olive oil and saffron. Its wines are among the best in the world. Jerez gave us sherry, Oporto port. The cheeses and cured meats are extraordinary and now, thankfully, more readily available outside the areas of production. These are the culinary building blocks of a citadel of good cooking. How I wish that I was sitting now in a bar in old Madrid, a glass of chilled fino on the table and a little dish of olives, thinking about where to go for lunch.

The first holiday you spend somewhere beautiful and excitingly foreign with someone you love colours your feelings about the food of that place forever and it creates expectations for the rest of your life. These few recipes are things that I ate once upon a time in just such a way. They remind me of how much more there is yet to explore and how much waits undiscovered.

CLAMS WITH GARLIC, PARSLEY AND HAM

The ritual of picking up the little shells, sucking out the tiny nuggets of clams and then dipping a piece of bread in the sauce has a nice – kind of elemental – feel to it. Though this dish is quick and easy to make, the resulting flavours are complex.

serves 8 as a tapa, or 4 as a first course

5 tbsp olive oil
115 g (4 oz) Serrano or other mountain ham, finely diced
3 garlic cloves, finely chopped
3 tbsp dry sherry
1 kg (2¼ lb) carpetshell clams (palourdes)
2 tbsp finely chopped parsley

Put the olive oil in a large shallow saucepan. Add the ham and fry gently over a low heat for 1–2 minutes, stirring. Add the garlic and cook for another minute.

Turn up the heat to high and add the sherry and, as it bubbles, dump in the clams. Stir and toss, then cover tightly. Cook for about 3 minutes, or until all the clams have opened. Stir in the parsley and serve in warmed bowls.

CHICKEN BREASTS WITH TOMATO, PEPPERS AND MOUNTAIN HAM

Spain produces some of the finest tomatoes and peppers in the world. The ham is of the Serrano type, usually eaten raw but here diced and cooked. It is very salty, so take this into account when seasoning.

serves 4
675 g (1½ lb) ripe plum tomatoes
500 g (1 lb 2 oz) red and yellow peppers
1 hot red chilli
3½ tbsp olive oil
115 g (4 oz) Serrano or Parma ham, cut in a piece
4 chicken breasts
salt and pepper
2 garlic cloves
3 tbsp dry sherry
handful of flat-leaf parsley
bread, to serve

Blanch the tomatoes in boiling water for 15 seconds. Refresh in cold water and skin. Cut into quarters, strip out the seeds and pulp and discard, or add to a stock. Reserve the tomato petals.

Destalk the peppers, cut out and discard the seeds and white placenta, then cut the flesh into strips. Destalk the chilli and shred.

Put 2½ tablespoons of the olive oil in a frying pan and fry the peppers and chilli over a low heat until soft.

Dice the ham and put in a large frying pan with 1 tablespoon of the olive oil. Fry gently over a low heat until the fat runs and the ham starts to brown. Remove with a slotted spoon and reserve.

Season the chicken breasts with salt and pepper and shake a little flour over the skin. Lay them to fry in the ham fat and olive oil skin side down, and fry over a low-to-medium heat, turning after 8 minutes. Cook the other side for about 6 minutes. Remove and keep warm.

Turn up the heat under the pan, add the garlic and deglaze the pan with the sherry. Return the ham to the pan and, when all liquid has evaporated, add the peppers. Toss to coat.

Spoon the peppers into 4 warmed plates. Slice the chicken breasts at an angle and arrange on top. Garnish with a little finely chopped parsley and serve with a basket of bread on the table.

GRILLED TUNA WITH ALLIOLI AND MASHED POTATOES

Allioli is the Catalan version of *aïoli* and, like a really authentic *aïoli*, does not contain eggs, simply being an emulsion of garlic paste and olive oil painstakingly worked up with a pestle and mortar and seasoned only with salt. This is not easy to achieve and it is very fragile, with a tendency to split if you even look at it the wrong way. Colman Andrews writes at length on the subject and he as much as says it is almost too difficult even to try and make a bona fide *allioli* and admits that most Catalan restaurants include eggs in the mixture, just like a mayonnaise.

My own efforts have pushed me away from the pestle and mortar towards a hand-held electric whisk. I use some dry mashed potato for the base and roast the majority of the garlic, only including one raw clove. Whether I am entitled to call this emulsion *allioli* is debatable. What I do know is that, in combination with the seared tuna and the mashed potatoes, it makes a dish you have to feel good about.

serves 4
4 tuna steaks, each about 200 g (7 oz)
olive oil, for brushing
salt and pepper

FOR THE ALLIOLI AND MASHED POTATOES:
1 head of garlic, plus 1 extra clove
1 kg (2¼ lb) floury potatoes
300 ml (½ pint) extra-virgin olive oil

First make the *allioli*: preheat the oven to 190°C (375°F, gas 5). Wrap the head of garlic in foil and bake for 45 minutes. Remove, unwrap and, when cool enough to handle, cut the top off to expose the insides of the cloves and squeeze these out into a mixing bowl. Smash and finely chop the raw garlic and add to the bowl.

Boil the potatoes until done and mash them dry. Add 2 tablespoons of the potato to the garlic.

Preheat a ridged grill pan. Brush the tuna with olive oil and season generously with salt and pepper.

Add about 1 teaspoon of salt to the garlic pulp and potato, and beat with an electric whisk, adding the oil at first a few drops at a time and, as it coheres, pour in the remaining oil in the thinnest stream you can manage. (I use a Kikkoman soy sauce bottle for this, which dispenses the oil at the perfect rate for mayonnaise-type sauces.) Reserve.

Put 2 tablespoons of the *allioli* into the mashed potatoes and whisk in, then add olive oil until you have a smooth purée. Transfer to the switched-off oven to keep warm.

Briefly grill the tuna for about 1½ minutes on each side. Transfer to large warmed plates. Put a spoonful of allioli on top of each steak and put a mound of potatoes on each plate. Offer the remaining *allioli* in a sauceboat for people to have more if they want to.

TROUT ON POTATO TORTA WITH ALLIOLI

The trout are coated with seasoned flour and sautéed in a mixture of olive oil and butter until the skin is crisp. They are served on individual potato tarts made of interleaved wafer-thin potato slices baked with goose fat, the assembly being finished with a fried garnish of garlicky strips of Bayonne ham. The *allioli* is the perfect accompaniment. For the baking of the potato tarts you will need four small crêpe pans, cake tins or pizza trays that can go in the oven.

serves 4
4 small trout, cleaned and heads and tails removed
60 g (2 oz) flour
1 tbsp olive oil
15 g (½ oz) butter
1 garlic clove, finely chopped
85 g (3 oz) Bayonne or Serrano ham, cut into strips
chopped flat-leaf parsley, for garnish
Allioli (see previous recipe, using 2 tbsp potato)

FOR THE POTATO TORTA:
675 g (1½ lb) baking potatoes, scrubbed but not peeled
5 tbsp melted goose or duck fat
1 garlic clove, finely chopped
salt and pepper
sprig of thyme, chopped

First make the potato torta: preheat the oven to 200°C (400°F, gas 6). Slice the potatoes thinly on a mandoline grater. Rinse under cold running water, then squeeze dry in a cloth.

Brush the pans or baking tins with the melted fat. Put the garlic in a mixing bowl with the remaining fat. Season with salt and pepper and add the chopped thyme. Add the potato slices to the bowl and turn to coat. Arrange them in overlapping concentric circles to fill the base of the pans.

Bake for 25–30 minutes, when the tops will be golden-brown and the potatoes will have shrunk in from the edge.

Meanwhile, prepare the trout: season the flour quite

heavily with salt and pepper and put on a plate. Press the trout in it to coat both sides, shaking off any excess.

About 10 minutes before the potato torta will be done, put a large heavy-based frying pan over a medium heat and, when it is hot, add the olive oil and butter. As the butter foams, lay in the trout and turn the heat down slightly. Fry for about 4 minutes, then turn and give the other side about the same time. The flesh must be cooked around the bone. Using a fish slice, remove to a warmed plate.

Put the garlic and the ham strips in the pan, add the remaining butter and stir-fry for a minute or 2.

Put a potato torta on each of 4 warmed plates, then put a trout on top of each. Spoon over the ham and the buttery pan juices and scatter over a little parsley before serving with the *allioli*.

PAELLA

The round, shallow metal pan with handles on both sides in which paella is cooked is called a *caldero*. The ingredients of a paella may be very simple and limited – say chicken or rabbit, snails and broad beans – or a luxurious mixture of meats and shellfish and beans, a celebratory feast for a high day and the sort of mixture visitors to Spain expect when they order a paella. The rice is the key ingredient, just as it is in a risotto, and the type of rice is similar, being short- rather than long-grained. I use Italian risotto rice, as it makes a cracking paella too; the difference in execution being that the cooking liquid is added all at once and not gradually. You will be able to find a risotto rice easily, but the right Spanish rice is harder to come by. Good saffron is vital and is added here towards the end of cooking, when it delivers maximum impact.

The duck gizzards are optional but, being first simmered for two hours in the chicken stock, give it and the paella a remarkable depth of flavour and they are delicious in their own right with the rice.

serves 6
30 duck gizzards (optional)
1.25 litres (2¼ pints) chicken stock
150 ml (¼ pint) dry white wine
2 bay leaves (optional)
6 ripe plum tomatoes
115 g (4 oz) green beans
175 g (6 oz) broad beans, blanched and peeled
16 large raw unpeeled prawns
30 saffron strands
5 tbsp olive oil
225 g (8 oz) onion, diced
400 g (14 oz) Vialone or Arborio rice
salt and pepper
4 chicken breast fillets
handful of flat-leaf parsley, chopped, to garnish

If using the gizzards, simmer them in the chicken stock and white wine for 2 hours with the bay leaves. Strain the cooking liquid through a sieve into a measuring jug and discard the bay leaves. If reduced, top up to 1.1 litres (2 pints) with water. Reserve the gizzards.

Blanch, refresh and skin the tomatoes. Quarter, discarding the pulp and reserve.

In a pan of rapidly boiling salted water, first cook the green beans for 3–4 minutes, refresh in cold water and reserve. Cook the broad beans for 8 minutes, or until done. Refresh and reserve.

Remove the prawn heads, keeping them for use in a stock. Butterfly the prawns by cutting open down the back and removing and discarding the intestinal thread. Reserve.

Put the saffron to soak in a ramekin with 2 tablespoons of hot water.

In a large *caldero* or heavy casserole, put

4 tablespoons of the olive oil over a low heat and sweat the onions until soft and translucent. Stir in the rice, turning to coat, then pour over the stock. Turn up the heat to moderate and bring to the boil. Stir in the gizzards, if you are using them. Lower the heat to a simmer, season and cook without stirring for 20 minutes.

While the rice is simmering, brush the chicken breasts with the remaining olive oil, season with salt and pepper and fry over a low-to-medium heat in a heavy-based frying pan, starting skin side down and turning after about 8 minutes, to cook the other side for about 6 minutes or until just cooked through. Remove to a cutting board, skin side up.

When the rice has been cooking for 20 minutes, dice the tomato pieces and stir in with the saffron and its soaking liquid, the prawns and the beans. Continue to cook for 5 minutes, when all the liquid should have been absorbed. The rice on the bottom may have formed a crust, which is considered desirable so long as it has not burned. Carve the chicken breasts at an angle into bite-sized slices and stir in.

Turn off the heat, cover the pan and leave to stand for 10 minutes. It should be served warm rather than hot. Serve on large plates with a little finely chopped parsley scattered on top.

VALENCIAN ORANGE CHICKEN

In this part of Spain, famous for its sweet juicy oranges, there are at least two dishes that combine chicken breasts with oranges: *pechugas de pollo en salsa de naranja* and *pechugas de pollo con naranjas*, the difference being that in the former the chicken is cooked in orange juice while in the latter it is sautéed in butter and olive oil and served with an orange sauce. The first is simpler and, I think, nicer.

serves 4

4 chicken breast fillets
2 tbsp olive oil
salt and pepper
60 g (2 oz) unsalted butter
300 ml (½ pint) freshly squeezed orange juice
8–10 mint leaves
boiled long-grain rice, to serve

Brush the chicken breasts with olive oil and season generously with salt and pepper.

Lay them, skin side down, in a non-stick frying pan over a low heat. After 5–7 minutes, when the skin is crisp and golden brown, turn them and add the butter to the pan.

Turn up the heat to moderate and pour round the orange juice. Cook at a fast bubble, until the meat feels firm to the press of a finger, about another 5 minutes. Remove the chicken breasts to warmed plates.

Chop the mint leaves and stir into the sauce. Turn off the heat and leave to stand for 1 minute for the mint to infuse before spooning over the chicken.

Serve with boiled long-grain rice.

DUCK WITH NEW POTATOES, PEAS AND ASPARAGUS

Duck legs are the ideal joint to make *confit* (page 117) or stews. There is no waste and they are good value. Here they are lightly salted and marinated with vinegar. After rubbing with spices, they are slowly pan-fried with a little duck or goose fat until the meat is tender and the skin crisp.

serves 4

4 duck legs
salt and pepper
1 tsp coriander seeds

2.5-cm (1-inch) piece of cinnamon stick
2 cloves
1 tsp allspice berries
1 tsp black peppercorns
1 tsp dried chilli flakes
500 g (1 lb 2 oz) asparagus
500 g (1 lb 2 oz) new potatoes, scrubbed
500 g (1 lb 2 oz) peas in the pod, or 200 g (7 oz) frozen peas
1 tsp sugar (optional)
2 tbsp duck or goose fat
3 tbsp extra-virgin olive oil
4 spring onions, cut across at an angle into 2.5-cm (1-inch) lengths
2 garlic cloves, chopped
2 tbsp finely chopped flat-leaf parsley

Cut through the joint to separate the legs into drumsticks and thighs, and rub 2 teaspoons of salt into them. Leave at room temperature for 2 hours. Rinse under cold running water and pat dry with kitchen paper.

In a small, heavy-based pan, toast the coriander seeds, cinnamon, cloves, allspice berries and peppercorns over a low heat for 2–3 minutes or until aromatic. Grind with the chilli flakes to a powder. Rub this into the duck and leave to stand for another 2 hours.

Prepare the vegetables: cut the asparagus into 2.5-cm (1-inch) lengths, discarding the woody base (or use these in a vegetable stock or soup). In a large pan of rapidly boiling salted water, first cook the potatoes, transferring to cold water briefly before draining. Then blanch the asparagus pieces, but not the tips, for about 4 minutes or until done, refreshing them in cold water and draining in the same way; do the same for the tips but only blanch for 1 minute.

If using freshly shelled peas, add the sugar to the water and cook them for 8–10 minutes, or until just tender. Refresh, drain and reserve. Replace the blanching water with fresh water and return to a simmer.

In a large heavy-based frying pan, melt the duck or goose fat over a moderate heat and lay in the duck pieces. As they start to fry, turn down the heat and cook for 15 minutes. Turn, giving the other side 10–12 minutes. Remove to a warmed plate and reserve.

During the last 5 minutes of cooking the duck, add the olive oil to the pan, turn up the heat to moderate and sauté the spring onions. As they wilt, add the garlic and stir-fry for a minute.

Return the vegetables to the fresh simmering water for 1 minute. If using frozen peas, add them now. Drain the vegetables well and add to the frying pan. Season with plenty of pepper and a little salt, and turn to coat with the onions, spices and oil. Remove from the heat and add the parsley, turning gently with a spoon to mix through.

Put a drumstick and thigh on each warmed plate, mound the vegetables next to them and serve immediately.

HOME-SALT COD AND BLACK-EYED PEA SALAD

The idea of salting cod at home came from Alastair Little when we were working together on *Food of the Sun*, our book which redefined a number of classic Mediterranean dishes. He had been experimenting with salting cod for his restaurant, finding the fashionable use of commercially produced salt cod overblown. Ever a doubter, even of his usually faultless good taste, it was only when I salted some cod in my own kitchen that I was convinced of its desirability. Well, that is putting it mildly.

serves 4
Maldon sea salt
450 g (1 lb) cod fillet, any pin bones removed
350 g (12 oz) black-eyed peas
2 bay leaves
2 hot red chillies
juice of 1 lemon
4 tbsp extra-virgin olive oil
salt and pepper
bunch of rocket
handful of chives, chopped, for garnish

FOR THE GREMOLATA:
grate zest of 1 lemon
1 garlic clove, finely chopped
2 tbsp finely chopped flat-leaf parsley

The day before: scatter 1–2 tablespoons of the salt in a Swiss roll tin or suitable dish large enough to hold the cod fillets lying flat. Lay the cod on it, skin side up, and scatter a thin layer of salt on top. Cover with cling-wrap and put a weight on top. Refrigerate overnight. Put the peas to soak overnight.

Next morning, rinse the fish and pat dry. Clingwrap and refrigerate until ready to make the salad. Use the same day.

Drain the peas and put in a pan with fresh water to cover generously. Bring to the boil and boil hard for 5 minutes. Drain and cover with fresh water again by about 2.5 cm (1 inch), then add the bay leaves and chillies, bring to a simmer and cook until the peas are just tender, about 45 minutes. Drain and remove the aromatics.

About 30 minutes before you want to serve, slice the cod thinly like smoked salmon and lay on a porcelain dish, dress with lemon juice and leave to marinate.

Make the gremolata by mixing all the ingredients in a bowl.

In another bowl dress the drained cooked peas with the gremolata and half the olive oil and toss to coat evenly. Taste and season with salt and pepper if you think it needs it.

Mound the rocket on individual plates and arrange 2 or 3 slices of cod around it. Divide the black-eyed peas equally, mounding them on top of the rocket. Dribble a little of the lemon juice marinade over each serving, pouring the remaining olive oil on top. Scatter with chives and serve.

CHICKEN AND CAPER BERRIES IN CRAB MAYONNAISE

The combination of shellfish with chicken has a long tradition in the Mediterranean kitchen. The caper berries give the dish a rather more Spanish flavour, making it a hybrid dish to eat close to any border. Caper berries are the fruit of the caper bush and a speciality of Andalucia, where they are most often lightly pickled in sherry vinegar and brine. The caper bush grows wild in volcanic soil and thrives in arid habitats. Caper berries are delicious straight from the brine as a nibble with a glass of sherry.

The chicken, crab and mayonnaise can all be prepared the day before and refrigerated overnight. The dish then takes only minutes to assemble and serve. It is very rich and is best balanced with a lightly dressed salad of watercress or rocket, and a basket of bread for which no butter will be required.

serves 4

1 chicken, about 1.35 kg (3¼ lb), poached (page 76)
225 g (8 oz) picked white crab meat
300 ml (½ pint) mayonnaise
300 ml (½ pint) thick Greek-style yoghurt
1 tbsp Dijon mustard
85 g (3 oz) caper berries, drained
30 g (1 oz) flat-leaf parsley, finely chopped
salt and pepper
finely chopped chives, to garnish

Cut the chicken meat into bite-sized pieces. Put in a mixing bowl with the crab.

Separately beat together the mayonnaise, yoghurt and mustard. Add the caper berries and fold in with the finely chopped parsley leaves. Season to taste.

Mix all together and transfer to a serving bowl, scattering finely chopped chives over the top.

Chapter 16
The USA

The food of the silver screen

My first American train ride was a short one, from Grand Central Station to a little place called Tarrytown. 'Return to Tarrytown,' I said to the ticket clerk. He gave me a long-suffering look. 'You too, Mac.' Since I had not asked for a 'round-trip ticket', he thought I was just another quaint Englishman using an antiquated salutation, a 'Get thee back to Tarrytown,' by way of greeting.

This was my first experience of the two cultures divided by a common language. The year was 1973 and the Americanization of Britain was still at an early stage. No Jerry Springer trailer-trash or Oprah touchy-feely; no cheap flights to Florida, no McDonald's or pizza home delivery, only three TV stations and they all shut down with the national anthem by midnight, and no touch-tone dialling. In every and any popular sense I was in a foreign land.

But such a land and such a joy. I was already in love with New York, my first gateway, long before I went there; my childhood spent going to the cinema four times a week. I longed to order a Jack Daniels on the rocks in P. J. Clarke's. I dreamed of hanging out at the Algonquin. And I wanted to eat real American food, about which I had strong but entirely positive feelings in general, if rather hazy in particular. What was clam chowder? What cut was a strip sirloin and would it really be too big to eat? Please toss me a chopped salad. Pretzels... what is a pretzel? Hot dogs on the street with steam coming out of a grating right next to the vendor's cart. When the moon hits your eye like a big pizza pie, that's *amore*. Pile me shaved pastrami on rye so tall it won't fit in a wide-open mouth and be rude when you do it, while you put that fat pickle on the side. A real hamburger in a sesame seed bun and run it through the garden... The Maine lobster with the drawn butter? I want one.

Heading south for mint juleps, I'd travel on a train so I could hear the horn sound, a great mournful blast through the long night, waking to a morning hot and humid enough to stick a seersucker jacket to my back. The Big Easy for sugar-dusted beignets at the Café du Monde, lunching off gumbo, jambalaya and dirty rice in the French Quarter. Slide down to Key West from Miami on a Greyhound bus, then go west, young man. Palm trees and freeways, Hollywood and the Beverly Hills Hotel. Sprinklers making rainbows on green baize lawns. Driving past orange and lemon groves. Do you really have an avocado tree in your garden?

Small town America waited: homecoming queens and watching ball games on the bleachers – the what? – drinking a bottle of Dr Pepper so cold your finger cuts a line through the frost on the glass. And what could it taste like, this soft drink? And root beer. Somebody told me it was like that funny red toothpaste in your mouth, like fizzy Euthymol, and it was. Cherry cobbler, apple pie à la mode, chocolate brownies, popcorn in buckets, these were the stuff of dreams fed by the flickering light that cut through the cigarette smoke of the movie theatre like a knife through Håagen-Dazs mocha ripple. A movie theatre, not a cinema screening pictures, but honest-to-God movies. At last I was there, the land of my heroes, Faulkner, Fitzgerald, Hemingway, McCullers, Updike, Wolfe, and Gonzo Thompson.

I stepped off that plane all those years ago and it was as foreign as anywhere else I had ever been, but it was also like coming home. I was there, not another member of the audience watching an image on a screen but right there three-dimensionally. It was still there when I turned round. I became, in Ralph Waldo Emerson's words, a transparent eyeball, for I was at last *in* the movie.

Inevitably, in this land of the automobile, it was a road movie, where so many perceptions are framed by windscreens and side windows. In the country you drive for hours, days even, and nothing changes. 'No gas this route 1,000 miles', a sign urgently warns. Well, of course there is, but it is up the off-ramp at every cross-road and maybe as much as 100 yards from the interstate.

I love the long outskirts roads into every anonymous town, all bearing the same mix of commercial jumble. A drive-in muffler shop sits next to a beautician, the mortician beside a poodle-parlour the bright-lit window of which overlooks a car lot, while at regular intervals fast-food outlets give off a whiff of Fritol: Dunkin' Donuts, McDonald's, Burger King, Dairy Queen, Pizza Hut, all the usual suspects.

I'm only 24 hours from Tulsa and when I get there it is full of churches, for it is the buckle on the bible belt. Georgie Fame and I are there for a wedding – he to play, me as best man. Reading a telegram from Akio Morita to the groom I refer to a currently popular T-shirt: 'Sony – from the people who brought you Pearl Harbor' – and the room hisses with loathing, for, by ugly coincidence, it is the anniversary of the bombing and many of the people at the reception had lost family or friends when the Oklahoma went down.

We are taken to admire the Oral Roberts centre, the world's first big-time TV evangelist's preposterous campus, hospital and bible university built with the donations of the gullible. Their money is counted in The Prayer Tower, above which burns an eternal flame. Oral indeed.

America is full of American names: Crespo C. Dollar Jnr, Zoop Dove, Flip Spiceland, Carlton Sheets and Skip Riddle. Everything bursts with a quality that – despite its more absurd, sad and bad manifestations – I fall deeply in love with.

Twenty-five years of visiting and travelling and – from time to time – living in the US have never really completely removed that feeling and I still get a kick out of just being there. Now I am, as people like to call it, 'confined to a wheelchair' or 'wheelchair-bound', some (though not all) of America is where I choose to be because legislation there has made it accessible to me. By the way, I must have a different wheelchair from every other cripple because mine lets me get in and out of it to go to bed or sit on an aeroplane seat or go for a swim, no chains, no binding straps, no pin-down. I use mine, and since MS summarily removed the use of my legs six long years ago, it has accompanied me from Sydney to Maui to... you name it. Have chair, can travel, international meals on wheels.

I guess, since this is the first time I have ever come out on the subject, it is as good a time as any to address the obtuse question I am frequently asked, can you still cook? There is nothing in the kitchen that cannot be done seated that is done standing up and, yes, I cook every day. Some things are more difficult to do sitting down, like rolling pastry (where you need pressure) and carving (where you need leverage), but nothing is impossible. There is no such thing as a disabled cook, only disabled food – which may or may not be cooked by very fit people. I never wrote standing up and I have always preferred to eat sitting down. This is my seventh food book since fate decided I should be permanently seated. End of story. Well, end of that particular story.

And so I took my chair west. I wrote in *Cutting Edge*, my book about California and the cooking inspiration it had given me, that in some ways it is now what France once was. 'California is a place where you find affordable excellence round every corner, where bakers produce wonderful bread and drinkable wine is to be had for $5 a bottle. It is a place where the emphasis will always be on pristine ingredients and where people go to farmers' markets and do not automatically buy their fruit and vegetables drenched in pesticides and packed in plastic from supermarkets.' Not surely that contentious, but it irritated a lot of people who want to dismiss California as frivolous and irrelevant. Love it or hate it, the impact of mixing ingredients from the global kitchen has been huge, and this is where it all began, this phenomenon rather unfortunately described as 'Pacific Rim'.

The better chefs, though, have been as much influenced by Mexican cooking as by the peasant Italian dishes of the Southern Mediterranean, and by the culinary maelstrom of Southeast Asia, where Thai, Vietnamese, Cambodian, Malay and Indonesian styles fuse as well as co-exist. I wrote that this new kitchen was a place 'where Japan can meet France in one bowl, where Italy and China unite on the same plate'. I should also have said that fusions of this sort start out looking and feeling odd, but over time we forget that they are the product of cross-cultural combining. Think of Central and South America, the food of whose countries is the product of a 400-year-long fusion between Spain and Portugal and the New World.

The handful of dishes which follow are not about fusions, at least not in the contemporary sense, though the Creole cooking of New Orleans is about as melting pot as you can get. They are just things I loved and have worked on a bit. And they all make me wish I was there right now.

It must begin with a sandwich, though what the world outside the USA calls a sandwich and what Americans know to be a sandwich, and the difference between them, is as huge as that between real and virtual sex. The Earl of Sandwich, a gambling dissolute and therefore not all bad, is credited with its invention. Unwilling to leave the whist table, he had his servant bring him a piece of meat between two slices of bread and so earned his place in history. As the Earl immediately understood, a perfect sandwich is not defined by too many things shoved willy-nilly together – a current confusion – but by absolute simplicity.

In these terms, a good hamburger must be the absolute American sandwich for, though most of us do not think of it as such, a sandwich it surely is. It is made only from minced beef seasoned with salt and pepper. Anything else is added in the bun, like rings of raw sweet Vidalia onion, a dill pickle, ketchup and mustard.

HAMBURGERS

It is important to use good beef, but this should have at least a 15 per cent fat content and better still about 20 per cent or the burger will split and taste dry and chewy. The best way to get the right proportion of lean to fat is to discuss it with your butcher and have him mince a selected piece of meat for you, as they always do in France. Blade bone or flank steak are perfect.

As you will see, for optimum flavour and juiciness, I recommend that hamburgers be cooked medium-rare. Yes, I know that undercooked meat can kill. I live and eat dangerously. I don't dismiss E-coli lightly, but there is a way round it if you are worried, because the bacteria live on the surface and are killed by high temperatures. In a hamburger you eat the bacteria from the surface of the meat because they have been minced into the middle of the patty, the bit you want to leave under-done. If you have a mincer, the get-out is to lay the piece of meat for the hamburgers in a smoking-hot pan for 15 seconds on each plane, then mince it. No worries, mate, as burger addicts say in Australia.

makes 6
900 g (2 lb) minced beef (see above)
salt and pepper
6 hamburger buns

Spread the meat out, season with salt and pepper, and divide into 6 equal portions, then form these into balls, squeezing gently between your hands to compact. The dilemma is how hard to squeeze. If you pack them too loosely they will fall apart, but squeeze too tight and they will cook tough and dry.

The best way to cook them is in a heavy non-stick frying pan, preheated over a low flame and then turned up to medium a minute before you start cooking. Turn once, giving both sides the same exposure. Hamburgers this size will cook to medium-rare in 5 minutes.

The quality of burger buns you buy is not terrific. They taste better, though, if you split them and toast the cut surface on a smoking-hot grill pan, as this gives them a smoky taste, cuts the sugar and improves the texture.

DILL PICKLES

This is a recipe for making the pickled cucumbers to go with your burgers. Use the small fat cucumbers which will fit whole, sitting upright, in a 2-litre (3½-pint) kilner jar.

makes 1 kg (2¼ lb)
4 garlic cloves, peeled
2 hot dried red chillies
5 tbsp white wine vinegar
1 kg (2¼ lb) small cucumbers
20 black peppercorns
bunch of dill, well washed and drained
85 g (3 oz) sea salt

Put the peeled garlic cloves and the chillies in a ramekin, cover with the white wine vinegar and leave for 1 hour. Sterilize the kilner jar (see above) in boiling water.

Wash the cucumbers. Put the garlic, red chillies and vinegar in the jar with the peppercorns. Pack as many cucumbers as you can into the jar, adding the bunch of fresh dill when it is half full, so that it sits in the middle.

In a pan, bring 1.5 litres (2½ pints) of water to the boil with the sea salt. Turn off the heat and, when cool, pour this over the cucumbers. They must be completely covered. Seal tightly.

Leave for 7 days before opening and eat within 3 weeks. Once open, keep refrigerated.

SEARED TUNA CAKE WITH CARROT STRIPS AND CHILLI RÉMOULADE

This is my homage to the modern sandwich in a bun, very West Coast. The fried carrot sounds most unsuitable, but it is in the form of thin strips deep-fried until crisp, and these are sweet and entirely appropriate. The tuna is minced and cooked just like a hamburger; the crust seared outside and rare in the middle.

serves 4

500 g (1 lb 2 oz) tuna fillet, trimmed
1 tbsp Kikkoman soy sauce
salt
2 tbsp sesame seeds
1 tsp cracked black pepper
flour, for dusting
oil, for deep-frying

2 large carrots
4 hamburger buns
2 tsp wasabi (page 163)
1 recipe-quantity Chilli Rémoulade
2 tbsp groundnut or sunflower oil

FOR THE CHILLI RÉMOULADE:

6 spring onions
2 tbsp flat-leaf parsley
2 anchovy fillets
2 hot red chillies, deseeded
2 tbsp chives
1 tbsp capers
575 ml / 1 pint thick mayonnaise
1 tbsp Dijon mustard
3 tbsp tomato ketchup
juice of 1 lemon
1 tbsp Worcestershire sauce

Make the rémoulade: chop the spring onions, parsley, anchovies, chillies, chives and capers and beat into the mayonnaise, with the other ingredients. If worried about eating raw eggs, use a good quality, commercial mayonnaise as the base. The strong flavourings will mask any inadequacies.

With your sharpest knife, cut the tuna into the smallest pieces you can manage, or put through the coarsest plate of a mincer. Put in a bowl with the soy sauce and a pinch of salt and mix thoroughly with a fork. Form into 4 balls, squeezing gently to compact them, then shape into fat cakes, making them taller than they are wide, as they are going to be cooked raw in the middle.

Put the sesame seeds and pepper on a plate and press the cakes in to coat both sides. Shake over a little flour and reserve.

Heat oil for deep-frying to 180°C (350°F). Heat a ridged grill pan. Put a heavy-based frying pan over a low-to-moderate heat.

Using a potato peeler, cut the carrots lengthwise into strips. Split the hamburger buns. Mix the wasabi to a paste with water and stir into the rémoulade.

Deep-fry the carrot strips until soft. Remove and reserve, turning the temperature of the oil up to 190°C (375°F) after you have done so.

Toast the buns on the cut surfaces on the smoking grill pan to stripe them and reserve.

Turn the heat to high under the frying pan. When it is smoking-hot, swirl in the oil and immediately lay in the tuna cakes, searing each side for 1½ minutes to give a crisp crust, but leaving them raw in the middle.

Sit them on the bottom halves of the buns on warm plates. Plunge the carrot strips back into the oil for a minute or two to crisp them, then drain on kitchen paper.

Put a spoonful of chilli rémoulade on top of the tuna cakes and arrange the carrot on top.

Sit the tops of the buns against the cakes at an angle and serve at once, putting the remaining rémoulade in a bowl on the table for people to help themselves.

EGGS BENEDICT

This construction of poached eggs bathed in hollandaise and presented on toasted English muffins is one of the best-known and best-loved dishes on the brunch menu. As American as brunch itself – the 'English' muffin was an American invention – eggs Benedict is very rich, hollandaise being a sauce of egg yolks and butter, but unquestionably delicious if your constitution is up for it.

serves 4
salt and pepper
1 tbsp wine vinegar
4 very fresh eggs
2 English muffins
15 g (½ oz) butter
4 slices of ham or grilled bacon
1 tsp paprika

FOR THE HOLLANDAISE SAUCE:
3 tbsp lemon juice
4 egg yolks
125 g (4½ oz) diced unsalted butter

You want 2 pans of water on the hob, one to poach the eggs and the other to act as the bottom half of a double boiler for the sauce. For the poaching, put on a wide shallow pan of lightly salted water and the vinegar to boil. You want the water to bubble, but not too hard.

Bring the second pan to a simmer and have the lemon juice ready for the sauce. Put the egg yolks in a bowl over a pan of simmering water in which the base of the bowl sits just above the water but does not touch it. Whisk in 45 g (1½ oz) of the butter, a few pieces at a time, then whisk continuously until the butter melts. Add another 45 g (1½ oz) of butter and continue whisking vigorously. As the sauce starts to thicken, whisk in the remaining butter. When it is fully incorporated, remove the bowl and continue whisking off the heat for 1½–2 minutes. If the sauce splits at any point, immediately beat in a tablespoon of boiling water.

A teaspoon at a time, add the lemon juice, whisking in each time until fully incorporated before adding the next. Season with salt and pepper to taste and return the bowl over the hot water, whisking continuously until it is as thick as mayonnaise, which should take 3–5 minutes. At this point, remove the bowl from the heat.

Break the 4 whole eggs, one at a time, into a saucer and slide them into the simmering vinegared water. Poach for 2–3 minutes. Remove with a slotted spoon and trim the ragged edges with scissors. If the eggs are really fresh this will not be necessary, as the whites set in a neat round or oval.

To serve, split the English muffins and toast the flat side only, lightly buttering each. Put a slice of ham on top, then sit an egg on the ham and spoon the hollandaise over the eggs. Sit the top half of the muffin at an angle on the first, not touching the yolk. Sprinkle a little paprika on the hollandaise and serve at once.

SHRIMP COCKTAIL

Is the prawn cocktail British, French or American? All three countries may lay claim to having invented the sauce Marie Rose which distinguishes it, but I think that the essential ingredient, bottled tomato ketchup, bats the ball firmly into the US court, where the dish is called shrimp cocktail. You can make it with scampi or langoustines if you are feeling grand. Australian freshwater yabbies make a perfect cocktail in the Southern Hemisphere, while chunks of lobster tail elevate it another step up the ladder of the sublime, only you need to change its name accordingly. The sauce is also lovely with crab. Current restaurant trends embellish prawn cocktails with funny fruit salads, something to be avoided. Romaine lettuce – what we call Cos – is the leaf of choice, sweet and crisp, the perfect foil.

What makes this particular version so good is the attention paid to the court-bouillon, the poaching liquid, which, despite its aggressive use of acids and aromatics, does not dominate the prawns but rather brings out their natural flavour. The amount of salt used has been carefully calculated to give a salinity akin to that of the sea. Adding salt to the ice slurry in which the prawns are rapidly cooled after cooking prevents loss of flavour.

If you don't have any fresh horseradish root to grate, mix a teaspoon of green wasabi powder (page 163) to a paste with water and stir this in with the other ingredients.

serves 4

1 kg (2¼ lb) large raw prawns, peeled and deveined, heads and shells reserved
1 Cos lettuce
2 tbsp extra-virgin olive oil
2 tsp lemon juice
chopped parsley, to garnish

FOR THE COURT-BOUILLON:

600 ml (1 pint) dry white wine (can be sour)
3½ tbsp white wine vinegar
1 tbsp black peppercorns
1 tbsp coriander seeds
2 bay leaves
handful of parsley stalks
3 lemons, quartered
salt and pepper

FOR THE COCKTAIL SAUCE:

300 ml (½ pint) thick mayonnaise
2 tbsp tomato ketchup
1 tsp Tabasco sauce
2 tsp freshly grated horseradish
1 tbsp lemon juice
2 tsp brandy
1 tbsp chopped flat-leaf parsley

The court-bouillon is made in two stages: in a large saucepan, put the prawn heads and shells with the wine, vinegar and 2.25 litres (4 pints) of water and bring to the boil. Lower the heat and simmer for 20 minutes, then strain through a sieve into another pan.

Add the peppercorns, coriander seeds, bay leaves, parsley stalks, lemon quarters and 3 tablespoons of salt. Bring to the boil and boil hard for 5 minutes.

Add the prawns, stir, then turn off the heat. The

prawns will be cooked in about 2–2½ minutes, their flesh becoming firm and opaque.

While they are cooking, fill a mixing bowl with water and add a tray of ice and 1 tablespoon of salt. As soon as the prawns are done, transfer them to this ice slurry and stir in. Leave for 2 minutes, then drain and refrigerate, if not using immediately.

To serve, mix all the sauce ingredients together in a bowl, season with pepper and stir in the prawns, tossing to coat.

Cut the Cos leaves across into 5-cm (2-inch) strips. In another mixing bowl, make a dressing with the olive oil, lemon juice and a little salt and pepper. Toss the lettuce in this, then mound in the middle of each of 4 large plates. Spoon the prawns neatly on top and scatter a little chopped parsley over all.

PO'BOY SANDWICHES

Po'boy sandwiches, cut from crisp-crusted baguettes and stuffed with fried oysters, are the old fast food of New Orleans. They have been a local speciality since the end of the eighteenth century and probably got the name in the early 1800s. Po'boys were served all day, but were best known as a comfort snack after a night of depravity in one of the brothels or gambling dens to be found on and around Bourbon Street in the French Quarter, in the same way that onion soup has been eaten by successive generations as a pick-me-up in the early hours of the morning in Paris's Les Halles. Bourbon Street is still pretty depraved, though now it is tourists who flood the topless bars and juke joints of the Big Easy.

Poor is hardly the way to describe an oyster sandwich in Europe, where at the time of writing one native English oyster costs £2 at the fishmonger and more in a restaurant, though oysters are still cheap in New Orleans. Today's po'boys are filled with deep-fried oysters, but whether or not this was always the case I am not sure. Deep-frying was already commonplace in the eighteenth century and the practice of egging-and-crumbing shellfish or coating them in batter had been known for 200 years or more, so probably so, though I have also come across references to sandwiches made with shallow-fried oysters. The advantages of deep-frying are that it makes the oysters bulkier, gives them a nice crunchy coating and makes them go further. It is what you would be served in New Orleans today.

Allow 6–8 large Pacific (rock) oysters for each sandwich, though you would be more likely to get a dozen in New Orleans. The kind of bread you use makes all the difference. A ficelle is perfect. Otherwise a section of baguette is *de rigueur*. The tangy taste of crème fraîche works best, but you can substitute double cream.

serves 2
oil for deep-frying
12–16 oysters
60 g (2 oz) unsalted butter
2 ficelles or 1 baguette
2 eggs, beaten
60–85 g (2–3 oz) fine dry breadcrumbs
½ tsp Tabasco sauce
squeeze of lemon juice

Preheat the oven to 200°C (400°F, gas 6). Preheat oil for deep-frying to 190°C (375°F).

Open the oysters, reserving the juice in the shells.

Melt the butter over a low heat. Split the bread lengthwise, brush the cut surfaces with the melted butter and put to crisp for 5 minutes in the oven.

Roll the oysters in the beaten egg, then toss to coat in the crumbs. Repeat this sequence to give a double coating.

Deep-fry for 2 minutes. Remove and drain on paper towels.

Mix the Tabasco with the oyster juices and lemon juice. Arrange the oysters along the sandwiches and dribble the mixture over them. Shut your eyes and you can hear the addictive see-saw swinging violin and piano accordion of a zydeko band and the crash and stamp of the dancing.

JAMBALAYA

Cajun people came to Canada from South Western France and their first colony in Nova Scotia was called Acadia. Driven out by the British, many of them moved to the largely French settlement of Louisiana, where they became known as Cajuns, developing a spicy cooking style that mixed local ingredients with basic French techniques.

Perhaps the most famous Cajun dish is jambalaya, a highly seasoned rice dish typical of southern Louisiana. It may include any combination of chicken, beef, pork, sausage (*andouille*), seafood and ham. It is thought the name comes from the French *jambon* for ham, *à la* and *ya*, a West African word for rice. *Andouille* in Louisiana is a coarsely chopped and highly spiced smoked pork sausage.

I have, to a degree, deconstructed the original recipe – which I find overcooks both the rice and the prawns – and reworked it, using less fat than is traditional. Jambalaya is also usually made with green pepper, to which I have an aversion in the majority of recipes which call for its inclusion. They are basically unripe and their flavour, or rather the lack of it, reflects this. They don't taste as sweet as ripe red or yellow peppers, and when cooked turn an ugly khaki colour. For me, red is best, though I do include lightly cooked green peppers in Shrimp Creole (page 270) for no logical reason.

serves 4

350 g (12 oz) long-grain rice
115 g (4 oz) smoked ham
115 g (4 oz) smoked sausage
2 tbsp corn oil
225 g (8 oz) diced onion
2 celery stalks, strings removed and sliced
1 red pepper
2 garlic cloves, chopped
2 bay leaves
150 ml (¼ pint) chicken stock
500 g (1 lb 2 oz) canned chopped tomatoes
4 skinned chicken breasts
12 large peeled raw prawns
60 g (2 oz) unsalted butter
4 spring onions, thinly sliced
1 tbsp parsley leaves, to garnish (optional)

FOR THE CAJUN SEASONING MIX:

2 tsp hot cayenne or chilli pepper
2 tsp ground black pepper
2 tsp dried oregano
½ tsp dried thyme
1 tsp salt

Steam or boil the rice until just cooked. Drain, fluff with a fork and reserve.

Stir the spice mix together in a bowl and reserve. Cut the smoked ham and smoked sausage into neat 1-cm (½-inch) dice. Fry them in the oil in a flameproof casserole over a moderate heat, stirring, until they exude their fat and start to brown. Add the diced onion, sliced celery and diced pepper, turn down the heat and sweat until soft but not browned.

Add the garlic, bay leaves, seasoning mix, chicken stock and tomatoes with their juice. Cut the chicken breasts into bite-sized pieces, stir in and bring to the boil, stirring. Turn down the heat and simmer until the chicken is just cooked, 5–8 minutes.

Stir in the prawns and continue to cook for 2 minutes more, stirring and turning to ensure even cooking. Add the cooked rice, the diced butter and sliced spring onions. Stir and mix thoroughly over the lowest heat for a couple of minutes. Cover with a lid, remove from the heat and leave to stand for a final 2–3 minutes, when the rice should be heated through.

Serve in large warmed soup plates. Scatter over a few whole leaves of parsley if liked.

CRAB AND AUBERGINE PIROGUE

Pirogue is the Cajun name for the wooden canoe used for fishing and getting about the swampy bayous and lakes of Louisiana. It also describes any vegetable hollowed out and filled, in this case aubergine with crab in a spicy béchamel. Large courgettes are also nice this way and look more like pirogues.

serves 4
2 large aubergines
1–2 tbsp olive oil
45 g (1½ oz) unsalted butter
4 spring onions, thinly sliced
2 garlic cloves, finely chopped
45 g (1½ oz) flour
1 hot red chilli, cut into tiny dice
2 tsp paprika
450 ml (¾ pint) milk
150 ml (¼ pint) dry white wine
1 bay leaf
1 tsp dried oregano
freshly grated nutmeg
salt and pepper
2 egg yolks
2 tsp mustard powder
350 g (12 oz) picked crab meat
60 g (2 oz) Parmesan cheese, grated

Preheat the oven to 220°C (425°F, gas 7). Cut the aubergines in half and hollow them out, leaving 1 cm (½ inch) of flesh on the skin. Shave off a little piece from the curved side of each half so they will sit upright steadily and brush all over with olive oil. Put on a baking sheet.

Melt the butter in a pan over the lowest heat. Add the spring onions and sweat, stirring from time to time, until soft. Add the garlic and then stir in the flour, chilli and paprika. Cook, stirring, for a minute, then whisk in the milk and white wine. Stir in the bay leaf, oregano and nutmeg, and season with salt and pepper. Bring to the boil, lower the heat and simmer for 20 minutes, stirring frequently.

Remove and discard the bay leaf. Off the heat, whisk in the egg yolks and mustard. Return to the heat and cook, stirring for 2 minutes. Turn off the heat and stir in the crab meat and Parmesan. Taste and adjust the seasoning, if necessary.

Bake the aubergine shells for 8–10 minutes, removing before they start to crumple. Fill with the crab mixture. Shake over a few crumbs and dot with butter. Return to the oven until bubbling. Serve very hot.

SHRIMP CREOLE

There is no such thing as a prawn in America, where everything – irrespective of size – is called shrimp. Creole describes the culinary style of New Orleans and is distinct from Cajun food, being the product of the city's historic government by the French, Spanish and Italians at different times. It is said that Creole developed as cooks originally from West Africa worked for different nationalities, taking something from each and fusing it with the knowledge of their own culture while using local ingredients. It is generally thought of as more complex and sophisticated than Cajun food, though I am not sure this is true. As an impartial observer I would say that there are obvious similarities. Indeed, you only have to compare this with jambalaya to see them.

Shrimp Creole is a rich treatment with complex spicing. Cooked in two stages, much of the fat used in the first sauté and stock-making can be skimmed off and discarded if you prefer. Even so, I have significantly reduced the butter. Famous Southern chef Paul Prudhomme stresses the importance of the shrimp heads in their contribution to the flavour. I maximize this element by puréeing the shells before incorporating them in the stock. The use of goose fat is my idea, where a Creole cook might use lard or chicken fat.

serves 6
1 kg (2¼ lb) large raw prawns, heads and shells on
850 ml (1½ pint) fish stock
1 bay leaf
350 g (12 oz) long-grain rice
60 g (2 oz) goose fat
300 g (10½ oz) onions, peeled
4 celery stalks, strings removed and thinly sliced
1 green pepper, deseeded and cut into 1-cm (½-inch) dice
2 garlic cloves, sliced paper-thin
1 tbsp paprika
500 g (1 lb 2 oz) canned Italian tomatoes, puréed
1 tbsp Encona hot pepper sauce or Tabasco sauce
2 tsp oregano
1 sprig of thyme
salt and pepper
60 g (2 oz) unsalted butter
8 basil leaves

Peel the prawns. Devein them and butterfly them open (see page 217–18). Rinse and refrigerate until needed.

Purée the heads and shells and add to the fish stock with the bay leaves. Bring to the boil, lower the heat and simmer for 20 minutes. Pass through a fine sieve, pressing to extract every bit of juice from the shells. Reserve.

Steam the rice until done (page 308) and reserve.

Melt the goose fat in a frying pan and, over a low heat, sweat the onions until translucent. Add the celery and diced green pepper, turn up the heat and fry, stirring until the onions start to brown. Add the garlic and paprika and fry for a minute.

Pour in the stock and the puréed tomatoes. Add the hot sauce, oregano and thyme. Bring to the boil, lower the heat and simmer for 20 minutes. Taste and season with salt and pepper.

Stir in the prawns, then turn off the heat. Leave to stand for 3 minutes then stir in the rice, followed by the butter. Put on a lid and leave to stand for 5 minutes.

Spoon into warmed soup plates. Shred the basil, scatter it over and serve immediately.

BLACKENED SNAPPER

Blackened redfish was the Louisiana dish which caught the international imagination in the early Eighties, when Cajun food was briefly all the rage. With the passage of time it is possible to look back and recognize this as a great dish, which properly uses a local redfish but for which you can substitute red snapper, pompano or even cod or haddock fillets, if no redfish is to hand. This version has all the right flavours, but uses less butter than is traditional. It also replaces with fresh garlic and onion the garlic and onion powders of the proprietary Cajun spice mixes you buy.

serves 4
4 snapper fillets, each about 225 g (8 oz)
1 tbsp paprika
1 tsp salt

1 tsp cayenne
2 tsp freshly ground black pepper
½ tsp dried thyme
½ tsp dried oregano
60 g (2 oz) unsalted butter
3 garlic cloves, sliced paper-thin
2 spring onions, thinly sliced
2 tbsp olive oil
1 lemon, quartered, to serve

Skin the fish fillets and make sure any pin bones have been removed.

In a bowl, mix together the paprika, salt, cayenne, ground pepper, thyme and oregano, and reserve.

In a small pan, melt the butter. Add the garlic and the spring onions and leave to infuse over the lowest heat for 10 minutes, then strain through a muslin-lined sieve into a second bowl, discarding the garlic and onion.

Brush the fish fillets on both sides with olive oil. Scatter half the seasoning in a tray, then lay the fillets on top, pressing down gently. Scatter the remaining mix over, press in and turn to give an even coating.

Heat a large heavy dry frying pan until red hot – at least 5 minutes at maximum. (Don't do this to a non-stick pan or you will ruin it.) Lay the fillets in the pan and dribble a teaspoon of the flavoured butter on top of each. Switch on the extractor or open the door, as acrid black smoke billows. Give them 2 minutes, turn and give them another 1–2 minutes, before serving on warmed plates with lemon quarters, spooning over the remaining flavoured butter.

SHRIMP AND MUSSEL GUMBO WITH STIR-FRIED OKRA

When slow cooked, as it traditionally is in a gumbo, okra produces a mucilaginous extract that has a thickening effect and gives the dish its rather slippery quality. This recipe is a deliberate deconstruction because I don't like that aspect at all, preferring the okra to be only just cooked, the way they generally eat it in Southeast Asia. Gumbo filé – powdered sassafras leaves – gives gumbo its unique flavour and its roots were used to make root beer. Sassafras grows wild through much of North America and was always used by native Americans to thicken and flavour stews, though it was first highly valued by Europeans in the seventeenth century, when it was erroneously thought to cure syphilis.

serves 6

1 kg (2 lb) mussels, bearded, scraped and washed
1 kg (2 lb) large raw prawns, heads and shells on
3 tbsp olive oil
115 g (4 oz) onion, diced
2 celery stalks, strings removed and sliced as thinly as possible, plus the leaves for garnish
1.1 litres (2 pints) fish stock
1 bay leaf
250 g (81/2 oz) canned Italian tomatoes, puréed
1 tbsp sassafras powder (gumbo filé)
1 tsp dried oregano
400 g (14 oz) long-grain rice
5 tbsp dry white wine
salt and pepper
finely chopped flat-leaf parsley, to garnish

FOR THE OKRA:

285 g (10 oz) okra
3 tbsp olive oil
115 g (4 oz) onion, thinly sliced
2 garlic cloves, sliced paper-thin
1 tbsp paprika
1 tbsp Encona hot pepper sauce or Tabasco sauce
1 sweet red pepper, roasted, peeled and chopped

Soak the okra in a bowl of iced water for 1 hour. This helps them retain crispness when cooked.

Remove any beards from the mussels, scrape them and wash them well. Peel and devein the prawns, reserving the heads and shells. Rinse the prawns and set aside.

Put the olive oil in a wide shallow heavy-based saucepan (which has a lid) and, over a low heat, sweat the onion and celery stalks until soft.

Blitz the reserved prawn heads and shells in a food processor until puréed. Put in a saucepan with the fish stock and bay leaf. Bring to the boil, lower the heat and simmer for 20 minutes. Strain through a sieve into a large saucepan, pressing with the back of a spoon to extract every last drop. Add the puréed tomatoes, filé powder and oregano, and bring to a simmer.

Meanwhile, steam the rice as described on page 308.

Add the white wine to the pan of onion and celery and turn up the heat to moderate. As it boils, add the mussels, toss and put on the lid. Cook over a high heat until done, about 4 minutes or until they have all opened.

Drain through a colander, adding the liquid to the broth. Return the mussels to the pan and put the lid back on. Reserve.

Cook the okra: drain the okra in a colander, leave them to dry out, then top and tail them. Put the oil in a large heavy-based frying pan over a low heat and sweat the onions until soft and translucent. Turn up the heat to high. Add the okra with the garlic, paprika, hot sauce and roasted pepper. Fry, tossing, for 3–4 minutes. Turn off the heat and reserve.

Taste the simmering broth and season as necessary. Add the prawns and turn off the heat. After 3 minutes, when they will be just cooked, stir in the rice, followed by the okra and finally the mussels. Put on a lid and leave to stand for 4–5 minutes.

Serve in large warmed bowls, scattering over the finely chopped celery and parsley leaves.

CHICKEN ÉTOUFFÉE

A roux made with vegetable oil and flour that is cooked for as long as an hour is a Louisiana cooking technique that is unique to the region, imparting a distinctive flavour to much of the food. Traditionally, Louisiana cooks use lightly cooked and coloured roux with dark meats and dark long-cooked roux with light meats.

Four distinct stages are recognized by Paul Prudhomme: a pale roux as a sauce base (the one you would use for a béchamel); a light brown roux, used with beef and game dishes; a dark brown, nutty-tasting roux for chicken, pork and veal; and a black roux which is used for gumbos. The last is said to be very difficult to achieve, the difference between black and burned obviously being a very fine line.

In this chicken étouffée – literally 'smothered chicken' – the roux is cooked for 20–25 minutes, when it takes on a deep golden-brown colour.

serves 4

6–7 tbsp corn or groundnut oil
45 g (1½ oz) flour
225 g (8 oz) onions, diced
2 garlic cloves, finely chopped
2 celery stalks, thinly sliced
300 ml (½ pint) dry white wine
2 litres (3½ pints) hot chicken stock
bouquet garni of thyme and a bay leaf
½ tsp dried chilli flakes
salt and pepper
4 chicken legs
60 g (2 oz) unsalted butter
1 red pepper, deseeded and diced
1 red onion, diced
350 g (12 oz) long-grain rice
2 tbsp finely chopped flat-leaf parsley
small bunch of chives, finely chopped

Put 4 tablespoons of the oil in a heavy-based saucepan over a moderate heat and, when it is shimmering-hot, remove from the heat and whisk in the flour. Return to the heat, turn it down a little and cook this paste, whisking continuously, for about 20 minutes, when it should be a dark, reddish-brown colour. If you stop whisking for even a minute, it will stick and burn and will have to be thrown away. Watch out for it spitting too. The paste is super-hot and if you get any on your skin it will give you a very nasty burn, because it sticks to the skin like liquid sugar. Prudhomme calls it 'kitchen napalm'.

Remove from the heat and stir in the diced onion with a wooden spoon. Continue stirring, off the heat, for 2–3 minutes, then add the garlic. Return to a low heat and add the celery and cook, stirring, for 1–2 minutes.

Pour in the dry white wine and bring to the boil, then add 850 ml (1½ pints) of the chicken stock and bouquet garni. Add the chilli flakes and season with salt and pepper. Bring back to the boil, lower the heat and simmer gently.

Put 2–3 tablespoons of the oil in a large frying pan and fry the chicken legs over a medium heat, turning to brown them all over. Transfer to the sauce and simmer for about 40 minutes, or until tender when pierced with a skewer.

About 25 minutes before you calculate the chicken is going to be finished, put the butter in a large saucepan and fry the diced red pepper and red onion over a moderate heat, stirring, for 2–3 minutes.

Stir in the rice, then pour over the remaining simmering chicken stock. Stir, add 1 teaspoon of salt, then bubble for about 15 minutes, stirring from time to time, until all the liquid has been absorbed or evaporated, leaving the rice cooked.

Stir in the finely chopped parsley and then mound on 4 large warmed soup plates. Put a piece of chicken on top, ladle the sauce over and scatter over some chopped chives to finish.

SLOW-FRIED PORK CHOPS WITH BOSTON BAKED BEANS

Boston baked beans are another good way of cooking haricots – what Americans call navy beans – and almost as easy as opening a can. Unlike Heinz, your authentic pot of Boston baked beans does not contain tomatoes, but I think is nicer when it does. It does indisputably contain salt pork however, the recipe for which is on page 125, masquerading under its French name, Petit Salé.

serves 6

600 g (1¼ lb) haricot beans, soaked overnight
1 tbsp paprika
3 tbsp olive oil
6 pork chump chops
1 onion, chopped
500 g (1 lb 2 oz) canned chopped tomatoes
60 g (2 oz) muscovado sugar
125 ml (4 fl oz) molasses or black treacle
3 tsp Colman's mustard powder
350 g (12 oz) piece of salt pork (page 125)
1 bay leaf
salt and pepper

The day before: put the beans to soak in water. Mix the paprika to a paste with the oil and brush the chops with this. Leave to marinate in the fridge overnight.

Next day, when ready to cook: preheat the oven to 150°C (300°F, gas 2).

Bring the beans to the boil, throw away the water and cover with fresh. Return to the boil and pour the beans and water into a casserole.

Put the onion, canned tomatoes and their juices, the sugar, molasses and mustard powder in a food processor and blitz to a purée. Stir this into the beans.

Cut the salt pork into 4 and push the pieces

beneath the surface with the bay leaf. Bring to the boil on top of the stove, cover and put in the oven.

Bake for 4 hours, taking off the lid from time to time and stirring. If it seems to be drying out, stir in a few tablespoons of hot water and take the lid off for the last half hour. Taste and season with salt and pepper.

When the beans are nearly ready, dry-fry the pork chump chops over low heat, turning them after 10 minutes and giving them 8–10 minutes on the other side. Serve the chops with the beans. Although not very American, the beans also go well with duck *confit* (page 117).

CAJUN GARLIC STEAK AND CHILLI BÉARNAISE

Garlic powder has its advocates but include me out. My reaction to opening a jar is that it needs to visit the oral hygienist fast. Fresh garlic is such a magical thing that the use of halitosis powder in its name seems an act of criminal folly. All this by way of saying that garlic powder does not feature in this seasoning though it does in most Cajun meat rubs. Instead, the steaks are marinated overnight in garlic juice and lemon. This has the advantage of imbuing the steak with the flavour of garlic without the bitterness which comes from searing pulped garlic at a high temperature. Before grilling they are dried then coated in pepper, mustard, fennel and chilli. This means that when they hit the super-heated grill pan the smoke given off will challenge the most efficient of extractors. It is therefore best cooked on a day when you can have the doors and windows open or grill on a very hot barbecue (page 201).

serves 4

4 rib eye steaks weighing 200-225 g/ 7-8 oz each
8 cloves of garlic, peeled
juice of 2 lemons
2 tbsp olive oil
1 tbsp black peppercorns
1 tsp chilli flakes
1 tsp fennel
2 tsp Colmans mustard powder
1 tsp salt

FOR THE CHILLI BÉARNAISE

60 g/ 2 oz shallots, peeled and diced
1 tbsp chopped tarragon
1 tsp black peppercorns, coarsely crushed
1 tsp chilli flakes
4 tbsp red wine vinegar
6 quarters Olive Oil Tomatoes (page 309)
200 g/ 7 oz unsalted butter
4 egg yolks
salt and pepper
2 tsp chopped tarragon

Chop the shallots and put in a small saucepan with 1 tbsp chopped tarragon, the coarsely crushed black peppercorns, chilli flakes and red wine vinegar. Bring to the boil and evaporate the vinegar while stirring until you have a moist residue – about 1 tbsp. Sieve to remove the pepper and chilli and put in a food processor. Dice the tomatoes and reserve.

Melt the butter over a low heat. Switch on the processor at full speed and add the egg yolks. Continuing to process, add the melted butter in a thin stream through the feeder tube. Transfer to a bowl over simmering water, stirring with a wooden spoon until thick and spoonable. Taste and season with salt. Just before serving, stir in the tomato dice and the 2 tsp chopped tarragon.

Chop the garlic finely. Put in a food processor with the lemon juice and blitz for 2–3 minutes. Put a piece of butter muslin over a bowl and pour and scrape this mixture into it. Wind it up and squeeze out as much

liquid as you can. Put the steaks in a ziplock bag, add the marinade and refrigerate for 24 hours, removing 2 hours before you want to cook.

Put an unoiled ridged grill pan over a medium heat and leave it for 5 minutes.

Pat the steaks dry and brush with the oil. Coarsely grind the pepper, chilli flakes and fennel. Mix with the mustard powder and salt. Coat the steaks in this on both sides, tapping off any excess.

Turn up the heat under the grill pan to maximum. After 3-5 minutes, when the pan will be incandescent, lay the steaks on at an angle of 45°, turning after 1 minute and three more times to give a neat cross-hatch and a total cooking time of 4 minutes for a rare finish. Remove to a warmed plate to stand for 4 minutes before serving with chips or on top of wild mushroom potato cakes (page 50) with a mound of caramelized onions on top (page 124). Offer the chilli béarnaise in a sauceboat.

SUCCOTASH

A dish from the southern states of the USA, succotash is a sauté of corn and broad beans and was originally a Native American word describing, one imagines, something along these lines, though without the bacon this recipe suggests including. You can use frozen beans and corn when neither vegetable is seasonally available.

serves 4

500 g (1 lb 2 oz) broad beans, shelled weight
salt and pepper
115 g (4 oz) piece of smoked streaky bacon or pancetta
175 g (6 oz onions
1 red pepper
1 hot red chilli
1 tsp ground cumin
1 garlic clove, finely chopped
3 tbsp corn oil
½ tsp oregano
225 g (8 oz) frozen corn kernels
15 g (½ oz) butter
handful of coriander leaves or flat-leaf parsley

Blanch the broad beans in salted boiling water until just done. If using frozen beans, cook for 4 minutes less than the pack instructions suggest. Refresh in cold water to stop them cooking, drain and reserve.

Cut the bacon or pancetta into fat matchsticks and fry gently in a large shallow pan until they start to brown. Remove with a slotted spoon and reserve. Dice the onion, add to the pan and fry until soft and translucent but not browned.

Deseed the red pepper and cut it into 5-mm (¼-inch) dice. Cut the chilli into the thinnest strips. Stir these into the pan and cook until the peppers have softened, then add the cumin and the reserved bacon. Turn up the heat, then add the garlic with the corn oil and the broad beans. Sauté for 2 minutes, season with salt and pepper and add the oregano. Add 4 tablespoons of water and stir in the frozen corn. Cover with a lid, turn down the heat and cook for 2 minutes.

Drain, put in a warmed serving bowl and top with the butter. Scatter over some chopped coriander leaves or flat-leaf parsley, as you prefer, and serve with grilled or fried meat.

Chapter 17
The West Indies

Magical memories evoke magical flavours

Memory of place, wholly or in part, defines memory of taste. It might be said that we have no precise memory of taste, as we have no accurate recall of ecstasy or of pain. We know in a general way that something was either very nice or very nasty, but we do not literally relive the experience. It becomes an idea that we wish to experience again and that we seek out and dream about or hope most fervently that the dark side does not revisit us. So with locations that are idyllic holiday destinations, and there are few places as beautiful or as alluring as the islands of the West Indies. Magical memories evoke magical flavours.

The food of the West Indies today is another example of fusion cooking that has resulted from the multiple settlements which included, over the centuries, English, Spanish, Dutch, French, West African and Asian. It may be compared to the Creole cooking of New Orleans, sharing with it the dubious engine-room of slavery, with African cooks working in the grand houses of whichever national master held sway.

Thus West Indian food has been influenced by successive waves of colonization and cultural domination, though it is, of course, also given unique definition by the tropical islands and their indigenous produce, including heady allspice, also known as Jamaican pepper, and the aroma which underpins jerk seasoning.

Much of the island food today reflects the demands of American tourists and is cooked on the grill, appropriately enough since the very word barbecue comes from *barbacoa*, itself derived from *boucain*, French for buccaneer and the pirates who first took the Carib Indians' cooking technique and made it their own.

Some of the dishes I have cooked have long histories and are complex in their spicing and execution. Many of the traditional dishes – like salt fish and ackee, and pepperpot – have their roots firmly in the 18th century, and the recipes have changed little in 200 years. I have taken the liberty of reinterpreting them.

SALTFISH AND ACKEE

Saltfish is salt cod, the story of which is told by Mark Kurlansky in *Cod, A Biography of the Fish That Changed the World* (Jonathan Cape 1998). For anybody who cares remotely about the conservation of fish, it is required reading – a description that usually implies an exercise in self-mortification, a duty or a chore. *Cod* is none of these things and grips you from the first page. The story of the great fish and its role in history is fascinating, and told by a man who has been a professional fisherman as well as a tireless researcher.

Salt cod was one of the foods that made slavery possible, a cheap source of protein so heavily salted it did not go off in the tropics. Salt cod bound for the West Indies was of a lesser quality than that sold to the primary markets of Spain and Portugal, something still true to this day. With cod's depletion it has become expensive, so expensive Jamaicans joke that saltfish and ackee, their national dish, is now an international dish because only tourists can afford it.

Ackee is a West African fruit brought to Jamaica by Captain Bligh in 1793 and after whom it takes its botanical name – *Blighia sapida*. Poisonous when unripe, the fruit is about 7.5 cm (3 inches) long and hangs from trees that are handsome with their glossy dark-green leaves. They must be fully ripe – that is, bursting open – before they are safe to eat. When this happens, three large black seeds are revealed, surrounded by the creamy white flesh in two lobes. Ackee must be washed, the skin casing and seeds discarded before cooking, the remaining creamy flesh being the edible part. You can buy them safely from West Indian markets and they are also sold in tins. When cooked they look like firm scrambled egg.

The recipe section of Kurlansky's book is an absorbing collection of traditional dishes from cooks over the centuries and this one comes from contemporary chef Alphonso McLean of the Terra Nova Hotel in Kingston, Jamaica. Caribbean saltfish dishes always involve shredding the fish, because it is of low quality. The saltfish, barely soaked, is hard and salty. The dish depends on this for flavour, though only a small amount is used. 'Soak 115 g (1/4 lb) salt cod for 20 minutes. Boil the fruit from a dozen fresh ackee for 5 minutes. Heat vegetable oil in a skillet. In the countryside we always used coconut oil but here I use soya oil. Add chopped onions, scallion [spring onion], thyme and ground black pepper. Then add minced scotch bonnet chilli, the ackee and crumbled saltfish.' Here is my version:

serves 4
500 g (1 lb 2 oz) salt cod (page 256)
24 fresh ackee
225 g (8 oz) onions, diced
4 tbsp groundnut or sunflower oil
2 sprigs of thyme
4 ripe plum tomatoes, quartered and pulp discarded
4 spring onions, shredded
1 tsp dried chilli flakes
pepper

Soak the cod for 48 hours in plenty of cold water, changing it regularly, until desalinated.

Discard the skins and shiny black seeds of the ackee. Put the creamy-coloured flesh in a colander and wash under running water, rubbing very gently with your fingers as the fruit is delicate and rough handling will cause it to break apart. Leave to drain.

Sweat the diced onion in the oil in a heavy-based frying pan over a low heat. When softened, turn up the heat to moderate and fry the onion, stirring continuously, until golden but not too brown.

Add the ackee and thyme. Cook, stirring, for about 3 minutes. Add the tomato pieces and half the shredded spring onion and then scatter over the chilli flakes. Chop the cod into bite-sized pieces and stir in. Turn down the heat and cover with a lid. Cook for 3–5 minutes, when the cod will be opaque and just cooked.

Serve as soon as the cod is done, grinding plenty of pepper over and with the remaining spring onion scattered on top.

COD AND PRAWN PEPPERPOT WITH CHILLI AND CORIANDER DUMPLINGS

Pepperpots in Jamaica are catch-all one-pot dishes, usually of chicken or beef, with an underpinning of salt pork. This fish variation would have been made with salt cod – very much a West Indian staple to this day – but for which we can beneficially substitute fresh cod.

Dumplings seem unlikely food in a hot humid place but obviously stem from the 18th century, when considerations of climatic appropriateness were not dietary concerns. These dumplings are very light, bound with egg white and containing a little butter for fat rather than the traditional suet. When steamed rather than simmered in water, they are even lighter.

serves 4

500 g (1 lb 2 oz) canned chopped tomatoes
115 g (4 oz) salt pork in a piece (see page 125) or pancetta, cut into lardon strips
3 tbsp corn oil
225 g (8 oz) onions, diced
3 garlic cloves, cut into paper-thin slices
1 sweet red pepper, deseeded and diced
2 Scotch bonnet chillies, shredded (or about 1 tbsp Encona hot pepper sauce)
2 tsp paprika
1.1 litres (2 pints) fish stock or light chicken stock
1 bay leaf
2 sprigs of thyme
400 g (14 oz) spinach, stalks removed
800 g (1¾ lb) cod fillets, skinned and any pin bones removed
12 large raw prawns, peeled and deveined
finely chopped spring onion, to garnish

FOR THE DUMPLINGS:
175 g (6 oz) self-raising flour, plus more for dusting
60 g (2 oz) unsalted butter
white of 1 egg + 1 tsp water
1 tsp dried chilli flakes
1 tbsp chopped coriander leaves
¼ tsp salt
¼ tsp pepper

First make the dumplings: put the flour and butter in a food processor and blitz briefly to a crumb. Add the other ingredients and work until they ball – just a few seconds will do it. Remove to a floured surface, divide into 8 and roll gently into balls. Put on plates and reserve. Bring the steamer water to the boil.

Purée the canned tomatoes with their juices in a food processor and reserve.

In a dry flameproof casserole or heavy-based saucepan, sweat the salt pork or pancetta lardons until they start to exude their fat. Add the corn oil and sweat the onions until soft and translucent. Add the garlic, red pepper, chillies and paprika. Cook, stirring, for 2 minutes. Add the puréed tomatoes, stock, bay leaf and thyme. Bring to the boil, lower the heat and simmer for 20 minutes. Remove and discard the bay leaf and thyme stems.

The dumplings take about 20 minutes, so put them in the steamer over boiling water when you start simmering the pepperpot.

Stir the spinach into the pepperpot. When it has wilted, cut the fish into large chunks and stir in with the prawns. Continue to simmer until just done, 3–4 minutes.

To serve, ladle into large warmed soup bowls, put 2 dumplings in the middle of each and scatter over a little finely chopped spring onion.

MATETE CRAB RISOTTO

Matete is a small island near Guadeloupe in the French Antilles, known for its slate-grey mud crabs. A walk beside the Thames can be the answer to any supply problems. We now have them in large numbers, some escapees from a crab *gulag* having discovered that the muddy river banks of London are a home from home. They start the year small, but they can get up to 1 kilo or larger. They have big, powerful claws and a nasty disposition. Any crab may be substituted, preferably ones wearing rubber bondage bands.

serves 4

4 mud crabs, each 225–300 g (8–10½ oz)
850 ml (1½ pints) shellfish stock
250 ml (8 fl oz) dry white wine
1 whole fresh Scotch bonnet chilli
2 celery stalks
2 bay leaves
1 tsp dried oregano
1 tsp black peppercorns
1 tsp coriander seeds
1 tsp ground turmeric
salt and pepper
5 tbsp olive oil
115 g (4 oz) pancetta, cut into lardon strips
115 g (4 oz) red onion
2 spring onions, thinly sliced
2 garlic cloves, cut into paper-thin slices
350 g (12 oz) Vialone or Arborio rice
1 tbsp sweet paprika
handful of coriander leaves, finely chopped, to garnish
2 limes, to serve

Kill the crabs by cutting them in half between the eyes with a cleaver. Twist off the claws, crack with the back of the cleaver and reserve. Pull out the body pieces from the shell. Cut each of the parts in half so that each has legs attached. Pull out and discard the stomach sacs.

Scrape the juices on the work surface into a saucepan. Add the stock and the wine, the chilli, celery stalks, bay leaves, oregano, peppercorns, coriander seeds and crab shells and bring to the boil, then turn down to a simmer. Simmer for 20 minutes, then strain through a sieve into a measuring jug. You want 1 litre (1¾ pints), so top up with water if needed.

Pour this into a clean saucepan and return to a simmer. Add the turmeric to it with 1 teaspoon of salt. Fish the chilli out of the sieve, shred it and reserve.

Put 1 tablespoon of oil in a large, shallow heavy-based pan over a low heat. Fry the pancetta in it until the lardons start to colour. Add the remaining oil, then stir in the diced red onion and sliced spring onion and sweat until soft. Stir in the garlic and turn up the heat to moderate.

Add the rice and paprika and stir to coat. Start adding the stock, a ladleful at a time. After it has absorbed 4 ladlefuls, stir in the crab and the shredded chilli. Continue adding the stock and stirring until it is all used up and you have a creamy risotto texture. Adjust the seasoning, if necessary.

To serve, spoon on to a large warmed serving dish. Scatter over finely chopped coriander leaves. You pick the pieces of crab up and suck out any flesh. There isn't much, but the bits look pretty and they will have helped give the rice a terrific flavour. Serve with lime halves on each plate.

CORIANDER AND GINGER CHICKEN WITH LIME

Indian flavours suffuse Caribbean cooking. This is a curry by another name, given a nice sour note by the lime marinade. Serve it with Rice and Peas (page 285).

serves 4
4 chicken legs
6 limes
1 tbsp coriander seeds
½ tsp black peppercorns
15 g (½ oz) coriander, including roots and stems
60 g (2 oz) flour
2 tbsp corn or groundnut oil
30 g (1 oz) unsalted butter
225 g (8 oz) onions, diced
2 garlic cloves, chopped
1 Scotch bonnet chilli, shredded
1 tbsp caster sugar
300–600 ml/ ½–1 pint chicken stock
salt
5-cm (2-inch) piece of root ginger, peeled and grated
150 ml (¼ pint) thick yoghurt
coarsely chopped coriander leaves, to garnish

The day before: cut the chicken legs into drumsticks and thighs. Put them in a zip-lock bag with the juice of all the limes plus the grated zest of 2 of them. Refrigerate overnight.

Next day, remove the chicken from the marinade and pat dry, reserving the marinade.

Toast the coriander seeds in a small pan over the lowest heat until aromatic. Grind to a powder with the peppercorns and reserve.

Detach the coriander leaves and reserve. Scrub the coriander roots gently. Chop them and the stems finely and reserve.

Dust the chicken pieces with flour and brown them all over in the oil over a moderate heat. Remove to a saucepan or casserole in which they will just fit in a single layer.

Add the butter to the frying pan, lower the heat and fry the onions gently until they start to colour. Stir in the garlic, the coriander roots and stems and shredded chilli. Continue frying until the garlic starts to colour, then stir in the coriander and pepper powder. Cook, stirring, for 2 minutes, then add to the chicken.

Pour over the marinade, sprinkle over the sugar and add enough chicken stock just to cover the chicken. Season with a little salt and bring to the boil. Lower the heat and simmer, uncovered, for 45 minutes, or until the chicken is tender enough to pull from the bone.

Put the grated ginger in a piece of butter muslin and ball it to extract as much juice as you can over the chicken, discarding the dry pulp. Stir in the yoghurt, turn off the heat and leave to stand for 5 minutes before serving.

Serve with the coarsely chopped coriander leaves scattered over.

JERK CHICKEN

Jerk describes an aromatic and chilli-hot marinade paste, common throughout the Caribbean, and the meats barbecued with it. While everybody has their own version, some with as many as 20 ingredients, most include chillies, onions, lime juice and allspice. The right chilli to use is the Scotch bonnet, which is indigenous to the West Indies, its pronounced fruit flavour the result of evolving in a tropical climate with extremes of heat, sunshine and high humidity.

A small round red capsicum that looks like a brightly coloured lantern and very like Mexico's hottest chilli, the habanero, the Scotch bonnet is actually hotter than the habanero, which puts it up there with the hottest chillies on earth. If you can't find any, use Encona West Indian pepper sauce, which is made from Scotch bonnets and bursts with their

fruit flavour. It is now to be found in every supermarket.

Everywhere you go on the islands you find jerk barbecues, usually built out of old oil drums. You could cook your jerk chicken with a whole jointed bird, chicken legs only or whole chickens or poussins split through the back and opened out (spatchcocked). You can also make it with pork or lamb, marinating in exactly the same way before cooking.

serves 4

1 free-range chicken, about 1.35 kg (3 lb)

FOR THE JERK PASTE:

175 g (6 oz) spring onions, finely chopped
2 tbsp corn or groundnut oil
2 garlic cloves, finely chopped
2 Scotch bonnet chillies, deseeded and finely chopped (or about 1 tbsp Encona hot pepper sauce)
3-cm (1¼-inch) piece of root ginger, peeled and grated
1 tsp ground allspice
1 tsp dried thyme
¼ tsp ground cinnamon
¼ nutmeg, grated
2 tbsp dark rum
grated zest and juice of 1 lime
salt and pepper

One or two days ahead, make the jerk paste: sweat the spring onions in the oil until soft and translucent. Add the garlic and the chillies or hot pepper sauce, the grated ginger, allspice, dried thyme, ground cinnamon and grated nutmeg.

Stir in and continue to cook for 2 minutes. Add the rum and the zest and juice of the lime, turn up the heat to moderate and cook, stirring, until you have a dark paste. Add ½ teaspoon of salt and ½ teaspoon of black pepper and leave to cool.

Remove the legs from the chicken and cut through their joints to separate them into drumsticks and thighs. Cut off the breasts with the wings, chopping through the wings to leave the small bone attached. Use the carcass and wings for stock.

Rub the paste into the chicken pieces, put them into a zip-lock bag and refrigerate for 12–48 hours, turning from time to time.

Jerk should be cooked over charcoal to give it that authentic smoky flavour of the beach barbecue, but good results can be achieved under a grill. Wipe off excess marinade before cooking and grill at least 12 cm (5 inches) from the heat source to prevent charring the outside before it is cooked through to the bone. Turn frequently as you grill, starting skin side to the heat. It will take 15–20 minutes.

RICE AND PEAS

Rice and peas is the Jamaican dish everybody has heard of, even if they have never eaten it. The name is slightly misleading, because the peas are actually red kidney beans. On the islands, rice and peas crops up everywhere and at every meal, including breakfast where it may be eaten on its own. It is the kind of thing which goes with anything, from plain grilled fish to spicy stews. Try serving with Jerk Chicken (page 283), Coriander and Ginger Chicken with Lime (page 283), or jerked racks of lamb. Because it is eaten so often, large quantities are often made and stored in the fridge, portions being steamed or microwaved to reheat when wanted.

serves 6

300 g (10½ oz) dried red kidney beans, soaked in cold water overnight
3 tbsp corn or groundnut oil
1 Scotch bonnet chilli, shredded (or about 2 tsp Encona hot pepper sauce)

3 garlic cloves, chopped
350 g (12 oz) long-grain rice
600 ml (1 pint) coconut milk
1 tsp fresh thyme, chopped, or 1/4 tsp dried
salt and pepper
2 spring onions, shredded

Bring the kidney beans to the boil and boil hard for 10 minutes, then drain, rinse and cover with fresh water by 2.5 cm (1 inch). This rids them of the toxins they contain, which can otherwise cause upset stomachs. Return to the boil, lower the heat and simmer until tender, 1–1 1/4 hours.

Heat the oil in a large saucepan over a moderate heat. When shimmering-hot, quickly stir-fry the chilli and garlic, then add the rice. Stir to coat, then add the beans with the coconut milk, thyme and 600 ml (1 pint) of water. Season with a little salt and pepper, stir thoroughly, then bring to the boil. Cover with a lid, turn down to the lowest heat and simmer gently for 20 minutes, stirring at regular intervals. After 15–20 minutes the rice should be done, with all the liquid absorbed; if not, turn up the heat a little and evaporate any excess, stirring continuously or the rice will stick and burn.

Transfer to a warmed serving dish and scatter over the shredded spring onion to serve.

CALALOO

Calaloo is the young green leaves of eddo and taro, edible tubers of the dasheen family. It has a flavour rather like strong spinach and can be bought fresh in West Indian markets. For those who do not have such specialized shopping facilities to hand, it is also available canned in brine (something I cannot recommend) and you sometimes find it frozen. If you can't get it, substitute spinach.

Calaloo gives its name to the best-known of all the Island one-pot dishes, calaloo soup. This is more of a soupy stew with local variations, but all containing dasheen leaves, crab and okra, the last giving it a glutinous texture like a Louisiana gumbo. Again, the okra is only just cooked, because I don't like the slippery effect of slow-simmered okra. Indian and Southeast Asian treatments usually give okra a preliminary soak in cold water before a brief stir-fry. This helps deliver a crisp and fresh result.

If you do not want to cook a live crab, use cooked crab from the chill section of the supermarket. Canned crab, like canned dasheen, is not a very desirable option.

serves 4
900 g–1 kg (2–2 1/4 lb) live crab, cooked and picked, or 275–315 g (10–11 oz) cooked crabmeat
3 tbsp corn or groundnut oil
115 g (4 oz) pancetta or unsmoked streaky bacon in a piece
225 g (8 oz) onions, diced
3 garlic cloves, chopped
1/2 tsp dried thyme
salt and pepper
450 ml (3/4 pint) shellfish stock or light chicken stock
600 ml (1 pint) coconut milk
2–3 tsp Encona chilli sauce
450 g (1 lb) okra, stalks removed
450 g (1 lb) calaloo or spinach, chopped
chopped chives, to garnish
sliced warm baguette or crisp rolls, to serve

Put the oil in a large pan over a low heat. Cut the pancetta or bacon into lardons and fry gently until they start to colour. Add the onion and sweat until soft. Stir in the garlic, thyme and 1/2 teaspoon of pepper. Fry for 1 minute.

Turn up the heat and add the stock. Bring to the boil, lower the heat and simmer for 15 minutes.

Add the coconut milk, a pinch of salt, the chilli sauce and the okra and calaloo or spinach. Turn up the heat and bubble for 3 minutes. Stir in the crab meat and cook for another minute.

Ladle into large warmed soup bowls and garnish with finely chopped chives. Serve with a basket of sliced warm baguette or crisp rolls.

PORK CHOPS WITH RUM, GINGER AND GARLIC

These chops are given classic West Indian flavours through marinading and are then fried slowly with a light allspice coating until tender and aromatic. They should be at least 3.5 cm/ 1½ inches thick and have a decent edging of fat.

serves 4

4 thick-cut pork chops with an edging of fat
7.5-cm/ 3-inch piece of ginger, peeled
juice of 2 limes
5 tbsp groundnut or corn oil
500 g(1 lb 2 oz) brown onions, peeled and thinly sliced
salt and pepper
1 tbsp allspice berries

FOR THE SAUCE
juice of 4 limes
1 tbsp demerara sugar
150 ml (¼ pint) chicken stock
50 ml(3 tbsp) dark rum
4 cloves garlic, peeled and finely chopped
1 tsp chilli flakes
2 tsp cornflour
45 g/ 1½ oz unsalted butter

TO FINISH
green parts of 2 spring onions

Four hours ahead, remove the chops from the fridge, slash the skin at intervals and put them in a dish in which they can just sit in one layer. Chop the ginger and purée in a food processor with the lime juice. Pour and spread over the chops. Turn after 2 hours. After marinating for 4 hours, scrape the marinade from the chops – patting them dry and reserving – and put the marinade in a saucepan.

Put 3 tablespoons of oil in a frying pan over a medium heat. Add the onions and stir to coat. As they start to fry, turn down the heat and cook, stirring at regular intervals, for about 20 minutes when they will have collapsed and have started to colour.

Meanwhile, brush the chops with oil and season generously on both sides with salt and pepper. Grind the allspice berries and press into both sides of the chops.

Put 2 tablespoons of oil in a heavy-based or non-stick frying pan and place over a medium heat until the oil shimmers. Lay the chops in and turn the heat to low. Fry for 6-8 minutes and turn. Give them 6 minutes on the other side and remove to a warmed plate to rest.

Add the juice of 4 limes, the sugar, chicken stock, rum, garlic and chilli flakes to the ginger marinade in the saucepan. Bring to the boil, turn down the heat and simmer for 5 minutes.

Mix the cornflour to a paste with water and whisk in. Return briefly to the boil, stirring as it thickens. Taste and season with salt and pepper. Pass through a sieve into another pan, working through with a wooden spoon. Put over a medium heat and whisk in the butter in small pieces, then remove from the heat.

Turn up the heat under the onions and fry, stirring continuously, for 2-3 minutes until golden. Turn off the heat and reserve.

Put the chops on 4 large warmed plates, spooning the sauce over and round them. Mound the onions on the chops. Scatter thinly sliced green onion over all and serve with boiled rice.

Chapter 18
Desserts

Elaborate puddings are not for me

You do not need many desserts in your repertoire to ensure that regular guests are never served the same thing twice, and many recipes are capable of seasonal variation. I have tried hard not to include too many recipes which are largely generic in their preparation and, as far as possible, have resisted the temptation of recycling old favourites. If you think that is stating something that should not need stating, then you have been very forgiving in your trawl through the cookbook shelves recently.

Desserts are not automatic inclusions in every menu. Rich puddings are surely for infrequent enjoyment and one's selection must be tempered by a number of variables including what precedes it. I am always pleased to conclude any meal with a plate of fruit that has been chosen for its ripe perfection and that has been prepared so that all I have to do is eat it. Fruit salad in a light syrup remains a perfect conclusion to any meal no matter how simple or complex and one that everybody appreciates. And the weather as well as the seasons should help shape our choice of what is most appropriate to eat.

Nothing here is described as 'wicked' or 'sinful', words that some find go irresistibly with puddings. Samuel Johnson said: 'Read over your compositions, and when ever you meet with a passage which you think is particularly fine, strike it out.' The same is true of adjectives and food. There should be a computer program called hyperbole-eliminator that could be run in parallel with spell-check. I need it as much as anybody else.

WINE-POACHED QUINCE WITH ZABAGLIONE ICE-CREAM

Quince is one of the most beautiful of fruits, its pale golden skin with a slight green tinge making it a favourite subject in Renaissance still-lifes. When first taken from the tree, the skin has a downy and slightly sticky fur that soon gets rubbed off. The quinces are picked and sold unripe and usually need two to three weeks at room temperature before they are ready, turning from green to yellow as they do so and giving off a scent of tropical fruit with a hint of apple.

They must be cooked, for even when ripe the flesh is hard and unyielding until it is simmered with sugar. Then its yellow flesh, the colour of salted butter, turns guava-pink and explodes with flavour. When buying, choose the largest and smoothest fruit; they are easier to peel and yield more flesh.

It is difficult to know why quince disappeared from our tables for decades, perhaps just because they have to be cooked. Anyway, the fruit is now being rediscovered in a big way and has become a fashionable dessert in restaurants.

Poaching in a wine syrup is as good a way as any to cook them and here they are served warm with ice-cream. The wine does not have to be a fine dessert wine – a not-terribly-good Riesling will do.

Zabaglione, a frothy custard whipped in a copper bowl at the table and flavoured with Marsala, is a lovely rich dessert. It also makes a great ice-cream. If you have no Marsala, Sicily's complex sweet wine, substitute an Oloroso sherry.

serves 4

4 large quinces, about 1.5 kg (3¼ lb) in total
150 g (5 oz) caster sugar
1 bottle of sweet white wine

FOR THE ZABAGLIONE ICE-CREAM:
8 egg yolks
200 g (7 oz) sugar
100 ml (3½ fl oz) Marsala or sweet sherry
250 ml (9 fl oz) whipping cream

Well ahead, ideally the day before, make the ice-cream: bring a pan of water to the boil. In a bowl which will sit over the water and using an electric whisk, beat the egg yolks and sugar until pale and frothy and doubled in volume.

Put over the water and continue whisking until you have a custard. Remove the bowl and allow to cool. While it is still warm, fold in the Marsala or sherry. Whip the cream to soft peaks and fold into the custard.

Put into an ice-cream maker and churn until set. Transfer to a plastic container with a lid and freeze for 12 hours, but no longer than 24 before eating. It won't go off if kept longer, but the flavours dissipate and the longer you freeze home made ice-cream, the more pointless making it yourself becomes.

Peel the quinces, quarter them and remove the hard cores with their pips. Put the flesh in a pan into which they will fit in a single layer without touching. Pour over the sugar and wine, then bring to the boil. Turn down the heat and simmer for 45 minutes. Turn off the heat and leave to cool in the syrup.

Transfer the ice-cream to the refrigerator about 15 minutes before you want to serve, to allow it to mellow.

To serve, put 4 pieces of quince in each bowl. Warm the syrup and pour over and round the fruit. Add a scoop of ice-cream just before taking to the table. Left-over syrup can be used in a sorbet or frozen and used again.

The quinces are also delicious served in combination with warm zabaglione as a custard, or with a crème anglaise.

COCONUT BANANA FRITTERS WITH HOT MANGO SAUCE

For this you want bananas which are at an early point of ripeness, still firm and only pale yellow.

serves 4
oil for deep-frying
115 g (4 oz) rice flour or Chinese Green Dragon wheat flour
350 ml (12 fl oz) coconut milk (page 233)
30 g (1 oz) icing sugar
¼ tsp salt
4 bananas
2 tsp desiccated coconut

FOR THE MANGO SAUCE:
75 g (2¾ oz) caster sugar
2 ripe mangoes
1 tbsp dark rum

First make the mango sauce: put the sugar in a saucepan with 150 ml (¼ pint) water and bring to the boil. Lower the heat and simmer for 5 minutes. Cut all the fruit from the mangoes (see page 47) and put in a food processor. Switch on at full speed, pouring first the syrup and then the rum through the feeder tube until you have a smooth sauce. Return to the pan over the lowest heat and keep warm.

Preheat oil for deep-frying to 190°C (375°F).

Whisk the flour, coconut milk, sugar and salt in a bowl until you have a smooth thick batter. Peel the bananas and cut them across into 3 equal pieces, discarding the tips. Cut each of the 3 pieces in half lengthwise.

Dip the banana pieces in the batter, allowing excess to drip off before frying in the oil until crisp and golden brown. Drain on kitchen paper.

Divide the sauce between 4 plates; put the banana pieces on top. Scatter over a little desiccated coconut and serve immediately before the batter goes soggy.

GRILLED PINEAPPLE WITH CACHACA AND LEMON VANILLA ICE-CREAM

If you have no *cachaca* (see page 219), use brandy or dark rum. This dish is quick, easy and delicious, and what more could you ask of a pudding. You could serve the pineapple with a plain vanilla ice, or whipped cream if preferred.

Pineapples are mostly sold unripe and can take up to a week to ripen in a warm room, when they will turn from a green-tinged hard fruit to a golden colour and smell sweetly of pineapple. When ripe they give to pressure from your thumb around the stem.

serves 4
1 large ripe pineapple
85 g (3 oz) muscovado sugar
60 g (2 oz) unsalted butter
3 tbsp cachaca or brandy or dark rum

FOR THE LEMON VANILLA ICE-CREAM:
6 egg yolks
juice and zest of 2 lemons
700 ml (1¼ pints) whipping cream
115 g (4 oz) sugar
1 vanilla pod, split

The day before, make the ice-cream: in a pan, whisk the eggs and lemon juice, then whisk in half the cream with the sugar. Add the split vanilla pod and seeds and cook over the lowest heat, stirring, until it is thick enough to coat the back of a spoon. Pass through a sieve into a bowl and fold in the remaining cream.

When cooled to hand-warm, churn in an ice-cream maker until set. Transfer to a plastic box with a lid and freeze.

Quarter the pineapple lengthwise and cut out the hard core. Separate the flesh from the skin by running the knife between them, then cut downwards into bite-sized pieces.

Preheat an overhead grill.

Put the sugar, butter and spirit in a small saucepan over a low heat and stir until the sugar melts. Whisk and brush the pineapple with this before grilling about 12.5 cm (5 inches) from the heat. Brush with the sugar mixture until it is all used up.

As the top of the pineapple starts to colour and the sauce caramelizes, remove to serving plates. Serve with a scoop of ice-cream on the side.

APPLE FRITTERS

Apple fritters, followed by a glass of Calvados, always transports me back to Honfleur, the pretty little Normandy port where so many Impressionists painted and got laid. Use eating apples that are very crisp and not overly sweet. Granny Smiths are fine for the job. The fritters one eats in France are usually made with Golden Delicious, but I think the contrast of sugar with a slightly tart apple is best. Indeed, Bramleys make excellent fritters, though Granny Smiths are the next best thing here.

serves 6
6 apples (see above)
juice of 1 lemon
4 tbsp Calvados or brandy
60 g (2 oz) sugar
oil, for deep-frying
icing sugar, for dusting
clotted cream or crème fraîche, to serve

FOR THE BATTER:
175 ml (6 fl oz) warm beer
7-g (¼-oz) sachet of easy-blend yeast
150 g (5 oz) flour
1 egg, separated, plus white of 1 extra egg
2 tbsp sunflower oil
¼ tsp salt
30 g (1 oz) sugar

Make the batter by whisking together the warm beer with the yeast, then whisking in the flour, egg yolk, sunflower oil and salt. Cover the bowl and leave to stand at room temperature for 3 hours.

Peel the apples, core them and slice across into 5-mm (¼-inch) rings. Put them in a bowl with the lemon juice, Calvados and sugar. Turn with a spoon to coat and leave for about 45 minutes.

Preheat oil for deep-frying to 190°C (375°F).

Whisk the egg whites to soft peaks, add the sugar and continue to whisk until stiff. Fold into the batter, starting with a spoonful and stirring this in, before folding in the rest with a plastic spatula.

Coat the apple rings in the batter and fry in batches, taking care not to overcrowd the oil. They take about 4 minutes per batch and should be turned halfway through. Remove to kitchen paper in a warm oven while you fry the rest.

Transfer them to a basket lined with a table napkin and dredge with icing sugar. Serve immediately with a bowl of clotted cream or crème fraîche. If left to stand the batter will go soggy.

APRICOT BREAD AND BUTTER PUDDING

The man who probably did more to reinvent this, once basic, pudding was the late Michael Smith, who started the trend of redefining traditional British dishes about 15 years ago, though some would say that the credit is due to Francis Coulson of Sharrow Bay, who died in 1998. Others might champion Anton Mosimann. It seems that a number of people thought about the possibilities around the same time.

In this recipe, the bread element has been reduced, the milk is enriched with cream and eggs to make a smooth custard, and the apricots are plumped with brandy. Use the kind of dried apricots which do not need soaking in water. Apricot brandy is the ideal liquor to macerate the fruit, but any spirit will do.

serves 6–8

115 g (4 oz) no-soak dried apricots
150 ml (¼ pint) apricot brandy, or cooking brandy, rum or whisky
175 g (6 oz) caster sugar
600 ml (1 pint) milk
600 ml (1 pint) single cream
1 vanilla pod
4 eggs
100 g (3½ oz) apricot jam
about 85 g (3 oz) softened butter
8 slices of crustless white bread
45 g (1½ oz) slivered almonds
icing sugar, for dusting

The day before, put the apricots in a screw-top jar with the apricot brandy, cooking brandy, rum or whisky or whatever is to hand. Add 30 g (1 oz) of the sugar to the jar and shake. Next day, put the milk, cream and the split vanilla pod in a pan over a low heat and bring slowly to the boil. Turn off the heat and leave to infuse for about 20 minutes.

Beat the eggs and remaining caster sugar in a large bowl until they form a smooth foaming mixture.

Drain the apricots, returning the alcohol to the jar to macerate more fruit later. Put the apricots in a food processor with the jam and blitz to a purée.

Butter the slices of bread and make 4 sandwiches with the purée. Cut across to make triangles and arrange, overlapping, in a buttered ovenproof dish.

Pour the milk and cream mixture through a sieve on to the eggs and sugar, whisking to make a custard. Ladle this carefully over the bread and leave to soak for 20 minutes.

Preheat the oven to 160°C (325°F, gas 3). Place the dish in a bain-marie and pour in water to come halfway up the sides. Bake for 45 minutes, or until firm but still pliant to the touch.

Serve warm or refrigerate overnight and serve very cold. Just before serving, scatter the almonds on top and dust with icing sugar. Sharp seasonal berries go well with it.

BRANDIED CHERRY COBBLER WITH LEMON VANILLA ICE-CREAM

A classic American dessert is given a more sophisticated flavour by baking the cherries with cherry brandy. The sweet buttery crust goes particularly well with ice-cream, here the rich home-made lemon vanilla from the Grilled Pineapple recipe on page 291.

serves 8

1 kg (2¼ lb) ripe cherries, stoned
115 g (4 oz) caster sugar
3 tbsp cherry brandy or brandy
45 g (1½ oz) unsalted butter, cut into small dice
1 recipe-quantity Lemon Vanilla Ice-cream (page 291)

FOR THE COBBLER TOPPING:

125 g (4½ oz) self-raising flour, plus more for dusting
30 g (1 oz), plus 2 tsp caster sugar
pinch of salt
85 g (3 oz) chilled unsalted butter, diced
4 tbsp single cream

Preheat the oven to 220°C (425°F, gas 7).

Put the cherries in a 20-cm (8-inch) square baking tin and scatter the sugar over them. Drizzle the brandy on top, then dot with the butter.

Make the cobbler topping: put the flour, 30 g (1 oz) of the sugar and the salt in a food processor. Add 60 g (2 oz) of the butter and pulse-chop to mix to a crumb. Switch to full speed, then add the cream through the feeder tube. Stop as soon as the dough balls, about 20 seconds.

Roll the dough out on a lightly floured surface to make a 23-cm (9-inch) square which should have an even 6 mm (¼ inch) depth. Fold the dough over the rolling pin and carefully unroll it into the baking tin so it sits on top of the cherries. Trim off any overhang and tuck the pastry down around the edges to cover the cherries completely. Melt the remaining butter and brush the top with it, then scatter over the remaining 2 teaspoons of sugar.

Put it in the oven and bake for 40 minutes, when the cherry juices will be bubbling around the edges of the golden brown crust.

Leave to cool a little, then serve the cobbler warm rather than seething-hot. Cut it into squares and serve on plates with a scoop of the lemon vanilla ice-cream on the side.

BLINTZES

Blintzes, sweet cheese-filled pancakes, are thought to be Hungarian in origin and are found on menus throughout Eastern Europe and in Israel, where they are offered with many different fillings. Raisins may be included and, if so, will benefit from an overnight maceration in brandy, rum or whisky. Use my standard Drunken Sultanas (page 309). Grated lemon zest is another possibility, or candied peel or even shredded Seville orange zest.

makes 12

115 g (4 oz) flour
300 ml (½ pint) milk
salt
2 eggs
groundnut or sunflower oil
30 g (1 oz) unsalted butter
icing sugar, for dusting

FOR THE FILLING:

85 g (3 oz) macerated raisins, currants or sultanas
500 g (1 lb 2 oz) dry cottage cheese
225 g (8 oz) cream cheese
2 egg yolks
85 g (3 oz) caster sugar
2 tsp ground cinnamon
zest of 1 lemon

Soak the dried fruit for the filling in an appropriate spirit for at least 1 hour and preferably overnight.

Make the pancake batter: whisk the flour with the milk and a pinch of salt. Add the eggs and 1 tablespoon of the oil, and whisk until smooth. Leave to stand at room temperature for 1 hour.

Mix the filling ingredients thoroughly together in a bowl with a fork, adding the raisins or sultanas last.

Preheat the oven to 190°C (375°F, gas 5).

Heat an 18- or 23-cm (8- or 9-inch) frying pan or crêpe pan over a low-to-medium heat and, when hot, wipe with kitchen paper dipped in oil. Pour in about 2 tablespoons of batter, swirling to coat the base and make a thin pancake. As it sets, turn and give the other side only a few seconds. Then remove to a cloth, stacking them and folding the cloth over to keep them covered as you go along.

Melt the butter in a small pan and remove from the heat. Use some of it to brush an ovenproof dish in which the 12 filled pancakes will just fit in a single layer.

Put 1½–2 tablespoons of the filling on each pancake, fold over the sides and roll up, tucking in the ends, and arrange them in the dish. Bake for 15–20 minutes.

Serve hot, dusted with icing sugar.

BEIGNETS WITH HOT JAM AND CRÈME ANGLAISE

Beignets, simple pillow-shaped doughnuts with a generous dusting of sugar, are eaten warm at breakfast in New Orleans' famous and cavernous Café du Monde. Serve them just-cooked with some hot sieved jam and a rich custard and you turn a breakfast basic item into an excellent pudding. These are flavoured with lemon and cinnamon.

The basis of the best doughnuts is a light sweet bread dough and clean oil at 190°C (375°F), the temperature at which the exterior of the doughnut is rapidly sealed to stop absorption of oil and hot enough to cause the dough to expand rapidly, giving an airy texture. Fried dough produces a different result to baking the same mixture, a soft but chewy texture and a delightful uniform golden-brown exterior.

The dough is very hard to work by hand and is best made in a food mixer with a dough hook. You need to make at least this amount of dough or there will be too much yeast. This sounds illogical but is simply practical, something you only appreciate when you start trying to halve or quarter 7 g of tiny yeast granules. The dough will keep in the fridge for 2 days in a zip-lock bag. Even in the fridge it will rise and then fall when the bag is opened. When you take it out of the fridge it will be noticeably stickier and wetter than when it went in. Just knead with a little flour and divide into balls. Leave covered with a cloth to rise for an hour and then fry as before.

If you are using a deep-fryer, change the oil and clean the interior. Any neutral-tasting oil will do, but I am currently keen on corn oil for deep-frying.

makes 12-16

400 g (14 oz) strong white bread flour
200 g (7 oz) soft plain flour, plus more for dusting
¼ tsp salt
7-g (¼-oz) sachet of easy-blend yeast
175 ml (6 fl oz) milk
85 g (3 oz) softened butter
2 eggs
85 g (3 oz) caster sugar
zest of 1 lemon
½ tsp ground cinnamon
oil for deep-frying, plus more for greasing
icing sugar, to serve

FOR THE JAM SAUCE:

300 g (10½ oz) black cherry or blackcurrant jam
1 tbsp lemon juice
2 tbsp bourbon, rum, brandy or whisky

FOR THE CRÈME ANGLAISE:

1 vanilla pod
600 ml (1 pint) single cream
5 egg yolks
175 g (6 oz) caster sugar

Sift the flours into a bowl with the salt and yeast. Heat the milk until it feels warm to the touch, then pour it into the mixing bowl. Turn the mixer on at the lowest speed and pour in the flour. Add the butter, a piece at a time, and when fully incorporated, add the beaten eggs, one at a time. Shake in the sugar, the lemon zest and the cinnamon and run the machine for 8 minutes, turning up to full speed for a final minute.

Turn the sticky dough out on a heavily floured surface and finish kneading by hand, incorporating a

little more flour if the dough is too sticky to work, until you have a smooth elastic ball. Brush this with a little oil, place in a lightly oiled bowl and cover with cling-film. Leave to rise at room temperature for 2 hours, when it should have at least doubled in size.

Remove from the bowl and knock down by kneading it lightly, then divide into 20 equal pieces. Roll these into balls then flatten them into rectangles. Put them on a lightly floured tray, cover with a cloth and leave to rise for 40–50 minutes, when they will have again doubled in size.

Make the *crème anglaise*: bring a pan of water to the boil. Split the vanilla pod and put it in another pan with the cream. Set over a low heat and bring to the point where it is just below boiling.

While these are heating, whisk the egg yolks and caster sugar together in a bowl that will sit over the water without touching it. Beat until you have a pale creamy mixture which falls in ribbons from the whisk. Off the heat, slowly whisk in the hot cream. Then put the bowl over the simmering water and cook, stirring with a wooden spoon, until it forms a custard thick enough to coat the back of a spoon. This will take 10–12 minutes. Pour through a sieve into a bowl and reserve. Cover with punctured cling-film to prevent a skin forming. Rinse the vanilla pod, dry and keep for another time.

Heat oil for deep-frying to 190°C (375°F).

Fry the beignets in small batches of about 4 at a time, being careful not to over-crowd the pan as this will cause the temperature to drop below sealing point. Fry for 1–2 minutes on the first side, turn and give them a further minute on the other side. When done, drain on kitchen paper.

Make the jam sauce while you are frying the last batch: melt the jam in a pan with the lemon juice and 2 tablespoons of water. When hot, stir in the rum, brandy or whisky,

The beignets are best eaten minutes from the pan. To serve, spoon some jam sauce on one side of a plate, putting some custard on the other. Sit 2 beignets on top and dust with icing sugar through a sieve.

CARAMELIZED APPLE TART WITH CINNAMON ICE-CREAM

The combination of hot caramelized apples, crisp pastry and cold cinnamon ice-cream is delicious. You can use all the leftover egg white to make meringue.

serves 4
500 g (1 lb 2 oz) puff pastry
30 g (1 oz) caster sugar
675 g (1½ lb) Granny Smith apples (4 large)
1 egg yolk, beaten, for the glaze
30 g (1 oz) muscovado sugar

FOR THE CINNAMON ICE-CREAM:
700 ml (1¼ pints) milk
6 cinnamon sticks
6 egg yolks
200 g (7 oz) caster sugar
½ tsp ground cinnamon
450 ml (¾ pint) double cream

Well ahead, make the cinnamon ice-cream: bring water to a simmer in a saucepan into which you can place a bowl in which to cook the custard.

Put the milk and cinnamon sticks in a pan and bring to the boil slowly over a low heat.

Whisk 6 of the egg yolks and the sugar together in a metal or glass bowl, until pale and creamy. Pour the scalded milk through a sieve into this mixture, whisking to incorporate.

Put the bowl over the simmering water and cook, stirring, until the custard coats the back of the spoon. Remove from the heat.

Add the ground cinnamon and, when cooled to

warm, whisk in the cream. Put in an ice-cream maker and churn until set. Transfer to a plastic box with a lid and freeze for at least 4 hours or overnight.

Ideally eat within 24 hours, removing from the freezer 10–15 minutes before serving.

Make the tarts: preheat the oven to 200°C (400°F, gas 5).

Roll the pastry out to a thickness of about 6 mm (¼ inch), scattering on the caster sugar as you roll. Cut out 4 rounds with a diameter of 15 cm (6 inches). Incise a circle 1 cm (½ inch) in from the edge on each, cutting to about half the depth of the pastry, and place on a baking sheet.

Peel and core the apples, then quarter and slice them thinly, preferably on a mandolin. Arrange them, overlapping, to cover the inner circle of each pastry round. Brush the pastry edge with the beaten egg yolk.

Bake for 15–20 minutes. Remove and scatter the brown sugar over the apple slices and caramelize with a blow torch or under a hot grill.

Serve with a scoop of ice-cream to the side or on top of each.

NECTARINE TARTE RENVERSÉE

A *tarte tatin* can also be made with any firm fruit, when it becomes a *tarte renversée* or upside-down tart and sod the apples. The cut fruit is baked sitting in caramel, with the pastry lid becoming the base when the cooked tart is inverted for serving. Nectarines or peaches are nicer here than the pears which usually substitute for apples. You want to use them when just ripe but still firm. The buttery caramel and nectarine juices which soak into the pastry when the tart is turned upside down mean that even industrial puff pastry tastes good.

However, it is worth tracking down proper butter puff pastry. There will be a baker near you who makes it and many are happy to sell you sheets of raw dough which you can then freeze. If you can find somebody to make perfect butter puff pastry, then there seems little point in doing it yourself. There are better ways to spend your kitchen time.

One of the most frequently used items in my kitchen is a 25.5-cm (10-inch) heavy-based frying pan with a rounded slope up the side rather than a straight edge. It was one of the first decent French pans I bought 25 years ago. You can stick it over the highest heat and leave it until the iron goes grey and hot enough to melt non-ferrous metals, and it sort of shrugs uncomplainingly. I removed its long wooden handle six years ago when looking for the ideal device for baking a *tarte tatin* for *Keep It Simple* and then could never fix it back again. This means not only that it can go in the oven, but the piece that sticks out where the wooden handle was attached makes a perfectly good handle without it. It looks a bit odd, but I strongly recommend you do the same thing with one of your pans, though not one with a non-stick surface because you can't put in a hot oven or over a high heat without ruining it.

serves 8

12 nectarines, about 1.8 kg (4 lb) in total
juice of 1 lemon
85 g (3 oz) caster sugar
60 g (2 oz) unsalted butter
500 g (1 lb 2 oz) butter puff pastry, defrosted if frozen
vanilla ice-cream or clotted cream, to serve

Preheat the oven to 190°C (375°F, gas 5). Peel the nectarines, cut them in half and turn in the lemon juice in a bowl to prevent discoloration.

Put the sugar in the frying pan or other suitable ovenproof pan (see above) over a low heat to melt it. Turn the pan from time to time to prevent patch burns in the sugar. The colour must be a dark caramel.

As soon as it is, remove the pan from the heat and dot the surface with small pieces of butter, then pack the nectarine halves on top, cut side upwards, which should use up 20 halves. Fill in any gaps with wedges cut from the remaining 4. They shrink during cooking, so the tighter you pack them, the better.

Dot the top of the nectarines with butter and put the pan back over a low heat for 5 minutes to melt the butter and start the nectarines cooking.

Roll the pastry out to about the thickness of a pound coin and, using a plate with a circumference slightly larger than the pan as a template, cut out a circle. Fold the circle of pastry in half then again to make a quarter. Lay this on one quarter of the pan and unfold to cover, tucking the edges of the pastry inside the pan.

Put into the oven and bake for 20–25 minutes, when the nectarines will be cooked and the pastry will be well-risen. Remove from the oven to a rack and leave to cool for 10 minutes.

Cover the top of the pan with a flat serving plate or round wooden cutting board and invert. Sit the plate on a flat surface, thump the bottom of the pan and lift away from the tart.

Cut into wedges and serve warm with a scoop of vanilla ice-cream or some clotted cream.

KEY LIME PIE

The 'key' in the name is a reference to the type of small strongly flavoured lime which grows in Florida, and is named after the Florida Keys, the chain of tiny islands connected by a highway on stilts that curls in a tail to Key West, America's most southerly town – just 80 miles north of Cuba – and the place which claims Key lime pie as its own. A proper Key lime pie has a base made from Graham crackers, a less sugary and less salty version of digestive biscuits which,

despite pedants' claims to the contrary, substitute perfectly well for them in this context. I prefer it made in a standard sweet pastry shell and to make the filling much less sweet than you tend to find in Florida. Without green colouring it does not come out like something Marge might cook for Homer in *The Simpsons*. Add a few drops for that authentic cartoon green.

serves 8

8 eggs, separated
170 g/ 6 oz caster sugar
400 g (14 oz) canned sweetened condensed milk
juice and zest of 12 limes plus 3 drops green food colouring
one 25-cm (10-inch) sweet pastry shell, baked blind in a tin with detachable base

Put a pan of water on to bring to the boil.
Whisk the egg yolks and 150 g/ 5 oz of the sugar

together in a bowl which will sit just above the water without touching it. Add the condensed milk, lime juice and food colouring to the mixture and whisk in vigorously.

Put the bowl over the simmering water and stir with a wooden spoon until it forms a custard thick enough to coat the back of a spoon, or even thicker. Over water this can take 30 minutes. If confident, you can get there faster by cooking the custard in a saucepan over the lowest heat. If it splits push it through a sieve into a food processor and blitz it briefly; this will usually pull it back together again. When thickened, stir in the lime zest. Pour into the pie shell and refrigerate for 4 hours or overnight.

Preheat the oven to 180°C (350°F, gas 4).

Whisk the egg whites to soft peaks. Continuing to whisk, gradually add 60 g/ 2 oz caster sugar until thick and smooth.

Spoon or pipe this meringue on top of the lime filling, making sure it makes an airtight seal with the base around its circumference. Bake for 25–30 minutes, when the surface will be crisp and streaked with golden brown, the meringue within quite soft and chewy.

Allow to cool to room temperature, then refrigerate for 1 hour before serving.

LIME AND PISTACHIO BAKLAVA

The stickiest, sweetest and richest of pastries, baklava is best eaten in small amounts with a cup of espresso or very strong and bitter Turkish coffee.

Frozen filo is great stuff, but it dries out faster than an Irish builder, so keep it covered with a barely damp cloth as you work. You need to find a suitable container in which to layer it. A 5-cm (2-inch) deep non-stick rectangular 23 x 17.5-cm (9 x 7-inch) baking tin is ideal. You will need to cut the pastry to fit, so it makes sense to find a tin which will just take half or quarter of a sheet neatly filling the base to the edges.

serves 12

500 g (1 lb 2 oz) caster sugar
juice and zest of 8 limes
1 tsp vanilla essence
500 g (1 lb 2 oz) filo pastry
200 g (7 oz) unsalted butter
250 g (8½ oz) unsalted pistachio nuts

Put the sugar, lime juice and zest in a saucepan with 500 ml (18 fl oz) water and bring to the boil over a low-to-medium heat. As soon as it bubbles, turn the heat right down, add the vanilla essence and simmer for 6–7 minutes. Do not stir. Remove from the heat and, when cool, pour into a jug and refrigerate.

Preheat the oven to 180°C (350°F, gas 4). Cut the filo sheets and stack them, covered with a dampened tea towel. Melt the butter in a pan over a low heat. Pulse-chop the nuts coarsely in a food processor and reserve.

Brush the base of the tin (see above) with butter, then brush a sheet of filo and lay it in it. Brush a second sheet and lay it on top. Scatter over a thin layer of nuts and repeat with 2 sheets of filo, interleaving with nuts until you have used them all up, finishing with 3 sheets of buttered filo and hopefully achieving a depth of 5 cm (2 inches).

Cut all the way through the pastry to the base in a cross-hatch to make diamond shaped bite-sized pieces.

Sit the tin on a baking sheet and bake for 45 minutes. Turn up the heat to 200°C (400°F, gas 6) and give it another 5–10 minutes to brown the top.

Remove from the oven and pour over the cold syrup. When cool, refrigerate for 24 hours before separating into pieces to serve.

MUSCAT PASTRY CAKES WITH CHAMPAGNE SABAYON

Rather than cakes, these are squares or fingers of puff pastry stuffed with a mixture of dried fruits and chopped apples.

makes 8
500 g (1 lb 2 oz) butter puff pastry at room temperature
500 g (1 lb 2 oz) sharp apples
60 g (2 oz) muscovado sugar
225 g (8 oz) sultanas, soaked for at least 48 hours in brandy
60 g (2 oz) candied lemon peel
2 tsp ground allspice
1 egg

FOR THE CHAMPAGNE SABAYON:
4 egg yolks
115 g (4 oz) caster sugar
150 ml (¼ pint) champagne
150 ml (¼ pint) Grand Marnier or other orange-flavoured liqueur

Preheat the oven to 200°C (400°F, gas 6).

Roll out the pastry to a thickness of 5 mm (¼ inch), then trim and cut into 2 equal rectangles. Put one of them on a lightly greased non-stick baking tray.

Peel and core the apples, then and dice them and fry in the butter. When golden and starting to soften, add the sugar and toss to coat.

Remove from the heat and stir in the sultanas, candied peel and allspice. Spread the mixture on the pastry rectangle on the baking tray. Put the other rectangle on top, pressing down gently. Using a scalpel or sharp knife, cut a neat cross-hatch all over the top, then cut almost all the way through the top pastry to make 16 squares and brush with egg yolk.

Bake for 15–20 minutes, when the pastry will be well risen and golden brown. Transfer the cooked pastry to a rack to allow to cool slightly, then cut into squares along the indentations.

While it is baking and cooling, make the sabayon: bring a large pan of water to a simmer. Put the egg yolks, sugar, champagne and liqueur in a metal bowl and whisk hard until the mixture is smooth and trails a ribbon from the whisk when it is lifted from the bowl. Position the bowl over the pan of simmering water – the base should just be above the surface of the water. Continue to whisk for 8–10 minutes, until you have a creamy custard.

Finish the pastry by dusting with icing sugar and serve still warm, with the sabayon poured around.

Options: the cakes can be left to cool completely and eaten for tea without the sabayon.

FIORE DI MANDORLO

Sicily grows 18 different types of almonds, a nut central to the island's cooking and one which, together with the extensive use of honey and spices, is a product of Arab occupation. The biscuits are good with an espresso and a grappa after lunch, followed by a bit of a cavort.

makes 30 biscuits
butter for greasing
450 g (1 lb) ground almonds
225 g (½ lb) caster sugar
6 tbsp clear honey
1 tsp ground cinnamon
zest of 1 lemon
whites of 1–2 eggs
icing sugar, for dusting

Preheat the oven to 150°C (350°F, gas 4) and lightly grease a baking tray with butter.

In a bowl, mix together all the ingredients, initially using just the white of 1 egg, adding a little more if needed until you have a firm paste, then knead until smooth.

Divide into about 30 little balls. Place them so they do not touch on the prepared baking tray, press them down to flatten slightly, and bake for about 20 minutes.

Transfer to a rack to cool and dust with icing sugar before serving.

CINNAMON JUNKET

Junket describes cream or milk set with rennet, a coagulant extracted from the stomachs of ruminants, which is also used in cheese-making. It is pronounced to rhyme with tenet not beret, as I heard celebrity chef Rose Gray do recently on television. It was a popular dish in Tudor times, its popularity carrying through to the 18th century, when frothy syllabubs captured the public imagination. Liquid rennet extract makes junket very easy to prepare, though to make it foolproof you will need to use a thermometer and the milk must be full-cream. Skimmed or UHT milk will not work. You can halve the amounts for 4 people, and experiment with different flavours – for example, vanilla makes a delicious junket.

serves 6

1.1 litres (2 pints) full-fat milk
1 tbsp caster sugar, plus more for dusting
4 tbsp brandy
1 tsp ground cinnamon
2 tsp rennet
300 ml (½ pint) clotted or double cream, to serve
freshly grated nutmeg, to serve

In a pan, gently heat the milk to blood temperature, 37°C (98–100°F).

In a china serving bowl, dissolve the caster sugar in the brandy, stirring. Pour in the warm milk, then add the cinnamon and rennet, stirring gently to mix evenly.

Leave undisturbed at room temperature to set, which will take about 1½ hours.

The proper Devon way of serving it is with clotted cream with a little nutmeg grated over the top and dusted with sugar.

TAPIOCA WITH CREAM AND SAFFRON

Also called manioc, tapioca is the starchy extract of cassava root. For more than a century it was the dread stuff of institutional desserts, but is now making a comeback. When milk puddings first became popular in the 18th century, they were made rich with eggs and cream, cooked with fortified wines and extravagantly filled with sultanas and currants plumped in liquor. These adult and indulgent desserts were not what some of us remember of school tapioca – slithery, slippery and thin in the bowl, for which 'frogs' spawn' was, if anything, a kind description. Children today, introduced to tapioca via a more sympathetic route, may well fall in love with it.

serves 4

300 ml (½ pint) single cream
300 ml (½ pint) milk
1 vanilla pod
zest of 1 lemon
15 g (½ oz) unsalted butter, plus more for the dish
3 eggs
75 g (2½ oz) caster sugar
12–16 saffron threads
60 g (2 oz) tapioca

fresh strawberries or raspberries, or a spoonful of good raspberry jam, to serve

Put the cream and milk in a pan. Split the vanilla pod and add it with the lemon zest. Over a low heat, bring almost to the boil, remove from the heat and leave for the flavours to infuse and the liquid to cool to hand warm.

Preheat the oven to 160°C (325°F, gas 3) and butter a gratin dish.

In a bowl, whisk the eggs with the sugar and saffron. Pour on the milk and cream mixture through a sieve, add the tapioca and beat to mix evenly.

Pour into the buttered gratin dish, stand this in a roasting tin and put in the oven. Pour water just off the boil into the tin to come halfway up the dish and bake for 1 hour 15 minutes.

Serve warm, with fresh strawberries or raspberries or with a spoonful of good raspberry jam – an addition that used to be called 'nose-bleed' at school.

MANGO AND BRANDY SMOOTHIES

Watch any Australian soap and you will find that the young apparently spend much time in cafés drinking milk shakes whizzed up with ice-cream called smoothies. These are, of course, very wholesome young people and about as credible in their fresh-faced, calcium-rich snacking as a snake-handling Southern Baptist passing the money bucket. You never see a fat one, for example, which is surprising as these are not the kind of shakes that induce rapid weight loss. Two a day and they would need to get their surfboards reinforced.

Somewhere between an alcoholic milk shake, a fruit purée and an ice-cream, this adult variation makes a nice pissy way to end a summer lunch. Sweetness can be moderated with a squeeze of lemon if liked.

serves 4
2 ripe bananas, peeled and sliced
350 g (12 oz) ripe mango flesh (see page 47)
125 ml (4 fl oz) brandy
4 tbsp Cointreau
30 g (1 oz) caster sugar
juice and zest of 1 lime
600 ml (1 pint) vanilla ice-cream

Put all the ingredients except the ice-cream in a food processor or blender and blend until smooth.

Add the ice-cream and continue to process until everything is incorporated.

Pour into chilled glasses and serve immediately with milk-shake straws and long-handled spoons.

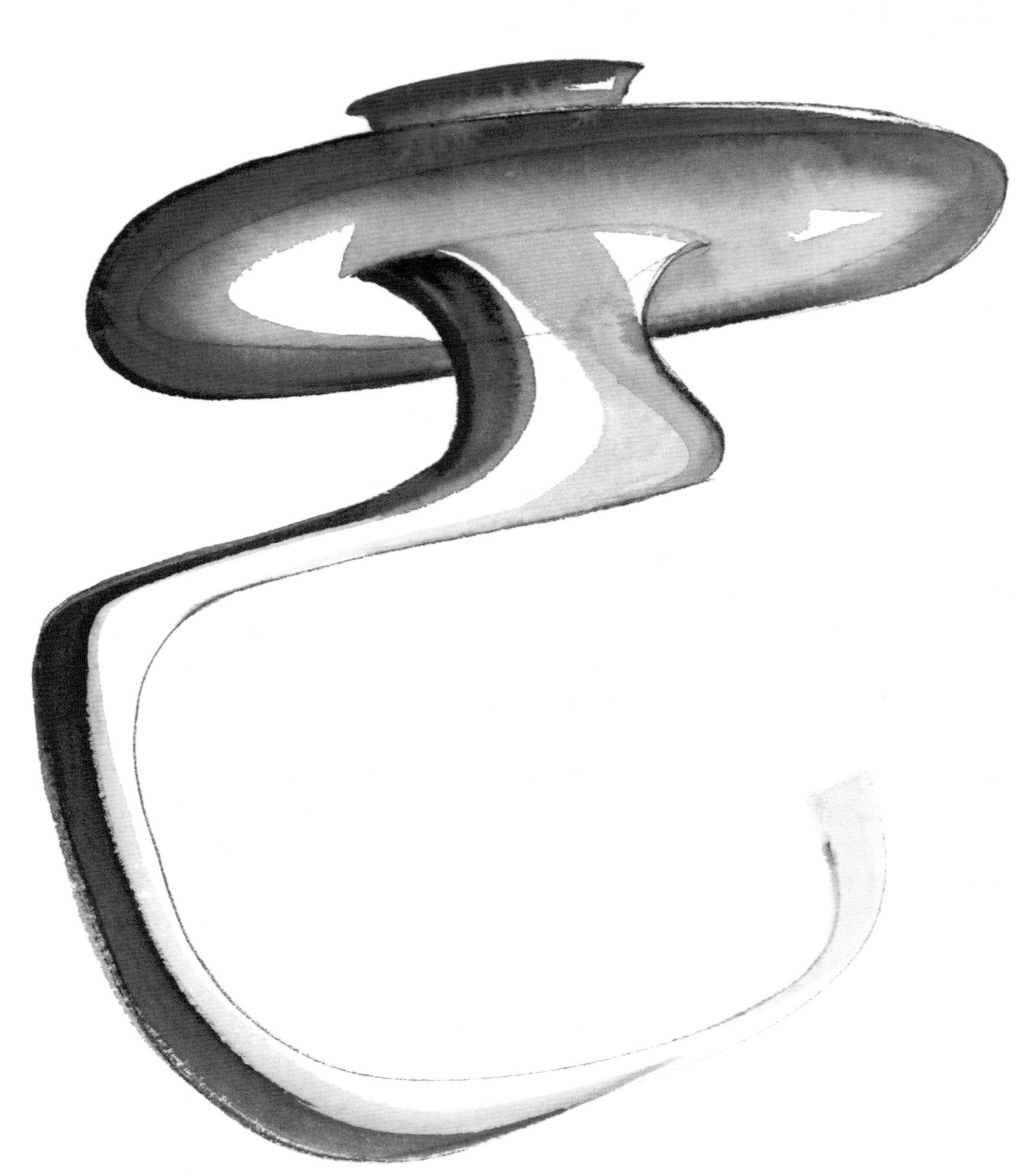

Chapter 19
Baking & Basics

The essential bases

Once upon a time mothers taught their daughters to cook after a fashion, or so I have been told. The exclusions from this broad statement are huge and it certainly does not imply that they were taught correctly. What is certain is that sons were not taught how to cook anything, since the very idea challenged deep rooted mores and conventions. Today's Delia Smith phenomenon suggests that the number of mothers passing on the most basic cooking information has dwindled even further. For today's daughters and sons – for a boy showing an interest in the kitchen is no longer viewed as an aberrant tendency with unfortunate sexual implications – Delia has become their virtual cookery mother.

Recent research suggests that an awful lot of people do not know the difference between a tablespoon and a dessertspoon, that television cookery programmes in the main do not communicate how-to-cook information effectively and are watched purely as entertainment – cooking as game shows with chefs as celebrities. Millions of people are interested in food and more and more eat out, but the majority do not really want to spend time in the kitchen. We have arrived uncomfortably in the age of gastro-pornography, a place in which that sold as a book about food and cooking is often a voyeuristic exercise, designed not to be read and cooked from but flicked through and coffee-tabled. These are style books put together by designers for whom text is an irritation. That is why you often see text reversed out white against a shiny and brightly coloured background which at best makes what has been written readable only with an effort or, in the worst examples, makes your eyes go funny like an out-of-synch video game.

Despite the negative impact of television and celebrity on publishing, keen private cooks continue to obtain information and ideas selectively from books. If you are reading this then you are almost certainly such a cook, and I have therefore limited this section. Why fill pages with generic information that you already know or can readily access? I would however remind you that we are all prone to accept too much in an unquestioning way, for the kitchen is cluttered with received opinions. Onion skins, long accused of turning a stock bitter, do no such thing, though they have the merit of giving your broth a burnished mahogany sheen. Old bitter aubergines are not made mellow by salting, remaining just as bitter but now inedibly salty. Seasoning meat just before it goes on a grill does not draw moisture from within the meat. These are old wives' tales disguised as knowledge, received wisdom that is anything but wise.

On the subject of stocks I would make the following general points, since their quality is key to so many of the dishes. When making chicken stock, do so at a lower temperature and for a longer period than most cookbooks recommend. Eight hours with the water steaming but not bubbling will reward you with a jewel-bright, flavour-packed consommé. Fish and shellfish stocks should be cooked at a bubble but for no longer than 30 minutes or they may turn cloudy and bitter. Vegetable stocks may be boiled hard but the ingredients will also have given whatever they have to give within 30 minutes. Once strained, all stocks can be boiled hard to reduce and then, for convenience, frozen as cubes in trays.

CIABATTA

Ciabatta or slipper bread, so called because of its flat, oval shape, is a soft white loaf characterized by large irregular holes in the dough and by a firm, chewy crust. It is most easily and consistently made by breaking some of the rules, giving the dough a lengthy secondary proving in the fridge. The dough is quite wet, almost a batter, so you need lots of flour on your work surface. This recipe is very versatile and can be used for pizzas or rolls immediately after its first rise.

makes 2 ciabatta

700 ml (1¼ pints) of hand-warm water
7-g (¼-oz) sachet easy-blend yeast
1 tsp sea salt
¼ tsp caster sugar
1 tbsp olive oil, plus more for brushing
900 g (2 lb) strong white wheat bread flour, plus more for dusting

The day before: put the hand-warm water in the bowl of a food mixer with the yeast, salt, sugar and tablespoon of oil. Using the dough hook and starting at the lowest speed, pour the flour into the liquid and work for 8–10 minutes. Increase to full speed for 1 minute, when you will have an elastic dough that is resilient and sticky.

Turn out on a well-floured surface, knock down and shape into a ball. Brush with a little oil and put in a lightly oiled bowl large enough to allow the dough to treble in size. Cling-wrap the top and leave to rise in a fairly cool environment. If you leave dough to rise in a hot place it will do so too quickly and will produce a heavier loaf.

After 3 hours the dough should have risen above the top of the bowl in a sticky and elastic mass. Transfer to a heavily floured surface, knock down again and knead by hand for 2–3 minutes. It could now be baked as focaccia.

For ciabatta, divide into 2 pieces, put into zip-lock bags and chill for 24 hours before baking.

Next day: remove the dough from the fridge an hour before you want to bake. This long chilling will give the bread a fine, crisp crust and a light interior with large holes.

Line 2 shallow baskets with drying-up cloths and dust heavily with flour. Take the dough out of the bags, dust with flour as it will be sticky and pull gently into ovals, dropping them into the lined baskets. Dust the top with flour and leave to rise for 45 minutes.

Preheat the oven to 250°C (475°F, gas 9). Put 2 heavy baking sheets in the oven to heat. If the oven is not large enough to have them both on one shelf, then you will need to bake them separately. Spray the oven with water, close the door and leave for 30 seconds to generate steam. Take out the baking sheets and upend the baskets, so the dough rolls out on to the sheets. Bake for 30–35 minutes, turning the temperature down to 220°C (425°F, gas 7) for the last 10–15 minutes. Remove to a rack to cool.

NAAN

Naan is a relatively flat, leaf-shaped bread from the north of India, baked in a clay tandoor oven. There are a number of things about the tandoor, a clay oven shaped like an Ali-Baba pot and fired with charcoal, that give naan bread its unique and delicious characteristics. The raw dough is slapped just under the lip of the oven in a round. As it cooks in a minute or two in the intense heat of around 400°C (600°F), gravity pulls the dough downwards so that, at the point when it is cooked, the naan has acquired its distinctive leaf shape, the surface bubbled and crisp, the interior soft and elastic. You can't do all that without a tandoor and even with one, it is a skilled and specialized job. This method, using an ordinary oven, produces a surprisingly authentic naan.

makes 12 naan
300 ml (½ pint) warm water
300 ml (½ pint) yoghurt
1 tbsp liquid honey
1 tsp salt
7-g (¼-oz) sachet of easy-blend yeast
about 900 g (2 lb) strong white bread flour, sifted, plus more for dusting
groundnut or corn oil, for brushing

Put the warm water and the yoghurt in the bowl of an electric mixer fitted with a dough hook. Switch on at the lowest speed and add the liquid honey, salt and yeast. Gradually pour in the flour and work for 10 minutes, when you should have a smooth, elastic ball of dough coming away cleanly from the sides of the bowl. If it is too sticky, shake over a little more flour until it does.

Remove to a lightly floured surface and form into a ball. Put into a large bowl, brush with oil and cover. Leave to rise at room temperature for 1½ hours, when it should have more than doubled in size.

Preheat the oven to the hottest it can get. If you have a multi-function oven with the potential to combine grill and fan, then this will deliver the highest temperature. Ideally put in a baking stone. If not, use a heavy roasting tin. Knock down the dough and divide into 12 pieces, rolling each piece into an oval about 1 cm (½ inch) thick.

Flour and slide directly on to the hot stone or tin and bake for 4–5 minutes, when they will be well risen and flecked with colour. Stack, wrapped in cloth. Reheat for 1 minute before serving.

CORNBREAD

Both cornbread and spoonbread from the southern states of the USA are made from cornmeal – polenta – though spoonbread has a preliminary cooking in a double-boiler before baking.

For cornbread, the best flavour is achieved using bacon fat, but you can substitute butter, lard or olive oil. Cornbread is best eaten warm and well buttered. You can stir various things into the batter to give the bread a different character. Crisp pieces of bacon, for example, or fried onions or blanched corn kernels (frozen corn dunked in boiling water for 1 minute and drained).

375 g (13 oz) cornmeal
2 tsp baking powder
450 ml (3/4 pint) milk
1 egg, beaten
1 tsp salt
1 tbsp melted bacon fat, lard, goose fat or olive oil, plus more for greasing

Preheat the oven to 200°C (400°F, gas 6).

Mix together the cornmeal and baking powder, then whisk in the milk, beaten egg and salt. Stir in the melted fat or olive oil.

Grease a rectangular cake tin or roasting tin with fat or oil, pour in the corn batter and bake for about 40 minutes, when the top will be golden and the bread firm to the touch.

Turn out and cut into squares while still hot and eat it buttered.

SPOONBREAD

Spoonbread is best eaten warm and is normally spooned from the tin, hence its name.

600 ml (1 pint) milk
225 g (8 oz) cornmeal
1 tsp salt
2 tsp baking powder
2 eggs, separated
butter, for greasing

Preheat the oven to 190°C (375°F, gas 5). Bring a pan of water to the boil over which the mixing bowl can sit.

Bring the milk to the boil and remove from the heat. Put the cornmeal in the mixing bowl with the salt and baking powder. Pour over the hot milk and mix together to a smooth batter.

Set the bowl over the boiling water and cook for 20 minutes, stirring from time to time. Remove from the heat and leave to cool until just warm.

Whisk the egg whites to soft peaks. Beat the egg yolks and stir them into the corn porridge, then fold in the whites.

Grease a 20-cm (8-inch) round cake tin generously with butter and pour and scrape in the batter. Bake for 35–40 minutes and serve warm.

STEAMED RICE

A rice steamer is one of the most useful and cost-effective pieces of kit you will ever buy. It cooks every type of rice to perfection and is fool-proof. It also then keeps the rice hot and in perfect condition for up to 4 hours. This is really helpful and has the bonus of freeing up space on the hob. The steamers are not expensive, usually £30–£40 – the price of a saucepan. If you cannot be persuaded to invest in one, the following formula steams rice perfectly, though you must follow it to the letter.

serves 6
500 g (1 lb 2 oz) Thai jasmine rice or Japanese glutinous rice

Put the rice in a saucepan which has a tight-fitting lid, and add a little cold water. Swirl to wash and pour off. Add 750 ml (27 fl oz) of cold water and bring to the boil. Immediately turn down the heat to its lowest setting. Cover tightly with the lid and cook for precisely 15 minutes. Do not lift the lid.

After 15 minutes, turn off the heat and leave undisturbed for 10 minutes to finish cooking and for the rice to absorb exactly the right amount of water to give a perfect result. Only now should you remove the lid and serve.

OLIVE OIL TOMATOES

It is odd to think that only five years ago the sun-dried tomato was an exotic and recent discovery outside Sicily and southern Italy. It was picked up by innovative chefs and rapidly became a fashionable ingredient. In its wake, the home-dried tomato enjoyed a similar popularity, partly because the slow oven treatment intensified the flavour. For many people, sweet tomatoes that tasted of tomato were a novelty and, it must be said, remain so to this day.

There is a wider understanding now that tomatoes grown in the sun are superior to those raised in greenhouses in cooler climates. The plum tomato from southern Spain, North Africa or Southern Italy is a thing of beauty, intensely red, plump and bursting with flavour. When such tomatoes are stewed very slowly in olive oil in the lowest oven, they become remarkable. The oil may be added to and used up to three times, acquiring its own intense flavour and making, with very few additions, a fine dressing.

Mediterranean vine-ripened tomatoes are at their best from May to September in Britain. If sold on the vine, then they are ripe and should be ready to eat. Most tomatoes, however, are sold unripe and will benefit from 4 days on a sunny windowsill or in the warmth of the kitchen, to allow them to come to full ripeness.

makes about 450 g (1 lb)

2.25 kg (5 lb) ripe plum tomatoes
2 tsp chopped fresh thyme leaves
30 g (1 oz) caster sugar
2 tsp salt
300 ml (½ pint) extra-virgin olive oil, plus more for storing

Preheat the oven to 110°C (230°F, gas ¼).

Scald the tomatoes in boiling water for 15 seconds, plunge immediately into cold water for 5 seconds and then skin. Cut in halves or quarters as you prefer, then strip out the seeds and pulp and discard.

Arrange the tomato halves in single layers on 4 Swiss roll tins. Sprinkle with the thyme, sugar and salt. Sprinkle over the olive oil, distributing it evenly.

Put in the oven. You will obviously need to use at least two levels to fit the trays. After 3 hours, switch the top and bottom trays. Give them another 1–2 hours, or until they have started to dry.

Use immediately or store in a jar in more extra-virgin olive oil to cover, adding the juice of ½ a lemon to prevent mould forming.

PIRI-PIRI SAUCE

Commercially produced piri-piri sauce is not easy to find outside Portugal, but a version can easily be made at home. Every family probably has a different recipe. This is only one way of doing it. Some people make the sauce without vinegar, but it is included not only for flavour but also as an antibacterial agent. In the absence of acid, nasty things can grow. The inclusion of cornflour as a thickening agent is also not very traditional.

This is a nice sauce to play with and modify with successive attempts. There is some disagreement about the oil to use. These days it is usually something like sunflower or groundnut oil, but these are relatively modern creations and it must originally have been made with a later pressing of olive oil.

makes about 600 ml (1 pint):

85 g (3 oz) hot dried red chillies
4 tbsp wine vinegar
2 tsp salt

100 ml (3½ fl oz) sunflower oil
100 ml (3½ fl oz) olive oil
2 tsp cornflour

Make the sauce at least a month ahead: put the hot dried red chillies in a bowl, pour over 300 ml (½ pint) boiling water and leave to soak for 30 minutes. Put the chillies and soaking water in a food processor with the wine vinegar and blitz to a paste.

Transfer to a saucepan, add the salt and the oils, and bring to a simmer. Mix the cornflour to a paste with cold water and add to the chilli mixture, stirring in and cooking until it thickens slightly. When cool, pour into sterilized bottles, seal well and leave for a month before using, shaking from time to time.

BEAN PURÉE

Any dried beans can be cooked and flavoured this way.

serves 4-6
350 g (12 oz) dried haricot beans, soaked overnight
1 head of garlic, plus 2 extra cloves
2 bay leaves
1 sprig of rosemary
2 celery stalks
1 tsp chilli flakes
salt and pepper
about 125 ml (4 fl oz) extra-virgin olive oil
175 g (6 oz) onions, diced
handful of flat-leaf parsley

Drain the beans, put them in a pan of fresh water and bring to the boil, throw the water away and cover again with fresh cold water by 2.5 cm (1 inch). Cut across the top of the head of garlic to reveal the cloves and bury it among the beans. Add the bay leaves, rosemary, celery and chilli flakes, and bring to the boil. Lower the heat and simmer for 1 hour, or until the beans crush easily. Discard the bay leaves, rosemary sprig and celery. Drain the beans, reserving the cooking liquid and garlic head. Put the beans in a food processor and season with salt and pepper. Squeeze the cooked garlic from the skins and add to the beans.

Sweat the onion in 2 tablespoons of the oil until soft and translucent. Finely chop the remaining 2 garlic cloves and stir them in. Cook for a minute, then transfer to the food processor with the beans. Blitz to a smooth paste, adding some of the reserved bean cooking liquid until you have a smooth purée. Finish by pouring 3–4 tablespoons of olive oil through the feeder tube until incorporated. Taste, adding more salt and pepper if needed.

Serve while still warm, with finely chopped parsley scattered on top.

SALSA VERDE

2 garlic cloves
85 g (3 oz) flat-leaf parsley
30 g (1 oz) fresh basil
2 tbsp capers
1 tbsp Dijon mustard
1 tbsp red wine vinegar
150 ml (¼ pt) extra virgin olive oil
salt and pepper

Put all the ingredients in a food processor and purée. Continuing to process, add the oil through the feeder tube until incorporated. Season with salt and pepper to taste.

DRUNKEN SULTANAS

Fill jars three-quarters full with sultanas. Add 2 tablespoons of caster sugar and fill to the top with brandy or rum. Leave for at least 24 hours and preferably a week, shaking from time to time. These are really useful in both sweet and savoury dishes; raisins may be treated the same way.

SAVOURY TART PASTRY

This will keep in the fridge for a week and also freezes well.

makes about 450 g (1 lb), enough for one 24-cm (9½-inch) round tart shell
125 g (4½ oz) butter
250 g (8½ oz) flour
1 egg
¼ tsp salt

Dice the butter and leave to soften. In the sort of average warm kitchen this takes about 30 minutes from taking it out of the fridge.

Sift the flour on to a work surface and make a well in the centre. Put the butter dice in the well, break in the egg and add the salt. Use your fingertips to rub these together, adding more flour from the outside as you work.

When all has cohered, moisten with 2 tablespoons of water and knead with the heel of your hand, making 3 turns, when you should have a silky smooth ball of dough. Wrap in cling-film and allow to rest in the fridge for at least 1 hour before use.

SWEET PASTRY

This is the classic short *pâte sucrée* of the French professional kitchen.

makes 675 g (1½ lb)
300 g (10½ oz) flour
150 g (6 oz) butter
100 g (3½ oz) caster sugar
2 eggs
grated zest of 1 lemon

Follow the same method as for the savoury pastry above, but rub in the butter and sugar before adding the eggs and the lemon zest. Then add the 2 tablespoons of water right at the end, before the final kneading.

Again, chill for at least 1 hour before rolling.

Food processor sweet pastry
275 g (10 oz) flour, sifted
100 g (3½ oz) icing sugar
pinch of salt
150 g (5 oz) unsalted butter, cut into dice and softened
2 eggs

Put the flour, sugar, and salt in a food processor and pulse for 5 seconds to mix. Add the butter and pulse-chop to a crumb.

Whisk the eggs lightly, switch on the machine and add the eggs through the feeder tube, working until the dough balls, which takes 45–50 seconds.

Cling-wrap the dough and refrigerate for at least 2 hours before rolling.

Index

Page numbers in *italic* refer to the illustrations